Cognitive Rehabilitation: Models for Intervention in Occupational Therapy

Edited by

Noomi Katz, Ph.D., OTR
Chairperson, Advanced Graduate Program,
School of Occupational Therapy,
Faculty of Medicine,
The Hebrew University, Jerusalem, Israel

With 14 Contributing Authors

Foreword by Elizabeth J. Yerxa

Andover Medical Publishers
Boston London Oxford Singapore Sydney Toronto Wellington

Andover Medical Publishers is an imprint of Butterworth–Heinemann.

Every effort has been made to ensure that the drug dosage schedules within this text are accurate and conform to standards accepted at time of publication. However, as treatment recommendations vary in the light of continuing research and clinical experience, the reader is advised to verify drug dosage schedules herein with information found on product information sheets. This is especially true in cases of new or infrequently used drugs.

∞ Recognizing the importance of preserving what has been written, it is the policy of Butterworth–Heinemann to have the books it publishes printed on acid-free paper, and we exert our best efforts to that end.

Library of Congress Cataloging-in-Publication Data

Cognitive rehabilitation : models for intervention in occupational therapy / edited
  by Noomi Katz : with 14 contributing authors.
     p.   cm.
  Includes bibliographical references and index.
  ISBN 1-56372-038-8 (case bound)
  1. Cognition disorders—Treatment.   2. Occupational therapy.
  I. Katz, Noomi.
  [DNLM: 1. Cognition Disorders—rehabilitation.   2. Occupational
  Therapy—methods.   WM 450.5.02 C676]
  RC553.C64C66   1992
  616.85′88906515—dc20
  DNLM/DLC   91-47069
  for Library of Congress   CIP

British Library Cataloguing in Publication Data

Katz, Noomi
  Cognitive rehabilitation : models for intervention in occupational therapy
  I. Title
  362.1968
  ISBN 1-56372-038-8

Butterworth–Heinemann
80 Montvale Avenue
Stoneham, MA 02180

10 9 8 7 6 5 4 3 2 1

Printed in the United States of America

Contents

Contributors   v

Foreword   vii
Elizabeth J. Yerxa

Preface   xi

Introduction: Comparison of Cognitive
    Approaches in Occupational Therapy   xv
Noomi Katz

1   Cognitive Disabilities   1
    Claudia Kay Allen

2   The Use of the Cognitive Disability Frame of
    Reference in Rehabilitation of Cognitively Dis-
    abled Older Adults   22
    Linda L. Levy

3   Use of the Cognitive Disability Frame of
    Reference in a Short-Stay Private
    Psychiatric Hospital   51
    Esta-Lee Stone

4   Cognitive Organization: A Piagetian
    Framework for Occupational Therapy in
    Mental Health   77
    Noomi Katz and Noga Ziv

5 A Dynamic Interactional Approach to
   Cognitive Rehabilitation   104
   Joan Pascale Toglia

6 A Dynamic Approach for Applying Cognitive
   Modifiability in Occupational Therapy
   Settings   144
   Naomi Hadas and Noomi Katz

7 The Process Approach for Cognitive-Perceptual
   and Postural Control Dysfunction for Adults
   with Brain Injuries   167
   Beatriz C. Abreu and Jim Hinojosa

8 A Neurofunctional Approach to Rehabilitation
   Following Severe Brain Injury   195
   Gordon Muir Giles

9 Cognitive Rehabilitation: A Retraining
   Approach for Brain-Injured Adults   219
   Sara Averbuch and Noomi Katz

10 Viewing Cognition through the Lens of the
   Model of Human Occupation   240
   Elizabeth DePoy and Janice Posatery Burke

11 Nonverbal Learning Disabilities in the
   Adult Framed in the Model of Human
   Occupation   258
   Sharon A. Cermak and Elizabeth Murray

Index   292

Contributors

Beatriz C. Abreu, Ph.D., OTR/L, FAOTA
Clinical Associate Professor, Director of Occupational Therapy Services, University of Southern California, University Hospital, Los Angeles, California

Claudia K. Allen, M.A., OTR, FAOTA
Chief, Occupational Therapy Department, Los Angeles County, University of Southern California Psychiatric Hospital; Clinical Assistant Professor, University of Southern California, Los Angeles, California

Sara Averbuch, M.A., OTR
Instructor at the Occupational Therapy Department, Tel Aviv University, School of Health Professions, Ramat Aviv, Tel Aviv, Israel; Senior Occupational Therapist, Leowenstein Rehabilitation Hospital

Janice P. Burke, M.A., OTR, FAOTA
Associate Professor, Occupational Therapy Department, Jefferson University, Philadelphia, Pennsylvania

Sharon A. Cermak, Ed.D., OTR, FAOTA
Associate Professor of Occupational Therapy; Co-Director, Center for Therapeutic Science, Boston University, Sargent College; Faculty Emeritus, Sensory Integration, International, Torrance, California

Elizabeth DePoy, Ph.D., M.S.W., OTR/L
Assistant Professor, Department of Social Work, University of Main, Orono, Maine

Gordon M. Giles, Dip. Cot. OTR
Director of Clinical Services, Bay Area Recovery Center, San Francisco, California

Naomi Hadas, M.A., OTR
Instructor at the Occupational Therapy Department, Tel Aviv University, School of Health Professions, Ramat Aviv, Tel Aviv, Israel; Editor, *The Israel Journal of Occupational Therapy*

Jim Hinojosa, Ph.D., OTR/L, FAOTA
Associate Professor, Director of Advanced Graduate Program, New York University, Department of Occupational Therapy, New York, New York

Noomi Katz, Ph.D., OTR
Associate Professor and Chairperson, Advanced Graduate Program, School of Occupational Therapy, Faculty of Medicine, The Hebrew University, Jerusalem, Israel; Chairperson, Board of The Israeli Society of Occupational Therapy; Editor, *The Israel Journal of Occupational Therapy*

Linda L. Levy, M.A., OTR/L, FAOTA
Associate Professor, Occupational Therapy, Temple University, College of Allied Health Professions, Philadelphia, Pennsylvania

Elizabeth Murray, Sc.D., OTR
Assistant Professor of Occupational Therapy; Research Associate, Center for Therapeutic Science, Boston University, Sargent College, Boston, Massachusetts; Assistant Director of Occupational Therapy, Shriver Center; Faculty Emeritis, Sensory Integration International, Torrance, California

Joan Pascale Toglia, M.S., OTR
Chief, Occupational Therapy, Department of Rehabilitation Medicine, The New York Hospital at Cornell Medical School, New York, New York

Esta-Lee Stone, M.S., OTR/L
Director of Rehabilitation Services, Fuller Memorial Hospital, South Attleboro, Massachusetts

Noga Ziv, OTR
Instructor at the Occupational Therapy Department, Tel Aviv University, School of Health Professions, Ramat Aviv, Tel Aviv, Israel

□ □ □
□ □ □
□ □ □

Foreword

Elizabeth J. Yerxa

Dr. Noomi Katz and her co-authors are to be congratulated on making this substantial contribution to the theory and practice of occupational therapy for patients with cognitive disabilities. This book with its international scope cannot fail to excite us with its breadth. For depth I found the case reports particularly compelling and helpful in understanding the practical, "real-life" aspects of occupational therapy for this group of patients. More importantly, these reports provided valuable glimpses into the daily life experiences of people who have great challenges to meet in adapting to their worlds. The occupational therapy literature needs many more such comprehensive, sensitive, and detailed case reports to enable us to understand the perspectives of such individuals in order to help them achieve greater efficacy and satisfaction in their daily activities.

This book demonstrates a fact that all occupational therapists know in their deepest consciousness: it is very difficult to be a good occupational therapist. The complex issue of human beings engaged in occupation and interacting with their environments in the presence of often profound disabilities cannot be simplified or reduced to diagnosis, standardized testing, or mechanistic theory. Nor can it be either effective or ethical. Occupational therapists are committed to enabling people to function in their own environments by engaging in patterns of daily activity which are both satisfying and provide "connectedness" with the daily routines of their cultures (Beisser, 1989). This commitment extends to viewing every human being as possessing the potential to act on and exercise some control over events in his or her environment. Such an optimistic view includes people with impairments, disabilities, or handicaps called "cognitive disabilities."

The eleven chapters in this book reveal that occupational therapists may wear many different "pairs of glasses" when they work with patients described as having cognitive disabilities. The reader may ask, how may I assess each theoretical perspective and the occupational therapy program connected with it? For the pair of glasses presented is one of several which have or will be recommended. Are the lenses worn by medicine, neuropsychology, cognitive science, or behaviorism appropriate for occupational therapists to wear while looking at their patients?

Let us remind ourselves that when we employ concepts such as "I.Q.", "cognitive levels," or "schema" we are choosing one description (of many possible). In this sense words are metaphors, drawing attention to constructs which theorists believe are important to name and notice (Rorty, 1989). Such metaphors are constantly changing. For example, the lenses through which society viewed "mental illness" changed dramatically over the centuries, reflecting differences in social values and power relationships (Foucault, 1965). Kuhn (1970) overturned the world's view of science by showing that scientific knowledge evolved through revolutionary changes in points of view rather than by simple accretion of facts.

There is nothing wrong with using metaphors. The problem arises when the metaphors we use lead to a diminishment of people's opportunities, curtail our expectancies, or when we mistake the metaphor for "reality." As Bateson (1979) noted, the map is not the same as the territory it describes. The metaphor is not the same as the person it describes.

In choosing an appropriate pair of glasses through which to view our patients and their needs, occupational therapists may wish to employ three criteria for relevance: (1) ethics, (2) scholarship, and (3) pragmatics. First, each approach can be examined for its ethical assumptions. To what extent does this theory and the practice emanating from it have a "good fit" with the values, beliefs, and assumptions of occupational therapy—for example, with occupational therapy's optimistic view of human beings and their capacities?

Second, each approach can be evaluated according to its scholarly foundation. To what extent is this view grounded in the broad, interdisciplinary knowledge required for understanding the complex person who not only has a "body" but engages in interaction with an environment, deriving meaning from such engagement?

Third, each approach can be assessed according to its outcome. To what extent does this point of view enable occupational therapists to help patients meet the challenges of daily living in their environments, with satisfaction (even joy!) to themselves and others? This judgment will not be made on the basis of experiments, standardized tests, and statistical tools. It will be made individual by individual within the real environments which create the challenges and demands.

The Soviet psychologist Vygotsky is cited in several of these chapters. Luria, his colleague, observed:

Unlike many previous investigators of handicapped children, Vygotsky concentrated his attention on the abilities such children had, abilities which could form the basis for developing their full potential. It was their strengths, not their deficits, that interested him most. Consistent with his overall approach, he rejected simple quantitative descriptions of such children in terms of unidimensional psychological traits reflected in test scores. Instead, he relied on qualitative descriptions of the special organization of their behavior.

Luria, 1979 (p. 53)

Vygotsky, in this quote, sounded like an occupational therapist.

By evaluating each approach according to these criteria, occupational therapists may feel more confident that they have chosen a good pair of glasses, one that enables them to both envision and help create better life opportunities for people who have disabilities. In a world to which increasing numbers of people with severe, chronic disabling conditions must somehow adapt and meet the challenges of a complex, technologically advanced civilization, occupational therapy has important work to do.

References

Bateson, G. (1979). *Mind and nature: A necessary unity.* New York: Bantam Books.

Beisser, A. R. (1989). *Flying without wings: Personal reflections on being disabled.* New York: Doubleday.

Foucault, M. (1965). *Madness and civilization: A history of insanity in the age of reason.* New York: Random House.

Kuhn, T. S. (1970). *The structure of scientific revolutions,* second edition. Chicago: The University of Chicago Press.

Luria, A. R. (1979). *The making of mind: A personal account of Soviet psychology.* Cole, M. and Cole, S. (Eds.). Cambridge, Mass: Harvard University Press.

Rorty, R. (1989). *Contingency, irony and solidarity.* Cambridge, England: Cambridge University Press.

Preface

The purpose of this book is to provide a comprehensive, state-of-the-art "knowledge base" on cognitive theoretical approaches in occupational therapy for adolescent and adult patients with cognitive dysfunctions in various clinical populations, such as brain-injured patients, psychiatric patients, geriatric patients, and learning-disabled adults.

Cognition is a basic, universally human trait that underlies every human function and crosses over all specialty areas in occupational therapy. The development of cognitive theoretical approaches in occupational therapy, which integrate knowledge on cognition from different scientific disciplines with occupational therapy tenets and principles, is relatively new and unique. As such, this book is special and timely. It is intended to mark a turning point for an important special area in occupational therapy.

By a cognitive theoretical approach in occupational therapy, I mean a cognitive intervention model that consists of (1) a theoretical base, which integrates various scientific concepts with occupational therapy principles and postulates; (2) intervention, including evaluation procedures, assessment instruments, and treatment methods; (3) specification of the target populations; (4) research (if it exists) to support the approach; and (5) implications for further knowledge development of the approach.

In line with this conceptualization and criteria, only cognitive approaches that provide these components were included in the book. Not included are works that relate only to subcomponents of cognition (such as perception) or that have developed instruments and treatment methods in occupational therapy but without an underlying theoretical base.

Cognition is conceived of as a target of intervention in cognitively dysfunctional individuals, as well as an avenue for intervention using cognitive concepts and instruments—in much the same way occupation or activity is the target (outcome, as well as the avenue) method of intervention in occupational therapy. Hence, cognitive interactions with occupation and activities are necessary components of a cognitive theoretical approach in occupational therapy.

Cognition is further conceived of as a global term, incorporating areas of attention, orientation, perception, praxis, visuo-motor organization, memory, thinking operations, executive functions, problem solving, planning, reasoning, and judgment. Thus, this book includes cognitive approaches that look at cognition or cognitive disabilities from their global and multiple components aspects (i.e., information processing abilities, cognitive organization, or cognitive modifiability).

This is the first book, to my knowledge, that presents the various cognitive approaches in occupational therapy in one volume. Some of them are outlined clearly for the first time, providing in addition to the material in each chapter extensive references for more complete study of each approach. The contributors to this book are leading professionals in the area of cognition in occupational therapy, and I am extremely appreciative of their cooperation and the in-depth work they present. The book is intended to stimulate knowledge development in the area of cognition and occupation/activity for intervention in occupational therapy, as well as for research related to components of occupational science.

In the Introduction, I compare the approaches, discussing similarities and differences and urging the readers to continue the process of conceptualization and research in this area.

The book consists of 11 chapters, starting with three chapters that relate to cognitive disabilities theory originated by Allen. This theory is the most established cognitive approach in occupational therapy. Allen elaborates in the first chapter her theory in more general terms, applying it to all populations with brain dysfunctions causing disabilities in doing an activity. She states that such disabilities should be the focus of rehabilitation.

Levy and Stone expand on Allen's theory in different directions. Levy (Chapter 2) discusses the application of Allen's model in the rehabilitation of the physically and/or cognitively disabled elder. Levy describes in this chapter her extensive theoretical work on the adaptation of activities and the cognitive disability model for the aged population and their caregivers. Stone (Chapter 3) continues Allen's original focus on psychiatric practice, but elaborates the frame of reference by using information processing and neuroscience concepts of attention. She provides more dynamically oriented intervention techniques for problem solving and activities of daily living evaluation within a short-term psychiatric hospitalization.

Katz and Ziv (Chapter 4) present a piagetian framework for intervention in mental health, emphasizing patients' cognitive organization as the central foci of function and dysfunction. Piaget's notions of genetic epistemology which subsumes development, thus enabling the understanding of adult thinking processes, is the focus of this approach.

Toglia (Chapter 5) presents a dynamic interactional approach to cognitive rehabilitation. Cognition is viewed as a dynamic interaction between the individual, the task, and the environment. Information processing and metacognition are central concepts. Methods of assessment and treatment are outlined that reflect this dynamic view of cognition and its application to brain-injured and schizophrenic patients. While Toglia integrates dynamic concepts from various theories, Hadas and Katz (Chapter 6) describe the application of Feuerstein's dynamic theory for cognitive modifiability and mediated learning experience in occupational therapy. They present applications for patients with cognitive, emotional, and/or adaptational dysfunctions.

The next three chapters center on brain-injured patients, each emphasizing a different perspective to the same population.

Abreu and Hinojosa (Chapter 7) focus on a process approach, looking at cognitive-perceptual and postural control dysfunctions in brain-injured adults. Their approach is grounded in information processing theory, learning theories, neuropathology, and the therapeutic use of activities. Giles (Chapter 8) presents a neurofunctional approach to rehabilitation with emphasis on severe brain injury. The focus of the approach is the retraining of real-world skills. Averbuch and Katz (Chapter 9), in contrast, focus on cognitive retraining in rehabilitation based on the assumptions that generalization and transference also occur in functional areas. Their theoretical base is grounded in neuropsychological and cognitive psychology theories.

The last two chapters utilize the model of human occupation as the framework for their approach. DePoy and Burke (Chapter 10) introduce two conceptualizations of cognition, constructivist and information processing. They provide a general analysis of cognition using the model of human occupation, followed by application to patients with cognitive dysfunctions. Cermak and Murray (Chapter 11) outline an approach for intervention of adults with nonverbal learning disabilities. They center on the identification and remediation of cognitive-perceptual and nonverbal deficits using the model of human occupation as a framework for guiding assessment and treatment.

Essentially, the order of the chapters is of no importance. Each chapter is complete on its own, and can be read alone or in any sequence the reader chooses. However, all chapters together provide a wide range of knowledge bases and clinical applications in occupational therapy for adolescent and adult populations with cognitive dysfunctions. It is my hope that the book will inspire further study and knowledge development in the area of cognition in occupational therapy.

Noomi Katz

Introduction: Comparison of Cognitive Approaches in Occupational Therapy

Noomi Katz

In 1961 Reilly gave an outstanding Eleanor Clark Slagle lecture (1973) where she provided the profession with a major hypothesis: "That man, through the use of his hands as they are energized by *mind* and will, can influence the state of his own health" (p. 88) (emphasis added). She further states that our profession has an obligation to acquire and develop the knowledge that will lead to competence in serving this hypothesis and to make it applicable to a wide range of medical problems. Accordingly, our focus in this book is on one major component of the hypothesis, namely, the role that cognition plays in human health.

The authors that collaborated in this book make an important contribution to our knowledge on how the interaction between cognition—mind and actions—activities, and occupations influences patients' state of health. They provide multiple ways to approach the problem of cognitive dysfunctions and to intervene with various patient populations. As mentioned in the preface, each of the approaches described disseminated and outlined a knowledge base that leads to intervention methods in occupational therapy.

The purpose of this introduction is to compare the approaches presented in the book on a few parameters that seem important to me. The comparison is not exhaustive, it intends to highlight a few points and to invite readers to use the information in the book for clinical application, as well as a basis for research and continuing knowledge development. The comparison follows the components that were used in describing the cognitive theoretical approaches in occupational therapy: a theoretical base, target populations, evaluation procedures, treatment methods, and research.

Theoretical Base

Source

The sources for the theoretical bases of the various approaches are presented in Table 1. What appears from this comparison is that the therapeutic use of activities, activity analysis, adaptation, and intervention are integrated by all authors as part of their theoretical base. Basic occupational therapy principles of purposeful activity, doing and function in daily activities or occupations are presented as fundamental to all approaches.

Two existing occupational therapy models or theories are utilized, cognitive disabilities (Allen, 1985) (Chapters 1, 2, and 3) and the model of human occupation (Kielhofner, 1985) (Chapters 10 and 11). In the approaches presented in these chapters, additional bodies of knowledge from other disciplines were added to extend or refine the approach and adapt it to the target populations (physical dysfunctions with cognitive disabilities; elderly people; psychiatric short-term treatments; brain-injured patients in the community; dementia; or non-verbal learning disabilities in the adult). Sources for these additions are cognitive psychology, information processing, neuroscience, and neuropsychological concepts.

The other six approaches are newly formulated cognitive approaches in occupational therapy. Two of them, Toglia's dynamic interactional approach (Chapter 5) and Abreu and Hinojosa's process-oriented approach (Chapter 7) have their starting point from the model of cognitive rehabilitation presented by Abreu and Toglia (1987). Both approaches integrate multiple perspectives into their occupational therapy approach. They also focus on dynamic or process orientation and the use of information processing concepts. However, Toglia's emphasis on the dynamic aspect is much stronger and she uses additional concepts of metacognition and social interactions, transfer of learning, and generalization to formulate a dynamic interactional approach. Abreu and Hinojosa integrate learning theories, especially motor learning and postural control, with information processing and activity intervention.

The remaining four approaches are based predominantly on one or two sources. The behavioral learning aspect is a major part of the neurofunctional approach presented by Giles (Chapter 8) together with concepts of cognition from neuropsychology. Neuropsychology is also the basis for the cognitive retraining approach together with concepts from cognitive psychology (Averbuch & Katz, Chapter 9). Katz and Ziv (Chapter 4) utilize Piaget's framework, while Hadas and Katz (Chapter 6) are using solely Feuerstein's theory of cognitive modifiability.

Table 1   Sources for the Knowledge Bases of Cognitive Approaches

Chapter 1: Cognitive disabilities
  neuroscience, psychiatry and neurology,
  activity analysis
  information processing,
  activity in Soviet psychology,
  ICIDH–WHO 1980–typology of disability,
  Law's definitions of competence,
Chapter 2: CD with the elderly
  cognitive disability theory,
  activity analysis–Soviet psychology (operations, results, meaning)
  gerontology–aging process–physical, cognitive, social
Chapter 3: CD in short-term psychiatric
  cognitive disability,
  information processing,
  neuroscience–attention, problem solving
  activity analysis–activity in Soviet psychology
Chapter 4: Cognitive organization–psychiatry
  Piaget epistemological and developmental theory
  psychopathology and cognition
  activity analysis and intervention
Chapter 5: Dynamic interactional
  dynamic approach to cognitive rehabilitation (individual, task, environment)
  information processing
  cognitive psychology–metacognition
  task analysis
Chapter 6: Cognitive modifiability
  Feuerstein theory: mediated learning experience
  cognitive modifiability, dynamic approach of learning
Chapter 7: Process oriented approach
  information processing
  learning theories–motor and cognitive
  neuropathology
  cognitive–perceptual and postural control
  therapeutic use of activities–activity analysis
Chapter 8: Neurofunctional approach
  learning theories; cognitive science
  neuropsychology–attention, memory, problem solving
  activity analysis–functional behavioral analysis
Chapter 9: A retraining approach
  neuropsychology
  cognitive psychology
  activity intervention
Chapter 10: Cognition and MOHO
  constructivism–Piaget
  information processing
  model of human occupation
Chapter 11: Non-verbal learning disabilities–MOHO
  learning disabilities–non-verbal
  perceptual cognitive deficits
  model of human occupation

We can visualize a continuum where on the one end exists a general model in occupational therapy, that of human occupation, which guides the intervention with cognitively dysfunctional patients/clients. In the middle, the only existing cognitive disabilities theory in occupational therapy is extended and refined conceptually and clinically. While, on the other end, newly developed occupational therapy approaches are presented, some more complete and elaborate, such as Toglia's, and the others less so. Most important in my view is that all approaches, as mentioned already, integrate cognition with activity intervention, which makes them occupational therapy approaches.

Assumptions or Premises

One major distinction may be drawn between those approaches which assume that cognitive impairments can be modified and treated directly, further assuming that generalization will occur to other areas and activities. Other approaches assume that generalization cannot be expected and suggest that direct training and practice of functional activities have to be performed. The later premise is part of Allen's cognitive disabilities theory and Giles' neurofunctional approach.

The other approaches assume that cognitive structures can be modified through training, and may be generalized to additional areas. However, this generalization will not occur by itself; generalization has to be practiced as well, but not every single task has to be trained. As Toglia (1991) states, based on recent studies in cognitive psychology, transfer of learning or generalization should be part of the learning process. This emphasis is most strongly made by Feuerstein's theory of mediated learning experiences.

The disinction made leads also to the difference between the premise that we have to adjust the task and the environment to the person's capabilities versus the focus on the individual's adaptation to the existing environment. These two premises are combined to some extent in many of the approaches, but the main focus on one or the other changes.

Target Populations

Age

Adolescents and adults are the target populations for whom the approaches in this book are intended. The age ranges are not specified in any of the approaches, but in general the age range applies from adolescence throughout the life span. Only one approach has a more limited age population and that is Levy's application of cognitive disabilities model to the elderly.

Etiology or Diagnosis

All approaches were developed for intervention with individuals with cognitive dysfunctions. Etiology or diagnosis is not the major consideration. The dysfunctional performance, the qualitative deficits in behavior that cognitive impairments or disabilities cause, are the focus of intervention.

Allen's cognitive disabilities model is intended for patients with central nervous system problems, with or without physical dysfunctions, who have difficulties in acquiring new information and adjusting to change. This may include psychiatric patients; patients with brain injuries, stroke, dementia, addictions; and elderly patients with cognitive and physical dysfunctions (Chapters 1 through 3).

Psychiatric patients are also the target population in the piagetian framework, which focuses on cognitive organization (Chapter 4), and in the dynamic approaches (Chapters 5 and 6), which describe applications to schizophrenic patients.

Brain-injured patients are the main target population in most of the chapters (notably 5, 7, 8, 9) but all approaches are applicable also to patients with cerebral vascular accidents and other neurologically based cognitive impairments. Patients with brain injuries and dementia are the populations presented in Chapter 10 using the model of human occupation; however, this model, as the authors state, may be used for guiding intervention with psychiatric and learning disabled populations as well. Finally, a specific adult population—one with non-verbal learning disabilities—is the target population of the approach presented in Chapter 11, where the model of human occupation is also used as a framework for intervention.

The cognitively dysfunctional person is the central focus of the intervention approaches; however, within the cognitive disabilities model, Allen, Levy, and Stone emphasize that caregivers or family members are also included in the target populations together with the patient.

Setting and Stage of Illness

The approaches in general are applicable to hospitalized patients as well as to clients in recovery phases including rehabilitation centers and at home in the community. However, some focus more on the treatment phase in the hospital and others, such as the approaches guided by the model of human occupation, are applied more in the community. The stage of illness (as it influences the patients' performance), the level of severity, and the type of cognitive dysfunction may determine the appropriateness of intervening with a specific approach. All approaches share the final aim of rehabilitating the patient/client in his or her environment.

Evaluation Procedures and Research

Table 2 shows a comparison of the variety of evaluation methods and instruments utilized. Each approach is in accordance with its theoretical assumptions and target population in using the appropriate evaluation procedure.

The evaluation methods can be divided along the dimension of formal assessment (i.e., structured, standardized, psychometric, quantitative) versus naturalistic evaluation (i.e., qualitative, observation, interview, functional assessment, etc.). Another dimension is dynamic versus static assessment within the formal category. Structured assessment instruments are presented in the cognitive disabilities model, in the piagetian framework, in the dynamic interactional approach, in the retraining approach, and, interwoven with treatment, in cognitive modifiability. Except for the last approach mentioned, all others have developed or adapted instruments as part of the occupational therapy approach. Dynamic assessments are developed by Toglia and partially by Stone, while the piagetian tasks are originally process based. Abreu and Hinojosa present a scale for reporting assessment results. The LOTCA and RBMT as well as ACL and RTI are the most "static" assessments among the occupational therapy instruments. All instruments are assumed to relate directly to functional performance and to daily life activities. Cermak and Murray in Chapter 11 provide an additional list of structured tools often used by occupational therapists.

The other group of approaches emphasize observations on functional performance in activities of daily life, history and role analysis, gathering information with questionnaires, checklists, interviews, etc. The neurofunctional and the process-oriented approaches and the approaches guided by the model of human occupation are in this category. However, information from standardized testing of other professionals in the team is considered valuable and an important addition to the evaluation of occupational therapy. Formal assessment can be performed by occupational therapists but is not an integral part of the approach.

Conversely, I should emphasize that all approaches in the first category mentioned integrate functional evaluations and observations as well.

Concomitant with the kind of instruments utilized, relevant research is also provided. Research data on measurement properties are reported or are in process for the more structured instruments. Research studies related to the more naturalistic methods do not currently exist. In general only a few research studies are reported in all approaches. The studies available center on reliability and validity of the instruments and on their differentiating power between groups. All methods of evaluation have to be further studied, with either quantitative and/or qualitative research methods, in order to substantiate their assessment power as the basis for treatment planning and rehabilitation recommendations.

Treatment Methods and Research

One fundamental and unifying method exists in all occupational therapy approaches reported in this book, namely, the use of activity, task, or occupational analysis. The cognitive components of analysis may differ depending on the theoretical concepts utilized in each approach. What is considered activity may also be defined differently, including tabletop and/ or computer exercises, crafts, or self-care, work, and leisure activities. This also relates to the underlying assumptions of patients' potential for generalization. When the approach assumes generalization occurs then exercises can be beneficial; but if it does not, then direct practice in necessary daily tasks is essential.

In addition to activity analysis, most approaches also emphasize environmental analysis and adaptation. Here, too, the differences between approaches center on whether the patient's potential for cognitive modifiability is assumed (thus, he or she will be required to adapt to existing environmental circumstances) or whether the environmental demands must be changed and adapted to the patient's present capacity.

Case descriptions are provided in most chapters. These cases are intended to present the readers with examples of how the approach is applied. The case studies can help the readers in understanding the approach described and can also serve to evaluate the completeness and stage of development of the approach.

Thus, in every approach consistent theoretical bases, concepts, and assumptions, with consistent evaluation procedures and treatment methods and consistent characteristics of the patient population form the first criterion for the merit of the approach. The second criterion is available research data to support the effectiveness of the intervention. While, the first criterion seems to be adhered to, the second is almost nonexistent regarding treatment effectiveness. Only in the neurofunctional approach, in which Giles reports on single-case and small-group studies, has research been shown that demonstrated the efficacy of functional task training with brain-injured adults in specific areas.

This state of the art also reflects the occupational therapy profession in

Table 2 Comparison of Target Populations, Evaluation and Treatment

	Population	Evaluation	Treatment
ch 1:	Psychiatry Brain damage Dementia Addiction	Allen Cognitive Level test Routine Task Inven- tory Scratch pad assembly	Task analysis Task demands adapted to pa- tient's capacity Caregiver guidance Placement recom- mendations
ch 2:	Elderly Cognitively and Physical	Functional assess- ment Assessing cognitive levels	Activity analysis Compensatory strate- gies Caregiver guidance
ch 3:	Psychiatry, Short-term	ACL-PS Clinical assessment ADL assessment process	Activity analysis Evaluation clinics Family guidance
ch 4:	Psychiatry	Piagetian cognitive tests	Activity analysis Individual and group
ch 5:	Brain injury Schizophrenia	Dynamic Interac- tional Assessment– DIA Instruments: DVPA, TCA Deductive reasoning, CMT	Functional training Compensation Multicontext: Strat- egy, metacognition, task analysis
ch 6:	Brain injury Psychiatry Adaptational problems	Instrument Enrich- ment Instruments for eval- uation and treat- ment	Individual Also groups
ch 7:	Brain injury CVA, brain tumor	Activity and environ- mental analysis for assessment and treatment; Natu- ralistic methods and Standardized tests, Scale for re- porting scoring of performance	Activities in 3 phrases: Detection Discrimination Hypothesis genera- tion Environmental de- sign
ch 8:	Severe Brain Injury	Neurofunctional as- sessment Observation in real life: Initial screen- ing of performance components	Retraining of real world skills task analysis Prompts, Reinforce- ment

Table 2 *(continued*

	Population	Evaluation	Treatment
		Structured and general; also questionnaires, rating scales, Checklists, standardized tests	
ch 9:	Brain damage Neuropsychologically impaired, learning problem	LOTCA RBMT Premorbid information Sensorimotor, ADL	Retraining of cognitive components in graded levels, building strategies, Transfer to real life situations
ch 10:	Brain injury Psychiatry, Geriatric Learning disabilities	Evaluation guided by the subsystems of MOHO; Neuropsychological battery by a team member; Structured observations, Role checklist, interview, OT instruments as indicated by each case	Activities of daily life, Environmental adaptations Work & leisure roles
ch 11:	Adult Nonverbal learning disabilities	Evaluation guided by the MOHO: subsystems, environment and history, List of tools; observation; reports of other professional	Strategies for coping with daily life tasks Community intervention

general. Research efforts, which have increased steadily in recent years, focused mainly on evaluation instruments. This is true also in the two existing models utilized in this book, cognitive disabilities and human occupation. Only a small body of studies exists on the effectiveness of intervention methods in occupational therapy. Therefore, all the authors emphasize the necessity and importance of planning and performing studies on the efficacy of occupational therapy cognitive approaches for further knowledge development and clinical application.

Summary

This book provides theoretical foundations for occupational therapy intervention with cognitively dysfunctional populations. A variety of theoretical approaches are presented, some similar to the others and some different. As Toglia states at the end of her chapter, "In the absence of evidence that demonstrates that one cognitive rehabilitation approach is better than another, clinicians need to continue to keep broad perspectives, critically analyze the results of their treatment, and ask many questions" (Chapter 5, p. 139). I would add that clinicians, theoreticians, and researchers should critically analyze the knowledge base presented here. They should design studies to support each approach, as well as compare among them, to understand and explicate the conditions appropriate for each intervention method.

All approaches need further development, refinement, and validation. Some are farther along the way than others; all provide the interested professional with many questions and postulates to explore. The major premise underlying this area in occupational therapy is the causal relationship between cognition and purposeful activity or occupation. Cognition is assumed to be a major determinant of human functional performance. Questions about these relationships should be asked and studied. The range of adolescent and adult patient populations who suffer from various types of cognitive disabilities is extensive. Occupational therapists are involved in treatment of these patients in all stages of their illness and in all settings from the hospital to the community. Thus, it is our professional duty and privilege to extend our knowledge base to enable the best possible intervention for these patients.

More recently a whole new challenge was put forward in our profession, that of the development of occupational science (Yerxa et al., 1989; Clark et al., 1991), namely, the basic science underlying occupational therapy intervention. Clark and colleagues (1991) present a model of the human subsystems that influence occupation as an organizing heuristic. Within this model information processing is conceived of as a ". . . subsystem which deals with the cognitive operations that are used by humans to organize behavior" (p. 303).

Yerxa et al. (1989) stress the need for understanding the relationship between engagement in occupation and health (p. 1). This book's contribution to the beginning of occupational science is in exploring and conceptualizing about the role cognition or information processing plays in the interaction between occupation and health.

Considering the 30 years that have passed since Reilly stated her hypothesis, occupational therapy has made a large step forward in knowledge development: From Reilly's assertion in 1961 that "occupational therapy can be one of the great ideas of 20th-century medicine," to aspiring to become a profession with a basic underlying science of occupation in the twenty-first century (Yerxa et al., 1989). Hard work lies ahead of us, but it is exciting to be part of a dynamic process of professional growth and change.

References

Abreu, B., & Toglia, J. P. (1987). Cognitive rehabilitation: A model for occupational therapy. *American Journal of Occupational Therapy, 41,* 439–448.

Allen, C. K. (1985). *Occupational therapy for psychiatric disease: Measurement and management of cognitive disabilities.* Boston: Little, Brown.

Clark, F. A., Parham, D., Carlson, M. E., Frank, G., Jackson, J., Pierce, D., Wolfe, R. J., & Zemke, R. (1991). Occupational science: Academic innovation in the service of occupational therapy's future. *American Journal of Occupational Therapy, 45* (4), 300–310.

Kielhofner, G. (1985). *A model of human occupation, theory and application.* Baltimore: Williams & Wilkins.

Reilly, M. (1973). Occupational therapy can be one of the great ideas of 20th-century medicine. In *The Eleanor Clark Slagle Lectures 1955–1972* (pp. 87–105.) Rockville, MD: American Occupational Therapy Association.

Toglia, J. P. (1991). Generalization of treatment: A multicontext approach to cognitive perceptual impairments in adults with brain injury. *American Journal of Occupational Therapy, 45* (6), 505–516.

Yerxa, E. J., Clark, F. A., Frank, G., Jackson, J., Parham, D., Pierce, D., Stein, C., & Zemke, R. (1989). An introduction to occupational science: A foundation for occupational therapy in the 21st century. *Occupational Therapy in Health Care, 6* (4), 1–17.

1

□ □ □
□ □ □
□ □ □

Cognitive Disabilities

Claudia Kay Allen

A cognitive disability reflects an individual's incapacity to process the information necessary to do ordinary activities safely. Six cognitive levels outline the degree of the disability, from profound disability (at level 1) to functional safety (at level 6). The disability is caused by a medical condition that restricts the way the brain operates. The restriction becomes apparent when something abnormal occurs. When the information needed to learn in order to adapt is not processed, doing activities can be dangerous and social assistance is required to protect the disabled person. Social assistance maximizes the cognitively disabled person's remaining abilities while protecting him or her from harm (Allen, 1985; Allen & Earhart, in press).

My focus in this chapter on disability is consistent with the classification systems published by the World Health Organization (WHO) in the *International Classification of Diseases* (ICD 9) (9th Revision, 1980) and the *International Classification of Impairments, Disabilities, and Handicaps* (ICIDH) (1980). ICD 9 is divided into three subheadings: etiology, pathology, and manifestations that represent the medical model. ICIDH contains the subheadings of impairments, disabilities, and handicaps and is concerned with the consequences of health problems. The medical model is driven by the cause of the problem but outcomes are not. Outcomes can have a variety of causes and are driven by the individual's learning to adapt to restricted abilities and learning how to use his or her remaining abilities to the full potential.

Cognitive Disability Theory

Cognitive disability theory is concerned with learning, as affected by accidents of nature. When this learning method is restricted by a disease process, the individual's ability to do activities safely is also restricted. The theory attempts to describe those restrictions, but identifying restrictions is really a secondary goal. The primary goal is identifying remaining abilities. The remaining abilities are what therapists try to tap in practice to help people with disabilities adapt to their disabilities. The sequence of remaining abilities describes the way new abilities are acquired and the transition from one degree of ability to another (Allen & Earhart, in press).

The cognitive levels measure one's capacity to learn to adapt to a disability. An individual adapts to a disability during the process of doing an activity. To engage in activities the individual must process information through the sensorimotor system. The sensorimotor system is an open method of learning by forming sensory associations, utilizing stored sensorimotor models, inventing new sensorimotor models, and speculating about possible motor actions (Miller, 1981; Allen & Earhart, in press).

The cognitive levels are arranged in an ordinal scale to describe distinct sensorimotor models as follows: automatic, postural, manual, goal directed, exploratory, and planned actions (Allen, 1982; 1985). A decimal system has been added to the original six levels to be more sensitive to change. The range of the cognitive level is from .0 to .9. Thus, at level 4, goal-directed actions range from 4.0 to 4.9. The cognitive levels are based on an aggregate of information that is used to guide motor actions. An aggregate is a whole that is greater than the sum of its parts. Two aggregates are formed within each cognitive level, at .0 and .4. The aggregate formed at .0 guides the motor action named in the title of the cognitive level. The aggregate formed at .4 incorporates all of the external sensory information related to the motor action. The cognitive levels are concerned with how information is combined into wholes to form sensorimotor models (Allen & Earhart, in press).

Descriptive models are superimposed on the cognitive levels to outline the way that the wholes are formed. People begin to process the information for the next cognitive level in the previous level at .5. Attention to level 4 information, for example, begins at 3.5. The range of the descriptive model is from .5 to .4. The descriptive model outlines the behavior that indicates that the information required to form the next aggregate is being processed. For discussion purposes the descriptive behaviors are named awareness, movement, action, activity, variation, and speculation. The relationship between the cognitive level and the descriptive model is displayed on Table 1, whereas Table 2 provides a brief outline of the descriptions. For a more elaborate description see Allen & Earhart (in press).

Fortunately a pattern for learning each model can be identified. An aggregate for motor actions forms at .0. At .2 the motor actions are oriented to external information. By .4 the model is integrated by forming an aggregate of all related external information. At .6, the system is open to information from the next cognitive level in a rather haphazard and unpredictable man-

Table 1 Superimposing the Descriptive Models on the Cognitive Levels and Sensorimotor Models

Descriptive Model Behavior	Level	Sensorimotor Model Learned
	0	Coma
Awareness	0.9	
	1.0	Automatic Actions
Movement	1.5	
	2.0	Gross Motor Actions
Action	2.5	
	3.0	Manual Actions
Activity	3.5	
	4.0	Goal-directed Activities
Variations	4.5	
	5.0	Exploratory Actions
Speculations	5.5	
	6.0	Planned Actions

ner. The .8 level forms a composite of information that, as a sum, is easily broken down into the parts. This sum is organized into a whole aggregate at .0. The odd numbers form sensory associations for the information of the next higher even number. The odd-numbered sensory associations are precursors to acting on the information within the even numbers. This pattern of learning is observed in each of the cognitive levels (Allen & Earhart, in press).

The range of the total scale is 0.9 to 6.0, with a total of 52 potential scores. Each score represents a mode of performance, which is *a pattern of behaving or problem solving.* The modes are in hierarchical order, with each succeeding mode adding more information. An ordinal scale can be safely assumed, but criteria for establishing an interval scale for learning and behavior are uncertain (Allen & Earhart, in press).

Table 2   Modes of Performance

A brief description of the modes of performance is provided to give the reader an impression of the degree of specificity outlined. These descriptions can be given greater clarity by applying them to common activities, like preparing food, as well as common processes, such as cutting (Allen & Earhart, in press).

Level 0: Coma
Coma is a prolonged state of unconsciousness with a lack of a specific response to stimuli.

0.9 Generalized reflexive actions are total body responses for no apparent reason or as a global response to stimuli.

Level 1: Automatic Actions
Automatic actions are a response to a stimulus initiated by someone else and are invariable reactions to the stimulus.

1.0 Withdrawing is a specific response to a noxious stimulus. Moans may be heard.

1.2 Responding is a specific response to stimulation of one of the five senses such as sniffing, blinking, salivating, or licking. Moans and grimaces may be elicited.

1.4 Locating stimuli is turning the head or tracking with the eyes to find a stimulus or follow a moving stimulus. Hand over hand feeding may be used by placing a hand over the patient's hand and guiding the spoon to the mouth, which may elicit an associated movement of lifting the head up to clear the passageway. The attention span may be a flicker to a few seconds, and continuous cuing to eat may be required.

1.6 Rolling in bed may be initiated by someone else but completed by the patient. Smiles, grunts, and screams may be heard. The attention span may be momentary.

1.8 Raising body part is holding an arm, leg, head, or buttocks up against gravity with continuous cuing. An increased response to loved ones may be observed. "No" with resistance by pushing away may occur.

Level 2: Postural Actions
Postural actions are self-initiated, gross body movements that overcome the effects of gravity and move the whole body in space.

2.0 Overcoming gravity is the first self-initiated response, using trunk stability to stay seated upright. May stay seated until tired and indicate a desire to go to bed, which can be non-verbal. Recognition of own name may occur.

2.2 Righting reaction is a spontaneous use of the arms to keep from falling over to the side or backwards. Standing is to bring oneself upright and hold the position until tired or told to sit. May be able to say own name when asked.

2.4 Walking is on flat surfaces, with an awareness of large objects like furniture and doorways, until tired. Preseverative words, like "thank you" or swear words, may occur.

2.6 Directed walking has a location in mind (bathroom) but may not know where the location is. May walk until arriving at the destination and step up a curb or a step. May lift legs over the edge of a bathtub, place feet on wheelchair, or bang on

Table 2   *(Continued)*

closed doors. Most common destinations are bed and bathroom. Imitation of following a demonstrated direction of gross motor movements of the upper extremities and trunk occurs.

2.8 *Grabbing* is spontaneous reaching out to use grab bars, railing, and other objects to keep from falling. May hold on until a sense of postural stability is achieved or until pried loose. May gesture and use short phrases.

Level 3: Manual Actions
Manual actions are using the hands, and occasionally other parts of the body, to manipulate material objects.

3.0 *Grasping objects* is reaching for, picking up, holding, or throwing objects placed in front of them. These responses are apt to be very slow and may be sustained for a few seconds or until removed. May reject object by walking away. The object may be named.

3.2 *Distinguishing objects* is using the movement associated with an object as in distinguishing between a hair and a tooth brush. The object may be named. The movements may be stopped and started on command but the effect of the movement is not considered. May distinguish between home and hospital.

3.4 *Sustained actions* are one action on one object to change the location or exterior surface of an object for a minute or longer. The effect of the sustained action on the object is not considered. Objects may be placed in a left-to-right sequence if reading and writing follow that direction. Attention may be easily distracted by external stimuli. May name actions engaged in but may speak inaudibly or without consideraton of the comprehension of the listener.

3.6 *Noting the effects on objects* is starting, stopping, and placing according to a feature of the object. The shape or perimeter of the object may guide actions and may name shape. May wait for an effect when cued for a minute or two. May relate a personal message of a vital need to another person.

3.8 *Using all objects* is covering all space, using all supplies, and recognizing the task is done upon completion. Says, "I'm done" or stops working when sense of completion is achieved. May not ask for help when in discomfort by abandoning task or accepting discomfort. Timing is determined by the number of objects available or the size of the surface to be covered; social conventions for measuring time have no meaning.

Level 4: Goal-Directed Actions
Goal-directed actions sequence the self through a series of steps to match a concrete sample or a known standard of how the finished product should appear.

4.0 *Sequencing* is directing the self through known steps to complete a task or seeking instruction about the next step when not known. When distracted, redirects self back to the task. May recognize an error, unknown step, or out of the ordinary situation but may not identify what it is. May be disoriented to the day and date.

4.2 *Differentiating features* is pointing out the difference between two things according to one of the following properties of objects: linear measure, linear direc-

Table 2   *(Continued)*

tion, shape, color, and number up to two. Features are matched and differences
noted, one property at a time. Time may be measured in 1-hour increments, one
activity at a time. May ask about day and date.

*4.4 **Completing goal*** is complying with steps to match a standard of performance
according to the 4.2 features with the addition of number up to four and simultaneous consideration of horizontal and vertical axes. Two features are considered
simultaneously but only one pair at a time. Notices objects in plain sight until
about 3 to 4 feet in front of them. Follows a routine sequence of activities and
knows day and date. Initiates requests for supplies needed to match the standard
of performance.

*4.6 **Personalizing*** is individualizing a task by changing one of the above features or
changing tool use according to past experience. Scanning is looking around the
immediate environment and noticing objects and people that are in plain sight.
Initiates change in routine sequence of own activities. Knows two concurrent
schedules may exist, but may not negotiate schedule conflicts. May press harder,
with brute force, to change effects on objects or recognize when too much force
was applied.

*4.8 **Rote learning*** is memorizing a new sequence of steps to do a task by adding one
step at a time. May ask for verification of each step. A slow inspection of effects
on objects may be done after the task is done by rotating the object and inspect-
ing the end results. Knows how two concurrent schedules fit together and fits
own routine into that of others. May not recognize or initiate personal choice in
activity selection or scheduling priorities.

Level 5: Exploratory Actions
Exploratory actions are discoveries of how changes in neuromuscular control can
produce different effects on material objects.

*5.0 **Comparing and changing variations*** are changes in strength, pressure, or range
of motion applied to a material object that produce different effects. Continuous
comparison and change requires full attention while working; does not talk and
work at the same time. May not change pace of movement or rate of speech on
request. May get tired of doing continuous comparisons and question the need to
do the activity or reject the activity. Recognizes the need to make appointments
and schedule infrequent events, which may be forgotten or missed.

*5.2 **Discriminating*** is estimating the significance of the primary effects that actions
have on the outward appearance of objects while in the process of producing the
effect. May rotate objects while working on them to inspect effects. May explore
the effects on the surface properties of objects. Surface properties are the sheen,
texture, evenness, smoothness, and highlights of objects. Seeks tools and materials to alter effects, but these actions are apt to be impulsive. Unfavorable secondary effects are not considered and frequently occur. Depends on tangible remind-
ers to keep schedules and uses a watch, calender, appointment book, alarm clock,
or other memory aids.

*5.4 **Self-directed learning*** is initiating changes that improve the effectiveness or
efficiency of performance. Changes may include alterations in tools, sequence of

Table 2   *(Continued)*

steps, posture, or work space. Explores the spatial properties of objects. Spatial properties are the relationships between the parts and the whole. May consider different arrangements of parts for better balance or harmony in overall appearance. May argue with requests to change the pace of movements or request more time. May insist on own methods of doing things, choose to follow or disregard the schedule of others, and plan spare time activities around personal priorities.

5.6 Considering social standards is adjusting performance of the task outcome according to conventional expectations. Cultural trends, fashions and fads, politics, and conventional schedules may be considered and discussed. May compare two sets of instruction or substitute own method of doing something after comparison. May have an internal awareness of the passage of time and adjust pace upon request.

5.8 Consulting is seeking opinions about the expected effects on a task outcome and unwanted secondary effects. To consult one must assume that activities have the potential for unwanted secondary effects, and seek advice to avoid hazards. The future effects of the properties of objects are discussed and understood in the presence of the material objects. May initiate variations in own pace. May seek opinions of secondary effects of schedule changes.

6.0: Planned Actions
Planned actions estimate the effect of actions on material objects, but the objects do not have to be present for the estimate to occur. The significance of the effects of a sequence of steps permits anticipation of secondary effects. Two sequences of effects may be compared before the performance process begins. The human brain probably has a limited capacity to compare sequences of effects; seven may be the limit, with three or four more comfortable.

Consequences of Cognitive Disabilities

The social consequences of a cognitive disability are operationally defined in the legal system. In English and American jurisprudence the socially accepted standards of performance can be found within the definitions of ordinary and reasonable care, and a failure to exercise ordinary care is defined as negligence (Black's Law Dictionary, 1979). A cognitive disability occurs when a person lacks the capacity for ordinary care and requires assistance to avoid accidents, injuries, or negligence. The legal system can decide that a cognitively disabled person is not competent to manage his or her own affairs (Allen, 1985; Allen & Earhart, in press).

The full range of six cognitive levels is thought to be available for use by normal adolescents and adults. Fluctuation in the quality of thought used during the course of a day is regarded as normal. The human brain appears to conserve energy and use the minimum amount required to do a particular activity. Most of the time we get up and go to work automatically and do not engage in planning until the demands to do so are placed on us. A cognitive disability limits the range of thought available to a person when he or she encounters a higher cognitive demand (Allen & Earhart, in press).

Presumably, everyone experiences a cognitive disability during his or her lifetime, usually in response to fever or fatigue. Temporary cognitive disabilities are of little social consequence because social allowances are made for them. We adapt by taking some aspirin, going to bed, taking time off from work, and avoiding dangerous situations. Disabilities that extend beyond the usual social allowances (such as 2 weeks of sick time) require more social support. A cognitive disability is a consequence of a health problem (an ICD 9 diagnosis) that produces brain pathology. A loss of normal flexibility in responding to changing environmental demands occurs and becomes meaningfully apparent while the individual is in the process of doing a functional activity (Allen & Earhart, in press).

Cognitive is an umbrella term that contains two alternative explanations for behavior: motivation and learning ability. Motivation is assessed by asking the patient to select the activity. If the patient refuses to try any activity, ability cannot be evaluated. Therapists must be prepared to analyze any activity that the patient will agree to do. Standardized criteria are available for evaluating the cognitive complexity of any activity that is legal (Allen, 1985; Allen & Earhart, in press).

Therapists use observations of behavior to draw inferences about the patient's learning abilities. Unfortunately, these inferences tend to jeopardize the reliability of the therapist's assessment. To keep the assessment reliable, therapist's must rule out motivational explanations. The patient must be willing to try a new activity. I have long suspected that this explains our traditional use of crafts and our current use of computers; they are great motivators with lots of new learning to be gained. These activities work most of the time, but they are not new motivators for everyone; hence, the therapist's need for standardized criteria for activity analysis (Allen, 1985; Allen & Earhart, in press).

Profiles of the quality of functional activities associated with each cognitive level are available (Allen, 1985; 1988; Allen & Allen, 1987). We are in the process of making progress in describing the modes of performance (Allen & Earhart, in press). The profiles describe the behavior that is likely to occur (such as forgetting to turn off the stove or not getting the shampoo out of one's hair).

Patients functioning at level 4 and below do not, for all practical purposes, generalize. Patients whose maximum ability is level 5 do some gneralizing, but it is often ineffective and very inefficient. Generalization occurs in a reliable and efficient manner at level 6, when no cognitive disability is present. The learning theory describes the building blocks for generalization.

The theory can be applied to teaching people who have limited abilities to generalize (Allen, 1982; 1985; 1987a; Allen & Earhart, in press).

Target Population

The original description of cognitive levels was developed while I was working with psychiatric patients (Allen, 1982; 1985). The advantage of working with psychiatric patients is that they do not have physical disabilities that might explain their functional difficulties. By observing psychiatric patient's movements one can get a fairly clear picture of how a disabled brain guides functional activities. The behavioral criteria for psychiatric diagnosis have proven to be a great advantage as well (APA, 1987). Some behavioral difficulties are diagnosis specific, whereas other difficulties cut across diagnostic categories. Difficulties that are shared by people with different diagnoses are characteristic of a cognitive disability (Allen & Allen, 1987). The possibility that the learning theory might be helpful with a variety of learning difficulties was recognized during the early developmental stages, and great effort has been made to keep the theory open to different frames of reference.

Learning difficulties can be divided into the component parts of brain functions, listed as impairments in ICIDH (WHO, 1950). Examples of impairments include perception, attention, memory, orientation, and apraxia. While we might assume that there is a connection between an individual's impairments and his or her performance of activities, that assumption has not been validated. This assumption needs to be tested and clarified. One might also assume that an improvement in impairment tasks will generalize to improvement in many activities. My guess is that the first assumption can be substantiated, and that the second assumption can be substantiated, to a limited extent, at level 5, but that treatment failures occur at levels 3 and 4. Learning is situation specific at levels 3 and 4, and training may be more effective in the home or on the job. When the therapist cannot assume generalization is being made, teaching cannot be broken down into the components of thinking. At levels 3 and 4, teaching needs to be integrated into the specific activity that the individual will be doing.

To the extent that a therapist's services depend on the therapist's ability to teach a person how to do something, the therapist should evaluate that person's ability to learn. Therapist's have a tendency to assume that learning ability is within normal limits, and that assumption is often wrong. Numerous treatment failures are based on this erroneous assumption. All patients should be screened for a cognitive disability. Long-term caregivers often have learning difficulties too, but therapists may not be able to test them. In those cases, the therapist needs to understand the cognitive levels well enough to do an assessment on the spot, in any new activity that the caregiver will agree to do.

The target population then, includes patients and caregivers who have difficulties in acquiring new information and adjusting to change. An assumption is made that a medical problem explains the etiology, pathology, and manifestations of the reason for the difficulty, but services are not directed toward changing the reason for the difficulty. The primary emphasis is on living safely and better with a disability, with secondary attention to impairments and handicaps.

Intervention

Evaluation Methods

The Allen Cognitive Level test is a screening tool that can be used to quickly assess levels 3, 4, and 5. The patient is asked to imitate three leather lacing stitches: sewing, whip, and single cordovan stitch. Each stitch is done three times and the patient continues until an error is made that he or she cannot correct. The ACL has been around long enough for several versions to exist. The original was published in 1985 (Allen). Research studies prompted an expanded scoring scale (Mayer, 1988; Newman, 1987; Earhart & Allen, 1988). Visual impairments that interfere with seeing the stitches prompted a larger version (Allen, and Earhart, in press). And a capping effect, failing to make clear separations within levels 5 and 6, prompted a new method of giving the instructions (Josman & Katz, 1991). A test kit and testing manual for the 1990 version are available for purchase (Allen, 1990c).

The ease of administration makes the ACL a popular research tool, so much so that we know quite a lot about what these scores mean. The Routine Task Inventory is a functional description of behavior associated with each of the six cognitive levels. The original list of activities was taken from an inventory developed by Lawton and Brody (1969). Reliability and validity data are available for the original list of activities, based on caregiver reports (Heinmann, Allen, and Yerxa, 1989; Wilson et al., 1989).

An expanded version of the RTI is also available (Earhart & Allen, 1988) which includes two subscales for communication and work/leisure and the activities of doing child care and therapeutic exercise. A comprehensive review of the reliability and validity data on these instruments can be found in Katz & Heinmann (1990) and Allen & Earhart (in press).

A scratch pad assembly task was standardized for the first study done by Herzig (Allen, 1985). Richards (1983) established a significant correlation between the ACL and the scratch pad scoring criteria ($r = .726, p < .001$). Standardized procedures for checking safety awareness while cooking are available for people functioning at level 4. The tasks include making pudding and macaroni and cheese. An accurate or genuine relationship was found between the ACL score and the number of errors made while making macaroni and cheese ($\chi^2 = 9.295, p = .002$) (Alsberg, 1987).

Treatment Approach

The treatment approach varies according to the medical condition of the patient. During the acute phase, the patient is not medically cleared to engage in any activities. With a cognitive disability, the acute phase is most likely to occur when patients are on suicidal, homicidal, or elopement precautions. Learning may or may not be evaluated during this phase. During the post-acute phase the patient is medically cleared to engage in some activities. With a cognitive disability a change in the cognitive level can be expected during the post-acute phase, for a variety of medical reasons. Very little change in the cognitive level is expected during the rehabilitation phase. Treatment focuses on helping people adjust to their residual disabilities. The primary goal is the identification of remaining abilities that can still be used. Long-term care occurs when specially designed activities are required to utilize the person's remaining abilities. The treatment approach aims at maintaining the person's maximum ability to function by matching the person's cognitive level to the demands of the activity (Allen & Earhart, in press).

To permit comparisons between the approaches the same format is used to describe each approach as follows: patient condition, length of stay, occupational therapy outcome, methods, referral criteria, discharge criteria, and language from the WHO typologies recommended for documentation in the patient's record.

Post-Acute Phase

In this phase, the patient is being examined to establish a diagnosis, has a new diagnosis, or has an acute problem with a previous diagnosis. The medical stability of the patient or the need for diagnostic tests often determines the length of stay. The primary OT outcome is to recommend the least restrictive environment that the patient can function safely in at the time of discharge. Four methods are used to achieve this outcome. First, at the time of admission or referral an evaluation is done to establish a baseline of symptoms of the disease or injury that are most likely to produce impairment or disability. Second, the patient's progress is monitored to measure change in symptoms, impairments, and disabilities. Third, the point in time when functional stability is reached is identified. Finally, the meaning of residual symptoms and impairments is interpreted for the treatment team by describing the typical quality of performance to be expected in doing functional activities.

The evaluation of change is associated with other explanations of change such as natural healing and psychotropic drugs. Within this frame of reference, therapists use sensitive measures to evaluate the effectiveness of medical care, to identify the point in time when change has stopped, and to assist with necessary adjustments to any of the consequences of an illness. During post-acute care the therapist's unique knowledge is derived from his or her understanding of how cognitive losses are likely to affect the individual and the community. Within this context, there are three suggested referral criteria: (1) patients with a diagnosis that predicts a short- or a long-term disability; (2) patients with a severe disability who are likely to require assistance for functional safety at the time of discharge; and (3) patients with a disability that is mild enough for them to actively participate in functional activities. Discharge criteria are determined by the physician according to the medical stability of the patient (Allen & Earhart, in press).

The medical model predominates during the post-acute phase; diagnostic categories and symptoms can be found in the patient's record. Therapists should use the medical terminology to communicate common concerns to other members of the treatment team. Therapists use ICIDH terminology to communicate concerns about impairments and disabilities. When the problem-oriented record adheres to medical terminology, therapists may find it difficult to record impairments and disabilities in the chart. If DSM III-R (APA, 1987) is being used, requesting Axis V's inclusion of the problem list is effective. In other situations a general problem description like "functional limitations" helps establish a location for discussing impairments and disabilities. Within a hospital setting, documentation should address both of the WHO classification systems (Allen & Earhart, in press).

The unique knowledge of the therapist is applied to making discharge recommendations. Discharge recommendations may include warnings about safety hazards that may not be noticed by the patient, changes in the home or work environment that may protect people from injury or prevent property damage, recommendations for changes in legal status when the patient is unable to manage his or her own affairs, and suggestions for rehabilitation services when the patient needs and can benefit from help adjusting to a disability. On a medical team, the therapist can be the lone advocate for the help the individual needs to deal with the day-to-day consequences of a medical problem (Allen, 1985; 1987b; Allen & Earhart, in press).

Rehabilitation

Rehabilitation occurs after the medical condition has cleared but some reduction in the degree of impairment and disability can still be achieved, usually 7 days to 6 months after the onset of the diagnosis. The treatment setting can be inpatient or outpatient as determined by the patient's need for skilled care. The length of stay is determined by the rate of remission expected with the patient's diagnosis and the severity of the impairments. The primary OT outcomes are to facilitate return to maximal functional ability and to prevent secondary complications that produce further disability. These outcomes are achieved by: (1) obtaining a functional history prior to onset; (2) discussing anticipated changes in life-style and identifying priorities of the individual patient as well as any priorities of the expected long-term care givers; (3) improving the patient's neuromuscular status when needed and possible; (4) engaging the patient in doing prioritized activities to promote his or her adjustment to the loss of abilities; (5) explaining the short-term and long-term assistance needs of the patient and other care givers; and (6) teaching the use of desired adaptive equipment and environmental compensations to the patient and the caregiver.

Rehabilitation is the treatment process that helps the patients make the transition from acute care to custodial care. When change in the cognitive level has stopped, or reached a steady state, treatment goals shift to a focus on living with a residual disability. Safety is the primary concern of stabilization services. The cognitively disabled patient requires the assistance of another person to do his or her problem solving. Custodial caregivers are consulted and asked about their priorities in selecting treatment goals to ease the burden of care. Caregivers are instructed in effective treatment techniques, the removal of hazards, and any drilling needed for training procedures. During the stabilization process, therapists are expected to help the patient and the caregiver through the grief of a loss of cognitive ability. If one or both people deny a residual disability, therapists are obligated to warn them of the difficulties they are likely to encounter. Rehabilitation sets up a maintenance program for a disabled person in a long-term care setting as safely and functional as possible (Allen & Earhart, in press).

Admission and discharge decisions are still monitored by physicians, but the primary burden of responsibility for establishing criteria resides with the therapist. The suggested referral criteria are as follows: (1) patients with a new diagnosis and a prognosis for a physical and/or a cognitive disability; (2) patients with a long-term disability who have experienced a recent change in the severity of the disability; (3) patients with a severity of disability that produces a burden of care, on self or others, that can probably be reduced by improved neuromuscular status or environmental compensations; (4) patients with a cognitive disability that is expected to improve but needs to be monitored for functional safety and adjustment to the disability; or (5) patients with a disability that is mild enough to continue to engage in some functional activities. The rate and degree of change may be expected to be slower and smaller than the change observed during the post-acute phase. The modes of performance may detect these changes, and the accompanying descriptions of the activities of daily living should help therapists predict the importance of these changes (Allen & Earhart, in press).

Stabilizing patients at cognitive levels 3 and 4 tends to raise questions about the need for skilled occupational therapy services. Patients functioning at these levels can be trained to do functional activities, but they usually need a great deal of repetitive drilling before they can follow a procedure safely and consistently. A therapist's knowledge of the cognitive levels is useful in setting up the training procedure and correlating that knowledge with ways of adjusting to physical disabilities. Once the training procedure has been established the therapist should train a long-term caregiver in the therapeutic techniques that facilitate the repetitive drilling (Allen & Earhart, in press).

Warning people about safety hazards is a critical part of the stabilization process. Therapists ask the patient and the caregiver what activities they intend to do and inquire about activities the patient has enjoyed in the past. If cognitive levels specify safety hazards that are likely to be a problem in the intended activities, the therapist should use that knowledge to recommend ways of modifying the activity whenever possible. Some activities, like driving, cannot be done safely given the patient's current cognitive level and discontinuing the activity must be recommended. When people are functioning at level 4, warnings are frequently ignored. In a free society, the therapist may be in the uncomfortable position of recommending but not legally stopping the activity. It is tempting to say, "He is going to do it anyway. I'm going to make it as safe as possible." Perish the thought. Teaching the patient an activity that you basically consider unsafe places you in legal jeopardy. Instead, you should document your warnings and hope that the people involved come to their senses before anything serious happens. When necessary, therapists should take steps to initiate legal action (such as removing driver's licenses or obtaining a legal guardian) (Allen & Earhart, in press).

Rehabilitation helps the disabled person and the long-term caregivers adjust to impairments. An impairment is a loss at the organ level. The meaning of the loss will become clear when the individual is doing an activity, and grief is a natural response. Therapists are sensitive to the problems of going through grief reactions while helping people get on with the practical aspects of living with a disability. Rehabilitation is regarded as a transition period between acute medical care and long-term care (Allen & Earhart, in press).

The stabilization process ends when all of the significant reductions in the burden of care have been achieved. A significant reduction is one that is meaningful to the individual and/or his or her long-term caregivers. Other reductions may indeed be possible, and therapists often are pressured by co-workers to do it all. All is not recommended. If the activity lacks meaning in a given situation then it should not be addressed. The other form of improvement that therapists are sometimes pressured to pursue is a small, but insignificant, change in neuromuscular status. There is no need to pursue neuromuscular changes that are likely to have little impact on the burden of care or the performance of functional activities.

Perhaps the most difficult judgment call in setting discharge criteria occurs when patients or caregivers cannot go along with the available treatment process. When patients or caregivers disregard warnings for functional safety, in spite of the therapist's best efforts to demonstrate the hazards, they should be discharged. Some patients and caregivers are either unable or unwilling to learn what the therapist can teach. The use of adaptive equipment and environmental compensations must be learned to be effective. At the point in time that the therapist does not expect learning to occur, discharge should occur. As therapists, we have to recognize our own limitations in terms of the motivational and learning abilities that we cannot overcome.

During rehabilitation the terminology used in documentation places the emphasis on disability as related to the burden of care for the individual. Changes in symptoms and limitations are closely monitored and interpreted as they relate to doing functional activities safely. A practical, reality-based, jargon-free form of recordkeeping is recommended. Avoid medical terminology and try to use ordinary language.

Long-term Care

Long-term care is provided for those patients who have been safely stabilized in their long-term care situation. Most candidates for long-term care will probably stabilize at cognitive levels 3 and 4. Individuals at these levels of function, are usually too disabled to fit into normal community activities but not so disabled as to be bedridden or unable to participate in any activity. Occupational therapy probably began by providing activities for individuals at level 3 and 4. It isn't easy. Designing activities that these people can do successfully requires a tremendous amount of creativity. In the U.S., states used deinstitutionalization to avoid their traditional responsibility for providing cognitively disabled people with long-term care. Many of these people became homeless. We now know what happens when people who need long-term care, lack access to functional activities; alcohol and substance abuse are the replacements they seek. Long-term care is a traditional occupational therapy service that should not be abandoned, but rejuvenated.

Patients that require long-term care are those who have been, or will be, disabled longer than 6 months and have a handicap that prevents them from participating in an occupational use of time within the usual community schedule. Long-term care consists of providing an activity program for disabled people within the least restrictive environment that will ensure the safety of both the individual and the community. The length of stay is determined by the prognosis for continued participation in functional activities. The primary OT outcome is to maximize remaining functional abilities within a supportive context and to avoid secondary complications that could produce increased health and social welfare needs (Allen & Earhart, in press).

To participate in these programs people must be willing to accept other people with disabilities and handicapping conditions as their peers. The program must ensure that drug and alcohol abuse is controlled as well as behavior that is dangerous to the individual and others. Activities that match the person's current cognitive ability to function prevent these behaviors from emerging as they do in normal settings. In the U.S., certified occupational therapy assistants have the activity analysis knowledge required and can match activity demands to the disabled person's remaining abilities.

The methods used to achieve participation in a custodial care program include the following:

· Obtaining a functional history that identifies stored sensorimotor models that the individual might be able to use;
· Providing activities that are acceptable to the individual (by reviewing past and present interests) as well as activities that are apt to be rejected by the individual;
· Recognizing residual limitations that will require modification in the usual activity procedure for successful task performance and tactfully making the necessary modifications;
· Replicating a sense of the individual's normal place in history and culture as closely as possible;
· Replacing deviant behavior with behavior that is more socially acceptable;
· Arranging for participation in normal community events whenever economically feasible and socially acceptable;
· Arranging for access to social welfare and health care resources when needed;
· Working with the available social support systems to maintain the highest level of function by explaining the difference between "cannot" and "will not" to other people in the community;

· Assisting other caregivers in making the environmental changes that reduce the burden of care or improve functional abilities;
· Assisting advocacy groups and consumer groups in objectively describing the need for long-term care; and
· Facilitating departure from the long-term care system whenever changes in the disability or social conditions (such as money for supportive employment) permit.

Long-term care is indicated for those people who have a residual disability at level 4 and below. In most instances level 4 functioning places the individual in a severe social disadvantage. A loss of economic self-sufficiency is probably the biggest disadvantage, followed by long hours spent passively watching television or engaging in substance abuse. The recent passage of the Americans with Disability Act provides an opportunity to create programs in the areas of employment as well as access to public accommodations, transportation, state and local government services, and telecommunications. Therapists should build on their traditions of providing long-term care by championing the civil rights protections of people with a cognitive disability (Allen & Earhart, in press).

A long-term care program is not transitional, and individuals should be allowed to continue as long as the desire and need are present. Persons with disabilities should not be forced to resume an independent schedule of participation in normal community activities without special assistance. The most likely outcome of such an event is that the condition will worsen to the point where the individual can no longer do any functional activities. Effective long-term care protects the patient and the community.

Implications

Application of the cognitive disability theory is certain to raise concerns about how hard a therapist should push a patient to increase his or her abilities. Other concerns some have raised are about the limits on learning imposed by different biological abnormalities (such as mental retardation and brain damage). The modes of performance are more specific descriptions of patterns of behavior than have existed before and are apt to place different demands on therapists in practice.

In general therapists match the task demands to the patient's current mode of performance. Short-term goals also match the patient's current mode of performance. The most basic question is, what should therapists do about possible improvements in the patient's performance mode? Therapists should look for a change on a regular basis by probing for the next higher performance mode. The probe consists of offering a sensory cue from the next mode. When the information is processed, raise your evaluation of the mode as well as your short-term goals. When the probe is ignored, rejected, or causes frustration, continue to match task demands to the current mode and keep the same short-term goals. Do not continue to frustrate or demoralize people by insisting that they try to function at a higher level. Pushing people beyond their capabilities can lead to a fight or flight response that is harmful and must be avoided. Do not allow your professional ego to get caught up in a personal need to force people to improve (Allen & Earhart, in press).

Similar adjustments should be made for a decline in the performance mode. When information from the mode recently given causes frustration or confusion, rescue the patient by offering information from a lower mode. Reduce the information processing demands until the patient can process the information comfortably and then adjust short-term goals (Allen & Earhart, in press).

Long-term treatment goals are based on predicting change in the performance mode. The phase of the illness and the natural course of the illness are important factors to consider. The biggest changes in the performance modes are likely to be seen during the post-acute phase. Observing change does not mean that the therapist caused the change. The assumption that a measurement of change equals a cause of change is far too simplistic. Long-term treatment goals may predict what degree of change will occur without assuming a causal relationship. A patient may be functioning within mode 3.8, and the therapist may predict 4.4 within a month. The long-term treatment goal within this example is 4.4. The reason for the improvement could be natural healing or medical intervention. The importance of the prediction is helping others realistically cope with the consequences of health problems (Allen & Earhart, in press).

Long-term goals for a stabilized mode of performance produce increased responsibilities for therapists as well. While therapists have always been concerned about safety precautions, the performance modes make it necessary to issue warnings. A warning is more distinct and unmistakable than a caution; it speaks plainly and usually details in strong language possible harm or anything else unfavorable. The strength of the advice given should be proportional to the therapist's ability to predict. Because the performance modes are more specific, therapists can be more specific about warnings given (Allen & Earhart, in press).

Therapists must also remember that predicting human behavior is closer to forecasting the weather than replicating what will happen in a chemistry experiment. Therapists can warn people about what may happen and imply that there is a natural tendency for something to happen. There may be a natural predisposition for the patient to forget to turn off the stove, but what an individual actually will do is unknown. The therapist's obligation is to give authoritative and formal notice of easily understood events. The performance modes may hold therapists liable for issuing these warnings, which should be documented in the patient's record (Allen & Earhart, in press).

A greater involvement in issuing warnings suggests a greater involvement in working with families and other caregivers. The modes of performance make it possible to deal with the unfavorable aspects of a cognitive disability in a candid manner. Therapists can help others understand what exactly they need to adjust to, which makes adjustment and planning clearer.

Very little is known about the effects of quality long-term care. Clinical experience suggests that living on the street or in situations where there is nothing to do produces a gradual decline in the mode of performance. Living situations that maximize the person's current mode of performance need to be investigated. Reversal of decline, preventing decline, and ceiling effects may be measured by the modes of performance.

References

Allen, C. K. (1990a). Development of a research tradition. *Mental Health Special Interest Section Newsletter.* American Occupational Therapy Association, *13*(2), 1–3.

Allen C. K. (1990b). Activities: Cross-cultural similarities and differences. In *Proceedings of the 10th International Congress of the World Federation of Occupational Therapy.* Melbourne, Australia.

Allen, C. K. (1990c). *Allen Cognitive Level Test Manual* (with kit included). Coldchester, CT: S & S/Worldwide.

Allen, C. K. (1989). Treatment plans in cognitive rehabilitation. *Occupational Therapy Practice, 1,* 1–8.

Allen. C. K. (1988). *Cognitive disabilities.* In S. Robinson (Ed.), *Focus.* Rockville, MD: American Occupational Therapy Association.

Allen. C. K. (1987a). Occupational therapy: Measuring the severity of mental disorders. *Hospital and Community Psychiatry, 38,* 140–142.

Allen, C. K. (1987b). Eleanor Clarke Slagle Lectureship–1987: Activity; Occupational therapy's treatment method. *American Journal of Occupational Therapy, 41,* 563–575.

Allen, C. K. (1985). *Occupational therapy for psychiatric diseases: Measurement and management of cognitive disabilities.* Boston: Little, Brown.

Allen, C. K. (1982). Independence through activity: The practice of occupational therapy (psychiatry). *American Journal of Occupational Therapy, 36,* 731–739.

Allen, C. K., & Allen, R. E. (1987). Cognitive disabilities: Measuring the social consequences of mental disorders. *Journal of Clinical Psychiatry, 48,* 185–191.

Allen, C. K., & Earhart, C. A. (in press). *Treatment goals for cognitive and physical disabilities.* Rockville, MD: American Occupational Therapy Association

Alsberg D. (1987). *Safety implications of cognitive disabilities: Using cognitive theory as an adjuct to discharge planning.* Unpublished master's thesis, Rush University.

American Psychiatric Association (1987). *Diagnostic and statistical manual, 3rd ed.-Revised.* Washington D.C.: American Psychiatric Association.

Averbuch, S., & Katz, N. (1988). Assessment of perceptual cognitive performance: A comparison of psychiatric and brain injured adult patients. *Occupational Therapy in Mental Health, 8,* 57–71.

Black's Law Dictionary. (1979) (5th ed.) St. Paul, MN; Western Publishing Co.

Earhart, C. A., & Allen, C. K. (1988). *Cognitive disabilities: Expanded activity analysis.* Colchester, CT: S & S/Worldwide.

Heinmann, N. E., Allen, C. K., & Yerxa, E. J. (1989). The routine task inventory: A tool for describing the functional behavior of the cognitively disabled. *Occupational Therapy Practice, 1,* 67–74.

Josman, N., & Katz, N. (1991). Problem-solving version of the Allen Cognitive Level (ACL) test. *American Journal of Occupational Therapy, 45,* 331–338.

Katz, N., & Heinmann, N. (1990). Review of research conducted in Israel on cognitive disability instrumentation. *Occupational Therapy in Mental Health, 10,* 1–15.

Lawton, M. P., & Brody, E. M. (1969). Assessment of older people: Self-maintaining and instrumental activities of daily living. *Gerontologist, 9,* 179–186.

Mayer, M. A. (1988). Analysis of information processing and cognitive disability theory. *American Journal of Occupational Therapy, 42,* 176–183.

Miller, R. (1981). *Meaning and purpose in the intact brain: A philosophical, psychological, and biological account of conscious processes.* New York: Clarendon Press.

Newman, M. (1987). *Cognitive disability and functional performance in individuals with chronic schizophrenic disorders.* Unpublished master's thesis, University of Southern California.

Richards, G. E. (1983). *Evaluation of the Allen cognitive level test as an occupational therapy assessment tool.* Unpublished master's thesis, West Chester State College.

World Health Organization. (1980). *International classification of diseases,* (9th rev.). Geneva, Switzerland: World Health Organization.

World Health Organization. (1980). *International classification of impairments, disabilities, and handicaps.* Geneva, Switzerland: World Health Organization.

Wilson, D. S., Allen, C. K., McCormack, G., & Burton, G. (1989). Cognitive disability and routine task behaviors in a community-based population with senile dementia. *Occupational Therapy Practice, 1,* 58–66.

2 □□□ □□□ □□□

The Use of the Cognitive Disability Frame of Reference in Rehabilitation of Cognitively Disabled Older Adults*

Linda L. Levy

In the gerontological literature, one well-established tenet suggests human ability to maintain activity is central to adaptation, life satisfaction, and retention of desired social roles in the later years (Atchley, 1980; Burrus-Bammel & Bammel, 1985; Havinghurst, 1963; Havinghurst & Feigenbaum, 1968). Equally important to the maintenance of physical and emotional health is the sense of purpose and control that comes from carrying out day-to-day activities (Rodin, 1986; 1989). Yet when faced with common disabilities, the capacity to maintain active participation in preferred activities and social roles is compromised (Gorden, Gaitz, & Scott, 1976; Harris et al. 1975; Rodin, 1989; Trieschmann, 1987). A critical question for our profession is how can we best assist disabled older adults in their attempts to participate successfully in desired life activities and to maximize their independence, life satisfaction, and quality of life.

This chapter discusses the application of Allen's frame of reference for rehabilitating cognitive disabled adults to the elderly population in order to

---

* Portions of this chapter are adapted from *Topics in Geriatric Rehabilitation,* 4(4), 53–66, with permission of Aspen Publishers, Inc., © 1989.

maximize their participation in life-sustaining activities and desired social roles. At the outset, I should point out that the concept of rehabilitating patients with cognitive disabilities is relatively new in the gerontological rehabilitation literature, yet Allen's frame of reference has already made benchmark contributions to this rapidly developing area (Allen, Foto, Moon-Sperling, & Wilson, 1989; Chiu & Smith, 1990; Health Care Financing Administration, 1989; Kemp, 1988; Levy, 1986a; Levy, 1989). I should also note that gerontological rehabilitation is characterized by the simultaneous management of multiple, often multidimensional, disabilities. Accordingly, I present an analytic framework relating rehabilitative strategies that compensate for cognitive limitations and those that compensate for physical limitations. This framework will serve as a guide for conceptualizing interventions that compensate for the limitations experienced by the elder who is both cognitively and physically disabled. This conceptual framework is yet another contribution that Allen's frame of reference has made to the foundations of gerontological rehabilitation.

Literature Review

A brief literature overview is necessary to address issues that should be considered in conceptualizing rehabilitation strategies for the elder with cognitive limitations and to provide the reader with an interdisciplinary perspective for appreciating the key contributions of Allen's cognitive disability frame of reference.

Allen was the first to propose a comprehensive rehabilitation theory that would address the functional problems experienced by the elder with dementia.

Allen's cognitive disability frame of reference was introduced in the literature in 1986 (Levy, 1986a) and has already provided gerontological rehabilitation professionals with a broad conceptual framework for addressing many of the problems that had been identified in the literature. As will be seen, this framework (1) examines the causes of the symptoms of dementia; (2) provides guidelines for assessing the specific difficulties experienced by the individual; (3) describes viable intervention strategies for assisting individuals and their families in coping with the wide range of physical, psychological, and social problems that occur as the disease progresses; (4) provides guidance on how best to support the individual throughout the course of the disease; and (5) proposes a comprehensive and humanistic approach to care.

Dementia can be defined as the progressive, global impairment of orientation, memory, judgment, and all other aspects of intellectual functioning. Dementia, the single most common cause of cognitive limitations in the elderly, is also the most common cause of all disability in the aged and the most critical deterrent to quality of life in the later years (Butler & Lewis, 1973). Dementia persists as one of the most serious medical–social–economic problems facing society today (Aronson & Lipkowitz, 1981). It is the primary diagnosis in about 5% of adults over the age of 65 years. The incidence increases to 20% in persons aged 80 and over (Select Committee on Aging, 1987), and recent data reveal that it reaches 33% by the age of 90 and 50% by the age of 95 (OT Week, 1990). The fact that the incidence of dementia increases so sharply with age is cause for enormous health and public policy concern, given that so many people are surviving into advanced old age. Treatment possibilities for the disease are still limited and care for the basic illness is unknown (Levy, 1986b; 1987).

Studying the literature reveals a number of issues that are paramount in considering reasonable bases for intervention:

1. There is no medical treatment for senile dementia. However, there is compelling evidence that some of the psychological and social problems caused by dementia are amenable to intervention (Kahn, 1975, Levy, 1987). It is not reasonable to assume that intervention will restore cognitive functioning or reverse organic brain damage (Levy, 1987).

2. The major tenet of gerontological rehabilitation, i.e., to help the disabled elder reach his or her highest attainable level of skill and function, is equally essential to the satisfactory care of persons with dementia (Reifler & Teri, 1986).

3. Persons with dementia experience a progressive loss of cognitive and functional capacity that necessitates caregiver support from the earliest stage of the disease process. In this role, the caregiver needs assistance from knowledgeable and committed health professionals. For every American presently suffering from some degree of dementia, three close family members are estimated to be deeply affected by the emotional, physical, social, and financial burdens of caregiving (Weiler, 1987).

4. Most cases of dementia are not stable but produce progressive declines in function, and different functional issues arise in different stages of the disease. Caregivers must be familiar with the deteriorating functions common to the course of dementing diseases in order to maximize the functional capabilities that remain and to prepare themselves for the changes to come (Baum, 1990; Chiu & Smith, 1990; Levy, 1987).

5. Dementia is the principal reason clients are admitted to nursing homes: family members are often advised to place dementia patients

there (Brody et al., 1984). Yet nursing homes are generally over-crowded, inadequately funded, understaffed, and rarely able to offer adequate care. A traumatic event for any older person, relocating to a nursing home can be even more catastrophic for persons with dementia. Because of their significant cognitive limitations, these clients have considerable difficulty learning the routines in a nursing home and finding their way around. They often panic in their unfamiliar environments. High doses of tranquilizing drugs are frequently used to control these behaviors, but this only intensifies the problems (Levy, 1987).

6. There are significant advantages in caring for people with dementia in home and community settings rather than nursing homes (Zarit et al., 1981) and, accordingly, health policy efforts increasingly encourage institutional alternatives. The familiar home environment contributes significantly to the quality of life of the person with dementia; for example, within the home care is structured in such a way that people with dementia do not become precipitously disabled, and they might regain some measure of self-care independence (Fry, 1986). However, there is an essential corollary to considering home care for people with dementia: Caregivers must be provided extensive support to endure the enormous physical and emotional demands placed on them (Zarit et al., 1981). Yet, with significant caregiver support, institutionalization might be prevented or delayed (Fry, 1986).

7. Despite increased health policy concerns about institutionalization, the fact that family members always have assumed primary caregiving responsibilities for their relatives with dementia has been largely unappreciated (Gwyther & George, 1986). The overwhelming majority of those affected—clearly 75%—have been cared for in their homes and communities. However, it is just as important to recognize that caregivers are often overwhelmed by stress (Schultz et al., 1990; Levy, 1986b; Zarit et al., 1986; Gilhooly, 1984; Rabins et al., 1982).

8. What prompts caregiver stress and institutional placement are problems such as repetitive behaviors, poor self-maintenance, low rates of social activities, and bizarre conduct (Rabins et al; 1982; Swearer et al., 1988; Tobin & Lieberman, 1976; Zarit et al., 1980). It is not the cognitive or behavioral problems associated with dementia that cause caregivers to become severely stressed, depressed, or physically ill, but rather the caregivers inability to cope with them (Chiu & Smith, 1990; Kemp, 1988; Zarit et al., 1980). Recent studies indicate that family members who cope better with the problems associated with dementia have higher levels of self-efficacy—the belief that one is capable of performing a necessary behavior because one has the

requisite skills, knowledge, physical capacity, and motivation (Cummings, 1987; Gallagher et al., 1987). Hence, there is a critical need for programs to help caregivers develop a sense of self-efficacy to better cope with behavioral problems they encounter. Prior to the introduction of Allen's frame of reference, such programs were rarely offered because strategies that were effective in addressing these problems had not been reported (Levy, 1987).

9. The "environmental docility hypothesis" proposes that the environment plays an increasingly important role in determining functional behavior as competence decreases (Lawton & Nahemow, 1973). For the person with dementia, functional independence is maximized by structuring the environment so that the external demand either matches, or is only incrementally greater than, the level the individual is currently adapted to (Levy, 1987; Lawton & Nahemow, 1973). Prior to the introduction of Allen's frame of reference, the state of the art in this area of rehabilitation was limited to identifying general characteristics of the environment central to the maintenance of competent behavior in all older people. At the same time, the literature pointed to a pressing need for means to better isolate characteristics of environments that are specific to the cognitive limitations experienced by people with dementia throughout the progressively debilitating course of their disease (Levy, 1986b; 1987).

In this area of rehabilitation, we are challenged to have a realistic understanding not only of the individual's capacities and limitations but also of his or her needs, desires, and preferences. To this end, the cognitive disabilities frame of reference has proved to be particularly valuable. It presents an approach to rehabilitation that helps people with dementia lead as normal a life as possible given the disability that exists. This frame of reference offers us the means to identify intact cognitive capacities that can be reinforced and cognitive impairments to be compensated for in the performance of needed or desired activities. It also provides guidance for therapists designing environmental compensations for real-life practical problems. At the same time, it can be used to adapt *any* normal life activity so that the individual's previous interests and self-care routines can be pursued as independently as possible (Levy, 1987).

Further, Allen's model suggests intervention methods we can teach family caregivers, which can improve problem behaviors and may offset unnecessary long-term care placements. Hence, this frame of reference holds promise not only for enhancing the quality of life of the individuals with dementia and their caregivers but also for helping to ease a pressing health policy problem (Levy, 1987). The discussion that follows presents the application of Allen's approach to the problems experienced by the elder with cognitive disabilities such as dementia, with or without co-existing physical disabilities.

Activity Analysis

The influence of disabilities on activity participation is addressed first by means of a comprehensive process known as activity analysis. Simply stated, activity analysis breaks down a desired activity into its multifaceted components and examines how those components affect the activity participant (Cynkin, 1979; Llorens, 1986; Mosey, 1981). Considered in turn are the intrinsic properties of the activity (e.g., necessary tools, materials, and motor patterns); the component demands of the activity on sensory, perceptual, cognitive, affective, motor, and social capacities; and the environmental factors that promote or constrain successful completion of the activity. Activity analysis must be done before designing intervention strategies that will optimize capacities and compensate for the limitations presented by disability. Only after the essential components of a desired activity are identified can rehabilitative strategies be considered for modifying those components that exceed the functional capabilities of the disabled older adult.

Analyzing and modifying an activity to match the capacities and limitations of older adults who have cognitive disabilities with or without physical disabilities is a complex process. The factors involved must be considered at three different levels: operations, results, and meaning (Allen, 1987).

Operations

The term operations refers to the technical processes needed to successfully engage in an activity. The materials, tools, strength, endurance, attention, memory, problem-solving capacities, procedures, and neuromuscular patterns required to complete the activity must be considered. They are then compared to the results of a comprehensive assessment of the functional capacity of the disabled older adult. The functional assessment identifies operations that are limited by the disability as well as functional strengths. Compensatory strategies for accomplishing the activity are then developed.

Two major types of compensatory strategies are used: Activities can be modified by (a) capitalizing on remaining neuromuscular and cognitive capabilities or (b) modifying elements of the environment. To illustrate, when the therapist's assessment of the individual's functional capacities reveals that a specific motor pattern necessary to do the activity is not available to the individual, the therapist can adapt the activity to use the individual's remaining motor and cognitive capacities. For example, although two hands are ordinarily required to dress, if the individual has lost the use of one hand, he or she can learn to dress with one hand. The alternative strategy compensates for motor, sensory, or cognitive limitations by modifying elements of the physical or social environment. For example, button closures can be replaced with Velcro fastenings, which are secured with one hand; a raised toilet seat can be introduced to compensate for difficulty rising from a regular commode; or the living environment can be modified to provide the most effective kind of visual, auditory, and tactile stimulation to compensate for sensory limitations (Levy, 1986c).

Results

The therapist next considers the goals or results that are produced by the operations. Activities are performed with goals in mind and, ultimately, the success of any activity is measured in relationship to its goal. At this level, activities are carried out with specific goals; yet, the implicit goals may not always be those inferred by an observer. Various goals motivate individuals to pursue activities and range, for example, from the simple pleasure of moving, to an interest in seeing the effects of their actions, to an investment in producing a high quality end product. Results are a particularly problematic area for those experiencing cognitive limitations, because a cognitive disability limits their ability to achieve goals that are available to those without cognitive limitations. For the cognitively disabled, the seemingly simple intent of producing a satisfactory end product often exceeds their capacities, and results that are unsatisfactory by traditional standards are commonplace. Hence, the cognitively disabled individual must be provided with opportunities to pursue a broad range of activities that compensate for their limitations in conceptualizing traditional goals. Without this intervention, their opportunities to pursue activities with success are limited.

Meaning

The third hierarchical level in activity analysis considers the implicit or explicit meaning of the activity to the individual. The meaning of an activity is related to the individual's sense of himself or herself as competent (rather than incompetent) as well as his or her interests and values. It is also related to the individual's perception of meaningful social roles and the expectations of significant others for role performance. To be meaningful, then, activities must not only be consistent with one's interests, values, and expectations for success, but must also have some relationship to one's desired and expected social roles.

At this level of activity analysis, one must first consider the intent of occupational therapy at its most basic level, to enable the individual to maintain a sense of competence despite his or her disability through successful participation in valued life activities and social roles. At the same time, gerontological research amply demonstrates that these concepts are inextricably linked to survival. Seligman (1975), Langer and Rodin (1976), and others provide data that support the notion that individuals who are unconnected to their world and who expect consistent failure are especially prone to depression, accelerated deterioration, and even death (Banziger & Roush, 1983; Langer, et al., 1979; Mercer & Kane, 1979; Rodin, 1989; Rodin & Langer, 1977).

In the face of disability, the older individual and/or his or her caregiver is forced to reexamine the requirements and expectations of desired social roles. Ultimately it is the ability to carry out the activities that maintain those roles that determines which roles can be pursued successfully. Often, disabled older adults (and their caregivers) need assistance in objectively assessing their capacities and limitations in performing desired activities. They need to become aware of their functional potentials and to determine realistic, desirable, and perhaps new social roles. In addition, they must appreciate that severe cognitive disabilities limit the range of desirable activities that the individual can engage in successfully. In these instances therapists intervene by making available as wide a range as possible of activities adapted to capitalize the individual's strengths, including activities in the areas of self-care, work, and leisure. Thus, these individuals will have the opportunity to choose those activities that are most desirable, to utilize and sustain their physical and mental strengths, and to retain a sense of connection and role investment within their social world.

Special Aspects of Functional Assessment and the Older Individual

Occupational therapists couple the functional capability assessment of older individuals with activity analysis to design intervention strategies that facilitate their participation in desired activities and social roles. A comprehensive functional assessment serves to identify sensory, perceptual, cognitive, affective, motor, and social capacities that can be capitalized on and the specific nature of the limitations to be compensated for.

Unlike younger persons seen in rehabilitation, older persons are much more likely to have multiple diseases. Four of five persons over the age of

65 have at least one chronic condition and, with increasing age, are likely to have multiple disabling conditions (U.S. Senate, 1986). One study of community dwelling older adults revealed that 40% had more than four medical problems (Lopez-Aqueres et al., 1984). Hence, in gerontological rehabilitation individuals rarely have only one disease to contend with.

The leading chronic conditions causing activity limitations for the elderly are dementia (Katzman, 1976), followed by arthritis, hypertensive disease (including hemiplegias), hearing impairments, and heart conditions (U.S. Senate, 1986). Each of these conditions imposes varying limitations in activity that are related to the severity of the condition, the presence of complicating conditions, and the adaptive capacity of the individual involved. However, functional capability assessment reveals that the most common limitations imposed by these conditions are deficits in attention, memory, learning, and problem solving; they also produce decreased strength, endurance, coordination, balance, and range of motion. Rehabilitative strategies to address limitations imposed by these conditions will be discussed shortly.

There are also a number of functional limitations that occur as a natural consequence of the aging process which need to be considered because they confound the limitations imposed by diagnosable conditions. Age-related functional limitations include the following: For most people, the aging process leads to a slow but steady decrease in visual efficiency. It produces reduced visual acuity, a steadily decreasing ability to focus (accommodation), a reduced capacity to adjust to changes in illumination, a decreased resistance to glare, and a shift in color vision. To compensate for these limitations, the environment can be modified to control contrast, glare, and lighting which will aid acuity, visual field accommodation, and dark adaptation, as well as compensate for glare sensitivity (Levy, 1986c). Generally, these interventions involve the use of increased illumination of the activity environment, magnifiers, large print lettering for written words, supplemental tactile cues, and strong color cuing.

As aging advances, the ability to hear progressively lower frequencies declines. Specifically, age-related hearing losses result in a decreased ability to discriminate speech and increased difficulty in hearing high frequency sounds, especially soft consonants (e.g., c, ch, f, s, sh, th, and z). Hence, many messages sound garbled and are frequently misunderstood. It also becomes increasingly difficult to discriminate speech from background noises. To compensate for these limitations, one can generally modify the sensory environment by lowering the pitch of one's voice, the pace of one's speech and amplification, eliminate background noise (such as radio or television), and use supplementary visual and tactile cues (Levy, 1986c).

Age-related changes in the arteries and the heart contribute to a decline in cardiac output, losses in the capacity of the heart to respond and recover from extra work, a progressive increase in resistance to blood flow, and a consequent increase in systolic blood pressure (Menks, 1986). These changes result in a diminished supply of oxygenated blood which becomes a major cause of decreased stamina and endurance in older adults. Muscle weight and strength also tend to decline with age, compounding the problem of diminished strength and endurance induced by the cardiovascular system, especially in those activities requiring major muscle groups. In respiration, the aging process leads to decreased levels of expiration, and inspiration, due to factors such as atrophy of intercostal muscles, thickening of pulmonary walls, and thinning of alveolar walls (Menks, 1986). This further contributes to a decrease in oxygen content of the blood and results in limitations of stamina and endurance.

To compensate for these physiological changes in the heart, muscles, and lungs, the individual must utilize principles of work simplification and energy conservation. He or she must break down desired activities according to duration and severity of effort and organize work and leisure space to minimize the need for lifting, bending, and walking. They will need options for sitting in lieu of standing whenever possible and storing supplies in close proximity to their place of use. Note that caregivers can provide the structure and cuing required for individuals to utilize these principles if the individual is experiencing significant cognitive limitations.

In the skeletal system, bone mass tends to decrease with age and become more vulnerable to fracture, requiring increased awareness of potential environmental safety hazards that could cause accidental falls. The vertebral column becomes more compressed, loses flexibility, and shortens, all of which can be compensated for by modifying the height of work surfaces and by optimally placing supplies. Decreased cartilage mass also causes the head and neck to flex forward, and flexion in the elbows, hips, and knees. Increased energy is required merely to maintain balance (Jacobs, 1981). It should also be recognized that 80% of the population experience synovium degeneration in their joints resulting in joint stiffness and pain (Kane, Kane, & Arnold, 1985). To compensate for joint limitations, the individual must learn principles of joint protection to reduce joint stress and preserve joint structures.

Gerontological Rehabilitation and Physical Disabilities

As noted previously, rehabilitation strategies are derived from analyzing which essential components of the activity can be modified to compensate for limitations identified in the individual's functional capability assessment. To enable those with physical limitations to pursue desired activities, particular emphasis is placed on analyzing activities at the "op-

erations" level. The functional capability assessment will emphasize biological capacities such as joint range of motion, muscular strength, manual
dexterity, and balance. Functional capacities are evaluated through standardized tests as well as clinical observations and procedures. For the individual
with physical limitations, an activity analysis most often reveals that strategies should be designed to compensate for limitations in range of motion,
strength, dexterity, and balance. This can be achieved by modifying one or
more of the following major activity components: (1) position of the individual performing the activity, (2) the amount of resistance in the activity, (3)
the properties of materials and tools used, and (4) the procedures for performing the activity (Trombly & Scott, 1984).

At this point, I would like to underscore a key contribution provided by
Allen's cognitive disability frame of reference to the foundations of gerontological rehabilitation. Whenever a rehabilitative strategy requires new
learning (e.g., learning new procedures for carrying out a highly familiar
activity or learning to use an adaptive device to carry out a desired activity),
the cognitive demands of the activity markedly increase. This demand necessarily limits adaptation strategies when, as often occurs in the elderly, a
physical disability coexists with a cognitive disability. In these instances,
compensatory strategies that modify environmental elements must be emphasized and may include modifying the position of the individual performing the activity, the amount of resistance in the activity, and/or the properties
of materials and tools used. This principle provides therapists with means
to integrate their understanding of strategies designed to compensate for
cognitive limitations with those that compensate for physical limitations.

Changing the Position of the Individual

Activities can be adapted to compensate for limitations such
as poor sitting posture, decreased endurance, and lack of upper extremity
strength. Poor posture is induced by hemiplegia, arthritis, and osteoporosis.
It decreases vital capacity, reduces oxygen intake, decreases mental alertness,
and increases fatigue. To compensate for postural limitations, intervention
strategies modify environmental elements and might include the use of
environmental supports (e.g., a wheelchair cushion with a supporting seat
board or height modification of the work surface to accommodate reduced
sitting height). Similarly, individuals with generalized weakness and low
endurance should be cued to sit rather than stand whenever possible (e.g.,
use a high stool for meal preparation or laundry tasks), and materials should
be stored to minimize the need to bend, reach, or walk.

In addition, limitations in upper extremity strength can contribute to
dysfunctional positioning. In the case of hemiplegia, these limitations can

be compensated for by providing a lap tray or an arm sling to support the arm from excess gravitational pull and by the use of a splint to support the wrist and encourage functional grasp positioning during activity. Providing functional hand splints is another environmental strategy used both to align dislocated joints and muscles and to reduce pain for individuals with arthritis (Shah, Avidan, & Sine, 1981; Spencer, 1988; Trombly, 1984; Trombly & Scott, 1984).

Changing Resistance

Another environmental modification strategy involves the addition or deletion of resistance within an activity to compensate for incoordination, decreased range of motion, lack of upper extremity strength, and joint deterioration. For example, a weighted cuff can be placed directly on the client's wrist to reduce hand tremors. Moving a weakened hemiparetic extremity can be made easier with a mobile arm support or suspension sling that eliminates gravitational resistance. Because excess resistance increases joint destruction and pain, individuals with arthritis must select objects for use in their activities that are as light weight as possible (e.g., aluminum pans versus cast iron). Similarly, individuals with decreased strength or endurance induced by cardiopulmonary conditions should avoid lifting or carrying materials that weigh more than two to three pounds and should select clothing that avoids excess weight (e.g., a down coat versus a heavy wool coat) (Shah, Avidan, & Sine, 1981; Spencer, 1988; Trombly, 1984; Trombly & Scott, 1984).

Changing Property of Materials and Tools

Environmental modifications can also be made in materials selected for desired activities. Materials are most often adapted in relationship to their pliability, resistance, size, and texture as well as in relationship to the intensity of tactile, visual, and auditory stimulation that they provide. For example, limitations in muscle strength can often be compensated for by selecting materials that are more pliable and that offer less resistance (e.g., thin aluminum can be selected in lieu of heavy copper when metal tooling, thin muffin batters are more easily mixed than biscuit batters, paperback books can be selected rather than hardcover books). Coordination or visual limitations can be compensated for by enlarging sizes of recreational materials (such as puzzle pieces and chessmen) or craft materials (such as yarn and tiles). Tactile limitations can be compensated for by selecting materials that are highly textured.

Decreased muscle strength, range of motion, and coordination can also be compensated for by adapting the size and shape of tools. For example, limitations in pinch and grip strength can be compensated for by enlarging handles on tools of daily living (such as pencils, combs, toothbrushes, eating utensils, doorknobs, and faucet handles). Reach limitations can be compensated for by extending handles on tools (such as combs, bathing sponges, and eating utensils) as well as by using long-handled reacher tongs. Coordination limitations can be compensated for by using weighted utensils as well as by selecting heavier tools rather than lighter ones (e.g., a claw hammer instead of a tack hammer, a cast iron frying pan instead of an aluminum one, or the heaviest electric shaver rather than the lightest) (Shah, Avidan, & Sine, 1981; Spencer, 1988; Trombly, 1984; Trombly & Scott, 1984).

Changing Method of Performance

If the individual has only mildly impaired cognitive capacities, his or her physical limitations can also be compensated for by learning alternative methods for carrying out desired tasks. For example, individuals with hemiplegia can compensate for decreased range of motion and strength in the involved upper extremity by learning to use adaptive equipment for one-hand cooking or dressing. Individuals with arthritis can compensate for joint deterioration by learning how to avoid actions that contribute to joint stress and deformity. Individuals with low stamina and endurance can learn ways of organizing routines, materials, and work areas to make the most use of available energy. And, because fluctuating energy expenditures are detrimental for those with cardiopulmonary conditions, these individuals can learn to carry out activities at a moderate and consistent pace. To reiterate, however, strategies involving new learning have limited use when the individual is experiencing significant cognitive limitations.

Gerontological Rehabilitation and Cognitive Disabilities

As with physical disabilities, a cognitive disability limits the individual's ability to pursue desired life activities and social roles and to maintain a sense of purpose and control. However, a cognitive disability presents different challenges. Conceptualization of intervention strategies must compensate for the limitations in thought patterns that are prerequisite to participation in normal life activities (Allen, 1985; Levy, 1987). Similar to the analysis process used with physical disabilities, activity analysis and functional capability assessment here is used to determine which components in the desired activity the individual can and cannot do. Activities are then adapted to maximize use of carefully assessed capabilities and to compensate for limitations. Given the limitations imposed by a cognitive disability, however, therapists place particular emphasis on activity demands at the "results" level of activity analysis, in contrast to the "operations" level emphasis in rehabilitation of the physically disabled.

The analysis of activities for those with cognitive disabilities involves the identification and assessment of thought patterns that are by their very nature abstract. A brief review, therefore, of Allen's (1985) cognitive disability theory is required. This theory provides a basis for understanding rehabilitation strategies specific to the thought patterns that impose limits on successful activity and role participation.

Cognitive Disability Theory

A primary concern of cognitive disability theory is to identify the thought patterns that need to be assessed to determine whether an individual can perform a desired activity successfully, and that need to be compensated for in the event of cognitive limitations. To this end, Allen (1985, 1988) has proposed a hierarchy of six cognitive levels that describe the dimensions of thought that are processed in pursuing desired activities, as well as qualitative differences in functional capacities and limitations. Allen views three dimensions of thought as stages of an information processing model that are addressed at each of the six hierarchical cognitive levels. These include sensory cues, sensorimotor activities, and motor actions.

Sensory Cues. All information processing begins with sensory input from the environment. Allen identifies two sources of sensory cues that capture and sustain attention: those that arise from the individual's inner world (including subliminal and proprioceptive cues) and those that arise from the environment (including tactile, visual, auditory, and complex symbolic cues). At primitive cognitive levels, individuals can attend to only internal cues, such as musculoskeletal sensations. At more advanced cognitive levels, individuals can respond to progressively wider ranges of cues, including internal as well as environmental cues.

Sensorimotor associations. Sensorimotor associations are the interpretive processes that follow from sensory cues and refer to the goals implicit in performing an action. What Allen's cognitive disability model clarifies is that the implicit goal of the individual performing an action may not be consistent with the explicit goals of a given activity. As stated earlier, individuals pursue activities for various goals. At more primitive cognitive levels, an individual may only comprehend the motions involved in a desired activity (such as pushing a vacuum back and forth) and would not be able to comprehend the goal—or the result—that would be expected from an individual with higher cognitive capacities (i.e., a clean rug). Consequently, at more primitive cognitive levels, unintentional results become commonplace. Hence, therapists must recognize that the inability to comprehend traditional goals reflects a cognitive limitation that must be compensated for within the structure of an activity.

Motor actions. Motor actions are the final stage of Allen's information processing model and are elicited by sensory cues, guided by sensorimotor associations, and can be observed in activity performance. There are two types: spontaneous (self-initiated) and imitated (copied from another person). At more primitive cognitive levels, individuals are only able to initiate and imitate motor actions that are already very familiar behavioral actions. At more advanced cognitive levels, self-initated motor actions are more diverse and individuals are able to participate freely in desired activities.

Cognitive disability theory provides the means for analyzing the relative difficulty of any desired activity in terms of requisite dimensions of thought. From this analysis, environmental factors can be identified that facilitate or constrain the production of each dimension of thought. Rehabilitative strategies are derived from understanding how the environmental cognitive elements might best be modified within the structure of a desired activity to reinforce and capitalize on cognitive capacities and to compensate for cognitive limitations and, by doing so, place desired activities within an individual's range of comprehension and control. Specifically, therapists modify the structure of a desired activity in relationship to (1) the "sensory cues" that the individual is able to attend to while doing an activity at any given cognitive level; (2) the quality of "sensorimotor association" that the individual is able to comprehend, or the goal that motivates an individual to engage in activity at any given level; and (3) the degree of assistance required for the individual to most effectively complete a desired "motor action" at any given level (i.e., whether the desired motor action is best imitated from the therapist and/or caregiver, or can be successfully self-initated).

Clinical Application

Therapists use a variety of methods to assess cognitive functional capacities and limitations, which are defined in this frame of reference as the three dimensions of thought (sensory cues, sensorimotor associations, and motor actions) processed in the course of pursuing desired activities. One tool, the Allen Cognitive Level Test (ACL) (Allen, 1985), is a standardized leather-lacing task that has been discussed in detail in chapters (one and three). Scoring is based on the complexity of the lacing stitch that the individual is able to imitate, and a numerical score is assigned which represents the individual's cognitive level. The demands of this task may limit its usefulness with individuals who experience visual and fine motor coordination limitations as part of the normal aging process, or as a result of a coexisting physical condition. However, the validity of an "enlarged" ACL to compensate for these limitations is currently under research (see Chapter 1). The ACL is also of limited use for those experiencing cognitive limitations at the lower end of Allen's hierarchy. In these instances the Lower Cognitive Levels Test (LCL) (Allen, 1985) can be used to differentiate functional capacities and limitations. This task requires simple clapping in response to demonstration.

Perhaps the most useful tool to assess levels of cognitive capacities and limitations in the elderly is the Routine Task Inventory (RTI) (Allen, 1985), discussed in detail in Chapter 1. The RTI was designed as a practical observational measure of performance within Allen's framework for describing cognitive disabilities. It describes and assesses qualitative differences in the performance of a variety of routine tasks such as bathing, grooming, and managing money. Primary data for the assessment of the extent of cognitive disability is obtained through observing the performance of routine tasks the older adults needs and wants to do in his or her natural environment.

Assessment methodology has been developed further in the Cognitive Performance Test (CPT), a new instrument for assessing cognitive functional capacities and limitations in patients with dementia (Burns, 1990). The CPT is comprised of 6 tasks, including to dress, shop, toast, phone, wash, and travel. Each task has standardized equipment, set-up, and methods of administration that involve the sequential elimination or inclusion of sensory cues when difficulty performing is observed. Consistent with Allen's frame of reference, the deficits observed in the CPT predict functional capabilities on a wide variety of daily life activities. The CPT holds enormous promise for future research in this area of intervention. It provides a single standardized instrument to assess functional impairment across the deteriorating course of the disease, and provides the means to evaluate the effects of intervention on disease progression.

Cognitive Levels in Rehabilitation

In order to conceptualize a basis for rehabilitative intervention, the therapist must identify the patient's cognitive capacities, limitations, and the environmental factors that can be modified to enable successful participation in activities that support desired social roles. The discussion that follows will identify cognitive capacities, limitations, and associated environmental factors. It will provide guidelines for the design of environmental modification strategies required to capitalize on cognitive capacities and compensate for limitations, at each of the cognitive levels. It will also provide guidelines for conceptualizing rehabilitative strategies for older individuals experiencing both cognitive and physical disabilities, given that single disabilities rarely occur in the aging population and that multiple disabling conditions are commonplace (U.S. Senate, 1986). Therapists will find it useful to note that cognitive levels 1 and 2 are most often associated with severe hemiplegia, severe dementia, and acute head injuries. Levels 3, 4, and 5, are associated with moderate hemiplegia, moderate and mild dementia, and major mental disorders.

Cognitive Level 1

At the first cognitive level, *attention* is directed to subliminal internal cues (such as hunger, taste, and smell), and individuals are largely unresponsive to external stimuli. There is no *goal*, or reason, for performing motor actions; hence, few motor actions are being performed. *Motor actions* are limited to the potential to follow near-reflexive one-word directives, such as "sip" or "turn." With little (if any) purpose and few (if any) motor actions available, the individual has few cognitive capabilities to capitalize on. It is unrealistic to attempt to modify activities.

Therapists and caregivers find that an orienting response can be elicited by familiar gustatory and olfactory stimuli (e.g., favorite foods and spices, fragrant plants, hand lotion, and after-shave), a gentle touch or massage, or a family pet (Allen, 1985; 1988; Levy, 1986a; 1987). They will also find that the individual either actively resists or is uncooperative in efforts to provide required maximal assistance in grooming, bathing, and feeding. The individual may need to be fed or allowed to eat with the fingers. Walking and transfers from bed to wheelchair may be achieved with physical guidance.

Cognitive Level 2

At this level, *attention* is directed to proprioceptive cues from muscles and joints that are elicited by one's own highly familiar body movements. The *goal* in performing a motor action is to repeat the one-step motor action component of the activity for the pleasure of its effect on the body alone (i.e., on one's sense of positon and balance, or on sensory input to muscles and joints). *Motor actions* are limited to the ability to imitate, albeit inexactly, a one-step direction only if it involves the use of a highly familiar, near reflexive gross motor pattern. New learning is not possible.

Activities that can be successfully accomplished at this level are those that are adapted to capitalize on the capacity to imitate one-step familiar repetitive gross motor actions, and that compensate for the inability to comprehend a purpose beyond the sensation of movement. Therapists and caregivers will find that providing opportunities to imitate simple movement, calisthenics, and modified sports activities are the most useful, but one-step activities (such as folding laundry, chopping vegetables, and polishing furniture) can be imitated if these activities were near habitual prior to the onset of the disability. Similarly, most instrumental ADL activities can be accomplished provided the individual is provided with a model to follow. For instance, to enable the individual to wash his or her arms, the caregiver should take a washcloth and demonstrate washing his or her own arms (the washcloth can be dry). Spontaneous behaviors are largely unproductive or bizarre (e.g., sitting backward on the toilet and "driving" it like a car—flushing to "shift gears," constantly disrobing and redressing, reapplying the same lipstick over and over again). It appears as though individuals are searching for opportunities to apply very familiar gross motor patterns to the environment regardless of the context. Hence, it is critical that therapists and caregivers provide individuals with opportunities to imitate actions that are appropriate to the environmental context that will encourage functional performance and allow the individual to retain their dignity and role investment within the environment.

Therapists and caregivers find that, with demonstration, individuals at this level may cooperate by moving body parts to assist in activities such as grooming, dressing, and feeding, but they still need maximal assistance and direct supervision. With supervision, individuals may be able to eat unassisted foods that can be eaten with fingers, and this should be encouraged. They may also be able to use spoons and nonslip scoop-edged plates or bowls, although other utensils should not be used. At this level, it is helpful to serve all food in bowls, which are easier to manage with one-step motor actions. The therapist should recognize that, at this level, individuals are unable to determine what is edible and what is not. Hence, anything that could be mistaken for food should be removed (such as decorative artificial fruit and poisonous house plants). Aimless pacing is common, but the individual will walk in directions guided by companions. However, the environment should be structured to provide a safe space for wandering, with complicated push-button or combination locks on the doors and an unobstructed walkway within the living environment. To avoid voiding in unacceptable locations, individuals at this cognitive level should be escorted to the bathroom every 2 hours while they are awake, and wastebaskets or any other receptacles that could be mistaken for a toilet should be removed. Individuals at this level are easily confused when objects are hidden by doors, drawers, or closets. Whenever possible, bathroom and bedroom doors, should be left open and frequently used objects or treasured possessions placed on furniture surfaces or hangers where they can be easily seen.

Individuals in wheelchairs can often manage the repetitive movement required to propel the chair; however, they are unable to plan and direct that motion and will frequently run into objects or walls. In addition, they may not recognize their motor limitations and may attempt to get up and walk. In these instances wheelchair restraints may be indicated. Therapists and caregivers need to design environmental strategies and to provide continuous supervision that will protect individuals functioning at this level from safety hazards (Allen, 1985; 1988; Levy, 1986a; 1987).

Cognitive Level 3

At this cognitive level, *attention* is directed to tactile cues and to familiar objects that can be manipulated. The *goal* in performing a motor action is limited to the process of discovering the kinds of effects one's actions have on the environment. These actions are typically repeated to verify that similar results occur. *Motor actions* are limited to the ability to follow a one-step, highly familiar, action-oriented direction that has been demonstrated for the individual to follow. It is unrealistic to expect the individual to learn new behaviors.

Activities that can be successfully accomplished at this level are those that are adapted to capitalize on the individual's capacity to imitate one-step, familiar, repetitive actions that provide predictable tactile effects and compensate for the inability to follow multi-step directions or conceptualize a predictable result.

The individual should be provided with opportunities to participate in adapted activities which reinforce the relationship between one's actions and predictable tactile effects on the environment. Some possibilities include sports activities (such as swimming, biking, and playing "catch"); household maintenance activities (such as washing the car, mowing lawns, cultivating gardens, and hand-washing laundry); kitchen activities (such as washing and drying the dishes, peeling and chopping vegetables, and cleaning counter tops); and instrumental ADL activities demonstrated one-step at a time. As in the previous level, functional performance can be maximized by teaching caregivers how to present activities to the individual in a manner that will best promote productive motor actions.

Spontaneous motor actions include such unproductive behaviors as clicking dials on and off, using keys indiscriminately in locks, and pouring soup in the coffee maker. The individual will be drawn to anything that can be touched and manipulated. Hence, potentially dangerous appliances (like toasters, blenders, and coffee makers) should be hidden from view; if possible, stove knobs should be removed (or push buttons on the stove covered), and lawn and garden tools and chemicals should be hidden. It is just as critical at this level for the individual to be provided with opportunities for more productive "face saving" activities and acceptable uses of familiar tactile movement patterns that will enable a sense of competence, dignity, and role investment within his or her social environment. To reiterate, however, at this level the goal of an activity is not related to a specific outcome or end product but rather to the relationship between actions and their predictable effects. Consequently therapists and caregivers need to appreciate the need for the individual to do the same thing over and over again, even though by traditional standards this behavior might appear to be unnecessary. Opportunities to engage in activities that appear by objective standards to have no specific outcome, such as vacuuming the same area repeatedly and polishing the same spot on the car door, should be encouraged. Such activities should also be deemed acceptable.

Caregivers find that individuals are able to brush their teeth, wash their hands and face, and use familiar table utensils independently, although they need to be reminded to do these activities. In the absence of a concomitant physical disability, these individuals are also able to dress themselves. However, if the caregiver does not select clothing and hand items to the individual one at a time, errors are frequent. For example, underwear may be placed over trousers, clothes may be donned inside out or backwards, and nightclothes may be selected for daytime wear. Most self-maintenance activities must be broken down into one-step motor actions, and supplies for activities such as tooth brushing, shaving, bathing, and hair washing should be presented one at a time. Note that physically disabled individuals at this level will still require assistance in self-care activities such as dressing because the routines required to perform adapted self-care techniques often entail procedures that are not highly familiar.

For the individual with concomitant physical disabilities, the repetitive actions required to manage a wheelchair or a walker can be initiated. However, these individuals will not be able to manage safety concerns that entail two or three steps (such as applying wheelchair brakes or manipulating foot plates) nor will they be able to arrive at proper locations at proper times without an escort. To help an individual follow through on an activity mastered in therapy (e.g., wheeling one's chair to the dining room), caregiving staff must be instructed on the individual's need to be cued at each successive step of the activity. Individuals may benefit from adapted equipment that requires the use of familiar motor actions (e.g., traditional eating utensils with extended or built-up handles to compensate for limited range of motion or grasp) but will not be able to make use of adapted equipment requiring the use of unfamiliar motor patterns (e.g., reaching tongs to initiate pulling clothes over parts of the body). Therapists will also find that individuals at this level require one-on-one supervision to sustain attention to therapeutic exercises (Allen, 1985; 1988; Levy, 1986a; 1987).

Cognitive Level 4

Attention at this level is directed to tactile as well as visible cues, and it is sustained throughout short-term activities. The *goal* in performing a motor action is to perceive cause and effect relationships between a tangible cue and a desired outcome. *Motor actions* are limited to the ability to follow a two- to three-step, highly familiar, motor process that leads to the accomplishment of familiar goals. At this level, individuals can learn two- to three-step procedures that have visible and predictable results.

Activities that can be accomplished successfully at this level are those that are adapted to capitalize on this capacity to use two- to three-step familiar motor actions that have predictable visible results, and activities that compensate for the individual's inability to comprehend unpredictable results or to notice mistakes when they occur. At this level, individuals should be provided with opportunities to engage in simple, relatively error-proof, concrete activities that support desired social roles. This goal is best accomplished by incorporating into the individual's daily routine yard work, household chores (e.g., laundry, simple meal preparation, and shopping for a few familiar purchases), familiar sports and dance activities, simple board games and puzzles, letter writing or typing, and walks to familiar destinations.

Despite significant cognitive impairment, the individual appears to be less confused at this level because activities are pursued with specific outcomes in mind. Caregivers and therapists should encourage these individuals to engage in comprehensible concrete activities which will protect personal dignity and enable social role retention. However, they should not expect the individual to notice mistakes or solve problems when they occur, to retain directions out of context, to plan beyond the immediate situation, to generalize learning to new situations, or to anticipate safety hazards. Individuals at this level are more easily engaged in activities and therapeutic regimens than at previous levels because they want to achieve a desired outcome (e.g., "to get the job done"). Desired outcomes, however, are restricted to those that are concrete and predictable and that entail no more than a three-step process.

Caregivers find these individuals can complete familiar grooming activities, although they frequently neglect areas that are not clearly visible. For example, the back of the body may remain unwashed, shampoo may not be rinsed from the back of the head, and the individual may neglect to shave under the chin. Dressing can be accomplished relatively independently, although the backs of garments may be ignored. The individual can eat independently but may require assistance to season foods, share a limited quantity of food, open unfamiliar containers, or avoid burns. Individuals should be protected from invisible hazards from sources such as heat, chemicals, and electricity.

Therapists find that physically disabled individuals at this level can learn to follow an exercise program and wheelchair safety precautions but will require weeks of practice to master their skills. Adaptive equipment can be successfully introduced if the actions required are highly familiar, they involve no more than three steps, and the intended effect is highly visible. For example, the individual with hemiparesis can learn how to cut meat unilaterally with the use of a rocker knife, or an individual with arthritis can learn to use an electric can opener to reduce the joint stress caused by tight grasp. In addition, modified procedures such as those required in one-handed dressing (e.g., putting clothing on the hemiparetic side first and taking clothes off the unaffected side first) can be mastered after weeks of practice (Allen, 1985; 1988; Levy, 1986a; 1987).

Cognitive Level 5

At this level, *attention* is captured and sustained by the interesting properties of concrete objects. The *goal* of action is to explore the effects of self-initiated motor actions on physical objects and to investigate these effects through the use of overt trial and error problem solving. *Motor actions* are exploratory to produce interesting effects on material objects, and they extend to the ability to follow through on a four or five-step concrete process. The individual is now able to learn through doing. Hence, in the event of a concomitant physical disability, teaching new procedures that will compensate for physical limitations when carrying out desired activities becomes an appropriate rehabilitation strategy.

Many activities can be accomplished successfully at this level because in concrete activities (i.e., those involving familiar four- to five-step motor actions with visibly perceivable results), individuals function relatively independently. However, the cognitive limitations experienced by older adults at this level become apparent when these individuals attempt activities that require attention to abstract and symbolic cues (such as those that involve spoken and written instructions, diagrams, or drawings). Activities requiring attention to these cues will accentuate the disability and should be avoided.

Caregivers find that individuals can complete grooming, dressing, and eating activities without assistance. Household activities are carried out relatively independently, although the individual may require assistance to establish safety procedures and to anticipate hazardous situations. Cooking difficulties may be reflected in the inability to anticipate food burning or to anticipate the need to coordinate the timing of several dishes.

Because individuals at this level with physical disabilities are able to follow a series of demonstrated instructions that contain new information, they can follow a therapeutic exercise program and learn requirements within two to four sessions. In addition, most adaptive equipment can be successfully introduced, although attention to safety precautions may be neglected (e.g., the chaffing of a splint strap). The cognitive demands of strategies such as work simplification and energy conservation may be beyond the cognitive capabilities of individuals at this level. These techniques often require the individual to use abstract reasoning (for example, when prioritizing activities and organizing future routines), and the individual at this level is limited to concrete reasoning. When involved in daily routines, however, the individual can be cued by others to make use of such strategies (Allen, 1985; 1988; Levy, 1986a; 1987).

Cognitive Level 6

Attention at this level is captured by abstract and symbolic cues. The *goal* is to use abstract reasoning to reflect about the range of possible actions, including reconsidering old plans and creating new ones. Spontaneous *motor actions* are those that have been planned in advance and on which there are no restrictions on performance. Learning uses symbolic thought and deductive reasoning, and can be generalized to new situations. Theoretically, this level represents the absence of cognitive disability. Activity adaptations to compensate for cognitive limitations are not required (Allen, 1985).

Individuals at this level with a physical disability can be introduced to strategies that compensate for physical limitations by learning complex alternative procedures for carrying out activities or that require the individual to change life-long patterns in performing routine activities. For instance, individuals with arthritis can learn to change positions frequently and to avoid highly habituated positioning that increase joint deterioration (such as turning door knobs with two hands rather than one or using improper body mechanics when sitting, standing, walking, or climbing stairs). Because the individual can organize the home environment and plan a schedule for completing chores in light of priorities and energy constraints, he or she can learn more abstract activity adaptations (such as those that involve work simplification and energy conservation techniques) and incorporate them into his or her daily routines.

Summary

The process of conceptualizing intervention strategies for the cognitively disabled older adult requires familiarity with Allen's cognitive disability theory. Environmental elements that can be modified have been identified at each of the cognitive levels and include (1) the sensory cues that should be reinforced by the therapist or caregiver, (2) an appreciation of what goal is perceived based on those cues, and (3) the type and complexity of assistance and directions neessary to promote productive motor actions. Rehabilitative strategies maximize the individual's cognitive capabilities and compensate for limitations by modifying the cognitive demands and the structure of activities that support desired social roles.

The concepts are critical to the design of rehabilitation strategies for the older individual who is both physically and cognitively disabled. The presence of a cognitive disability limits the use of traditional strategies for compensating for neuromuscular deficits that require unfamiliar tools, modified procedures, or new learning; in these instances, compensatory strategies that involve environmental modifications are emphasized. Hence, concepts used to adapt activities for the cognitively disabled older adult are paramount when therapists consider the best activity adaptations that will compensate for both physical and cognitive disabilities.

A Note on Research

Allen's frame of reference is within the mainstream of both gerontological research and gerontological rehabilitation research, which is organized around the central concept of "quality of life." An optimal aging lifestyle is deemed the desired outcome. Quality of life is composed of a number of parameters including subjective evaluations of life-satisfaction (a sense of well-being) and self-esteem (a sense of self-worth), and objective conditions including functional status and socioeconomic status. In gerontological rehabilitation, this concept is further refined as the ability to function at the highest possible level of autonomy within the least restrictive environment. As Kane (1990) states, "Successful rehabilitation cannot leave a patient unable to function more independently in his or her usual daily life." Outcome goals in gerontological rehabilitation, then, are defined in terms of improved function and quality of life (Kemp, 1990). These, too, are the major outcomes that Allen's frame of reference seeks to promote.

However, to prove its worth and survivability, any rehabilitation strategy must first meet criteria of effectiveness. Given that the evidence of effectiveness is "improved functioning," an evaluation system is needed that will measure the individual's ability to function at maximum autonomy in his or her natural settings (Kane, 1990). To this end, Allen's conceptual framework has also made significant contributions. Preliminary studies of the Cognitive Performance Test (CPT) (Burns, 1990) demonstrate that it provides a reliable and valid measure of function in a population impaired with dementia. CPT holds promise for evaluating the effectiveness of interventions that attempt to improve the cognitively disabled older adult's ability to function within his or her natural living environment.

Conclusion

Allen's cognitive disability frame of reference presents an integrated approach to physical and cognitive rehabilitation that helps the disabled older adult maintain active participation in as many preferred activities and social roles as possible, given the disabilities that exist. Using principles derived from Allen's frame of reference, therapists are able to knowledgeably modify the multifaceted components of activities to allow the older adult with physical and/or cognitive limitations to still meet activity demands. Appropriately modified activities optimize these individuals' remaining strengths and capacities and compensate for their limitations. They enable the disabled individual to retain a sense of competence, control, and social role involvement. In this way, Allen's frame of reference contributes significantly to enhanced functional independence, life satisfaction, and quality of life in the later years.

References

Allen, C., Foto, M., Moon-Sperling, T., & Wilson, D. (1989). A medical review approach to Medicare outpatient documentation. *American Journal of Occupational Therapy, 43,* 793–800.

Allen, C. A. (1985). *Occupational therapy for psychiatric diseases: Measurement and management of cognitive disabilities.* Boston: Little, Brown.

Allen, C. A. (1988). Cognitive disabilities. In S. Robertson (Ed.), *Focus: Skills for assessment and treatment.* Rockville, MD: American Occupational Therapy Association.

Allen, C. A. (1987). Activity: Occupational therapy's treatment method. *American Journal of Occupational Therapy, 41,* 563–575.

Aronson, M. K., Lipkowitz, R. (1981). Senile dementia, Alzheimer's type: The family and the health care delivery system. *Journal of the American Geriatrics Society, 19,* 568–571.

Atchley, R. (1980). *The social forces in later life: An introduction to social gerontology,* (3rd ed.). Belmont, CA: Wadsworth Publishing Co.

Banziger, G., & Roush, S. (1983). Nursing homes for the birds: A control-relevant intervention with bird feeders. *Gerontologist, 23,* 527–531.

Baum, C. M. (1991). Addressing the needs of the cognitively impaired elderly from a family policy perspective. *American Journal of Occupational Therapy, 45,* 594–606.

Brody, E., Kleban, M., Lawton, M., & Moss, M. (1974). A longitudinal look at excess disabilities in the mentally impaired aged. *Journal of Gerontology, 29,* 79–84.

Brody, E., Lawton, M. P., & Liebowitz, L. (1984). Senile dementia: Public policy and adequate institutional care. *American Journal of Public Health, 74,* 1381–1383.

Burns, T. (1990). *The cognitive performance test: A new tool for assessing Alzheimer's disease. OT Week*, December 27. Rockville, MD: AOTA Inc.

Burrus-Bammel, L., & Bammel, G. (1985). Leisure and recreation. In J. E. Birren & K. W. Schaie (Eds.) *Handbook of the psychology of aging*, (2nd ed.). New York: Van Nostrand Reinhold.

Butler, R., & Lewis, M. (1973). *Aging and mental health: Positive psychosocial approaches*. St. Louis: C. V. Mosby.

Chiu, H. C., & Smith, B. A. (1990). Rehabilitation of persons with dementia. In B. Kemp, K. Brummel-Smith, & J. Ramsdell. (Eds.), *Geriatric rehabilitation*. Boston: Little, Brown.

Cummings, J. L. (1987). Neuropsychiatric aspects of multi-infarct dementia and dementia of the Alzheimer type. *Archives of Neurology, 44,* 389–394.

Cynkin, S. (1979). *Occupational therapy: Toward health through activities.* Boston: Little, Brown.

Fry, P. (1986). *Cognitive impairment and cognitive disorders. In depression, stress, and adaptations in the elderly.* Rockville, MD: Aspen Publications.

Gallagher, D., Lovett, S., & Zeiss, A. (1987). *Interventions with caregivers of frail elderly persons.* Palo Alto, CA: Caregiver Research Program.

Gilhooly, M. L. (1984). The impact of caregiving on caregivers: Factors associated with psychological well-being of people supporting a dementing relative in the community. *British Journal of Medical Psychology, 57,* 35–44.

Gordon, C., Gaitz, C. M., & Scott, J. (1976). Leisure and lives. In R. H. Binstock & E. Shanas (Eds.), *Handbook of aging and the social sciences.* New York: Van Nostrand Reinhold.

Gwyther, L., & George, L. (1986). Caregivers for dementia patients: Complex determinants of well-being and burden. *Gerontologist, 26*(3), 245–247.

Harris, L. (1975). *The myth and reality of aging in America.* Washington, DC: National Council on the Aging.

Havinghurst, R. J., & Feigenbaum, K. (1968). Leisure and life style. In B. Neugarten (Ed.), *Middle age and aging.* Chicago: University of Chicago Press.

Havinghurst, R. J. (1963). Successful aging. In R. H. Williams, C. Tibbitts, W. Donahue (Eds.), *Processes of aging.* New York: Atherton Press.

Health Care Financing Administration. (1989). Outpatient occupational therapy Medicare part B guidelines (DHHS Transmittal No. 55). In *Health Insurance Manual.* Baltimore: Author.

Jacobs, R. (1981). Physical changes in the aged. In M. Devereaux (Ed.), *Elder care: A guide to clinical geriatrics.* New York: Grune & Stratton.

Kahn, R. (1975). The mental health system and the future aged. *Gerontologist, 15* (1; pt. 2), 24–31.

Kane, R. L. (1990). Measuring the effectiveness of rehabilitation programs. In B. Kemp, K. Brummel-Smith, & J. Ramsdell. (Eds.), *Geriatric rehabilitation.* Boston: Little, Brown.

Kane, R. L., Kane, R. A., & Arnold, S. B. (1985). Prevention and the elderly: Risk factors. *Health Services Research, 19*(6), 945–1005.

Katzman, R. (1976). Prevalence and malignancy of Alzheimer's disease. *Archives of Neurology, 33,* 217–218.

Kemp, B. (1990). The psychosocial context of geriatric rehabilitation. In B. Kemp, K. Brummel-Smith, & J. Ramsdell. (Eds.), *Geriatric rehabilitation.* Boston: Little, Brown.

Kemp, B. (1988). Eight methods family members can use to manage behavioral problems in dementia. *Topics in Geriatric Rehabilitation, 4,* 50–59.

Langer, E. J., Rodin, J., Beck, C. et al. (1979). Environmental determinants of memory improvement in late adulthood. *Journal of Personality and Social Psychology, 27,* 2000–2013.

Langer, E. J., & Rodin, J. (1976). The effects of choice and enhanced personal responsibility for the aged: A field experiment in an institutional setting. *Journal of Personality and Social Psychology, 34,* 191–198.

Lawton, M., & Nahemow, K. (1973). Ecology and the aging process. In C. Eisdorfer & M. Lawton (Eds.), *Psychology of adult development and aging.* Washington: American Psychological Association.

Levy, L. L. (1987). Psychosocial intervention and dementia, part 2. *Occupational Therapy in Mental Health, 7,* 13–36.

Levy, L. L. (1986a). A practical guide to the care of the Alzheimer's disease victim. *Topics in Geriatric Rehabilitation, 1,* 16–26.

Levy, L. L. (1986b). Cognitive treatment. In L. J. Davis and M. Kirkland (Eds.), *Role of occupational therapy with the elderly.* Rockville, MD: American Occupational Therapy Association.

Levy, L. L. (1986c). Sensory change and compensation. In L. J. Davis and M. Kirkland (Eds.), *Role of occupational therapy with the elderly.* Rockville, MD: American Occupational Therapy Association.

Levy, L. L. (1989). Activity adaptation in rehabilitation of the physically and cognitively disabled aged. *Topics in Geriatric Rehabilitation, 4*(4), 53–66.

Llorens, L. (1986). Activity analysis: Agreement among factors in a sensory processing model. *American Journal of Occupational Therapy, 40,* 103–110.

Lopez-Aqueres, W., Kemp, B., Plopper, M., Staples, F., & Brummel-Smith, K. (1984). Health needs of Hispanic elderly. *Journal of the American Geriatric Society, 32,* 191–198.

Menks, F. (1986). Anatomical and physiological changes in late adulthood.

In L. J. Davis and M. Kirkland (Eds.), *Role of Occupational therapy with the elderly.* Rockville, MD: American Occupational Therapy Association.

Mercer, S., & Kane, R. (1979). Helplessness and hopelessness among the institutionalized aged: An experiment. *Health and Social Work, 4,* 90–116.

Mosey, A. C. (1981). *Occupational therapy: Configuration of a profession.* New York: Raven Press.

OT Week. (1990). Alzheimer's disease linked to normal aging. August 9. Rockville, MD: AOTA Inc.

Rabins, P., Mace, N., & Lucas, M. (1982). The impact of dementia on the family. *Journal of the American Medical Association, 248,* 333–335.

Reifler, B. V., & Teri, L. (1986). Rehabilitation and Alzheimer's disease. In S. J. Brody & G. E. Ruff (Eds.). *Aging and rehabilitation: Advances in the state of the art.* New York: Springer.

Riley, M. W., & Riley, J. W. Jr. (1989). The lives of older people and changing social roles. *Annals of the American Academy of Political and Social Science, 503,* 14–28.

Rodin, J. (1989). Sense of control: Potentials for intervention. *Annals of the American Academy of Political and Social Science, 503,* 29–42.

Rodin, J. (1986). Aging and health: Effects of the sense of control. *Science, 233,* 1271–1275.

Rodin, J., & Langer E. J. (1977). Long-term effects of a control relevant intervention with the institutionalized aged. *Journal of Personality and Social Psychology, 35,* 897–902.

Schultz, R., Visintainer, P., & Williamson, G. M. (1990). Psychiatric and physical morbidity effects of caregiving. *Journal of Gerontology, 45,* 181–191.

Select Committee on Aging. (1987). *Exploding the myths: Caregiving in America* (House of Representatives Publication No. 99–611). Washington, DC: U.S. Government Printing Office.

Seligman, M. (1975). *Helplessness: On depression, development, and death.* San Francisco: W. H. Freeman.

Shah, M., Avidan, R., & Sine, R. (1981). Self-care training for patients with hemiplegia, parkinsonism, and arthritis. In R. D. Sine, J. D. Holcomb, R. E. Roush, et al. (Eds.), *Basic rehabilitation techniques.* Rockville, MD: Aspen.

Spencer, E. A. (1988). Functional restoration: Neurologic, orthopedic, and arthritic conditions. In H. L. Hopkins & H. Smith (Eds), *Willard and Spackman's occupational therapy,* (7th ed). Philadelphia: Lippincott.

Swearer, J. M., Drachman, D. A., O'Donnell, B. F., & Mitchell, A. L. (1988). Troublesome and disruptive behaviors in dementia: Relationships to diagnosis and disease severity. *Journal of the American Geriatrics Society, 34,* 784–790.

Tobin, S., & Lieberman, M. (1976). *Last home for the aged: Critical implications of institutionalization.* San Francisco: Jossey Bass.

Trieschmann, R. B. (1987). *Aging with a disability.* New York: Demos Publications.

Trombly, C. A., & Scott, A. D. (1984). Activity adaptation. In C. A. Trombly (Eds.), *Occupational therapy for physical dysfunction,* (2nd Ed.). Baltimore: Williams & Wilkins.

Trombly, C. A. (1984). Activities of daily living. In C. A. Trombly (Ed.), *Occupational therapy for physical dysfunction,* (2nd Ed.). Baltimore: Williams & Wilkins.

U. S. Senate, Special Committee on Aging (1986). *Aging America, Trends and projections, 1985–1986.* Washington DC: U.S. Government Printing Office 498–116–814/42395.

Weiler, P. G. (1987). The public health impact of Alzheimer's disease. *American Journal of Public Health, 77,* 1157–1161.

Zarit, S., Todd, P. A., & Zarit, J. M. (1986). Subjective burden of husbands and wives as caregiver: A longitudinal study. *Gerontologist, 26,* 260–266.

Zarit, S., Reever, K., & Bachman-Peterson, S. (1981). Relatives of the impaired elderly: Correlates of feelings of burden. *Gerontologist, 21,* 158–164.

Zarit, S., Reever, K., & Bachman-Peterson, S. (1980). The burden interview. *Gerontologist, 20,* 649–656.

3

Use of the Cognitive Disability Frame of Reference in a Short-Stay Private Psychiatric Hospital

Esta-Lee Stone

This chapter describes the use of the cognitive disability frame of reference in an occupational therapy practice at a short-stay private psychiatric hospital. It applies information processing theory to the cognitive disability frame of reference and explains how this application structures and defines service delivery, including the purposes and goals of treatment, the assessment procedures, and treatment interventions. I also describe and discuss some of the neuroscientific concepts and postulates that provided the foundation for the clinical applications, hypotheses, and formulations included in the chapter.

Theoretical Base

During the last decade, psychiatric occupational therapy has been influenced by factors that have changed the practice's function and purpose, the nature of treatment assumptions, and the delivery of services. One variable that has contributed to this process has been the "remedicalization" of psychiatry. Remedicalization was explained by Pasnau (1987) as the "refocusing of scientific advances in neurobiology and neuroscience as they affect psychiatric diagnosis and treatment" (p. 147). The effect of advances in technology and neuroscience, or remedicalization, has also been addressed by occupational therapists. King characterized the use of new pharmacology, technology, and neuroscientific knowledge in the treatment of patients with mental disorders as a revolution (1983). The early stages of the revolution were attributed to the development and use of the major tranquilizers and the perpetuation to the technologies of the CT and PETT scans as well as the expansion of knowledge in the neurosciences.

In the 1989 Eleanor Clarke Slagle lecture, Farber identified the importance of neuroscientific knowledge in the present understanding of psychiatric illnesses and the relevance of this knowledge to psychiatric occupational therapy treatment approaches. Research in and knowledge about the neurosciences provide the theoretical constructs for the cognitive disability frame of reference, which is used extensively as the foundation for many psychiatric occupational therapy practices. The importance of this frame of reference is underscored by the proliferation of recent research which reaches conclusions similar to Allen's. For instance, Townes et al. (1985) suggest that the type and extent of impairment in psychiatric patients is independent of psychiatric diagnosis. In their research, they found that the severity of the psychiatric disorder and level of impairment were not necessarily related. Acutely ill psychiatric patients performed in the normal range on the verbal subtests of the WAIS and performed in the low-average range on tests of attention and visual-spatial problem solving. These same patients performed in the impaired range on test of general problem solving. On the basis of these findings, the authors suggest that a competency-based classification for psychiatric patients is likely to be far more useful in planning for treatment and discharge than one based on traditional psychiatric diagnosis. The authors reason that "treating the psychiatric patient by identifying areas of greatest competence will maximize treatment outcomes" (p. 41) and may prevent a patient from being asked to function in his or her area or areas of least competence. These authors believe that the latter approach is more likely to resolve rather than increase anxiety, depression, and other stress-related adaptations.

A study by David and Riley (1990) supports the finding that the level of impairment and dysfunction and the level of psychiatric symptomatology are not necessarily correlated. Their study found no significant relationship between the ACL scores, which measure dysfunction, and the level of the patient's psychopathology as measured by the Minnesota Multiphasic Personality Inventory.

Similarly, Erickson et al. (1986) suggest that the "patient's profile of competencies and deficits" (p. 259) rather than positive or negative symptoms (symptomatology or psychopathology) should be the focus of treatment especially for the development of rehabilitation approaches.

Neuropsychology focuses primarily on impairments or deficits that are caused by dysfunctions in underlying mental or physical structures. Disability is the primary focus of rehabilitation generally and occupational therapy specifically. Allen defines a disability as a limitation in task behavior that occurs as a consequence of an anatomical or physiological deficit in the human brain. In her Slagle lecture (1987), Allen states that disability should be the selected focus of occupational therapy study. By focusing on disability, rather than impairment or dysfunction when evaluating and treating the patient the therapist is able to assist the individual to produce satisfactory results when performing the routine tasks of life. This purpose is accomplished by recognizing both the assets and deficits in the patient's cognitive capacity, facilitating the patient's involvement in tasks where performance will be satisfactory, and either adapting or eliminating those tasks in which the patient will be less competent.

In an age when the neurosciences contribute so much to our understanding of the anatomy, physiology, chemistry, electricity, and function of various parts of the brain, it is ironic that scientists and practitioners are becoming increasingly aware that the brain's most important aspect is its intactness or unity or what we call the mind. Currently, what we call the mind cannot be deduced from studying the separate parts of the brain. One promising approach to this dilemma has been the information processing approach, which relies heavily on analogies from computer processing. This approach places emphasis on delineating the stages of processing and identifying the components presumed to be operating at these various stages.

Information Processing Concepts

The cognitive disability frame of reference is a behavioral hierarchy that proposes a relationship among mental disease, functional capabilities, and cognitive capabilities. It describes, at each level, the effects of mental disorders on patterns of thought or cognition. Using this hierarchy, the frame of reference also provides a descriptive classification system, and principles and procedures for analyzing activities. This frame of reference is important because it provides a methodology for understanding and improving the quality of performance of the cognitively disabled.

Allen developed the cognitive disability frame of reference heuristically, prior to the massive accumulation and dissemination of data in the neurosciences and without the benefit of information processing theory concepts and language. Mayer (1988) used the information processing literature to provide a conceptual framework to expand the theoretical concepts and assumptions used in Allen's cognitive disability frame of reference.

Information processing can be defined as "the way one collects, stores, modifies, and interprets environmental information or information already stored internally [in the brain or mind]" (Lachman, Lachman, & Butterfield,

1979, p. 6]. Information processing theory explains "how man adds information to his permanent knowledge of the world, how he accesses it again, and how he uses his knowledge in every facet of human activity" (Ibid). This process requires the manipulation of symbols and patterns in the mind. According to Mayer, when Newell et al. proposed the phrase, "system for information processing" (1988, p. 163) they were attempting to develop a theory of human problem solving.

Furthermore, human problem solving was explained by the Newell group as the use of strategies for processing information; these strategies had been gathered in the course of previous experience and stored in "the intrinsic cerebral systems" (Ibid). They believed problem solving was accomplished by a condition-action sequence called a production system, which joins together the system receiving information and the systems engaging in action. According to Newell et al. these production systems or condition-action sequences are the basis for human problem-solving behavior.

Problem-solving behavior involves first representing the problem—converting an initial state into a goal state. For instance, if the goal is to fashion a wooden frog from a craft kit, the first problem may be identifying the initial texture of the pieces in the kit, the texture of the goal state of these same pieces, and the differences between the two. The next step would be to select the operations, or task procedures, which would transform the initial textured state into the goal textured state. This selection process is called means-end analysis. The choice of operations could involve smoothing the pieces of wood by sanding manually or by machine. Selecting operators, either sandpaper or steel wool, or an electric sander, and choosing the grain of sandpaper or the kind of steel wool are choices which continue to exemplify means-end analysis. The individual needs a strategy or plan that guides his or her selection of operations or operators to help avoid a haphazard problem-solving approach.

Planning occurs when actions are executed in sequence in order to achieve a desired outcome or goal and involves organizing in one's mind a sequence of intended actions, recognizing if potential conflicts in the sequence exist, and reorganizing sequences to resolve conflicts. In order to engage in this process, individuals must be able to mentally manipulate symbols to create a goal structure, mentally hold the plan without acting upon it, and have a reliable enough memory to maintain the goal structure during the performance of an action or a series of actions. Planning may involve retrieving relevant information from long-term memory or gathering additional information about the task from the environment.

Returning to the example of fabricating a wooden frog from a kit, the plan might include sanding manually with both sandpaper and steel wool and using these operators in sequence to achieve the desired smoothness.

The plan may also involve retrieving information about the amount of pressure and rate of sanding speed from past experiences with sanding. However, if the wood used in the kit is unfamiliar, the plan might need to include information from the environment (either a book, or a person) about the properties of the wood (i.e., hardness) and its ease of splintering.

The execution of the motor sequence, the actual rubbing on the wood, is called a voluntary action; it contrasts with stereotyped responses to an immediate stimulus such as a reflex action. One important difference between the two forms of action is that the former involves processing of the subsequent effects of the action whereas the latter is generally thought to be a sensory-motor association.

Increasingly, neuropsychologists and cognitive psychologists are turning their attention to how people process and use information. Static notions such as IQ have been replaced by more dynamic concepts such as crystallized and fluid abilities (Erickson & Binder, 1986). Fluid ability involves problem solving in unfamiliar situations. Crystallized ability refers to intellectual functioning on tasks that call upon previous training, education, and acculturation. The concept of fluid ability is considered more useful clinically since this concept predicts the individual's adaptive abilities when stimuli and situations are novel. Fluid abilities have also been identified as being more vulnerable than crystallized abilities among the aged and various psychiatric populations (Ibid). In the past, using more traditional measures of intellectual functioning have led the clinician to miss deficits relevant to a patient's ability to adapt to community demands. Furthermore, estimates of a patient's rehabilitation potential based on well-learned skills, rather than the patient's potential to apply these skills in a variety of both new and old situations, can and has led to clinicians overestimating a patient's ability to respond in an adaptive manner. Unfortunately, there have been many cares where patients have experienced acute exacerbations of mental disorders following an attempt to adapt to unfamiliar situations in the community.

Mayer (1988) found that the Allen Cognitive Level test (ACL) measures a domain similar to the measures of fluid ability and could, therefore, be used to indicate learning potential or problem-solving potential in the cognitively impaired population.

Attention and Information Processing

Before presenting my application of information processing concepts and theory to the cognitive disability frame of reference, I will review the process of attention. Understanding the neural mechanisms that underlie this process is important for comprehending how information is processed by the human brain. Much has been written about the dimensions of attention. Attention is not a single simple phenomena but a complex multivariant phenomena; this knowledge may assist our understanding of the functional deficits which define the lower cognitive levels especially. Attention getting is the ability to detect changes in the environment, and refers to the process of showing interest in the external environment (De-Gangi & Porges, 1991). The process of attention begins to be operative at level 3. Attention getting includes the ability to orient to specific visual, auditory, or tactile stimuli, or the orienting reflex. It is an automatic response but does require active processing. The orienting reflex is important because it tunes up the appropriate receptor system, providing the best conditions for perception. The orienting response is crucial in determining whether the individual continues to respond to the stimulus if it is novel or intricate (novelty is anything that has not been previously experienced).

Novelty and complexity holds the individual's attention. The individual's ability to persist or maintain a consistent response within a continuous or repetitive activity is called sustained attention. Data from regional cerebral blood flow studies suggest that schizophrenics have difficulty in tasks that require sustained attention (Harvard Medical School Mental Health Letter, 1988).

One process that allows individuals to sustain and hold attention is known as selective attention. Selective attention is the ability to select or focus on one type of information to the exclusion of others. Since humans have a limited capacity for attention, screening out irrelevant stimuli is essential (Ibid). Some researchers have used dichotic listening studies to examine why patients with schizophrenia have difficulty ignoring information from irrelevant channels. Neural mechanisms of suppression and inhibition help individuals attend to those aspects of the environment that must be encoded to learn new information. They hypothesized that these mechanisms may be malfunctioning in some patients with schizophrenia (Saccuzzo and Braff, 1986).

There are two aspects of selective attention: active and passive. The voluntary aspect of selective attention is called active selective attention and is based on prior learning, training, and or experiences. It requires effort. Active selective attention is directed to either internal activity (thoughts) or external activity (actions). Passive selective attention is involuntary and effortless and is related only to objects that directly affect the sensory systems. In order for an individual to function, attention to routine sensory stimulation must be passive and involuntary. Learning cannot occur if the individual is attending to sensory stimulation from his or her body (DeGangi & Porges, 1991).

In a study that explored the relationship between effort and cognition in depression, researchers found that tasks that involved effort or active processing were disrupted more frequently by patients with depression than tasks which required passive selective attention. The authors conclude that the ability to sustain attention is an important component in understanding both the cognitive and behavioral problems in depression (Cohen et al., 1982).

One theory that explains the process of selective attention is the feature–integration theory. It hypothesizes that images are organized into separate feature maps. Each object has different features, all of which are not attended to during each examination because doing so would be too inefficient and exhausting. During the feature–extraction stage, information processing is automatic and focused mainly on simple features of a stimulus. In the next stage, feature integration, several features or a constellation of features are processed simultaneously. As the inputs have increasingly similar stimulus features, focusing becomes more difficult (De Gangi & Porges, 1991).

Attending to an old item in a new context or an unfamiliar item in an old context also requires selective attention, since changing contexts create novelty. When examined more fully, this aspect of selective attention may explain why patients with schizophrenia have difficulty with learning transfer.

Application of Information Processing and the Process of Attention to the Cognitive Levels

At cognitive *levels 1* and *2*, individuals are unable to perceive the task environment because they attend primarily to internal or subliminal cues (Mayer, 1988). Patients at level 1 are awake and aroused; the level of arousal can be enhanced but only for a few moments and generally not enough for them to engage with the environment or execute voluntary motor behavior. At *level 2*, patients spontaneously perform postural actions or familiar gross motor movements in response to proprioceptive cues. The patients seem to be aware of and will attend to their own bodily sensations; spontaneous or voluntary motor behavior seems to be an attempt to adjust themselves to these sensations. The ability of patients to attend to the external environment is still significantly impaired. Little spontaneous motor action occurs in response to the external environment, but patients can be cued to follow a caregiver or repeat a familiar gross motor movement that is demonstrated.

At *level 3* patients attend to and are aware of their own gross movements and are aware that their actions have an effect on the environment. They may not understand the effect nor be able to predict the effect at this level. In other words, the individual engages in the environment only through chance action not through planned or goal-directed action. Theoretically then, problem solving does not occur at this level since, by definition, problem solving is the use of information to achieve a goal. Attention at level 3 appears to be an example of the attention process described as the detect-react phenomena. The quantity or quality of active processing between detection and reaction is unclear, although at this level individuals process enough to imitate one-step directions when demonstrated for an unfamiliar task. Although spontaneous attention to the external environment is beginning to emerge, at this level, it is captured only by those environmental aspects the individual can experience manually or by touching; tactile properties of objects are the cues they attend to. Some of the individual's dysfunction at this level could be related to his or her voluntary active attention being focused on routine sensory stimuli such as the feeling of their clothing or shoes, hunger pangs, etc.

At cognitive *level 4*, patients are goal directed. We commonly observe at this level that patients may be able to develop plans but the plans are usually inefficient and ineffective. At the lower end of this level patients are unable to attend to the multiple stimuli or sets of stimuli necessary to formulate a plan. Patients often have difficulty shifting between sets of stimuli. If they attend to one variable or stimuli, they forget the other or others. For instance, a patient is given the task of choosing four items that cost no more than $20 from a list of groceries. At level 4, the patient may choose four items that cost more than $20 or twelve items that cost $20. Few patients at this level can successfully solve the problem using both the criteria of four items and $20. In information processing language, patients cannot identify and consider a number of operators or operations; the patient's problem space or their visualization of the problem is limited. In order for the patient to successfully complete a task, at this level, the therapist or caregiver must provide the operators and operations necessary for the patient to move from the initial state to the goal state. Again the root of the problem may be related to a deficit in attention; this time not in the attention-getting process but in the attention-holding process. Attention holding is the maintenance of attention when a stimulus is intricate or novel (DeGangi and Porges, 1991).

At the lower end of level 4, patients have difficulty recognizing problems; they may be able to say something is wrong but not what is wrong. At the upper end of the level, patients are more likely to recognize and identify precisely what's wrong because their attention is sustained long enough for them to match the state of their product to the goal state represented by the sample. However, at this stage patients often cannot identify all aspects of a problem, perhaps again because of attention problems. Not recognizing all aspects of a problem hampers the problem-solving process. Furthermore, even though patients at this level identify problems they still may not correct them. As you may recall, problem solving requires attention holding, effort, and persistence—all of which may not operate efficiently at level 4.

At cognitive *level 5* according to Mayer (1988) means-end analysis is emerging. Patients at this level attend to relationships between variables and therefore can develop plans. Although the plans are not always efficient or effective, the plans conceived by patients at this level are an improvement over those at the previous level. Although patients at this level are able to develop plans, they don't hold and test plans in their minds. They seldom consider the consequences of their actions before undertaking them, a crucial part of problem solving and planning. Patients at this level need verbal cuing to assist them in that part of the planning and problem-solving process that requires evaluating a plan and comparing one plan against another.

However, at this level, the quality of the individual's problem identification process is much improved. Problems, by definition, are discrepancies between what one is accustomed to and what one is presently experiencing; in other words anything that is novel is a problem. This description may provide another way of understanding Allen's hypothesis that what captures attention at level 5 is novelty and that purpose at level 5 can be characterized as exploration. Exploration may be that part of the problem-solving process, problem identification, which facilitates the identification of novelty. Problem identification may be fully functional at level 5.

At cognition *level 6*, symbolic cues are used to plan and solve problems in both familiar and unfamiliar situations. According to Allen (1985) there is no disability at this level.

The severe deficits in attention and, therefore, in information processing that occur at levels 1 through 3 and to lesser degrees at each of the higher cognitive levels have been addressed extensively in the neuroscientific literature. The AOTA self-study series, "Neuroscience Foundations of Human Performance," describes the basic foundations of attention. These include arousal, alerting, and sensory registration. Arousal is the transition from a sleeping to a waking state. Alerting is defined as the transition from waking to the attentive state necessary for active learning and adaptive behavior. According to the authors, transition from waking to alertness depends on registering sensory stimuli from the environment. If the individual attends to internal (auditory hallucinations) rather than external stimuli it would seem unlikely that he or she would be able to complete the transition from arousal to alertness and attention. Patterson et al. (1986) review research regarding the information processing deficits in schizophrenia. They hypothesize that much of the research data that describe information processing deficits in schizophrenia could be accounted for if, in some fashion, a primary stimulus fails to engage the attention of the schizophrenic. They suggest that in some patients with schizophrenia, as well as in other patients with thought disorders, the significance of a primary stimulus may be lost if the information conveyed cannot be used in time. Saccuzzo and Braff (1986) summarize research studies that also reveal deficits in the ability of patients with schizophrenia to maintain normal attention and therefore informational processing functions.

Activity and Task Analysis Based on Information Processing Concepts

Methods of analyzing activities compatible with the theoretical constructs and concepts of a frame of reference are usually considered essential. The cognitive disability frame of reference does include a system of principles and procedures to analyze activities. Another method can be used for analyzing activity that is consistent with the information processing approach. It is based on the *Concept of Activity in Soviet Psychology* identified in Allen's 1987 Slagle lecture as a "hierarchy for activity analysis." This method of activity analysis provides a schema for analyzing demands that are inherent to a task and can be thought about and understood apart from the capabilities of the individual performing the task.

The concept of activity as defined by the Soviets is a system not an event. The key to understanding the concept of activity is by comprehending the relationship between the parts of the system that define activity. The concept of activity has three levels: (1) the activity level, (2) the chain of actions level, and (3) the operations level. These three levels can be understood only in the context of the social system in which the activity occurs. Descriptions of these levels are based on their relation to one another rather than on any intrinsic properties they possess.

The Activity Level

The first part of the system is activity, a molar unit of life or ongoing behavior that mediates a person's connection with the world in which he or she lives. The mediation process occurs through thought (information processing), an internal activity, and through doing (performance), an external activity. A molar unit possesses a momentum of its own and is perceived as having meaning or intent (purpose) to the participants engaging in the activity. The momentum is produced by the doer's or actor's desire to perform (motivation) the activity. The desire to perform an activity is considered to be the object or the real motive. The real motive or object is determined by the social system of which the activity is a part. In other words, a society not only forms, socializes, and acculturates an individual but also indicates and defines the activities in which individuals engage. For instance, the activity of work defined by the royal family in England (the society) may be acting as an ambassador of good will; the real object or motive of this work may be maintaining the image of the crown and the royal family. Work in a psychiatric milieu (the society) is defined as participating in a treatment program; here the object may be optimal functioning. In summary, an activity is defined by its motive. Therefore, what distinguishes one activity from another is the object or real motive. What distinguishes work in the social system of the royal family from work in the social system of a psychiatric milieu, is the object of real motive: maintaining the image of the crown in the former and optimal functioning in the latter.

Chain of Actions Level

The basic components of a human activity, and the next level of the activity system, are the actions or the chains of actions that translate the activity into reality. A process is an action (reaching, gripping, pushing) when it is subordinate to the idea of achieving a result or a conscious goal (plugging in an electric cord). Human actions are either internal action (thoughts) or external actions (motor actions). A chain of actions is an aggregate of actions related to an overall goal. Human activities exist only in the form of an action or chain of actions. For instance, making a pie crust exists only in the form of the following chain of actions: spooning or shoveling, stirring, pressing, and pushing, etc.

One or a chain of actions can be used to realize different activities. For example, the action chain involved in cooking dinner can be used to feed one's family, cater parties, or recreate with friends. On the other hand, the same object or motive can give rise to different goals and can produce different actions. We all know that the object of earning a living can be expressed through different goals (i.e., manufacturing dresses, panhandling, constructing houses, evaluating function, or collecting unemployment). Each of these goals exists only in the form of specific chains of actions.

When individuals select (or know) a goal they consciously perceive the immediate result of their action or the goal state, the conditions of its attainment (or the completion standards), and the operations needed (or how the goal and the goals state can be reached). In other words, actions are guided by premeditated plans directed toward definite ends known in advance. At the end of the action, there is a result that already existed in the doer's mind. The goal of making coffee includes the perception of a black, steaming, aromatic, cup of coffee. The term completion standards describes the conditions of goal attainment, the features or properties of the results. Features or properties are the distinctive characteristics or outward appearance of physical entities. The completion standards of making coffee include temperature (how hot), color (black), and smell (aromatic).

The Operations Level

Operations, the third level of the concept of activity, are concerned with how something is done. Operations are defined not by the goal itself but by the circumstances under which the goal is accomplished. In other words, operations define how, where, and when an action should be performed. For example measurement operations is one way of identifying how something will be carried out (measure water, coffee). Placement operations (pouring water into the coffee carafe, spooning coffee into a receptacle, inserting a filter into the coffee container) identify where something is done. Conditions define how the action is mediated or what tools mediate the action (measuring cups, spoons, filters, coffee carafe).

Using the Concept of Activity

In order to use the concept of activity, the therapist must be aware of the relationship between the socially determined desire to engage in the activity and the activity itself. The concept is referred to in recent occupational therapy literature as shared social meaning (Pierce, 1991). For an individual with cognitive disabilities, this relationship is usually illusive since the cues to determine and understand the activity in its social context are complex and in many cases subtle. Even if a particular activity is familiar the context in which the activity occurs often changes.

Actions, goals, and operations taken together are tasks. Task analysis yields a description of the actions, goals, and operations which define a particular task. Since action, goals, and operations can only be understood in the context of the activity they define, task analysis can be considered to be a part of activity analysis, which describes the object or motive that an activity has for a particular social or cultural group. Activity analysis also defines the tasks which express the activity. Often in the occupational therapy literature, task analysis and activity analysis are synonymous. The concept of activity allows task analysis and activity analysis to be defined separately even though part of both their definitions describes the relationship between the two.

Task demands are the required actions, the socially defined goals, and the given standard of completion related to the goal state; task demands also include the operations required to perform the task. What the individual must do to meet the demands of any particular task can only be determined by defining the information processing processes (attention, planning, organization, etc.) required to meet particular task demands. Performance of routine tasks requires a combination of internal actions (thoughts) and external actions (voluntary motor actions).

We can determine task equivalency, a process that accurately and reliably predicts satisfactory performance on a routine task based on performance on an assessment task, by further developing this method for analyzing activities, tasks, and the demands of each. Delineating and defining levels of task complexity based on the information processing requirements of task demands is also an important adjunct to activity and task analysis. However, progress in understanding task equivalency and complexity depends on further understanding the brain's information processing processes.

Clinical Applications

Target Population

The cognitive disability frame of reference is applicable to and useful in understanding most psychiatric diagnoses. According to Allen (1988), psychiatric patients with organic brain syndrome and severe dementia are likely to function at *level 1;* occasionally patients with major mental disorders also perform at this level. *Level 2* includes patients with dementia and severe psychotic disorders. Patients at *level 3* have diagnoses of dementia, acute mania or acute schizophrenia. Some patients with severe depression function at this level. *Level 4* includes patients with mild dementia, acute mania and depression, and chronic schizophrenia. At *level 5* are patients with remitting affective disorders, schizophrenic disorders with good prognosis, personality disorders, and early onset dementia. Patients at *level 6* have affective disorders in remission and schizophrenic disorders with good prognosis. Occasionally patients admitted with depression function at this level.

Experienced clinicians identify that patients whose primary diagnosis is polysubstance abuse or alcoholism tend to score at level 4 or 5. However, many of the patients whose primary diagnosis is substance or alcohol abuse also carry a secondary diagnosis of major depression. Furthermore, patients who are diagnosed as schizophrenic or schizoaffective may also abuse or be dependent on substances. More patients are presenting with dual diagnoses, complicating the assignment of patients with particular disorders to a cognitive level. Depending on the length and the severity of the substance abuse, patients who carry dual diagnoses can score as low as level 2.0.

Intervention

In order to demonstrate the usefulness of the information processing approach within the cognitive disability frame of reference, three clinical applications are presented next. These examples can apply to the patient populations included above.

Allen Cognitive Level Test—Problem Solving

The first clinical application is the work of Josman and Katz (1991) who have developed a problem-solving version of the Allen Cognitive Level test, ACL–PS. They developed the new version to provide a more accurate evaluation of the patient's ability to problem solve. The authors were concerned that subjects who scored a 6 on the ACL demonstrated cognitive deficits, which were indicated by difficulties in planning and problem solving during performance trials in the occupational therapy clinic. They reasoned that the ACL does not require the subject to attend to symbolic cues, nor does it require independent planning. The ACL does require imitation at all levels, which should be unnecessary at level 6 or at the level where there is an absence of cognitive deficit and disability.

Josman and Katz's research findings supported their hypotheses that the ACL test requirement was too low for the processes described in Allen's cognitive level 6. The ACL–PS, which is their adaptation, has demands that match and differentiate the capabilities of the subjects at higher cognitive levels.

Josman and Katz (1991) suggest the following sequence of performance demands be used as guidelines for the presentation of the ACL to patients: (1) independent problem solving, (2) problem solving following verbal instructions, and (3) performance by imitation following a demonstration. They also suggest that during the patient's attempts to replicate each stitch by the aforementioned sequence, the therapist should evaluate whether the patient is using overt or covert problem solving. Overt problem solving involves trial and error and induction whereas covert problem solving involves deduction or the process of reasoning from general principles. In her new manual for describing the administration of the ACL, Allen incorporates part of this adaptation; subjects are asked to perform the single cordovan stitch independently before the stitch is demonstrated.

Measuring Changes in Patients' Performance [ACL Level] During Treatment and Stabilization

The cognitive disability frame of reference postulates that therapists can infer cognition by observing individuals while they spontaneously perform tasks. Therapists in a short-term psychiatric setting continually used the problem-solving processes and patient products in the occupational therapy clinic to evaluate the patient's performance status (cognitive level). They then reported the patient's performance status to the treatment team who used this data as one measure of the effectiveness of psychopharmacological interventions, the degree of stabilization of symptoms and cognitive status, and readiness for discharge. Important clinical decisions were often made on the basis of the occupational therapist's report; thus, at one point in the history of this practice, the methodology the therapists used to evaluate performance status was examined to increase the reliability and validity of the clinic assessment process. Therapists noticed during the assessment process in the occupational therapy clinic, that they generated hypotheses or inferences about a patient's cognitive level and capability to problem solve. Their hypotheses were based on observing spontaneous task behavior and were validated through probing or questioning. The therapist formulated and asked patients questions or probed them about how they achieved their results and about the quality of the results. These questions served to either clarify, confirm, or negate the therapist's understanding of the patient's cognitive processes and level of disability, which was determined initially from observing task performance.

The clinical reasoning of the therapists who were responsible for the occupational therapy clinic at various times was examined. Behind their questions was the assumption that there were two ways to determine whether the patient was engaging in problem solving: (1) was by observing behavior, and (2) was by determining the internal subjective happenings of the individual. Problem solving can be engaged in without any overt sign showing that it is occurring. Some of the questions asked and their underlying rationale are listed in Table 1.

Once the cognitive level had been verified, interventions were then designed to assist the patient produce a more satisfactory result. The commonalities in the therapists' reasoning and interventions formed the basis

Table 1 Sample Questions and Their Underlying Rationale

QUESTION: Have you finished? How do you know that you have finished?

RATIONALE: Does the patient have an image of the goal state? Can the patient compare the current state to the goal state? Can the patient identify completion standards?

QUESTION: Is yours the same as the sample?

RATIONALE: Can the patient compare the current state to the goal state?

QUESTION: What did you start out to do? Can you describe what you did?

RATIONALE: Did the patient have a plan? Was the plan efficient and effective?

QUESTION: Did your plan work?

RATIONALE: Can the patient evaluate the plan?

Table 2   Sample Script

If patient stopped working:
I notice you are sitting there; have you finished? How do you know that you are
finished? Did you do what you started out to do? Can you describe what you did?
Is yours the same as the sample? If you wanted yours to look like the sample,
how would you change it? Can you think of how you would do that? Did you
have a plan initially? Can you describe your plan? Did you try it out? Did it
work?

If patient makes an error: (deviates from standard directions or acceptable completion standards):
I would like you to stop working for a moment. Are you doing what you started out
to do? Can you describe what you are doing? Is yours the same as the sample? If
you wanted yours to look like the sample, how would you change it? Can you
think of how to do that? Did you have a plan initially? Can you describe your
plan? Did you try it out? Did it work?

If patient asks for assistance:
What did you start out to do? Are you doing what you started out to do? Can you
describe what you did? Does yours look like the sample? If you wanted yours to
look like the sample, how would you change it? Can you think of how to do
that? Did you have a plan initially? Can you describe your plan? Did you try out
your plan? Did it work?

If patient completes chain of action or task with no errors:
You did a good job. Did you have a plan? How did you decide when you were
finished with each part of the project and the project as a whole?

for the subsequent organization of these questions into a script. The script
is presented in Table 2.

In subsequent clinics, the script was followed as closely as possible in
an effort to structure and begin to standardize the evaluation process which
was the clinic's focus. The information processing stages were correlated
with the cognitive level stages on a theoretical basis. How closely the cognitive level assessment, based on task observations and responses to the
script, correlated to the patient's ACL level formed the basis of a research
project.

The first step identified for the research protocol (and in all subsequent
occupational therapy clinics) was that tasks were presented with verbal
directions and a sample. Directions provided only a list of the action chains
and goals of the task but not the operations. The sample provided a visual
representation of the completion standards. Conditions or tools were placed
in the patient's task space. Examiners attempted not to provide any directions with the sample. However, this methodology often elicited symptoms
in the lower level occupational therapy clinic because the task demands (the
absence of the presentation of action chains and goals) were so much higher

than the capabilities of the patients. The later methodology would have approximated the first step in the presentation of the ACL–PS suggested by Katz and Josman more closely. A third option, presenting directions without a sample, would demand that the patient independently problem solve on the basis of only symbolic cues; the patient would have to invent action chains, goals, and operations.

The protocol included an attempt at correlating the problem-solving processes and the cognitive levels. The therapists determination of the patients' cognitive levels based on the level of problem solving was determined by answers to the probe questions and task observations. Based on the therapists assessment of both the cognitive level and the problem solving deficits, interventions were made with the intent of improving the quality of the patients' performance. Initial study results using 28 patients produced a significant Pearson correlation of $r = 0.71$.

As work on this project continued, I identified literature which helped connect the investigation to other types of work. I identified similarities in our process to the one identified by Lidz as dynamic assessment, which is currently being used in neuropsychology and in cognitive rehabilitation. According to Lidz

> in this process (of dynamic assessment) the examiner is an active inter-
> vener who monitors and modifies the interaction with the learner in
> order to induce successful performance; the learner is prodded, di-
> rected, and reinforced into a role of active seeker and organizer of in-
> formation. The product of the assessment is modifiability or change in
> the functioning of the learner (1987, p. 3).

Some researchers and clinicians consider information from this type of assessment to be as important as the quantitative scores. How patients approach the task, the kind of errors they make, their ability to correct errors, and what they need to improve their performance are currently important rehabilitation foci.

Dynamic assessment provides an opportunity for voluntary motor actions to emerge that represent the potential for improved functioning. The therapist then has an opportunity to assess not only the patient's capability but the circumstances under which these capabilities can be utilized. This information provides data not only for treatment planning during hospitalization but also provides the foundation for good discharge planning and family and caregiver education.

Lidz (1987) describes the Survey of Cognitive Skills (SCS) developed by Meltzer, which assessed 3 components of problem solving. The examiner observes and rates the student during the process of problem solution. Part of the process is a probe/prompt/question stage. This last stage includes structured questions to elicit the student's awareness of critical task dimensions. This process appears similar to the process used in the occupational therapy clinic to determine the most effective interventions to help patients improve the quality of their task performance.

Activities of Daily Living Assessment Process

The activities of daily living (ADL) assessment process was developed over several years and continues to be modified. Development included (1) delineation of those routine tasks relevant to the cultural and socioeconomic level of patients, (2) a family interview to corroborate the patient's performance history and delineate future performance expectations, (3) a living-skills assessment based on Allen's Routine Task Inventory, (4) a home program format, and (5) a family education format.

The general purpose of the evaluation was to establish a process for not only determining patients' specific performance capabilities, but also determining what task modifications and supervision techniques would help patients most to improve their task performance. In this regard, the process and format for the ADL assessment process was one of dynamic assessment rather than static assessment.

The evaluation was designed with several specific intents: first, to determine whether the patient's repertory of routine tasks and activities and the quality of the patient's performance of these routine tasks and activities would match the performance expectations of caregivers/families. For example, prior to hospitalization, a young mother of two performed her child and home care activities only with the assistance and guidance of her husband who worked on an evening shift. The husband expected the patient to be able to perform these routine tasks competently without his assistance. This conflict in expectations was a source of family stress and was one of the precipitants to her being hospitalized.

Once the therapist has determined both the family's and the patient's expectations and has assessed the gap between these expectations and the patient's capabilities, the therapist must establish a more satisfactory match between the family's expectations and the patient's performance. In the case of the aforementioned young woman, the assessment focused on whether and under what circumstances the patient would be able to manage child and home care tasks independently and competently.

The team decides to initiate an ADL assessment when the patient's capacity to process information from the environment does not match the information processing capacity that will be required to meet current and future task demands from family/caregivers. The patient's cognitive capacity during treatment and stabilization is measured by task performance during occupational therapy evaluation clinics. Family or caregivers expectations were initially determined from chart data or psychosocial histories.

The following case material illustrates the absence of a match between cognitive capacity and task demands. A 65-year-old married woman with a long history of substance abuse was admitted. As a result of her initial assessment, it appeared that her task and activity demands included working a full-time job and managing two homes. Her cognitive capacity, indicated by initial ACL score and clinic performance during treatment and stabilization, improved from 3.2 to a low 4. At the level at which the patient had stabilized, it seemed unlikely that she would be able to do the planning, organizing, and problem solving necessary to efficiently and effectively manage these demands. A 30-year-old mentally retarded man was living in a community residence where the staff expected him to independently manage his own self-care, prepare simple meals with supervision, independently do his laundry, and attend a sheltered workshop. He became increasingly abusive. His cognitive capacity, indicated by initial ACL score on admission, was a 3.2. His clinic performance during treatment and stabilization was in the mid 3 range, which indicated that the patient was not goal directed and incapable of spontaneously performing tasks with even one-step directions. To meet the community residence's expectations, he needed a higher cognitive level.

Once the therapist has established that the information from an ADL assessment would contribute to improving the quality of the discharge plan, he or she should initiate the evaluation process. The specific goals of the ADL assessment process are to determine (1) which routine tasks the patient will be expected to perform, (2) which of these routine tasks and activities the patient can perform spontaneously, (3) what quality of performance is acceptable to both the patient and the caregiver/family, and (4) what degree and nature of assistance, task adaptation, and environmental adaptation will be necessary to produce performance results satisfactory to both the patient and the caregiver/family member. The ADL assessment process contains four components: case review, family interview, routine task assessment, and a family meeting.

The first component of the ADL assessment, case review, helps the therapist determine if and when patient's task performance is at baseline and alerts him or her to the existence and extent of present and potential functional problems. Case review has several aspects: analysis of a patient's course of functioning, occupational therapy clinic performance summary, medical test results, psychological test results, and initial discharge plans. Course of functioning describes an individual's functional performance over time with special emphasis given to premorbid functioning, functioning immediately following an illness, and functioning following the stabilization process. It is determined by gathering and analyzing a history of past and recent functional performance. Psychological test results, a part of case review when they have been ordered by the physician, can corroborate the ACL score by indicating how the patient uses what he or she knows (or thinks abstractly). By reviewing a patient's medical history, the clinician can better understand the task demands. The initial discharge plan outlines alternative residences and activities for the patient.

The second component of the ADL assessment process is the family or caregiver interview. The therapist's goal in this interview is to determine the expectations by the family members/caregivers following discharge as well as collect additional data on patient's recent performance and course of functioning. During the course of the interview, families/caregivers are introduced to the relationship between psychiatric illness, cognition, and routine task performance. Initially, a family interview was not included in the ADL evaluation process; the quality of a patient's recent and past performance was assessed by interviewing only the patient (who was at best biased and at worst unable to provide the therapist with enough data to form a reasonable assessment). The therapists used data from social service's psychosocial history to determine the family's perceptions of the patient's recent and past functioning; these data were colored by family dynamics and expectations to which we were not privy. In addition, earlier ADL assessments were conducted at a time when the average length of stay was 3 weeks and an assessment of all routine tasks could be scheduled and implemented. Currently the average length of stay is 11 days, especially in hospitals whose patients are admitted under an HMO contract. An assessment that evaluates only those tasks that the family or caregiver expects the patient to perform after discharge has been opted to be compatible with the current length of hospitalization. Last, engaging the family in a discussion of the patient's recent and past performance and their expectations for future performance early in the treatment process may increase the likelihood that the goals of the assessment process will be reached.

A patient's true functional status at the time of discharge would best be measured by assessing the quality of performance on the exact functional tasks he or she will be expected to perform, in the actual setting where he or she will be expected to perform, and with familiar equipment. Since this ideal method is generally not achievable in an inpatient setting, we have developed tasks that simulate those routine to the majority of patients, taking into account their cultural and socioeconomic group. Since one purpose of the ADL assessment process was to increase the likelihood of a match between family expectations and patient's performance, our concern was not could the patient do the task spontaneously but could the patient do the task under any conditions and what conditions were they? To answer this question, we used the dynamic assessment methodology. The process of dynamic assessment is now incorporated into the ADL assessment process. We present tasks using verbal directions and no sample; this methodology provides no or few clues to influence cognition and the quality of task performance. In our opinion, spontaneous behavior or behavior independent of any assistance can best be evaluated in this manner. The therapist observes spontaneous behavior, approximates the cognitive level, and notes focal deficits if any. He or she then changes the tasks or adapts them to match the patient's cognitive capacity. Various adaptations are based on the patient's cognitive level, amount of experience in performing the tasks and their prior knowledge of the task. The family's expectations of the quality of performance and their capacities (i.e., time available to supervise the patient, level of understanding etc.) are considered. If adapting the task or the activity to the family/caregiver demands appears impossible, the final adaptation is eliminating the activity or task.

Case Example

A 69-year-old widowed man was admitted because of anxiety and depression. In this case, the source of data was the patient and the social worker. Prior to hospitalization, the patient had had some difficulty concentrating on working in and managing his shoe repair business. He had stopped exercising, socializing, and was not managing the routine tasks of his life. At first, he depended on his sister to manage some of the activities of daily living and then, temporarily, moved into his daughter's home where she managed the routine tasks. The data in his sister's narrative were in sharp contrast to data from the patient's self-report. He reported having owned a successful shoe repair business since the age of 14 when he dropped out of school. He also reported being a successful investor in the stock market, acting for himself and friends. The patient reported that during his 44-year marriage, his wife had been his bookkeeper. He enjoyed socializing and was active in the community. Since his wife's death, his sister had been managing the bookkeeping and the check writing. His initial ACL score, 4.0, was indicative of a moderate cognitive disability. The only psychological testing ordered by the patient's physician had been projective testing; the psychologist noted in his test report that there was no evidence of dementia or focal deficits, although some concreteness was noted. His medical history indicated the recent implant of a pacemaker, high cholesterol, and CT scan abnormalities that suggested early stages of dementia. There was no agreement about the discharge plan which increased the importance of the assessment process. The patient's daughter was concerned about the patient's difficulty managing his business and routine life tasks; she was contemplating building an apartment for him in her garage. The patient was interested in living in an apartment independently. The patient's physician thought the patient should move to a nursing home.

In the occupational therapy clinic, the patient's ability to process information improved during the several weeks he was hospitalized; he progressed from being dependent on verbal cues to identify and correct errors on familiar tasks to spontaneously identifying and correcting errors on familiar tasks. At the end of his hospitalization, he needed verbal cues to correct errors on unfamiliar tasks. His difficulty using written directions to guide his task performance also became evident.

The patient's sister was interviewed. She described what she expected the patient to be able to do spontaneously and independently following discharge. She expected him to manage and conduct his business and prepare most of his own meals. She planned to retire and travel. According to her, recently the patient was unable to do simple computations or write letters or checks easily. She explained that the patient had always had difficulty reading, writing, and spelling which was why the patient's wife (and then she) had done the bookkeeping and the check writing. The patient had stopped cooking for himself and was eating his meals at his sister's or daughter's.

The activities identified for assessment, based on the families' performance expectations, were money management, meal preparation, and medication management. In addition, the therapist assessed the patient's level of problem solving in order to predict whether he could manage total independent living, an activity with which he had had no experience.

To evaluate money management capabilities, the therapist asked the patient to complete several shopping tasks, design a budget, make financial decisions based on the budget, write checks to pay bills, and balance his checkbook. When required to make change, the patient made errors which he globally recognized stating that something was wrong. The cue ("What is wrong, and can you fix it?") did not improve his performance. At this point, he explained his educational history and described what appeared to be a significant learning deficit. He could not do any mathematical procedures except addition of single column figures, or reason mathematically. His accuracy on simple computational tasks improved when he was given a pocket calculator, a tool he knew and had used successfully in his business. He did not know how to compute percentages, comparison shop (although he understood the concept), design and use a budget to manage his expenses (although again he understood the concept), make out checks, fill out a deposit slip, or balance a checkbook. He found these last three tasks difficult because he had never learned to write or spell in school. The therapist asked the patient to plan a menu for several days and generate a shopping list from this menu. He did not know about the relationship between diet and heart disease, and could not plan healthy and nutritious menus based on the general dietary principles that were given to him. However, with the assistance of recipe suggestions supplied by the hospital dietitian which factored in his basic and special nutritional needs, the patient demonstrated that he could plan meals and make a shopping list from the menus he generated.

He had no difficulty preparing a two-course lunch. He located equipment and ingredients in the kitchen; read and used the unfamiliar written directions to guide his preparation; measured ingredients accurately; turned on and adjusted the heat; used acceptable completion standards for cooking, washing, rinsing, and drying dishes; sequenced steps spontaneously and correctly; used time efficiently; and knew and applied safety standards.

Although he could state the medicines and dosages he was taking, he could not explain the specific relationship between the medicine and his heart condition or between the psychiatric medication and his depression. In the past, whenever he felt better, he had stopped taking his heart medicine without his physician's permission. He could describe an efficient, effective system he would use for monitoring his compliance with his medication schedule; however, when common medication problems were raised, he made errors in solving them. In summary all tasks that required using arithmetic or mathematical reasoning, spelling, and writing were too difficult or impossible for the patient to manage and complete successfully. We suspected he had focal deficits and/or significant learning deficits, but they were never corroborated except by the CT scans: neuropsychology testing had not been ordered. His difficulties related to general problem solving; he was unable to spontaneously take general principles and apply them to a particular situation. In both familiar and unfamiliar situations where mathematical reasoning or computations were not essential, the patient could recognize both general and specific errors. In familiar situations, he could produce efficient, effective solutions. In unfamiliar situations, the quality of his solutions was compromised; he could identify general problem solutions but could not develop a plan to apply a solution.

In the home program and the family meeting, the therapist suggested that since the patient's sister was interested in retiring and the patient did not have the knowledge, skill, or the experience to do the arithmetic and spelling necessary to perform the bookkeeping or check-writing tasks, they consider selling his business. The patient did not have the information processing skills necessary to make this decision; the therapist presented the family with an outline of how to verbally cue the patient to facilitate the decision-making process. If the patient did decide to sell his business, the family should provide the planning, organization, and problem solving necessary to complete this activity since selling the business would generate many problems unfamiliar to him. The therapist also suggested that the patient find a job as a shoe repairer to assist him in structuring his time; shoe repairing is a very familiar task and if he worked in another person's shop he would probably need to learn familiar tasks in a new context. In his community, the therapist identified literacy and math classes for adults with learning problems, and made initial contacts with the instructors. The specific classes he was referred to could help him learn basic arithmetic and spelling skills as well as improve his reading comprehension. Again, the therapist did the research for this task since the patient did not have the problem-solving capacity to deal with the community bureaucracy.

During the family meeting, the therapist explained the effects of depression on task performance using the patient's difficulty managing the familiar routine tasks associated with meal preparation. The difficulty patients have on tasks that require active sustained attention was explained in simple language. They were also told about the effect of medication on symptom reduction and improvement in performance, using the patient's performance in the occupational therapy clinic and in the kitchen as an example.

The family also learned about his residual cognitive disabilities (not being able to reason inductively) and the effect this disability has on his ability to spontaneously plan meals, develop a budget if his income changed, spontaneously design activities to organize his time, etc. The therapist underscored the functional sequelae of the CT scan findings (these had already been presented to the patient and the family). Managing change, which in essence is complex problem solving, would become more difficult. Family expectations were reviewed as was a synopsis of most of his particular task performance problems. Task performance problems are often discussed with the patient alone before the family meeting so that the patient is prepared. The therapist reviewed the home program, which included the kind of assistance and cuing the patient needed to perform tasks satisfactorily, and discussed adaptations with the family who negotiated the quality of the performance they expected. They were told certain tasks should be eliminated. The patient and his family decided to sell his business, and he decided to work in a similar business doing those tasks which were familiar and he did well; his children agreed to write his checks and manage his banking. The patient returned to his home to manage the remainder of the routine tasks with the adaptations that had been suggested.

Discussion

The future development of the ADL assessment process is twofold. A standard procedure or script to determine the conditions under and methods with which performance improves must be developed. Secondly, the demands of combining all routine tasks into a unified whole in order to function independently must be better understood. Often patients can perform individual routine tasks effectively. However, these same patients seem to have difficulty combining the tasks into activities and functioning independently; the whole seems to be greater than the sum of the parts. The essence of independent living appears to be the ability to adapt the performance of routine tasks in the ever-changing contexts of life experiences. I make this last statement based on intuitive knowledge gained through years of clinical experience. The task before us now is to translate this intuition into concepts and theory.

References

Allen, C. A. (1985). *Occupational therapy for psychiatric diseases: Measurement and management of cognitive disabilities.* Boston: Little, Brown.

Allen, C. A., Allen, R. A. (1987). Cognitive disabilities: Measuring the social consequences of mental disorders. *Journal of Clinical Psychiatry, 48,* 181–191.

Allen, C. A. (1987). Eleanor Clarke Slagle Lectureship–1987; Activity: Occupational therapy's treatment method. *American Journal of Occupational Therapy, 41,* 563–575.

Cohen, R. M., Weinggartner, H., Smallberg, S. A., Pickar, D., Murphy, D. L. (1982). *Effort and cognition in depression. Archives of General Psychiatry, 39,* 593–597.

David, S., Riley, W. (1990). The relationship of the Allen cognitive Level Test to cognitive abilities and psychopathology. *44*(6), 495–497.

Erickson, R. C., Binder, L. M. (1986). Cognitive deficits among functionally psychotic patients: A rehabilitative perspective. *Journal of Clinical and Experimental Neuropsychology, 8*(3), 257–274.

Farber, S. (1989). Eleanor Clarke Slagle Lecture, 1989: Neuroscience and occuational therapy: Vital connections. *American Occupational Therapy 43*(10), 637–646.

Harvard Medical School Mental Health Letter, 1988.

Josman, N., Katz, N. (1991). Problem solving version of the Allen Cognitive Level (ACL) Test. *American Journal of Occupational Therapy, 45*(4), 331–343

King, L. J. (1983). Occupational therapy and neuropsychiatry. *Occupational Therapy in Mental Health, 3*(1) 89–94.

Lachman, R., Lachman, J. L., Butterfield, E. C. (1979). *Cognitive psychology and information processing: An introduction.* Hillsdale, NJ: Lawrence Erlbaum Assoc.

Lidz, C. S. (1987) *Dynamic Assessment* N.Y., London: Guilford.

Mayer, M. (1988). Analysis of information processing and cognitive disability theory. *American Journal of Occupational Therapy, 42*(3), 176–185.

Newell, A., Shaw, J. C., Simon, H. A. (1958). Elements of a theory of human problem solving. *Psychological Review, 65,* 151–166.

Pasnau, R. O. (1987). The remedicalization of psychiatry. *Hospital and Community Psychiatry, 38*(2), 145–151.

Patterson, T., Spohn, H. E., Bogia, D. E., Hayes, K. (1986). Thought disorder in schizophrenia: Cognitive and neuroscience approaches. *Schizophrenia Bulletin, 12*(3), 461–472.

Saccuzzo, D. P., Braff, D. L. (1986). Information-processing abnormalities: Trait and state-dependent components, *12*(3), 447–459.

Townes, B. D., Martin, D. C., Nelson, D., Prosser, R., Pepping, M., Maxwell, J. (1983). *Journal of Counseling and Clinical Psychology, 33*(1) 33–42.

4

Cognitive Organization: A Piagetian Framework for Occupational Therapy in Mental Health*

Noomi Katz and Noga Ziv

Acknowledgment: We want to thank Liliana Tolchinsky Landsmann, Ph.D., for her major contribution to the development of this model and for her work on the assessment battery and research related to it.

In this chapter, we provide a theoretical perspective that integrates Piaget's cognitive framework with occupational therapy activity intervention for the evaluaton and treatment of psychiatric patients. The chapter includes (1) the rationale for using Piaget's theory, followed by the major concepts and assumptions utilized; (2) the relationship of this theory to mental health and to activity intervention in occupational therapy; (3) the

---

* We dedicate this chapter to the late Professor Yehuda Fried who inspired our work in this direction and guided occupational therapists in exploring the theoretical foundation of Piaget's theory, particularly its contribution to activity intervention in mental health. In the appendix to this chapter, Aviva Fried, MA, OTR, faculty member at the occupational therapy department at Tel Aviv University, provides a glimpse into her husband's early ideas relating to psychopathology and Piaget's theory.

evaluation process using a battery of tests and research findings; (4) treatment principles utilizing a compatible activity analysis, with an individual case example; and (5) implications for future development.

Theoretical Base

Because we focus in this chapter on cognitive structures, processes, and the organization of knowledge, we based our approach on the piagetian theoretical framework. This framework centers on cognitive issues from an epistemological perspective.

According to Piaget, our source of knowledge about the world is action. "Cognition is, at all genetic levels, a matter of real actions performed by the subject" and these actions "constitute the substance or raw material of all intellectual and perceptual adaptations" (Piaget in Flavell, 1963, p. 82). Piaget also notes that with cognitive development, intelligent actions become progressively internalized. They become increasingly schematic and abstract, broader in range yet reversible, and organized into systems of internal operations. Cognitive development proceeds from overt, slow-paced, simple, sensory motor actions that are transformed into quick and highly organized covert systems of intellectual operations, which characterize logical thought. Piaget emphasizes that the latter are actions just as surely as the former. Hence, all knowledge at all levels is linked to action (Piaget, 1971).

Piaget focuses on a broader theory of genetic epistemology which subsumes development, which allows us to understand adult thinking processes in light of a developmental perspective. Genetic epistemology is defined as "the study of the mechanisms whereby bodies of knowledge grow" (Flavell, 1963, p. 251; Piaget, 1971). One of the major premises is that, underlying any behavior of an organism, systematic structures exist that explain behavior. These structures are developed by balancing assimilation and accommodation, which in turn leads to adaptation. The twin processes of assimilation and accommodation explain all interactions between the individual and his environment.

Intelligence is first allied to biology and as such is considered as the very center of adaptation. Piaget argues that we inherit a mode of intellectual functioning, but we do not inherit cognitive structures. These develop in the course of intellectual functioning, and it is only through functioning that cognitive structures are formed. According to Piaget the mode of functioning or modus operandi remains constant throughout life. Two major functional invariants, organization and adaptation, are responsible for creating new structures the individual uses in his or her interaction with the environment. Hence, function and structure are closely interrelated.

Defining Concepts

Structure

Schema. A schema is a cognitive structure which refers to a class of similar action sequences. It is a concept, category, or underlying strategy; or an organized disposition to grasp objects on repeated occasions. In general, any organized behavioral pattern is termed a schema. Schemas, as structures that support actions, are both created and modified by intellectual functioning.

Operations. Operations are patterns of behavioral schemes or a more complete thought structure, like the operations of classification or conservation.

Function—Organization and Adaptation

According to Piaget, adaptation and organization are two sides of the same coin. Adaptation assumes an underlying coherence, and organizations are created through adaptations.

Cognitive Organization. Cognitive organization is a system of relationships among elements. Any intelligent action is always related to a system of acts of which it is one. Organization refers to the tendency of all species to systemize and organize their processes into coherent systems, to integrate structures into higher-order systems.

Cognitive Adaptation. Cognitive adaptation comprises an invariant process of assimilation and accommodation. An act that balances assimilation and accommodation constitutes a cognitive adaptation. Thus, adaptation refers to those organism-environment exchanges in which assimilation and accommodation are in equilibrium.

Assimilation. Assimilation refers to the integration of information into previous structures. It refers to any process whereby information is changed in order to make it part of the organism's existing knowledge, the reception of any new stimuli by the existing structures, and the understanding of the unknown by that which is known.

Accommodation. Accommodation is any adjustment the organism must make to the external world in order to assimilate information.

Self-Regulation—Equilibration

Self-regulation or equilibration are the processes whereby the individual organizes and adapt to his environment. "Self-regulations are the very nature of equilibration. . . . they come into play at all levels of cognition including the very lowest level of perception" (Piaget, 1977, p. 838). Piaget distinguished three kinds of equilibrium: first, the balance between assimilation and accommodation between the individual's known structures and new objects; second, equilibrium among the subsystems of the individual's schemes, namely, coordination among the various conceptual domains; and third, equilibrium between the individual's ability to differentiate and integrate knowledge at any given moment. Equilibrium also refers to differentiating all the individual's knowledge into parts and integrating the parts back into the whole. Equilibrium at any point is not a final state; there is always a tendency to go beyond it to a better equilibrium (Piaget, 1977).

Conceptual Domains

Our knowledge of the world is acquired, according to Piaget, through two kinds of knowledge: the factual (or physical, spatial knowledge) and the logico-mathematical (or symbolic and abstract knowledge). These two kinds of knowledge require two kinds of validation, factual validity and logical validity. Factual validity comes from direct knowledge of objects, whereas logical validity comes from the knowledge one deduces from his or her acts on and with objects. This is also, according to Piaget, the relationship between induction and deduction (Fried, 1984).

Developmental Stages

Conceptual domains are acquired throughout the stages of cognitive development from the sensory-motor period through the preoperational period, the concrete operational period, and the formal operational period. Namely, these are acquired from sensory-motor intelligence which is factual and linked to objects and movements, and thus to operational, representational, and conceptual thought (i.e., logical knowledge). This is a universal and unvarying course of progressive development, but the actual age ranges can change in different cultures and environments, and the extent of the highest stage of formal thought may be different for specific individuals. Social factors play an important role in intellectual development at all stages, but the interaction with the social environment (other individuals), varies in nature according to the individual's level of development or cognitive organization.

Centrism—Decentrism

In broad terms, cognitive development proceeds from an initial state of egocentrism to a state of social interaction in which the individual's actions are performed according to his or her understanding of others. Piaget uses the concept of centrism instead of egocentrism. He found that there are some people at age 18 and older who are sometimes self-centered and unaware of other views. In this sense they are in a state of centrism, although not in the same sense as a 5- or 6-year-old child's egocentric state. Thus, intelligence here is a way of looking at things from another viewpoint, being able to step away from one's own viewpoint and looking at other alternatives.

The Possible, Impossible, and Necessary

The ability to decenter (to consider alternative possibilities), logically transform operations in one's mind, and to understand the reversibility of acts and mental operations all lead to formal thought which comprehends what is realistically possible, what is impossible, and what is necessary. In other words, these processes lead to the understanding that things or acts can be possible but are not necessary, the understanding of multiple possibilities; the understanding that things have limits and can be impossible but that impossibility has to be questioned first. Impossibility limits action; removing it provides for the possible. Reality is, thus, an integration between the two poles of possible and necessary (Piaget & Voyat, 1979; Piaget, 1987).

Constructivism

The development of new knowledge is the development of possibilities through transformations. "Possibility in cognition means essentially invention and creation, which is why the study of possibility is of prime importance to a constructivist epistemology" (Piaget, 1987, p. 4). But one can speak of possibilities only relative to how an individual conceives reality and its possibilities as they develop with age.

In summary, Piaget suggests a constructive system that operates upon action and "reflection upon action" (Glick, 1985). "For Piaget, intelligence is an adaptive biological function. To know is to act, and in the absence of action, the question of knowledge becomes mute within Piaget's system. As any biological function, knowing implies structure, and to begin to know is to construct new structures" (Pufall, 1988). Normally individuals use equilibration to construct cognitive structures during an activity. These schemes are automatic. By using self-regulation in any new or different situation, these schemes allow the individual to assimilate the unkown into existing cognitive structures and change these structures simultaneously to accommodate and adapt to the new situation. This ongoing process allows individuals to acquire and develop new knowledge as children as well as when they become adults.

Mental Health and Illness

Based on Piaget's conceptualization, Fried (1978, 1984) states that mental health and illness are fundamentally problems of organization, and psychopathology is the science of mental organization and its disruptions. Piaget's own opinion on the subject of cognition and affect was that affective factors cannot change cognitive structures:

> I always sustained—without adventuring myself in the domain of pathology—that the affective factors play an indispensable role of motor (energy) in the development of normal thought, without modifying the cognitive structures (Gruber & Voneche, 1977).

> Affective life, like intellectual life, is a continual adaptation, and the two are not only parallel but interdependent, since feelings express the interest and value given to actions of which intelligence provides the structure (Piaget in Flavell, 1963, pp. 80–81).

Researchers working in this field have tried to characterize levels of cognitive organization according to diverse psychiatric populations (Apostel, 1981; Bunard, Zutter, Burgermeister, & Tissot, 1981; Fried & Agassi, 1976; Tissot, 1976; 1979). They agree, first, that the main problem is defining boundaries between mental health and mental illness and, second, that similar processes (assimilation and accommodation) are involved both in healthy and nonhealthy mental functioning. Despite this shared basis, two different assumptions emerge on the consequences of mental illness. According to the first assumption, mental illness predominately affects how individuals approach problems requiring abstract thought to be solved (Apostel, 1981; Fried & Agassi, 1976). This position sees nonhealthy mental functioning as being organized around a number of fixed principles that predetermine the type of solution reached by abstract problem solving. They attempted to formally describe the logic of pathological thinking by focusing mainly on paranoia and depression and then providing a theoretical and clinical analysis.

According to the second contrasting assumption, mental illness predetermines the type of solution provided for concrete problems as well (i.e., those problems dealing with objects) and is expected to influence every area of the individual's interaction with objects and persons (Bunard et al., 1981; Tissot, 1976; 1979). Focusing on schizophrenia, their main hypothesis was that inadequate mental operations are due to a disequilibrium between assimilation and accommodation. Schizophrenics would continually oscillate between complete assimilation as observed in symbolic games and complete accommodation as observed in pure imitation.

Based on this assumption and hypothesis, they attempted to functionally explain differences in performance of schizophrenic patients. Using their small sample of normal individuals as well as individuals with paranoia and hebephrenic schizophrenia who had all completed the Wechsler intelligence tests and a battery of piagetian tasks, they found first, as in most studies on cognitive performance, that cognitive impairment was primarily related to the duration of the disease. Young acute patients performed similarly to controls. The lowest performances were seen in long-term hebephrenic patients.

Second, in line with their hypothesis, they found that the deductive logical operations suffered less impairment than operations involving spatial representation, or experimental reasoning. The latter was less impaired because it calls for real objects to be assimilated into the thought process and for individuals to perform actions that are specific to certain characteristics of the objects. Patients had better results in some of the formal logical tests than in tests of elementary logic. In trying to explain this, Tissot suggests that "when one is dealing with the quantification of probabilities, the nature and the properties of the objects are of little importance. On the contrary, when the task is to classify geometric shapes or to arrange figures, the subject must be able to abstract some common property from the outer reality; in other words his classification scheme must assimilate various real objects through one of their common characteristics" (Tissot, 1976, p. 240).

In line with clinical knowledge, the findings suggest (according to Tissot) that schizophrenics retain mental operations they acquired before the onset of the disease. The question is, then, why are they unable to apply these operations? What causes schizophrenics to lose their ability to enact these operations?

According to Fried and Agassi (1976), "the cognitive impairment in schizophrenia is not that it is a primitive form of thinking, but that it is a low-level integrative principle, and a global one at that" (p. 88). Psychosis primarily impairs the thought process, causing an intellectual disturbance. The manic depressive state is characterized by the individual's inability to think about anything else (i.e., fixation on certain ideas). Emotional expressions are secondary to the thought impairment, even though the diagnosis may be affective.

In general, what these authors recommend is an approach that does not distinguish sharply between the intellectual and emotional, a premise we accept when using a cognitive framework for intervention in mental health. This basic assumption is shared by authors who perform intensive studies of schizophrenic cognition based on neurostructures, information processing, and hemispheric specialization (Margo, 1984). Models of information processing that combine perception and conceptualization have also been developed and studied. On the other hand, cognitive therapy for depression, which uses piagetian structural concepts, also assumes that affect and behavior are based on how the individual structures his or her world (Beck et al., 1976).

Occupational Therapy

Various theoretitians in occupational therapy used Piaget's concepts in their conceptualizations. Reilly (1974) discusses Piaget's work in relation to play, but she first recognized in his theory a cognitive adaptation model of behavior. Action or overt behavior is essential to knowledge, and play behavior forms the basis for learning. "Thinking is not for action, it is action" (p. 74) and reflects the internalization of action sequences into mental images. Children learn to develop concrete strategies into complex formal operations without concrete examples through play, and it prepares them to adapt as adults to the external world (Reilly, 1974).

Mosey (1970, 1986) uses part of Piaget's concepts when she breaks down cognitive adaptive skills in her developmental frame of reference. Llorens (1976) considers Piaget's developmental stages as part of her general developmental frame of reference.

Allen (1985) in the early development of her cognitive disability theory for adult patients with psychiatric disorders, applied central concepts of Piaget's theory (such as schemes, assimilation, accommodation, self-regulation, equilibrium) and conscious awareness of action. She also used basic concepts from the sensory-motor period to construct six cognitive levels, which can be used to assess a person's cognitive functional capabilities. Later, Allen found developmental theory for normal children was limited in its use with adult disabled patients. Although, she dropped the use of some of the concepts, she expanded the basic cognitive levels (Allen, 1988).

Recently, Depoy and Burke (see Chapter 10) utilized Piaget's constructivist notions as part of their theoretical basis for a cognitive intervention approach within the human occupation model.

As emphasized in the introduction and rationale, we consider Piaget's work from its epistemological and cognitive perspective to be fundamental to human functioning and, as such, it is an excellent source for understanding dysfunctional individuals.

Intervention

Target Population

The target population in this study is psychiatric patients, adolescents and adults, whose function currently or in the past was at higher cognitive levels. These are patients whose premorbid performance was good and who now present dysfunction such as problem solving, planning, or organization. They can also verbalize their response to acts they perform. Many of these patients are treated in half-open and open settings, outpatient clinics, and in the community. However, the major principles of adaptation can be applied to other populations as well.

Evaluation

The complete evaluation process consists of: (1) a background questionnaire and occupational history, (2) an activity checklist, (3) a performance schedule on a typical day (Katz & Allen, 1988), and (4) the cognitive assessment battery, which is described in the following section.

Assessment

The assessment battery was based on traditional piagetian tests refined in a careful field-testing process (Tolchinsky Landsmann & Katz, 1988). Interrater reliability was determined among three pairs of therapists who collected the data. The battery consists of eight tests that evaluate the subject's mode of understanding different physical, spatial, and logico-mathematical concepts. Table 1 displays the assessment battery according to conceptual domain and developmental stage within the piagetian framework. [Table 1 is based on the table presented in the Tolchinsky Landsmann and Katz's (1988, p. 78) article with two tests added, weight conservation and transitivity of sizes.] A short description of each test is provided (parts were described in the previous article and are repeated here for the reader's convenience).

Conservation of Weight

Weight conservation is tested by showing subjects two plasticene balls and asking them to agree or physically verify the same amount of plasticene in each. This step is important because if they do not establish

Table 1 Assessment Battery According to Conceptual Domain and Developmental Stage

Developmental stage	Conceptual Domain		
	Logico-mathematical	Physical	Spatial
		Weight conservation and the conservation of one's own weight	
Concrete Operational	Classification (class inclusion)	Conservation of volume	Conservation of horizontality without fluid
Formal Operational	Conception of chance Quantification of probability	Transitivity of sizes	

the balls are equivalent to begin with it will be impossible for them to predicate whether or not they are equal after they have been altered. After establishing that the balls are equal, the subjects are shown a scale that has two plates and are asked what the balance will be before one ball is placed on a plate. After the first ball is placed on the scale, subjects are asked what will happen when the second ball is placed on the other plate. Then, one of the plasticene balls is left on one of the plates to act as a baseline. The tester then changes the plasticene ball's shape twice (into a ring and into small pieces). After each modification, the subjects are asked whether the placement of the altered ball on the plate will cause a similar change in the balance of the scale. Scores reflect the range of the subject's ability to note operational conservation, their need for empirical verification, or their uncertainty and lack of conservation.

Conservation of Own Weight

The testers gave the subjects the following verbal description: Suppose you are weighing yourself on a scale. You looked at the scale and you weighed, let us say, 60 kg. Will your weight remain the same if you stand on one foot? And if you bend your knees and bow down? The answers describe how the subject's thinking adjusts when one's own body is involved.

Studies of children show that weight conservation is acquired earlier than volume conservation (Piaget & Inhelder, 1941).

Conservation of Volume

Volume conservation is tested by showing subjects two clay balls and asking them to agree or physically verify that the amount of clay in each is the same. As with weight conservation, if the subject cannot tell if they are the same, it is impossible for them to predicate volume conservation after the balls have been altered. After establishing their equivalence, one of the clay balls is placed in a 5×10 straightsided glass, half-filled with water.

The subjects are asked to anticipate what the water level will be before the clay ball is put into the glass. Once the first ball is placed in the glass, subjects are asked to anticipate what the water level will be for the second clay ball when placed in a second identical glass. Then, one of the clay balls is left inside one of the glasses to act as a reference glass. The tester changes the shape of the ball of clay twice. After each modification, the subjects are asked whether placing the altered ball into the glass of water will cause a similar rise in the water level. These procedures test the establishment of: (a) initial equivalence; (b) anticipation of the water level; and (c) that volume stays the same even after two transformations (Piaget & Inhelder, 1941; 1967; Piaget, Inhelder, & Szeminska, 1960).

Conservation of Horizontality

The subjects are shown a standing narrow-necked bottle with straight, parallel sides filled with water and asked to look at the water level. The bottle is then covered and placed in different positions (e.g., upside down, tilted). Subjects are asked to draw the bottle in the different positions including the surface of the water level corresponding to each position. The drawings should reflect the horizontality of the water level. The subjects' degree of verbal accuracy in justifying the drawings is also scored (Piaget & Inhelder, 1967; Piaget, Inhelder, & Szeminska, 1960).

Transitivity of Sizes

The subjects were shown a series of seven white circles of 10mm. height (A—G). Each circle was 0.2 mm larger or smaller than the adjacent one so that all appeared to be the same size. However, A (58.8mm across) could clearly be shown by superposition on G (60mm) to be smaller. The circles were presented on a blackboard in a zig-zag formation, in increasing order of size:

B   D   F

A   C   E   G

Subjects were presented with the circles and asked whether they looked equal in size based on their diameter. After subjects noted the similarily (or the dissimilarity) of the circles they were invited to verify their first impression by directly comparing the circles. A rule of comparison was then established: Only circle G could be moved to be compared with every other circle. The other circles can only be compared with the ones adjacent to them. Before starting the comparison, subjects are asked how they are going to compare the circles and why they think one way is better than another. The subjects were then asked to explain their findings. The testers recorded verbatim the initial anticipation, the full comparison procedure, and the conclusion and comments regarding equality or nonequality of the series. The subjects' scores reflect using a logic approach versus empirical, understanding the transitive nature of similar sizes, and awareness of a contradiction within or without the solution.

Classification of Geometric Figures

These tasks included the Riska Object Classification (ROC) test (Allen & Williams Riska, 1985) along with class inclusion questions (Katz, Josman, & Steinmetz, 1988). The ROC test is divided into two parts, unstructured and structured classification. The subjects are presented with 18 pieces of cardboard of three different shapes and three different colors. In the unstructured part the subjects are asked "to form groups that are alike" and to name the criteria that guided their grouping, while in the structured part subjects are provided with an example of a group (3 figures one of each color and shape) and are required "to form others like it." In both parts verbal and motor responses are scored.

For class inclusion subjects are presented with eleven of the same cardboard pieces and asked 12 questions, such as, "Are there more x than y?" that explore the subject's conception of the part–whole relationships existing between the pieces (Piaget & Inhelder, 1964; Katz, Josman, & Steinmetz, 1988, provide the questions). Categories for scoring were based on performance on all three parts of the classification task.

Conception of Chance

The subjects are shown 35 chips (15 yellow, 10 red, 7 green, and 3 blue). Exactly the same number and kind of chips is put into a box, and the subjects are asked to say which colors are more likely to appear if two chips are taken out. After two chips are effectively taken out, the subjects are required to explain the outcome, and the whole process begins again. The test describes the extent to which subjects take probability into account and differentiate it from chance (Piaget & Inhelder, 1975).

Quantification of Probability

The subjects are shown two kinds of coins, marked and unmarked. Two sets of coins, each containing a different proportion of marked versus unmarked coins are then presented to the subjects. Subjects are asked to select the sets where they would have the greatest chance of finding a marked coin on the first try. To select correctly the subject must calculate the ratio between favorable and unfavorable cases. For instance, one of the sets contains one marked coin out of two pieces while the other contains two marked coins out of three pieces. Ten different arrangements are used to test the subject's capacity for understanding probabilities that result from the proportion of favorable over possible cases (Piaget & Inhelder, 1975).

Scoring categories for all tests are presented in Table 2. Hierarchically organized categories for grouping the responses are built on the basis of detailed protocol analysis at the initial study. Scoring ranges from the correct operational thought to responses that implied reliance on or total dependence on the physical properties of the object. The range of scores are from 1 (high) to 5 or 6 (low) on all tests.

The assessment process is based on a clinical method used in psychogenetic studies, similar to Piaget's method in studying children's cognitive organization. It is an exploration process in which the subject interacts with the tester. The tester poses questions in order to understand and verify the subject's exact level of cognitive organization.

Research

We performed two studies using the assessment battery. The first study focused on an adult outpatient psychiatric population and a matched normal control group (n = 60) (Tolchinsky Landsmann & Katz, 1988). The second study focused on schizophrenic patients at different ages (adolescents and adults), at different stages of illness (acute and chronic), and (within the chronic group) on the difference between hospitalization and ambulatory settings. Subjects were placed into four groups of schizophrenic patients (n = 77) and two groups of normal control subjects (n = 44). A physician identified the schizophrenic patients according to the DSM-IIIR diagnostic criteria (1987). The control groups were matched by sex, age, and years of education, as were the adolescent and adult hospitalized acute patients (Katz & Tolchinsky Landsmann, 1991). We analyzed the cognitive performance of schizophrenic patient groups compared to normal control groups.

The findings in the first study suggested some higher levels of abstraction were retained by the psychiatric patients while lower levels were lost.

Table 2   Categories of Responses on All Tests

Conservation of Weight (CW)
1 Operational conservation
2 Factual identity
3 Empirical verification
4 Uncertain, doubtful, fluctuating
5 No conservation

Conservation of Own Weight (COW)
1 Operational conservation
2 Factual identity
3 Empirical verification
4 Uncertain, doubtful, fluctuating
5 No conservation

Conservation of Volume (CV)
Initial equivalence (IE)
1 Immediate acceptance
2 Acceptance after elongated process
3 Qualitative identity
4 Uncertainty/empirical
5 Uncertainty/qualitative
6 Nonacceptance

Anticipation of water level (AWL)
1 Correct based on volume
2 Correct based on weight
3 Without generalization
4 Only personal appreciation
5 Impossibility or
  Incorrect/deformation of observation

Conservation after two transformations
  (CV)
1 Operational conservation
2 Conservation without reason
3 Based on weight only
4 Factual identity
5 Empirical verification
6 No conservation

Conservation of Horizontality (CH)
1 Correct drawing/external justification
2 Correct drawing/internal justification
3 Correct drawing/inflexible justification
4 Correct drawing/straight positions
5 Incorrect drawing/able to correct
6 Incorrect drawing/unable to correct

Classification of Geometric Figures (CF)
1 Hierarchical with abstraction
2 Two criteria or more simultaneously
3 One criterion and class inclusion
4 One criterion with spatial arrangement
5 One criterion incomplete
6 Preclassification/identity, collection

Transitivity of Sizes (TS)
1 Logic approach/transitivity, solution
2 Logic approach/solution
3 Logic approach/no solution
4 Empirical approach/solution
5 Empirical approach/no solution
6 Empirical approach/no contradiction

Conception of Chance (CC)
1 Adaptation of/chance and probability
2 No adaptation/chance and probability
3 No integration/chance and probability
4 Focus on facts/no rule explication
5 Personal explanations

Quantification of Probability (QP)
1 Probability and ratio
2 Difference positive/negative items
3 Absolute numbers not ratio
4 Other
5 Personal explanation

". . . we found that subjects' performance differs mostly in those tasks or subtasks requiring equilibrated consideration of the physical characteristics of the object. . . ." (p. 91).

This finding was not supported in the second study. In general, the performance level seemed to follow a developmental sequence. Task performance of concrete operations combined with the physical conceptual domain were retained by a higher number of patients. Next was the spatial domain.

Fewer patients retained the ability to solve higher level tasks of the logico-mathematical domain and formal operational stage. This result agrees with studies that suggest that patients with mental illness have an impaired ability to approach problems that require formal operations (Apostel, 1981). Still, there are patients whose cognitive performance were high or low on all tests, suggesting that there are individual differences in the effect of illness on cognitive organization.

Our results also suggest that additional variables such as age, length of illness (i.e., duration), and hospitalization are strongly related to lower cognitive performance within the schizophrenic patient groups. In general, acute adolescents performed higher than acute adults, followed by long-term patients in ambulatory settings. The lowest performance was seen in the long-term hospitalized group. Clearly, schizophrenic patients showed lower ability in cognitive organization compared to other diagnostic groups. But the results suggest that illness duration and hospitalization are particularly major variables in determining cognitive performance as well. This finding agrees with previous studies, all of which indicated that duration is the main differentiating variable between psychiatric patients' cognitive performance and normals (Bunard, Zutter, Burgermeister, & Tissot, 1981; Sollod & Lapidus, 1977; Tissot, 1976; Trunnel, 1964).

Treatment Principles

As in Piaget's theory, action is generally considered the source of knowledge, and therefore action is used in treatment. We used objects from the human and nonhuman environment as activities. We assumed that the use of object manipulation would help to stimulate the subjects' verbal and mental responses, which are assumed to help in cognitive organization. Therapists selected activities and adaptations according to the evaluation results of the patient's cognitive capabilities, and his or her specific areas of difficulties as identified during the assessment. The treatment goal is to enable the patient to participate in experiences in which he or she will acquire knowledge about the world through physical knowledge as well as logical-mathematical knowledge.

The assumption of the treatment process is that, gradual improvement in cognitive organization will occur within the patient's conceptual domains from concrete operations to the formal operations, and from actions with objects to abstractions. By using equilibrated mechanisms of assimilation and accommodations during these activities, the patient will adapt to his or her environment. When these cognitive processes are in equilibrium they will influence both the patient's affective domain and self-perception.

Both in development and in treatment, direct action with objects is central to providing the basis for logical organization and higher cognitive functioning. Through experience with materials and objects, the patient will acquire logical, objective, and deductive operations. Concrete experience is essential to the logical organization of an adult's performance. *This is occupational therapy's unique and special contribution to mental health.*

In general, the treatment process goes from disequilibrium of assimilation and accommodation to equilibrium and adaptation; from disintegration to better integration; from externally directed actions to internally represented actions; from concrete static situations to mobile transformations; from centrism to objective decentered thinking; and from a reality orientation that thinks only of the necessary to seeing reality as full of possibilities. Activity analysis is the basis for treatment adaptation. Activities are analyzed in relation to the different conceptual domains (Table 1); using the categories of evaluation within each thinking operations (Table 2); and the concepts defined in the theoretical base.

The treatment method, like the assessment, uses guided activities that provide interaction between the patient, the material, and the therapist. In a group situation, other members become an additional source of interaction. The patient acts and is asked to explain his or her acts. The therapist demonstrates and gives verbal or written instructions. The ultimate goal is knowledge organization (i.e., cognitive organization) leading to adaptive performance.

Activity Analysis

Example—Creating a Set of Ceramic Bowls

In this activity the materials include clay and paints, tools for working with clay, and an oven. The task is to create a set of six ceramic bowls of the same size. The bowls can have features (i.e., handles, ornaments, and colors).

Procedure. The therapist shows the patient two bowls of the same size but different in color and ornaments, one with handles and one without. The patient is then asked to create similar bowls. He or she is given directions for preparing the clay, making the bowls, burning, and coloring. The therapist guides the patient through the various steps of the task with demonstrations, stimulating verbal responses and explanations, during the performance of the task. The therapist observes and intervenes as necessary.

This activity is an example of *volume conservation,* a concrete operation in the physical domain. It is first analyzed, therefore, according to the *categories* used in the assessment (Table 2).

Initial Equivalence. Does the patient cut the same amount of clay material for each bowl easily, or does it take many tries and a lengthy process? Does he or she need empirical verification by weighing it in his or her hands or on a scale? Is he or she uncertain that the amount of material is equal: it can't be equal if the end result is different. To what dimensions of the clay does he or she relate; does he or she need sensory-motor exploration of touch, smell, or taste?

The therapist follows the process with questions such as: "How do you know that these are equal?" "What do you have to do to make them equal?" "Could you make all bowls equal using one ball of clay?"

Anticipation. Is the patient estimating the right amounts he or she needs when dividing the clay into balls to make bowls of similar size? Does he or she make one ball of clay and use it for comparison, or does he or she need external criteria? Is he or she able to visualize how the clay will be transformed to the finished colored and ornamented bowl? After presenting examples of ceramic bowls before and after burning, is he or she able to anticipate the color changes after burning?

Transformation. Does he or she understand the material can be altered by changing shapes or adding or subtracting clay, or that a number of different objects can be created from the same amount of material, sizes, shapes, etc? He or she will need to understand that color changes according to the facts and rules provided in written or verbal descriptions.

The activity is then analyzed according to *concepts,* such as the following:

Scheme. The patient has to comprehend the scheme of a bowl and its function of holding liquid or solid materials.

Assimilation and accommodation. Imitating the therapist's actions without adjusting his or her actions to achieve the required result is considered overaccommodation. Overassimilation occurs when the patient uses a ball of clay without referring to the real trask (such as creating an object that can't fulfill the function of a bowl), or when he or she decides that a certain raw color will turn out as he wants without reference to data provided. Overassimilation is also seen when the patient performs task steps according to his or her logic and not the routine way.

Reversibility. Reversibility refers to understanding how various materials and colors change; knowing which changes are reversible and which are not. Are their verbal explanations based on operational understanding or only on factual knowledge? The therapist asks the patient to perform acts that lead to reverse actions and their compensations.

Necessity and Possibility. Do patients understand that the order of actions is necessary; for example, you can't color before burning the first time. In contrast, do they understand the possibility of making different objects for different purposes, etc?

Centrism/Decentrism. Can the patient differentiate between using the objects himself or herself and giving them as a present to somebody else, to one or more people.

Cooking and baking are other activities that use operations of conservation that can be analyzed as well. Another area, that of classification in the logico-mathematical domain, can be analyzed using various ADL activities within the home and in shopping (see example in the following case).

Case Example

Rachel, a single woman aged 41 years, has been ill for the last 15 years and was diagnosed as having paranoia vera (delusional Paranoia disorder, DSM-IIIR, 1987). In the last few years, she has received treatment in a day center and experienced longer periods of remission. According to her occupational history, she lives alone but is a short distance from her parents. She works as a secretary but changes her job frequently because, she says, "people don't understand me or my mission to bring the Messiah." During periods when she was hospitalized, her psychotic fixation centered on the "mystic world," while when she was in remission the topic was less dominant but always present. Hospitalizations usually occurred after she had been fired because of problems at work. She would then also neglect her house, her self-care, and she would behave strangely by dressing in odd clothing, buying large amounts of food, and storing things in abnormal places.

Assessment. Rachel was very cooperative and tried to perform and answer the questions well. She talked constantly while performing the tasks and included her perceptions about the world and her place in it. In every response, she would try to adjust facts to fit into her personal system of thought (overassimilation).

Results. Rachel's performance along all battery tasks was low (see Table 3). She related mostly to irrelevant dimensions, gave personal explanations, could not relate to external reference points as in the "conservation of horizontality" where she did not relate to the table and drew the water line almost vertically parallel to the bottom in the tilted bottle (see

Table 3   Case Example Battery Results

Category	Score
Conservation of Weight: Uncertain, doubtful, fluctuating	4
Conservation of Own Weight: Uncertain, doubtful, fluctuating	4
Conservation of Volume:	
a. Initial equivalence: Uncertainty/qualitative	5
b. Anticipation of water level: Only personal appreciation	4
c. Conservation after two transformations: No conservation	6
Conservation of Horizontality: Incorrect drawing/unable to correct	6
Classification of Geometric Figures: One criteria incomplete	5
Transitivity of Sizes: Empirical approach/no contradiction	6
Conception of Chance: Personal explanations	5
Quantification of Probability: Absolute numbers not ratio	3

Figure 1). She realized she made a mistake but could not correct it although she tried. In a letter Rachel wrote after the testing session, she writes, "Do we also have to understand other people's viewpoints? . . . I changed my mind many times before I decided where to draw the water line. It came out that way because something guides me, the same thing also happened in other situations." It appears based on her performance on the tests and her response and difficulties in working with two systems were present in the tasks of transitivity and probability.

Rachel could not identify two criteria or conceive of two systems simultaneously. She had difficulty shifting to another way of thinking but was aware, saying that "she has no imagination, and that was her problem also in the past." In regard to the class inclusion questions she (as many paranoid patients do) said, "The question you ask does not fit. You can't ask a question like this. Don't think that I am nervous like the other patients. I only thought about the arrows and also about the 'mystic world.' It can't be." The same response and difficulties in working with two systems were present in the tasks of transitivity and probability.

Treatment. Treating Rachel incorporated two goals: providing her with an avenue to express the content of her inner world and, at the same time, helping her focus on cognitive organization. Rachel's main problem in cognitive domain terms was identified as overassimilation (i.e., relating to reality from personal explanations) or seeing the world only from an internal viewpoint that is centristic and linear. Her treatment was structured to provide her with activities that require accommodations hoping that a more equilibrated process will lead her to adapt better to reality. These

The water
is standing

The water
is falling

The water
is changing
forms

Figure 4-1 Patient's drawing of the water level in the conservation of horizontality.

activities will strengthen her logical knowledge as a result of her contact with objects through actions that require manipulating and changing materials in concrete operational tasks. Her treatment included tasks that incorporate simultaneous actions, that take into account another person's viewpoint, and that also focus on decentric and objective processes.

The treatment was carried out singularly and in groups. Activities included self-care and housekeeping, as well as secretarial work to simulate situations from her daily routine. A sample activity follows.

SELF-CARE—CHOOSING AN OUTFIT. This activity uses the logico-mathematical domain and is mostly based on classification operations, such as choosing clothes according to various criteria (i.e., time of day, weather, event or situation, colors, fashion, etc.). Dressing also requires combining two or more criteria to make combinations that work in different and changing situations (blouse and a sweater; shoes that fit a variety of outfits; same skirt with changing blouses for work and evening, etc.). As mentioned earlier, Rachel dressed in a very strange combination of clothes and, when asked, why would give an unrealistic answer. The treatment progressed gradually by using her clothes first, pictures second, and, finally, printed cards. These steps helped Rachel to organize herself. Each day she would plan her outfit with the therapist for the next day, taking into account various criteria. The next day, the therapist would check with Rachel what she chose and what possibilities and alternative she had planned. Eventually, the therapist explained the social meaning of dressing-up, as well as the concepts of personal style and taste.

This activity worked using schemes of clothing and their function, accommodating social and environmental conditions, responding to conditions that require a certain kind of clothes (like weather) but still retaining a wide range of possibilities even with this condition, and anticipating and planning in advance according to known information.

HOUSEKEEPING. *Laundry* is another activity that requires classification operations as well: sorting according to color or fibers, adjusting temperature and amount of detergent according to the above criteria, folding and arranging clothes in closets, etc. *Meal preparation* involves planning menus for a few days, having a shopping list arranged according to where food categories are found in a store, arranging food in kitchen closets; and preparing meals for family members while also taking into account their taste and preferences. *Secretarial work* involves developing a filing system according to importance (which is another classification task). In addition, Rachel learned to prioritize or sequence her activities in the proper order, such as by sending mail (writing a letter, preparing the envelope with address and the adequate stamp, going to the post office and sending the letter). Organization of an office room focuses on how equipment spatially arranges and accounts for functional considerations. Just as Rachel could not decenter from her internal system and consider the task according to external aspects during the conservation of horizontality task, she also arranged all her office with instruments located according to her own needs. She did not consider that another secretary would be using the same phone or filing cabinet and therefore things should be arranged to suit others as well. Thus, the therapist focused on ways instruments and furniture can be arranged in different positions for different purposes and conditions.

All activities were generally practiced in simulations at the day center first and later at home and in the community.

In group situations, treatment focused on taking into account viewpoints of the other members of the group. For example, in a group discussion about current events after reading a newspaper, Rachel was asked to react to the other participants' ideas; or in a cooking group, she was asked to plan the menu for lunch for all patients together with two more women. She had to accommodate her preference in food to those of the others and also take into account budget considerations, kitchen facilities, etc. She had to decenter herself from her inner world and adapt to the physical reality as well as to the social environment.

Implications for Further Development

The piagetian framework described in this chapter needs to be further developed in its theoretical organization and integration with occupational therapy concepts. The validity of the assessment battery, and the effectiveness of the treatment approach, should be studied. From our experience, this framework is most appropriate with patients who are able to verbally explain their actions and who had good premorbid cognitive functioning. Still, future studies should identify those populations that would benefit the most from this approach. For example, it appears that with psychogeriatric patients the principles of the approach could be used as well. The battery of assessment tests should be studied further and refined accordingly. Qualitative and quantitative procedures should be used in order to provide a complete account. We have found the tests of the formal operational stage to have less direct application to functional activities, while the concrete operational tests from all conceptual domains have direct relevancy. This preliminary conclusion should be studied as well. In summary, we think that this framework holds much promise for occupational therapy in mental health for the appropriate populations.

References

Allen, C. K., & Williams Riska, L. (1985). In C. K. Allen (Ed.), *Occupational therapy for psychiatric disease: Measurement and management of cognitive disabilities*. Boston: Little, Brown.

Allen, C. K. (1988). Cognitive disabilities. In S. Robertson (Ed.), *FOCUS*. Rockville, MD: American Occupational Therapy Association.

American Psychiatric Association. (1987). *Diagnostic and statistical manual of mental disorders, DSM-IIIR*. Washington, DC: Author.

Apostel, L. (1981). Some uses of deductive and inductive logic in the study of neurotic and psychotic disorders. In J. Agassi (Ed.), *Psychiatric diagnosis*. Philadelphia: Balaon Ins. Science Services.

Beck, A. T., Rush, A. J., Shaw, B. F., & Emery, G. (1976). *Cognitive therapy of depression*. New York: The Guilford Press.

Bunard, Y., Zutter, A. M., Burgermeister, J, J., & Tissot, R. (1981). Quelques aspects des activities cognitives du schizophrene. *L'Encephale, VII*, 153–179. (French).

Fried, Y. (1978). *Psychopathology: Introductory notes*. Tel Aviv: Ministry of Defence, Israel. (In Hebrew).

Fried, Y. (1984). *Jean Piaget: Psychology and method*. Tel Aviv: Ministry of Defence, Israel. (In Hebrew).

Fried, Y., & Agassi, J. (1976). *Paranoia: A study in diagnosis*. Holland: D. Reidel Publishing Co.

Flavell, J. H. (1963). *The developmental psychology of Jean Piaget*. Princeton, NJ: Van Nostrand.

Glick, J. (1985). Culture and cognition revisited. In E. D. Neimark, R., De

Lisi, & J. L. Newman (Eds.), *Moderators of competence.* Hillsdale, New Jersey: LEA.

Gruber, H. E., & Voneche, J. J. (Eds.) (1977). *The essential Piaget.* New York: Basic Books.

Katz, N., & Allen, C. K. (1988). *The development of standardized clinical evaluations in mental health.* New York: The Haworth Press.

Katz, N., Josman, N., & Steinmetz, N. (1988). Relationship between cognitive disability theory and the model of human occupation in the assessment of psychiatric and nonpsychiatric adolescents. *Occupational Therapy in Mental Health,* 8(1), 31–43.

Katz, N., & Tolchinsky Landsmann, L. (1991). A Piagetian framework as a basis for the assessment of cognitive organization in schizophrenia. *Israel Journal of Psychiatry and Related Sciences,* 28(4), 1–18.

Llorens, L. A. (1976). *Application of a developmental theory for health and rehabilitation.* Rockville MD: American Occupational Therapy Association.

Margo, P. A. (1984). Psychosis and schizophrenia. In *Theories of schizophrenia and psychosis. Nebraska Symposium on motivation.* Lincoln and London: University of Nebraska Press.

Mosey, A. C. (1970). *Three frames of reference for mental health.* Thorofare, NJ: Charles B. Slack.

Mosey, A. C. (1986). *Psychosocial components of occupational therapy.* New York: Raven Press.

Piaget, J. (1971). *Biology and knowledge.* Chicago: University of Chicago Press.

Piaget, J. (1977). Problems of equilibration. In H. E. Gruber, & J. J. Voneche (Eds.), *The essential Piaget.* New York: Basic Books.

Piaget, J. (1987). *Possibility and necessity.* Minneapolis: University of Minnesota Press.

Piaget, J., & Inhelder, B. (1941). *Le development des quantities chez l'enfant: Conservation et atomisme.* Neuchatel, Paris: Delachaux et Niestle.

Piaget, J., Inhelder, B., & Szeminska, A. (1960). *The child's conception of geometry.* London: Routledge & Kegan Paul.

Piaget, J., & Inhelder, B. (1964). *The early growth of logic in the child.* London: Routledge & Kegan Paul.

Piaget, J., & Inhelder, B. (1967). *The child's conception of space.* New York: Norton.

Piaget, J., & Inhelder, B. (1975). *The origin of the idea of chance in children.* New York: Norton.

Piaget, J., & Voyat, G. (1979). The possible, the impossible, and the necessary. In F. B. Murray (Ed.), *The impact of piagetian theory.* Baltimore: University Park Press.

Pufall, P. B. (1988). Function in Piaget's system: some notes for constructors of microworlds. In G. Forman, & P. B. Pufall (Eds.), *Constructivism in the computer age.* New Jersey: LEA.

Rielly, M. (1974). *Play as exploratory learning.* Beverly Hills, CA: Saga Publications.

Sollod, R., & Lapidus, L. B. (1977). Concrete operational thinking and psychopathology. *Journal of Abnormal Psychology, 2,* 199–202.

Tissot, R. (1976). Some aspects of cognitive activities in schizophrenics. In D. Kemali, G. Bartholini, & D. Richter (Eds.), *Schizophrenia today.* Oxford: Pergamon Press.

Tissot, R. (1979). *Introduction a la psychiatrie biologique.* Paris: Masson.

Tolchinsky Landsmann, L., & Katz, N. (1988). Concrete to formal thinking: Comparison of psychiatric outpatients and a normal control group. *Occupational Therapy in Mental Health, 8*(1), 73–94.

Trunnell, T. (1964). Thought disturbance in schizophrenia. *Archives of General Psychiatry, 11,* 126–136.

Intellectual Regression in the Schizophrenic with Paranoia

Aviva Fried

"Intellectual Regression in the Schizophrenic with Paranoia" was the title of a paper written by Yehuda Fried in January 1954. The complete article was written as part of a project within the framework of his studies at the Piaget Institute and the Medical School in Geneva. From that time on until his death in 1990, he developed his original theory which formed the basis of his research, excerpts of which are given below. As head of the Day Hospital at the Mental Health Clinic in Tel Aviv and professor of psychiatry at the Tel Aviv University Medical School, he devoted a great deal of his time and teachings to occupational therapists who worked with him.

Yehuda believed that occupational therapists had the practical and intellectual tools to progressively motivate and direct patients to reach various developmental levels of functioning, such as indicated by Jean Piaget. On the one hand he encouraged activity and a realization of their intellectual faculties by means of a rational symbolism such as suggested by Sechehaye. On the other hand Yehuda also felt that both approaches should take place simultaneously. He would have said, "One must attack the patient from every angle." This tactic, when applied to his own patients often brought about good results. It was noted that even when there was no visible improvement in the patient's condition or in his ability to function, the patient felt "well." This approach manifested itself in the patient's ability to participate in all activities, a fact that shows us that in this way one can reach the patient and speak to him or her in a familiar and comprehensible language, one by which the demands made on the individual are at a level at which he or she is "able" to fulfill.

From his original essay it appears that Yehuda's main concern was to find a way in which to help schizophrenic patients to reorganize their disturbed reasoning. The fact that he chose to work with schizophrenic patients with paranoid symptoms can be explained as follows: he believed that the content of their disturbed thinking process clearly indicated a logical structure.

A brief summary of his essay follows here: The results of the tests show us Piaget's unique contribution to psychopathology, one which was not recognized at all until this research was published. The question at the root of the research was as follows: "What changes, if any, occur in the level of intelligence of the schizophrenic patient with paranoia? Is it a gradual process? Intelligence enables man to adapt to the world around him. I found two reasons for treating and discussing hallucinations: (1) hallucinations characterize the egocentric thought processes of the patient; and (2) hallucinations as a symptom enable us to understand the essential expression of this particular type of thinking processes in our patients. (The expression, *essential*, was originally explained by the neurologist J. Jackson, who believed that the essential signs of the disease compensated for that which is missing due to the trauma.)

The work of Sechehaye (*The Symbolic Realization*, 1947) was vital to this essay. Sashi, in her attempts to rebuild the "Ego" in her patient, René, was amazed to discover the stages clearly described by Piaget in his work in the field of child psychology. First the sensory-motor stage appeared. This was followed by the representative stage, then the concrete, and finally the abstract stage.

The development of intelligence always precedes familiar, known principles. In order to advance, and sometimes at an accelerated pace, one has to remember that the abstract stage will not appear before the concrete one. Similarly the concrete stage will not precede the representative stage—this, initially manifesting itself as a phenomenon. This stage comes last—it cannot appear before the sensory-motorical is established (J. Piaget, *Introduction to Genetic Epistimology*, PUT, 1950).

The developmental symptom as present in the intelligence of the child, seen as a transformation in the forming of the ego, was first noted by M. Sashi in her rebuilding of the "Ego" in her patient, René. If in the development of the child's intelligence, there is a transformation from an egocentric thought process to a social one, then this change in the level of intelligence can beyond all doubt, be defined as a direct transformation and vice versa. This change is in fact a reverse *thinking* process: from the social to an egocentric stage. It is clear that if we find such a process in the patient, it would be only of theoretic value. However, it does also enable one to throw new light on several symptoms of the disease, especially when hallucinations are present. In fact, these hallucinations have a connection approximating egocentric thinking.

It is known that children who are in the operational (i.e., the prelogical) and concrete stage, tend to describe their dreams in the third person (Piaget, *The Representation of the Child's World*, 1926). They tell the dream as though it is happening to themselves but also as though external to their person. They separate themselves from the person they dreamt about and apply a realistic personality to the dream character, who is concrete and yet at the same time external to themselves.

Schizophrenic patients also differentiate between themselves and their delusions and give them a realistic objective status in reality. Comparatively speaking, it is obvious, and then the next question arises: Do the dream and the delusion not originate from the same source? It is also important to note that the patient tends to exaggerate his disassociation, and thus the symptom of hallucination appears.

The child disassociates himself from his dreams and he cannot differentiate between the internal and the external. Similarly, the patient disassociates himself from his delusions, if and when he retreats from reality, to a level in which he cannot differentiate between external and internal forces (between himself and others).

We can ask, at what level do patients who suffer from hallucinations function? Schizophrenic-paranoidal patients were examined from the point of view of their intellectual weaknesses. Was it memory loss, or a weakness in their thought processes? Perhaps it was a disturbance in the organization of their thought processes, in the logical structure of these thought processes. Here Piaget enters the picture, and the question then becomes: Are the loss of these logical steps in the thought processes in line with the development of thinking as described by Piaget in his work with children?

Occupational therapy tends to lean mainly on the allegations of Piaget, as expressed by Yehuda Fried: "The detail as well as the environment, both to the same degree and in mutual agreement, are equally responsible for, and determine the adaptation and development, thus maintaining a balance of both systems: assimilation and accommodation" ("Y. Fried: *Jean Piaget, Psychology and methodology*, 1984).

These ideas form the basis of what is done and what must be done within the framework of treatment in the field of occupational therapy.

5

□ □ □
□ □ □
□ □ □

A Dynamic Interactional Approach to Cognitive Rehabilitation

Joan Pascale Toglia

What one addresses in cognitive rehabilitation depends to a large extent upon how one conceptualizes cognition and the scope of cognitive functioning. Traditional cognitive rehabilitation approaches have been guided by the assumption that cognition can be divided into distinct subskills (Trexler, 1987). In this chapter, I propose a dynamic interactional view of cognition as an alternative to traditional deficit- and syndrome-specific approaches. In this dynamic approach, the clinician is urged to abandon classical taxonomies of dysfunction and instead to investigate dynamically the underlying conditions and processing strategies that influence performance. Assessment uses cues and task alterations to identify the individuals potential for change. Treatment incorporates a number of components: strategy training, practice in multiple situations, establishment of criteria for transfer, and metacognitive training, and consideration of learners characteristics to facilitate learning transfer.

Until now, cognitive psychology theories have not been used as a guide for cognitive rehabilitation assessment and treatment. This chapter represents an attempt to integrate the cognitive psychology theories of how normal people learn and generalize information with the rehabilitation of patients with cognitive dysfunction.

Cognitive dysfunction can be seen in people with developmental, neurologic, or psychiatric dysfunction. The theoretical concepts presented in this chapter are broad and apply to all populations. However, the specific assessment and treatment techniques described later have been developed for the brain-injured adult. Some of these techniques have recently been used with schizophrenic patients who manifest negative symptoms. Measurable cognitive impairment and structural brain abnormalities have been well documented in schizophrenic patients with negative symptoms (Crow, 1985). The neurological findings in this population provides justification for using techniques originally developed for the brain-injured population. Some adaptations, however, may be required for the psychiatric population as well as other populations.

The Scope of Cognition in the Traditional Approach

Traditionally, cognition has been viewed as a higher-level cortical function which can be divided into separate subskills such as attention, memory, organization, reasoning, and problem solving (Pedretti, 1983; Trexler, 1982). This view of cognition did not originate from theory of cognition; it was derived from psychometric models of intelligence testing and from localization approaches. Psychometric approaches in intelligence testing used techniques (such as factor analysis) to identify tests that tapped different mental abilities (Sternberg, 1986). Deficits were derived from performance analyses on specific tests. A poor performance on a specific test (such as a memory test) was assumed to reflect a deficiency in the specific skill (eg. memory) that the test was designed to measure. Localization approaches emphasized the correlation of specific skills and/or syndrome types to the location of the brain lesion (Trexler, 1982). This approach, in combination with the traditional psychometric testing, reinforced the assumption that cognition could be divided into distinct entities. In addition, models that proposed that the brain processes first simple then complex information provided support for the view that cognitive subskills are hierarchically arranged. The assumption that cognition is composed of separate hierarchical subskills and that cognitive dysfunction is defined according to separate syndromes or deficits is reflected in most current cognitive perceptual treatment programs (Trexler, 1987). The terms "deficit specific" (cognitive deficits defined according to performance on specific tests), "reductionistic" (cognition reduced to separate skills), or "transfer training" have all been used to describe treatment approaches that are based on this view of cognition.

Deficit Specific Approaches

Trexler (1987) describes the characteristics of a reductionistic or deficit specific approach as follows: (1) Cognitive subskills are hierarchical in nature; for example, more basic skills such as attention and memory are requisite to higher-order skills such as logical reasoning; (2) treatment involves repetitive practice on a specific tabletop or computer task until the patient reaches some identified criteria; and (3) the remediation program is organized into activities which address specific deficits, which are derived from test performance. For example, if the patient does poorly on a test that measures attention, his treatment is based on receiving a graded sequence of attentional activities. The parameters and methods of training are closely related to the materials used to evaluate the patient. This approach is similar to the transfer training approach used by Frostig & Horne (1973) in the early 1970s to treat perceptual motor problems in learning disabled children. In both approaches it is assumed that any improvements observed with a specific skill will affect performance on other tasks which involve the same underlying skill.

In some cases, the cognitive remediation program is organized around modules (such as an attentional module, reasoning module, etc.). All patients receive the same type of treatment activities within each module. The patient progresses from one module to another until a specific performance criteria is reached or until progress has plateaued (Ben-Yishay & Diller, 1983). Ready-made exercises or training modules have the advantage of being practical and easy to use by a beginning therapist. They also assure that each patient with a similar problem (as defined by standardized testing) receives the same treatment in the same way. This type of program lends itself readily to empirical research methods and outcome studies. Most of the literature on cognitive rehabilitation emphasizes deficit specific or reductionistic approaches (Trexler, 1987).

Limitations of the Deficit Specific Approach

The deficit specific approach does not describe how specific skills interrelate during cognitive processing and task performance. Factors such as reasoning, verbal comprehension, and visual spatial skills are useful in describing broad areas of strengths and weaknesses; however, as Sternberg (1985) points out "the information conveyed by factors is not specific enough for training" (Sternberg, 1985, p. 218). For example, labels such as "visual spatial" or "reasoning" do not specify what characteristics of visual spatial abilities or reasoning contributes to either high or low performance. Additionally, in the clinical setting one never observes isolated cognitive deficits. Cognitive problems often overlap and correlate with one another, which leads one to question the usefulness of this division (Toglia & Golisz, 1990). Recently Seron & Deloche (1989) have urged clinicians to abandon the classical syndrome-oriented approach used in classifying cognitive dysfunction. There is strong evidence that syndrome approaches are not sufficiently precise. Many classical syndromes (such as visual agnosia, Broca's aphasia, and

constructional apraxia) group patients together who present highly heterogeneous deficits (Seron & Deloche, 1989).

The Dynamic Approach

Another approach to cognitive rehabilitation has recently been
described by Trexler (1987) as the dynamic approach. In this approach, cognition is defined in terms of global capacities. Characteristics of a dynamic
approach include the following: (1) treatment is delivered in a reactive mode;
the individual's response determines how and what kinds of therapy will be
administered; (2) there is little emphasis placed on the absolute level of
performance on specific tests; and (3) there is no predetermined or prescribed
sequence of treatment activities. Specific skills such as spatial analysis and
recall are not addressed separately. The clinician operates as a detective with
each individual case and analyzes common underlying behaviors to account
for difficulty on a number of different tasks. This approach abandons classical
taxonomies of dysfunction.

One of the inherent limitations with the dynamic approach is the difficulty of performing empirical research when no two patients receive the
same treatment in the same way. This method is also time-consuming and
requires an experienced clinician. Very little has been written about the
dynamic approach. The following represents an attempt to further define
and expand the dynamic approach.

Theoretical Foundations for a Dynamic Interactional Model of Cognition

Cognition is generally defined as the individual's capacity to
acquire and use information in order to adapt to environmental demands
(Lidz, 1987). This definition encompasses information processing skills,
learning, and generalization. The capacity to acquire information involves
information processing skills or the ability to take in, organize, assimilate,
and integrate new information with previous experiences (Adamovich, Henderson, & Auerbach, 1985). Environmental adaptation involves using information that has been previously acquired to plan and structure behavior for
goal attainment. Thus, the ability to apply what has been learned to a variety
of different situations is inherent within the concept of cognition (Lidz,
1987). This description of cognition cuts across specific domains. Cognition
is not divided into distinct entities nor is it localized to the cortex. Instead
cognitive abilities and deficiencies are analyzed according to underlying processes, strategies, and potential for learning.

Essential to the conceptualization of cognition is the idea that cognition is an ongoing product of the dynamic interaction between the individual, the task, and the environment (see Figure 1). Cognition is not static; it changes with our interaction with the external world (Lidz, 1987).

The Individual

Individual factors that interact during information processing and learning include: structural capacity, strategies, metacognitive processes, and specific learner characteristics such as knowledge and motivation (Bransford, 1979; Brown, Bransford, Ferrara, & Campione, 1983).

Structural capacity refers to a physical limitation in the amount of information that can be processed at any one time. Although structural capacity is fixed, there are different ways to use this capacity efficiently. Efficient use of processing capacity is termed functional capacity. In contrast to structural capacity, functional capacity is modifiable and flexible; it is influenced by the environment and the kinds of processing strategies used by the individual (Flavell, 1985). Processing strategies and behaviors are defined globally as organized approaches, routines, or tactics which operate to select and guide the processing of information (Abreu & Toglia, 1987; Lidz, 1987). Individuals can introduce them to make more efficient use of the information processing system. For example, when confronted with a large amount of information the individual may automatically prioritize information and decide where to start, what to do first, second, and so on.

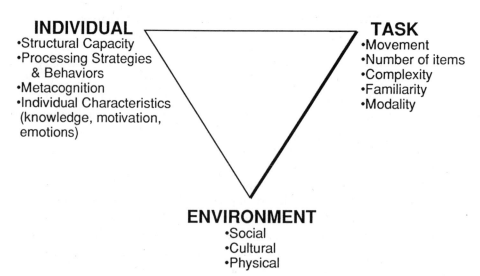

Figure 5-1 Dynamic interactional model of cognition.

The individual may select the most important stimuli and ignore the unimportant stimuli. He or she may organize or cluster related information together or decide to shift his or her attention among various stimuli (Abreu & Toglia, 1987). Which processing strategies the individual employs determine the depth at which information is processed, and they have been shown to be a critical variable in learning. In deep processing strategies, the individual discriminates important from unimportant information or tries to decide how new information fits in with previous knowledge. Surface-level strategies include memorizing words without actively elaborating or reorganizing the material to obtain meaning (Nolen, 1988). Information that is processed at deep levels is more easily understood and retained than information processed at shallow levels (Anderson, 1985).

Processing strategies and behaviors are the most observable aspects of a learner's performance and the aspects most accessible to intervention and modification. Evidence is accumulating that suggests by modifying processing strategies one can increase performance and that, unlike poor learners, good learners spontaneously apply these strategies (Lidz, 1987). Processing strategies can be divided into two types: situational strategies, which are effective in specific tasks or environments, and nonsituational strategies, which are applicable in a wide range of tasks and environments (Toglia, 1989a). These strategies are overseen and managed by metacognitive processes.

Metacognition refers to knowledge and regulation of one's own cognitive processes and capacities [Flavell, 1985]. The skills involved in metacognition include: the ability to evaluate task difficulty in relation to current skills, to plan ahead, to choose appropriate strategies, and to predict the consequences of action and monitor performance (Toglia, 1991). These skills are prerequisites to the flexible selection and application of strategies. They have been demonstrated to be critical in learning and generalization of new information (Belmont, Butterfield, & Ferretti, 1982).

The relationship of processing strategies and metacognition to a information processing model is illustrated in Figure 2. The broad stages of information processing (input, elaboration and output) can be used to classify cognitive function and dysfunction (Lidz, 1987).

Strategy selection and the information processing speed also depends partially on previous experience and knowledge. Past knowledge can guide the selection, organization, and representation of new information (Bransford, Sherwood, Vye, & Rieser, 1986). There are two types of knowledge. Procedural knowledge, or knowing how to perform, is acquired through practice and feedback. It is activated when the individual recognizes patterns associated with a given action sequence. Declarative knowledge, or knowing

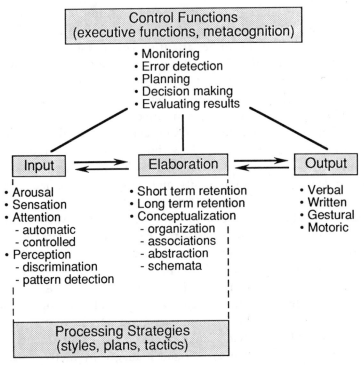

Figure 5-2 From stimulus to behavior: the processes influencing human performance. Information processing is broadly divided into three stages: input, elaboration, and output. The input stage involves the skills used in getting information from the external environment. The elaboration stage involves linking information with previous experience, or expectations, and formulating decisions or hypotheses. The output stage involves a verbal, written, gestural, or motoric response. Information processing can be driven by the external stimulus, or it can be driven by internal expectations and prior experiences. Processing strategies are the observable behaviors that are reflective of the input and elaboration of information. Control functions or metacognitive skills can influence all stages of information processing. This model can be used to categorize cognitive function and dysfunction. From: Toglia, J. P. and Fine, S. B. (1990). Applying cognitive rehabilitation to mental health: Assessment and treatment strategies for schizophrenia. With permission of the author.

about facts and things, is acquired when new information stimulates the activation of relevant prior knowledge. Organization and elaboration of new information are required to activate declarative knowledge (Gange, 1985). When people are presented with information in a way that helps them activate appropriate knowledge, it can have a powerful effect on their abilities to process information (Bransford, 1979).

The use of strategies, metacognitive skills, and previous knowledge to process information requires the individual's active participation. The individual's motivation and emotional state will influence the extent to which information is processed deeply and is monitored (Brown, 1988). Social learning theories state that one's motivation is influenced by the beliefs he or she has regarding his or her control over a situation (Bandura, 1986). The more an individual believes he or she has control over a situation, the better he or she will perform. Thus metacognitive skills and the ability to accurately estimate task difficulty and predict results are related to motivation. If the individual consistently overestimates his or her abilities and inaccurately predicts the consequences of his or her actions due to poor insight, he or she may perceive that he or she has no control over his or her performance and become discouraged.

Environment

The type of environment (social, physical, cultural) an individual is in can influence his or her ability to process information and adapt to demands.

The social environment has occupied a central place in some theories of cognitive development and includes the people with whom the individual interacts (Vygotsky, 1978; Feuerstein, 1979). Vygotsky (1978) and Feuerstein (1979) have argued that much of learning and higher cognitive skills are mediated through social interaction. For example in child development, an experienced adult guides the child through problem-solving activities and structures the child's learning environment by selecting, focusing, and organizing incoming stimuli. Social interactions can transform or mediate incoming information either to enhance or impede information processing (Jensen & Feuerstein, 1987). Gradually, the individual begins to internalize this external structuring and adopts regulatory activities on his or her own (Brown & Ferrara, 1985). Vygotsky (1978) describes the distance between the level of a child's unaided performance and the level that can be accomplished through guidance or collaboration with a more knowledgeable participant as the "zone of proximal development." Solving tasks with the assistance of a more knowledgeable person creates the zone of proximal development by tapping processes that "will mature tomorrow but are in the embryonic state" (Vygotsky, 1978, p. 86). The level of performance the child can reach unaided characterizes the cognitive skills that have already developed, while the zone of proximal development characterizes cognitive skills which are in the developmental stage (Brown & French, 1979). Vygotsky (1978) and Feuerstein's (1979) theories imply that what an individual can accomplish with guidance or external aid from a more capable peer indicates the individual's learning potential. This concept has direct implications for assessment and treatment of brain-injured adults. Cicerone and Tupper (1986) proposed that Vygotsky's definition of the zone of proximal development can be adopted as a guiding principle in the dynamic assessment of rehabilitation potential.

The physical environment includes the materials and objects that surround an individual. The cultural environment involves the values and expectations accepted by the person's cultural group. More familiar physical and cultural environments can influence the individual's ability to process information (Abreu & Toglia, 1987). Familiar environments provide contextual cues which can facilitate the access of previous knowledge and skills and guide in the selection and processing of new information.

The Task

The task can be divided into surface characteristics and conceptual characteristics. The surface characteristics of a task are easily observed. They include the number of items, their spatial arrangement and presentation mode, directions needed for the task, the type of stimuli, variable attributes, and/or active movement and postural requirements. The conceptual characteristics of a task cannot be directly observed. These include the underlying skills and strategies used to perform the task as well as the underlying meaning of the task to the individual (Toglia, 1991). The self-monitoring skills and processing strategies needed to perform the task are partially determined by task characteristics. For example, a patient may be unable to accurately sort 35 cards into meaningful categories; however when the number of cards is reduced to 15, the patient may have no difficulty. The ability to categorize (or to recognize the objects' similarities and differences) may be intact. However difficulty recalling which cards have been placed in which categories may interfere with the patient's ability to perform the task when a larger number of stimuli are involved. A larger number of stimuli requires additional strategies for keeping track of and organizing the material. It also requires closer self-monitoring skills. In addition, the body alignment, positioning, and active movement patterns used during an activity can require different processing strategies (Abreu & Toglia, 1987). By analyzing the task characteristics, one can understand the conditions that cause information processing to break down. This contrasts to the deficit specific approach, where the deficit is defined by the task. Thus, if the patient cannot do a categorization task, he or she is assumed to have a categorization deficit. The conditions which influence performance are not analyzed.

In addition to influencing the ability to take in and process information, task characteristics can also influence the ability to transfer learning. The closer two tasks are physically (or the more they share surface characteristics) the easier it is to transfer learning (Gange, 1970; Gick & Holyoak, 1983). Learning transfer can occur at different distances along a continuum. The extent to which learning transfer occurs can be defined according to task characteristics (Toglia, 1991). For example: (1) Near transfer, which is an alternate form of the same task (only one or two surface task parameters are changed); (2) intermediate transfer, which occurs when the new task shares some physical features with the original task but they are less obvious (three to six surface task parameters are changed); (3) far transfer, in which the task is conceptually the same but physically different (all task parameters are changed except for one or two); and (4) very far transfer, which occurs when what has been learned in treatment is transferred to everyday function.

Summary of the Dynamic Model of Cognition

In this model, cognition is viewed as a dynamic interaction between the individual (capacity, strategies, metacognition, and learner characteristics), the task, and the environment (social, physical, and cultural) (Bransford, 1979; Brown, Bransford, Ferrara & Campione, 1983; Lidz, 1987). The environment can mediate processing between the task and the individual. In some situations the task parameters may be the primary influence on information processing, in other situations the environment or individual characteristics may be the most influential. To understand cognitive function, one must analyze the interaction between all three components. Assessment and treatment reflect this dynamic view of cognition.

Redefining Cognitive Function and Dysfunction

Cognitive function, as previously described, requires the ability to receive, elaborate, and monitor incoming information. It involves the ability to flexibly use and apply information across task boundaries. Cognitive function includes the spontaneous use of efficient processing strategies, the ability to access previous knowledge when needed, and the awareness of one's cognitive capacity (Lidz, 1987). Processing strategies considered to be the most observable aspect of cognitive functioning have been defined broadly to encompass underlying processing behaviors and cognitive styles. Table 1 includes some of the observable processing strategies and behaviors which can underlie task performance in cognitive skill areas. There are too many possible strategies to include them all. As one can see there is considerable overlap between the different areas. Attention to detail (or the spontaneous comparison of stimuli) underlies performance in attention tasks, memory tasks, and visual processing tasks. The same underlying behaviors

Table 1 Cognitive Function: Underlying Elements

Structure	*Processing Strategies and Behaviors*
Attention	· Reacts to a gross change in the environment
	· Detects subtle changes in task conditions
	· Initiates exploration (search of the environment)
	· Searches for information in a planned, systematic manner
	· Inhibits automatic responses
	· Maintains goal-directed behavior
	· Is unhindered by internal or external distractions peripheral to the task
	· Sustains focus of attention on task (eye contact)
	· Persists with a repetitive activity over time
	· Paces and monitors speed of response
	· Reduces stimuli/Identifies irrelevant information (Cross out, sort, remove what is unnecessary)
	· Identifies relevant information (highlights, distinguishes critical details spontaneously, compares stimuli and chooses important facts)
	· Simultaneously attends to overall stimulus as well as details
	· Keeps track of rules, facts, pieces of information (external vs internal methods)
	· Allocates resources by placing greater effort and concentration on more critical aspects of the task
	· Easily disengages focus of attention when necessary
	· Follows changes in task, stimuli, or rules without error, withdrawal, or resistance
Visual processing	· Initiates active visual search
	· Plans and systematically explores the visual display
	· Sustains visual fixation on stimuli for appropriate length of time
	· Distinguishes critical features of the object or picture
	· Detects and compares subtle visual details
	· Attends to the overall configuration
	· Shifts scanning approach with different stimuli arrangements
	· Localizes information in space
	· Pays equal attention to all parts of the visual field or stimulus figure
	· Paces and monitors speed of response to visual information
	· Simultaneously keeps track of what is seen
	· Looks at the whole and divides it into parts
	· Recognizes the stimulus from different perspectives (Involves identifying critical attributes, visual imagery, and abstract thinking)
	· Can use visual imagery to describe objects or pictures that are not present
Memory	· Recognizes overall context
	· Recognizes most important details or information
	· Focuses, fixates on stimulus to be recalled
	· Sustains focus of attention on material to be remembered

Table 1 *(Continued)*

Structure	Processing Strategies and Behaviors
	· Spontaneously shifts focus of attention to the different stimuli to be remembered
	· Uses stimuli reduction methods (e.g., studies only a limited portion at one time and breaks the large amount into smaller, more manageable units)
	· Summarizes or identifies the main points or theme
	· Uses rehearsal (requires sustained repetitive activity)
	· Use association (requires ability to recognize similarities and differences between stimuli and organize information into concept categories)
	· Uses elaboration (The ability to link meaningless with meaningful information. Requires the ability to access previous knowledge and relate new information to old information)
	· Uses visual imagery
	· Initiates use of memory strategy (e.g., if unable to spontaneously recall, does not give up but persists in trying to use active retrieval strategies to trigger memory)
	· Spontaneously uses external aids to assist in recall
Problem solving	· Recognizes that an obstacle or problem exists
	· Predicts the consequences of an obstacle or action
	· Analyzes the conditions of the problem
	· Recognizes when information is incomplete and actively searches for needed information
	· Attends to relevant details, highlights or lists critical information
	· Prioritizes information
	· Distinguishes critical facts, assumptions, and irrelevant information
	· Summarizes the main issues
	· Simultaneously keeps track of all the relevant information; uses external aids when appropriate
	· Narrows down range of possibilities
	· Has ability to hypothesize (go beyond the here and now)
	· When problem is large, breaks problem up into two or more manageable subproblems
	· When stuck, re-examines the problem in a different way, re-organizes information differently, asks questions for clarification, talks aloud through each step, or brainstorms
	· Able to view situation or problem from different vantage points
	· Formulates a plan (sequence of action)
	· Shifts to alternate strategies, plans when needed
	· Classifies or groups related information together
	· Initiates the plan of action
	· Persists with the task in searching for a solution
	· Spontaneously checks work
	· Detects errors

can influence performance in a number of different skill areas. Terms such as attention, memory, visual spatial skills, and problem solving describe broad areas of function. They convey general information about the type of task but they do not describe the underlying processes needed to perform the task (Sternberg, 1986). The task's parameters and the environment determine the type and extent of the processing strategies required rather than the task itself. Cognitive function is described by defining the task parameters and environment as well as the underlying processing strategies that are needed to perform the task.

Cognitive dysfunction can affect functioning in all spheres of life: social and interpersonal, work, leisure, and daily living. In social situations, cognitive dysfunction may interfere with the individual's ability to accurately take in and integrate all parts of a situation. The patient may have decreased awareness of another person's verbal and nonverbal reactions and may have difficulty following conversations. His or her behavior may, therefore, be inappropriate to the context of the situation (Toglia & Golisz, 1990). Individual tasks may be performed inefficiently. The patient may be unable to decide what to attend to first, how to prioritize, or how to break the task into steps. Excessive time may be spent processing nonessential details. In addition, the patient may have difficulty keeping track of previous events and associating related information (Toglia & Golisz, 1990).

These problems reflect a reduced capacity to acquire and use new information. Cognitive dysfunction represents a decrease in the use of efficient processing strategies to select, discriminate, organize, and structure incoming information (Bolger, 1982; Melamed, Rahamani, Greenstein, Grosswater, & Najenson, 1985). In addition the patient's ability to access previous knowledge when needed and apply knowledge and skills flexibly to a variety of situations is diminished. These deficits may be observed in localized areas such as in visual processing or they may exist regardless of the modality involved. Table 2 provides a partial list of deficiencies in processing strategies, categorized according to the information processing model (as seen in Figure 2).

This categorization is based on Feuerstein's (1979) classification of cognitive deficiencies. Impaired cognitive functions found at the input phase include deficits in the quality and quantity of information obtained by an individual. Impairments at the elaboration phase include those factors that impede efficient use of available information and existing cues. Impaired output functions represent those factors that lead to inadequate communication of answers, solutions, and actions. Impaired control functions includes deficits in the ability to monitor and verify accuracy of performance. In some instances, the deficiencies observed may cluster predominantly at one stage of information processing (input, elaboration, output, or control functions) but overlap is frequently observed. Deficient functions are not completely

Table 2 Cognitive Dysfunction: A Redefinition

Information Processing Stages	Deficient Processing Strategies and Behaviors
Input	· Decrease in active exploration · Unsystematic, unplanned exploratory behavior · Tendency to overfocus on parts, details, one aspect of stimulus, or task · Overattention to detail · Impaired ability to consider two or more sources of information at once · Impaired ability to sustain focus of attention
Elaboration	· Decreased ability to shift focus of attention · Decreased ability to spontaneously compare similarities and differences · Decreased ability to recognize critical distinguishing features · Inability to select relevant from nonrelevant cues · Inadequacy in identifying a problem and subsequently defining it · Inability to internally manipulate data · Impaired inferential hypothetical (if) thinking · Impaired strategies for hypothesis testing · Impaired association, clustering, and detecting patterns of organization · Impaired ability to reason simultaneously about parts and wholes · Impaired reflection · Impaired ability to look beyond "here and now" and anticipate events, or plan future goals · Impaired flexibility and reversibility in thinking · Impaired ability to prioritize information · Tendency to lose track of information · Impaired ability to comprehend symbols and concepts · Inability to simultaneously hold in mind all the qualities of a situation, object or experience
Output	· Decreased persistance, sustained effort · Random, haphazard, trial and error approach · Impulsivity or slow reaction time · Blocking (an unwillingness to engage in a task after experiencing a failure) · Reduced stamina or energy (adynamia) · Irritability, lowered frustration tolerance
Control	· Decreased ability to evaluate task difficulty in relationship to one's capabilities · Decreased ability to predict the consequences of one's actions · Decreased error detection · Decreased self-control · Decrease in strategic behavior · Decrease in self-initiation · Decrease in planning · Decreased awareness of one's strengths and weaknesses · Difficulty generating goals · Unrealistic expectations and goals

absent but represent areas of weakness and vulnerability (Groveman, Brown, & Miller, 1985). The extent to which these deficiencies are observed depends upon the parameters of the task (e.g., number of stimuli, complexity, familiarity, etc.) and the environment. For example, a patient's tendency to overfocus on irrelevant details may emerge under certain task conditions, regardless of whether it is an attentional task, memory task, or visual-processing task. An improved ability to screen out irrelevant details may be observed in both visual spatial tasks and memory tasks. The underlying processes and behaviors that are interfering with the patient's performance in the majority of tasks are the components which are analyzed during assessment and targeted as priorities for treatment.

Dynamic Interactional Assessment

Assessments can be divided into two categories: static and dynamic. Static assessments, such as standardized cognitive screening instruments or neuropsychological tests, are based on traditional psychometric models. They define "here and now" performance. The objective of static assessments is to identify and quantify cognitive deficits. This information is necessary for diagnosis, monitoring progress, discharge planning, and patient or caregiver education regarding expected behaviors (Toglia, 1989b). In contrast, dynamic interactional assessment (also termed dynamic investigative assessment), seeks to identify and specify the conditions that have the greatest influence on performance. It attempts to estimate the conditions under which the patient is likely to succeed as well as to identify those conditions where the patient is likely to fail. This approach originated with Vygotsky's (1978) concept of the zone of proximal development. The principles of dynamic assessment have been used in standard assessments with learning disabled, mentally retarded, and normal children (Campione & Brown, 1987; Jensen & Feuerstein, 1987). I have adapted these principles and combined them with strategy investigation techniques for use with the brain-injured adult. The information gained from dynamic interactional assessment (DIA) is directly related to treatment planning. Both types of assessment are needed. The emphasis and extent of testing depends upon the purpose of assessment.

In some cases, a static assessment such as a cognitive screening battery may be unnecessary. Quantification and identification of deficits may have already been established through a neuropsychological evaluation. Once general deficits are identified, the role of the occupational therapist is to explore these deficits further. The therapist needs to specify which conditions increase or decrease symptoms and investigate the patient's use of processing strategies. This information is a necessary prerequisite for treatment. In situations where cognitive deficits have already been objectively identified by another discipline, it is not time or cost-efficient for the occupational therapist to assess all areas of cognitive perceptual function. For example, if the neuropsychological report indicates that visual spatial skills are intact while memory, organization, and problem-solving skills are impaired, the occupational therapy evaluation does not need to include visual spatial skills.

Dynamic interactional assessment is based on the dynamic interactional model of cognition described earlier. In this approach, the ability to learn and generalize information is central to the concept of cognition. Therefore the assessment of cognitive abilities includes estimates of the potential for learning and looks at how an individual goes about solving problems and dealing with situations. An observed problem with a specific task is often the result of interactions among multiple components including personality and emotional factors, task and environment variables as well as deficiencies in processing strategies and metacognitive skills. The DIA attempts to specify how external (task, environment) and internal (processing strategies, metacognition, motivation) components influence the ability to process information.

The dynamic interactional approach is individually focused, flexible, interactionist, and process oriented. The examiner does not simply observe behavior but attempts to change behavior. The assessment analyzes the use of processing strategies and metacognitive skills (self-monitoring, awareness) during task performance.

If the patient has difficulty with a task, the therapist alters test administration procedures and materials and probes patient responses. For example, cues or external aids may be provided, the task demands can be decreased, and/or the patient may be asked to explain why he or she chose a particular answer. DIA seeks to estimate the degree of change that is possible as well as to specify the means by which changes in performance can be produced (Toglia, 1989b). Assessment focuses on the individual's best performance or maximum level of function. It taps on weakened skills that lie beneath the surface but have the potential for function. Assessment within the zone of proximal development has been thought to discriminate differences in abilities not identified using conventional methods (Brown & French, 1979; Brown & Ferrara, 1985). Affected functions may exhibit a differing potential for change. Not all functions which are impaired show equal potential for restitution (Cicerone & Tupper, 1986).

In DIA, the examiner-examinee relationship is considered crucial. In standardized tests, the procedures are designed to provide the same environment for each examinee. Examiners are trained to remain neutral, not to question or add to the individual's response, and not to help the individual in any way. They have avoided the use of cues, questioning, task modifications, and interaction with the examinee in standardized testing because they can influence reliability and validity. DIA seeks to measure cognitive modifiability or the change that is possible under different conditions. Classical psychometric procedures cannot be accommodated easily for the measurement of change. Therefore DIA requires use of a nontraditional measurement model (Embretson, 1987).

There are several different test designs which can incorporate the use of dynamic testing procedures (Embretson, 1987; Toglia, 1989b). I am currently working on developing a number of different types of DIA assessments for the brain-injured adult. Some of the assessments have also been piloted with chronic schizophrenic patients. The individual assessments cover a range of tasks including sorting cards into categories, the contextual memory test (Toglia 1989b; Toglia, in press) and copying designs. Three examples (the dynamic visual processing assessment [DVPA], Toglia Category Test [TCA], and deductive reasoning tests) are presented in the following section. Each assessment was developed through videotape analysis of patients performing tasks with unstandardized cues and questions. From the videotape analysis, guidelines and sequences of cues and questioning were developed.

One limitation of DIA assessments is that they cannot be used to measure change over time. Another limitation is that extensive examiner training is required to use and interpret the assessments proficiently. In addition, the tests described in the following section require use of language skills, however, the principles of DIA can easily be adapted for aphasic patients by using graded tactile, motor, or visual cues.

Examples of Dynamic Interactional Assessment

The Dynamic Visual Processing Assessment

The Dynamic Visual Processing Assessment (DVPA) (Toglia & Finkelstein, 1991) consists of drawings of objects which are presented under different task conditions. Object perception, unilateral inattention, the ability to keep track of what is seen, and organization of scanning are analyzed as task conditions (number, arrangement, rotation, and familiarity) change. The test seeks to identify the specific task variables which influence the ability to process information. For example, it can determine the effect the number of items has on an examinee's unilateral inattention or his or her ability to keep track of what is seen. The test is progressively graded from simple to complex. Simple visual tasks are relatively automatic in nature and require little attention or effort. Complex visual tasks require effort, analysis, attention, and comparison of detail. The test begins at a middle level and moves up or down depending on the patient's responses. In addition, a cueing sequence is incorporated into testing to determine the amount and type of assistance that enhances performance. There are two types of cueing sequences: cues for errors of omission and cues for errors of misperception (see sample cues; Table 3). The DVPA uses cues within the initial testing situation. The use of cues and level of cueing indicates a lower ability. A comparison of local estimates of the person's ability is provided to determine the extent of learning effects from the cues. At the end of each cueing procedure, the examiner asks a standard question to investigate the patient's awareness of his or her errors.

A patient may have difficulty taking in and organizing visual information for many different reasons. For example, in some cases, a patient may have difficulty accurately perceiving objects because he or she overfocuses on details. In other cases, the patient may fail to attend to details. Still in other cases, the patient may approach the task in such a disorganized manner that he or she omits objects on the page. While in other cases the patient omits items because of unilateral inattention. The standard cues and questions are designed to help sort out the underlying difficulties. Preliminary results have shown that, in some brain-injured patients, processing problems (such as unilateral inattention, ability to keep track of information, object perception, and scanning organization) become predictably worse as specific task parameters increase in difficulty. For example, in one case, a patient with a right cerebral vascular accident, had no difficulty in attending to the left side when there was less than eight stimuli or when stimuli were presented in a well organized manner. However, when the eight stimuli were scattered, the patient had inconsistent omissions on the left side. When 16 stimuli were scattered, the patient consistently demonstrated 1-to-3 left-sided omissions.

Table 3 Sample Cues Used in the Dynamic Visual Processing Assessment

---

Are you sure you have seen (told me) all objects on the page? Could there be more?

There are still some that you didn't mention. Can you find them?

Look on the (right/left/upper/lower/middle) of the page.
  or
Can you think of a way to help you keep track of the objects? Try it.

Try moving your eyes all the way over here (place red line as anchor).
  or
Try pointing to each object you mention in an organized way. Start here (point) and
  go across to here.

The left-sided neglect was not present in tasks that had relatively few stimuli or when the stimuli were well organized. The patient had difficulty imposing organized scanning on a disorganized array with eight stimuli or more. Thus the DVPA is designed to explain the task conditions which influence the identification and organization of visual information. Cognitive perceptual deficits are not all or none phenomena. The clinician needs to understand the conditions under which the deficit is likely to surface as well as those where it is unlikely to surface.

The DVPA is in the preliminary research stage. We have developed a protocol and collection of reliability and normative data is in progress (Toglia & Finkelstein, 1991). The test uses the Rasch measurement model, a family of logistic psychometric models, to provide independent estimates of a person's ability and the stimulus difficulty. Rasch measurement provides a model for examining and accounting for the difficulty of the task along a common linear scale (Rasch, 1960). The task dimensions of amount, familiarity, spatial arrangement, and rotation will each be calibrated along four linear scales, so that a person's ability can be expressed as a function of the difficulty of each task dimension. Our first step is to determine whether patients of varying abilities fall along the hypothesized linear task continuum and, in future research, we will examine concurrent and predictive validity. We predict that an assessment that analyzes difficulty level according to task parameters rather than according to specific items may show closer correlations with functional task performance.

Toglia Category Assessment (TCA)

Two tasks that use plastic utensils of different sizes and colors are used to assess category flexibility and deductive reasoning. In the category assessment, the examiner asks the patient to sort 16 utensils into different groups so that the items in one group are different in one way from those of the other groups. The utensils differ from each other in color (red, white, and yellow), size (big or small), and utensil type (knife, fork, or spoon). When the patient correctly classifies the items according to one attribute (size, color, or type), he or she is then asked to sort the items again in a different way and then again in a third way. After each classification, the examiner asks the patient to explain how the groups are different. A standard sequences of cues are provided if the patient has difficulty (Toglia, 1990).

Use of the cues has helped to differentiate patients and their underlying problems. For example, one brain-injured patient sorted the utensils into spoons and forks. When asked to sort the utensils a different way, the patient shuffled the utensils around but ended up with the same two categories.

Again the procedure was repeated and the patient did the same thing. However when he was cued to attend to the individual attributes (size and color), he immediately sorted them in different ways. This indicated that the patient's underlying problem was a tendency to become stuck in one response. Another patient was able to sort the utensils into two separate groups but could not think of a third way to sort them. Although he was provided with maximum cues, the patient insisted there were only two ways (by color and type of utensil) to sort them. When the patient was shown the third method (by size), he denied his error and stated that size was not a good category. The patient's response to cues provide differential implications for treatment.

Deductive Reasoning

In using the test for deductive reasoning, a question game is used to investigate the ability to formulate and test different hypotheses. In this task the examiner tells the patient that he (or she) has to determine which utensil the examiner is thinking of, with the least amount of guessing and the fewest number of questions as possible. The patient has to ask questions that can be answered as "yes" or "no." The examiner does not actually think of an item, but answers "no" to all the questions (whenever possible) until there is only one possibility left. The answer is obtainable with three questions when eight utensils of two different colors (red or white), size (big or small) and type (fork or spoon) are used. For example if the following three questions are asked, the answer can be easily deduced; Is it red? Spoon? Small? The answer must be a white, large fork. If the patient does not solve the problem with three questions, another trial is given with a maximum of up to four trials. The examiner gives a standard sequence of prompts when the patient is unable to solve the problem with four questions. The test can be made more difficult by including a set of other colored utensils (Toglia, 1990). Preliminary analysis has revealed interesting patterns of responses. Two patients asked about each utensil, one by one: "Is it this fork?" "Is it this spoon?" When cued to narrow down the questions, one patient immediately generated an efficient set of questions. The other patient required maximum cues and still could not generate a different set of questions. In both cases the patient had the same initial baseline response but, again, there were significant differences in the way they responded to cues. These differences have different implications for treatment planning. In one case, the patient only requires a general cue to think of an alternate approach to the task. In the other case, treatment needs to focus on helping the patient to attend to and discriminate between the various attributes before attempting to solve a problem.

The category flexibility and deductive reasoning tasks are still in their initial stage of test development. We have developed a standard protocol with scoring guidelines and reliability studies are in progress.

Treatment

Dynamic interactional assessment seeks to estimate the patients potential for change. The extent to which this assessment reveals that the patient is aware of his or her errors, and is responsive to cues or task modifications, determines the treatment techniques and activities used. If DIA reveals that the patient's performance cannot be facilitated through cues or task modifications, then a functional approach, which has little or no requirements for transfer of learning, may be appropriate. On the other hand, if assessment reveals that the patient's performance can be facilitated with assistance or by changes in task conditions, then the therapist should use a multicontext treatment approach to help enhance the patient's ability to process information and use it flexibly across task conditions. These two different approaches to treatment are described in the following section. Therapists should remember that decisions regarding the patient's rehabilitation potential are based on a number of additional factors including the nature and expected course of the illness or injury, the length of time since onset, and the assessment results of other multidisciplinary team members.

The Functional Approach: Patients with Poor Learning Potential

The functional approach capitalizes on the clients' strengths (Neisdadt, 1990) and it can be divided into two techniques: domain-specific training and compensation/adaptations.

Domain-specific training involves repetitive practice of a specific functional task through the method of vanishing cues. It capitalizes on procedural learning, or learning for doing rather than learning facts or rules. Procedural learning is often preserved even in adults with severely involved brain injuries. In domain-specific training, the therapist breaks the task down into a series of small steps. Initially the patient may require maximum assistance to perform each step. Cues are gradually withdrawn until the patient can perform the task independently (Glisky & Schacter, 1988). Therapists may occasionally use rewards or positive reinforcement when the patient successfully completes each step. The learning acquired through domain-specific training has been characterized as hyperspecific and may be bound to the stimulus characteristics of the training situation (Glisky & Schacter, 1988).

In domain-specific training, the task and environment conditions remain consistent. Transfer of learning beyond near transfer level tasks is not expected and the deficient processing strategies underlying task performance are not addressed. Task learning is acquired through repetitive action or procedural learning. Some self-monitoring techniques or learning of rules may be taught but the emphasis is on action-oriented, procedural learning. Awareness or insight into one's cognitive perceptual problems is generally not required and is not addressed in treatment. However, in some cases where domain-specific training is used to teach a patient how to operate a compensatory device (such as a data bank watch for a patient with memory problems), insight is a prerequisite for treatment (Davis & Radomski, 1989). Use of behavioral techniques such as positive reinforcement and shaping, have been used with brain-injured adults who are severely impaired to increase participation and motivation (Giles & Wilson, 1988).

In some cases, the patient may view domain-specific training as a means of regaining lost skills. For example, an adult patient with a degenerative neurological condition was unable to write his signature legibly because he had visual spatial difficulties and had lost the visual image of specific symbols and letters. The patient was extremely upset over losing his ability to sign his name because he had been stopped from using his credit card and was unable to sign letters he had dictated. Through repetitive practice with gradually fading assistance, he regained the ability to write his signature legibly. He still could not write other words in script, and his visual spatial difficulties were still present on other tasks. The patient viewed his accomplishment as an improvement in his skills while the therapist viewed it as an example of task specific learning. The patient acknowledged that he had difficulties; however, he had resisted any suggestion of compensation or external adaptations because he did not accept the permanency of the deficit. In this particular case, domain-specific training was successful in building a therapeutic relationship and helping the patient become more functional. As treatment progressed, the patient gradually began to accept external aids and other compensation methods. In some cases, domain-specific training can be disguised as remediation. The patient may view his accomplishments as a sign that he is getting better: this practice increases motivation but it can also raise false hopes. The therapist will need to assist the patient in maintaining realistic goals.

Compensation or adaptation involves changing the task or environmental conditions to avoid or minimize the use of the impaired skill or deficient processing strategies (Neisdadt, 1990). Before initiating compensatory treatment, the therapist must consider the patient's metacognitive skills (such as awareness of one's limitations) and his or her emotional and personality characteristics. Compensation for a deficit assumes that the patient recognizes and accepts the need to compensate. A patient who is unable to recognize his or her errors, or predict when they are likely to occur, will not initiate the use of compensatory adaptations or strategies. The patient needs to accept the decision to attempt to circumvent the deficit rather than to change it. If the patient is not aware of the deficit or has not accepted that it exists, compensation may not be a successful starting point for treatment (Davis and Radomski, 1989). As Gianutsos stated, "Assisting individuals to engage in exercise directed toward restoration of function is often a more successful starting point for a clinical relationship than focusing on compensation. If exercise does not lead to improved function, the individual will begin to welcome and appreciate compensatory methods . . ." (Gianutsos, 1989, p. vii). Diminished awareness of cognitive capacity has been identified as a major problem in brain-injured adults. A greater incidence of unawareness has been documented in patients with right hemisphere lesions and frontal lobe damage however the phenomena is still poorly understood (Anderson & Tranel, 1989). In cases where the patient is unaware of his or her deficit, treatment may need to begin with activities that focus on the deficit areas. Treatment activities may also need to start considerably above the level of breakdown to help the patient recognize a problem exists. The multicontext approach that follows can also be used in the initial stages of treatment to help the patient understand the underlying nature of his or her difficulties. In this approach, awareness training techniques (such as self-estimation, role reversal, self-questioning, or error evaluation) may be used in a variety of different tasks to help the patient understand that the same problem interferes with performance in a number of different situations (Toglia, 1991). Once the patient is able to recognize errors when they occur, he or she may be willing to accept compensatory strategies.

In those cases where the patient does not show potential for change, treatment may also be directed towards helping the caregiver learn to manage the patient. Caregiver training may include techniques for minimizing confusion, helping the patient follow directions or attend to a simple task, or managing agitated behaviors.

The Multicontext Approach: Patients with Potential for Learning

The multicontext treatment approach is based on the dynamic interactional model of cognition. The goal is to improve the individual's capacity to process, monitor, and use new information flexibly across task situations. This approach includes methods to help the patient use his or her residual skills in the most efficient manner as well as attempts to restore cognitive function. Treatment activities focus on the areas of limitations rather than the areas of strengths. Task, environment, and individual components are manipulated to place gradually increasing demands upon learning and information processing. Components of the multicontext approach include strategy training, metacognitive training, use of multiple situations, task analysis (to identify levels of transfer), and consideration of learner characteristics (Toglia, 1991).

The multicontext approach involves practicing targeted processing strategies and self-monitoring techniques in a variety of situations and environments (Figure 3). Task and movement parameters are analyzed and graded to place progressively more demands on the impaired processing system and on the ability to transfer learning. The therapist uses a variety of tabletop, computer, gross motor, and functional tasks in treatment. Both individual and group activities are used to help the patient adapt to different environments. The goal is to help the patient relate the targeted strategy or self-monitoring technique to a variety of different experiences. The therapist avoids exclusive use of either functional activities or tabletop activities in treatment because, if what is taught is embedded in one context, the skills learned may be accessible only in relation to that specific context (Toglia, 1991).

Treatment involves identifying one or two processing strategies that the therapist would like to see the patient use in a variety of situations. For example, two processing strategies that may influence performance in a variety of situations include: (1) the ability to attend to relevant details, and (2) the ability to pace and monitor the speed of one's response.

Once the processing strategies targeted for treatment are determined, a detailed task analysis is required to choose treatment tasks which fall into the categories of near transfer, intermediate transfer, far transfer and very far transfer. Treatment generally begins at the level of where performance breaks down or the point at which the patient is able to successfully complete the task with only 1 to 3 cues. Task complexity is not increased until evidence of generalization is seen at all levels of transfer. In multicontext treatment, the underlying strategy or conceptual characteristics remain the same in all treatment tasks while the surface characteristics of the task gradually change as treatment is moved from near transfer to far transfer (Toglia, 1991). For

Change Environment
Change Movement Requirements ➡ Keep Strategy Consistent ➡ Transfer of Learning
Change Physical Characteristics of Task

Figure 5-3 Multicontext treatment.

Table 4   Levels of Transfer Distance

Transfer Level	Task	Changing Surface Characteristics	Example of an Underlying Processing Strategy Remaining Consistent
Starting	20 playing cards are scattered across the mat. Pick up only the red even-numbered cards.		Selectively attend to relevant detail and
Near	Pick up only the coins which are heads up	Only type of stimuli changed	Identify when response was too quick
Intermediate	Objects are placed in various locations. Throw bean bag to objects with letter "A" in their name or use a computer shape matching game	Type of stimuli, movement demands, rules, stimuli arrangement changed	
Far	Given a shopping list and a newspaper circular, circle the prices of items in the circular which are on the shopping list.	All surface characteristics changed	

example, Table 4 illustrates how the same underlying processing strategies, "attention to detail" and "monitoring the tendency to respond too quickly," are consistent across different tasks. By applying the same strategy or self-monitoring techniques to tasks which progressively differ in surface characteristics learning transfer is facilitated. When two situations are physically different, learning transfer becomes more difficult because the underlying similarities may not be recognized. In multicontext training, attention is drawn to the core similarity of the tasks and away from the surface similarities and differences. Applying the same strategy to different situations during treatment will demonstrate the range of the strategy's applicability and will allow the learner to understand the conditions in which it is useful (Brown & Kane, 1988; Brown, Bransford, Ferrara, & Campione, 1983).

During all treatment sessions, the therapist analyzes the processing strategies that the patient is or is not using and determines if the task could be performed in a more efficient way. In some cases, the patient may be asked to think of an alternative way of performing the task while, in other cases, the patient may be explicitly shown an alternative strategy and asked to repeat the task. Any improvements in the ability to initiate use of a processing strategy should be observed in a number of different tasks. For example, if the area that is targeted for treatment is "attention to relevant details," then improvement in this area should be reflected in attention tasks, visual spatial tasks, and memory tasks. Treatment is not deficit or task specific.

In the multicontext treatment approach, task grading, strategy training and practice in different situations need to be combined with metacognitive training to promote learning transfer. Metacognition includes two interrelated aspects: awareness of one's own cognitive processes and capacities and the ability to monitor performance (Flavell, 1985). Metacognitive skills (such as the ability to evaluate the difficulty of a task in relationship to one's own strengths and weaknesses, predict or anticipate the likelihood of problems, or recognize errors as they are occurring) are recognized critical components in the learning and generalization process (Belmont, Butterfield, & Ferretti, 1982). The patient can only move from a cued to an uncued condition when he or she has internalized the ability to estimate and self-monitor performance.

If the patient does not understand the full extent of his or her deficit he or she will be likely to accurately estimate the difficulty of tasks and will not perceive the need to approach the task in a more efficient way. Crosson et al (1989) divides awareness into three independent types: (1) intellectual awareness, which refers to the patient's ability to understand that at some level a particular function is impaired; (2) emergent awareness, which is the ability to recognize a problem when it is actually happening; and (3) anticipatory awareness, or the ability to anticipate that a problem may occur.

Awareness training techniques (such as self-estimation, role reversal, self-questioning and self-evaluation, and videotape feedback) have been recently described that address the different areas of awareness (Toglia, 1991). For example, in self-estimation, the patient estimates his or her performance before performing a task and after completing it. The emphasis is on realistically anticipating difficulties and estimating performance. Awareness training techniques are designed to teach patients to learn how to evaluate and monitor their own performance. They help the patient understand why errors may occur. Awareness training techniques can be integrated into daily treatment activities.

When planning and selecting treatment activities, the therapist needs to consider the learner characteristics of the patient, including motivation and individual personality characteristics, when planning and selecting treatment activities. In the multicontext approach, treatment activities are not predetermined. The activities chosen depend to some extent upon the patients premorbid personality and interests. If the patient used to enjoy competitive situations, then competitive game-like situations would be used in treatment. If the patient previously worked with numbers and finance, then treatment activities that involved numbers and money would be integrated into the total treatment program. Both functional and remedial activities are used in treatment. There are advantages and disadvantages to both. Functional activities require the integration of all performance components. Although they may be more meaningful for the patient, such activities do not easily lend themselves to strategy analysis, didactic interruptions, or manipulation of specific task parameters, all of which are characteristic of treatment. Remedial activities, on the other hand, can be easily controlled and manipulated to emphasize different strategies and skills (Ben-Yishay & Diller, 1983). Remedial tasks do not have to be limited to parquetry block activities or peg designs. They can incorporate use of meaningful and relevant stimuli such as stamps, coins, utensils, pencils, and pens, etc. But the activities are outside the realm of everyday function. Therefore, they require the therapist to make an extra effort to actively engage and motivate the patient. The therapist needs to create an atmosphere of challenge and support. The therapist's tone of voice and the manner in which he or she presents the activities is important in engaging the patient in treatment. For example, the therapist can enthusiastically say "Let's see if you can keep your attention strong and steady so that you will get a score of 90%. If you feel your attention withering away, stop and take a break. Ready? Let's give it all you've got." The therapist needs to clearly define the goals of each activity in concrete terms that the patient can understand (Ben-Yishay & Diller, 1983). Results should be graphed and plotted. Patients lose interest when they do not understand the purpose of the activity nor see any progress. If the patient cannot understand the relevance of an activity, it should be discarded.

The multicontext treatment approach is individualized and flexible. The patient's response to activities determines the subsequent course of treatment. If the patient has not shown any gains in treatment within a 2- to 4-week period, then treatment may attempt to address a different problem area (or a different underlying processing strategy) before concluding that the patient's performance has plateaued. The sequence of treatment is not predetermined.

Case Examples

The following case examples of a brain-injured adult and a patient with chronic schizophrenia illustrate the application of the dynamic interactional model to practice. Information gained from dynamic interactional assessment is summarized and the use of the multicontextual approach in planning and guiding treatment is outlined.

Case 1

F. is a 21-year-old male with s/p closed head trauma. He demonstrates subtle difficulties in balance; however, he is independent in ambulation without an assistive device. F. is independent in basic self-care skills; however, he makes frequent errors in higher-level ADL skills such as shopping, cooking, or money management. For example, his mother complained that everytime she sent him to the store with a shopping list of about ten items he would come back with only half of the items, and he never thought to check himself by looking at the list. He would also mix up appointments and things he was supposed to do. He liked to cook, but his mother observed that he sometimes forgot something he had put on the stove or in the oven.

Assessment Results

Input: F. demonstrated no difficulty in attention or visual discrimination when the task involved up to 8 to 10 stimuli. Beyond this amount, his approach became increasingly disorganized, and he demonstrated a tendency to omit important pieces of information. For example, on a task which involved identifying 16 pictures of rotated objects randomly scattered on a page, he consistently missed 1 to 2 items and repeated other items up to 3 times asking "did I say this one already?" With 1 to 2 cues he was able to perform the task in a more orderly fashion. He had no difficulty when the same task was presented with 4 or 8 items.

Elaboration: F. demonstrated the ability to recognize similarities and differences, make associations and group related information together; however, on unstructured tasks with more than eight stimuli he did not spontaneously use these skills to help him. For example, when he was asked to sort 25 cards into categories he appeared to lose track of the categories and sorting principle he had already established. He made two piles of clothing and put scissors with the category of furniture. However, when he was asked to carefully look through each pile and explain how the cards went together, he immediately self-corrected his errors. He had no difficulty sorting eight spoons and forks into three different categories; however, on a reasoning task that involved deducing a hidden item, he lost track of the questions he had previously asked. On a memory task involving recall of 20 items related to a restaurant, he recalled eight items but he did not appear to attempt to group related information together. When asked how he tried to remember, he stated "I just looked at them." He did not recognize that all the pictures were associated with a restaurant. When the second part of the test was administered and the patient was given a strategy to use, his recall performance improved to 14 items out of 20.

Output: F. frequently approached tasks in a haphazard and disorganized manner.

Control: F. acknowledged that he sometimes had difficulties with memory and concentration. He frequently had a vague sense that he was not on the right track but he did not stop to check himself. He consistently overestimated his performance. For example, on a memory task, he estimated he would remember 18 items and he only recalled eight. On the picture identification task in the DVPA, he admitted to sometimes losing track of his responses but he did not demonstrate awareness of omission errors until they were pointed out. In specific tasks, F. readily admitted his difficulties after he was provided with feedback on his performance.

Processing Strategies: F. often approached tasks in a random manner. He did not attempt to prioritize information or to group related information together (even though he had the underlying capabilities to do this), and he tended to lose track of information easily.

Learning Potential: F's performance was easily facilitated when he received 1 or 2 cues to help him initiate organizational strategies or when the amount of information he had to deal with at any one time was reduced.

Assessment Summary: F. can perform tasks that do not require the ability to keep track of a number of different things. He has no difficulty in discrimination or sorting tasks involving up to eight stimuli, and he was able to participate in a 1-hour session without being distracted by internal or external stimuli. However, on tasks that require effort, attending to detail, and tracking previous responses, F. demonstrates a tendency to lose track of information or omit important pieces of information. This interferes with his performance on a variety of different type of tasks including problem-solving tasks (where F. may omit an important variable), memory tasks, and tasks that require sorting multiple stimuli. On these tasks, F.'s approach is inefficient and, at times, appears to increase his memory and attention load. For example, on one sorting task, F. devised an elaborate number coding system to separate the categories but he then forgot which number represented each category. Although F. does not initiate use of efficient processing strategies, he appears to have the underlying capabilities to use them and when provided with only one or two general cues is able to use strategies successfully.

Treatment Plan

The first step in treatment planning is for the therapist to identify the processing strategy that he or she wants the patient to use in a variety of different tasks. In F.'s case the therapist felt that F.'s performance would improve in a number of different tasks if he could use the following two processing strategies: (1) self-monitoring strategies, in which he would predict the tasks where his tendency to lose track was likely to emerge and stop performing a task when he feels he has lost track; and (2) initiate use of efficient organizational strategies to assist in reducing memory load so that he can keep track of information.

The treatment goal was to get F. to approach all tasks in an organized manner or in a way that would reduce his memory load. The therapist chose activities that require using an organized approach for successful outcome within the categories of near, intermediate, and far level transfer tasks. The surface parameters of the task (such as movement and postural requirements, type of stimuli, and task directions) were gradually changed while the same underlying strategies were emphasized. In all treatment activities, F. was asked to predict on a scale of 1 to 5 whether he will have difficulty keeping track of the information (1 represented no difficulty; 2 represented possible difficulty, may lose track of one item; 3 meant he will lose track of two to three items; 4 meant he will lose track of four to five items or 4 to 5 times; 5 meant he will lose track of more than six items or more than 6 times). His original prediction was then compared with his actual performance. In addition, F. was asked at 3 to 5 minute intervals whether or not he felt he was keeping track of everything. Then F. was required to ask himself two questions which are written down on an index card. The questions include: "Have I used an orderly approach and grouped similar items together?" and "Have I missed any items?" Gradually, the therapist provided less structure for self-questioning and self-evaluation because the ability to self-monitor performance is necessary to be able to move from one level of transfer to the next. Once F.'s improvement in initiating efficient organizational strategies and self-monitoring strategies was observed in a variety of different tasks, the complexity of the activities was increased. A combination of gross motor tasks, tabletop tasks, and functional tasks were used to emphasize the same underlying processing and self-monitoring strategies. Examples of selected treatment tasks are as follows:

Sample Treatment Activities

Starting Activity: F. is standing and is asked to pick up various colored shapes spread all over the floor. He is told that any three-sided figure is worth 4 points and any four-sided figure is worth 6 points and any figure with five or more sides is worth 3 points. F. has to keep track of his score as he picks up the shapes. Initially F. picked up the shapes randomly and quickly lost track of his score without realizing it. During treatment, the patient's approach to the task was analyzed and he was helped to think of alternatives. He was also asked to evaluate the efficiency and success of his performance.

Near Transfer: F. is in a standing position and is asked to pick up playing cards spread all over the table and floor. If the card is an odd numbered he receives 6 points, if it is even numbered he receives 3 points, and if it is a picture card he receives 4 points. He has to keep track of the score. Again, an organized approach is required to successfully complete the task.

Intermediate Transfer: F. is presented with a tabletop game that requires figuring out the hidden object (a modified 20-question game). He has to generate efficient questions and keep track of previous questions and answers.

Far Transfer: First, F. is given a hypothetical sum of money to spend on nine holiday gifts for friends and relatives. He is given catalogs with gift items. He has to find nine gifts and stay within his budget, which requires him to keep track of how much has been spent and for whom he has already purchased a gift. Second, F. is given a stack of cards with phone numbers of local stores and restaurants. He is asked to think of two different ways the cards can be organized so that people will have an easier time finding the phone number they need. He is then asked to choose the method he thinks is more efficient. Third, he would like to get a job as a cashier in a local store. The task of a cashier is simulated and the patient recognizes that he is having difficulty keeping track of items that he has already rung up. His ability to spontaneously initiate a solution was observed.

Case 2

J. is a 36-year-old female with diagnosis of chronic schizophrenia with negative symptoms and some paranoid features. She recently showed improvements with Clozapine. Her occupational therapist had observed marked task impairment and reported that she was inattentive to the requirements of the task. For example, she did not wait for or ask for assistance and would continue performing a task obviously incorrectly without being aware of her poor results. She seemed oblivious to many aspects of the task and social environment. A dynamic interactional assessment was requested to provide insight into J.'s underlying cognitive problems and strengths (Toglia & Fine, 1990).

Assessment Results

Input: J.'s major problems were seen in the input. She was able to accurately perceive and attend to the task when there were only four concrete stimuli present. Once she was presented with a task that required her to identify eight pictures of objects arranged in a horizontal row, she began to have difficulty and made 1 to 3 omissions consistently. She did not systematically scan the items from left to right and instead named items in a random, haphazard fashion. When the eight objects were scattered and rotated she had difficulty focusing on the task at hand and made numerous misperceptions. Verbal cues did not facilitate her responses.

Elaboration: With the therapist's assistance (or structure for input) to help J. focus on the critical variables of the task, she was able to demonstrate her ability to recognize similarities and differences, make associations, and categorize information. When given 25 pictures of objects to sort into categories, she haphazardly created piles of cards, without really looking at them. When she was provided with maximum structure to help her focus on each individual card, she was able to correctly place it in an established category. When asked to sort knives and forks into two categories, she separated them into color. When asked to sort them a different way, she haphazardly sorted them into two random groups. When asked how the utensils were different from each other, she identified the three different attributes (size, color, and type) and then proceeded to sort them correctly. On a memory test involving recall of 20 items related to a restaurant theme, she only recalled five items. There appeared to be no attempt to group related information together. During stimulus exposure, she frequently looked around the room.

Output: At times her responses were slow, while at other times they appeared to be impulsive. Her actions were disorganized and she frequently proceeded in a task without a clear goal or plan in mind.

Control: J. was unable to detect errors and she was not able to use feedback when it was provided. She appeared to have no knowledge of what she could or could not do. For example, on a memory task she was unable to predict her score and stated that she was not sure if her score would be 0 or 20. After performing tasks she was unable to state how she thought she did on the task, often stating "I have no idea."

Processing Strategies: J. did not appear to initiate use of efficient processing strategies in structuring the input of information.

Assessment Summary: J.'s inattentiveness and disorganized approach characterized her performance on all tasks. She appeared to be unable to cope with more than a few visual stimuli at once. However, when stimuli were limited and she was asked to focus on one or two things at a time, she demonstrated many high-level skills. For example, she demonstrated the ability to understand similarities and differences, make associations, and establish logical sequences. In other words, when input of information was highly controlled and structured, she was able to organize and elaborate on this information. Verbal cues did not help J. in selectively attending to relevant aspects of the task. Her task performance improved when she was presented with controlled stimuli and they were graded so that she only needed to take in a limited amount of information at once.

Treatment Plan

The main treatment objective was to expand J.'s input capabilities. The processing strategies emphasized in all tasks included systematic exploration of the visual display and sustained focus of attention on the relevant aspects of the task. The therapist also encouraged J. to stop the task whenever she felt she was losing her focus of attention and emphasized these behaviors in a variety of different basic level tasks. Initially, the therapist stopped the task every time J.'s focus of attention started to fade. Gradually J. was required to identify, on her own, when she was losing her focus of attention. Treatment aimed to help J. effectively and accurately deal with more than four stimuli. Once her ability to systematically scan and sustain the focus of attention was demonstrated in all of the tasks listed below, the amount of stimuli and the complexity were gradually increased. The long-term objective was to improve J.'s task performance so that she would be able to participate in a sheltered workshop.

The therapist presented activities in a game-like, competitive fashion to heighten J.'s motivation. A point system was built into all activities, and plastic chips were given to J. as a concrete representation of her score. J. earned bonus points (or chips) for identifying the times when she was losing focus or making errors. In all activities, stimuli were presented in an organized fashion (e.g., linear row) to encourage systematic search.

Sample Treatment Activities

Starting Activity: Eight coins are presented in a horizontal row. J. is required to pick up only the coins that are "heads up." To help her focus and systematically scan the stimulus array, she is encouraged to point to each coin and state aloud whether the coin is tails or heads up. Gradually, the use of this additional structure is faded.

Near Transfer: The same task is repeated with postage stamps, playing cards, or objects. For example, J. is required to pick out all the stamps that are upside down, or all the even-numbered playing cards, or all the objects that have the letter "A" in their spelling.

Intermediate Transfer: First, J. is required to look through a magazine and pick out pictures of things that would be appropriate to wear to a party. Second, J. plays simple computer matching games.

Far Transfer: First, J. undertakes simple cooking tasks. Initially all items are pre-selected and each step is presented one at a time. For example, making jello or pudding, and slicing and baking cookies. Second, J. engages in simple craft activities. In a tile activity, J. has to copy an alternating two color sequence. She chooses the tiles from approximately six tiles of three different colors. The selection demands are gradually increased. Third, J. engages in simple role playing and problem identification. Two therapists roleplay a problem situation in an exaggerated manner. For example, the two therapists are playing a card game and one therapist is not paying attention (e.g., looking around the room, trying to find something in her pocket, etc.). The patient is required to identify the problem behavior and receives points for identifying the problem accurately. The activity requires little or no social interaction among the group members. The main requirement is sustained attention on the role-playing scene that is positioned in the center of the room.

Both case examples presented a treatment plan based on dynamic investigative assessment. My intent was to illustrate how the assessment and multicontext treatment approach can guide the selection and progression of activities. Although improvements were seen in both cases, the changes cannot be attributed to the occupational therapy treatment approach because many factors (such as other treatments) were not controlled for. The efficacy of the multicontext treatment approach needs to be objectively examined through research methods.

Summary and Implications for Future Research

In this chapter, I have presented a dynamic interactional model of cognition as a foundation for occupational therapy assessment and treatment of cognitive dysfunction. This model was contrasted to traditional deficit specific and syndrome-specific approaches which have been guided by a narrow conceptualization of cognition. In the dynamic interactional model of cognition, learning and the ability to transfer information flexibly across task boundaries is seen as an integral component of cognition. Therefore, learning potential and learning transfer is directly addressed in assessment and treatment. This dynamic approach to cognitive rehabilitation is still in its initial stages of development. In this chapter, samples of assessment and treatment techniques that have been developed for the brain-injured adult and recently piloted on patients with schizophrenia manifesting negative symptoms were presented. The dynamic interactional assessment uses cues and task modifications to determine the conditions under which the patient is likely to succeed as well as those under which he or she is likely to fail. This information is directly related to treatment planning. The multicontext treatment approach involves practicing the same processing strategy with a variety of selected tasks, movement patterns, and environments. Learning transfer occurs at different levels and treatment attempted to facilitate the transfer process by combining training in multiple situations with strategy training and metacognitive training. If the patient is unable to transfer learning, then an intervention program that does not require transfer can be planned.

This approach must be explored further with developmentally disabled and psychiatric populations. In addition, this approach should be compared with other cognitive rehabilitation approaches developed for the brain-injured adult. Different brain-injured adults may respond differently to various approaches. The level of severity, stage of recovery, and type of cognitive dysfunction may influence the approach that is most effective. The specific assessment and treatment techniques presented in this chapter rely heavily on verbal mediation. Patients with significant language impairment, decreased alertness or severe sensory-motor impairment may not be capable of responding to verbal cues. In these cases, the same theoretical concepts described in this chapter can be applied; however, the specific assessment and treatment techniques must be adapted. For example, assessment tasks that analyze a patient's response to nonverbal cues such as imitation, additional visual cues, tactile-kinesthetic cues, and changes in environmental context or task parameters could be developed. While awareness training techniques and self-monitoring strategies described in this chapter would not be appropriate for these patients, awareness of cognitive capacity and the ability to recognize and correct errors could be promoted through tactile, kinesthetic, or visual feedback.

Many of the assessment and treatment issues I have touched on have not been well investigated in the adult brain-injured or psychiatric populations. The principles of dynamic assessment have been researched with learning disabled, mentally retarded, and normal children but they have not been well tested with adult populations. The reliability and validity of dynamic interactional assessment methods in measuring learning potential and cognitive modifiability needs to be established in the adult brain-injured population. The extent to which dynamic interactional assessment methods measure task-specific learning versus generalized learning potential is debatable. Transfer probes, or tasks that differ in surface characteristics but require the same underlying skills, could eventually be added to dynamic interactional assessments. In addition, the measurement models used in dynamic assessment are being refined and expanded. Some controversy exists over how standardized the cues need to be and whether traditional measurement models of reliability and validity should be used. Other areas of future research include the utility of dynamic interactional assessment in planning treatment, predicting the patient's response to intervention, and predicting the patient's performance on functional tasks.

There are also some questions surrounding the treatment issues addressed in this chapter. For example, the concept of awareness of cognitive capacity and self-monitoring skills, despite its importance has been poorly researched in clinical practice. Present standardized test measures do not even include an assessment of this function. With the exception of a few small studies, the question of whether awareness and self-monitoring skills can be improved in the brain-injured adult has been practically unexplored. No one has attempted to analyze the awareness training techniques that are most effective with different brain-injured populations. The effect of the nature of the environment and the activity, on learning has also been virtually unexplored in the brain-injured adult. Comparing treatment that takes place in the same environment versus multiple environments must still be investigated. In addition, research needs to compare treatment that is conducted with the same graded tabletop or computer activity to treatment consisting of a variety of different types of activities. The conditions that promote and facilitate learning transfer have been investigated in normal adults and children but, again, this area has not been investigated with the brain-injured population. Strategy use and strategy training also needs further investigation. Can brain-injured adults be taught to use processing strategies efficiently? What strategies are hardest and which are easiest for different types of brain-injured patients to use? Are there qualitative differences in the processing strategies used or not used among different psychiatric patients? Finally, treatment conducted in a predetermined hierarchical sequence needs to be contrasted with programs that are not conducted in a fixed sequence. In other words, the reductionistic approach to cognitive rehabilitation needs to be compared to the dynamic interactional approach.

This chapter provided a theoretical foundation as a guide for assessment, treatment, and future research. In it, I touched upon many issues that need further exploration with the cognitively disabled population. In the absence of evidence that demonstrates that one cognitive rehabilitation approach is better than another, clinicians need to continue to keep a broad perspective, critically analyze the results of their treatment, and ask many questions.

Acknowledgments
This chapter was prepared with support from the C. Scribner Jr. Fund, Department of Rehabilitation Medicine, New York Hospital-Cornell Medical Center, New York, New York.

I would like to extend a special thanks to Susan Fine, MA, OTR, FAOTA, for assistance in applying this model to mental health and for stimulating many thoughts and ideas.

References

Abreu B. C., & Toglia, J. P. (1987). Cognitive rehabilitation: A model for occupational therapy. *American Journal of Occupational Therapy, 41,* 439–448.

Adamovich, B., Henderson, J., & Averbach, S. (1985). *Rehabilitation of closed head-injured patients.* California: College Hill Press.

Anderson, J. (1985). *Cognitive psychology and its implications.* New York: W. H. Freeman & Co.

Anderson, S. W., & Tranel, D. (1989). Awareness of disease states following cerebral infarction, dementia and head trauma: Standardized assessment. *Clinical Neuropsychologist, 3,* 327–339.

Bandura, A. (1986). *Social foundations of thought and action: A social cognitive theory.* Englewood Cliffs, NJ: Prentice Hall.

Belmont, J. M., Butterfield, E. C., & Ferretti, R. P. (1982). To secure transfer of training: Instruct self-management skills. In D. K. Detterman & R. J. Sternberg (Eds.), *How and how much can intelligence be increased* (pp. 147–154). Norwood, New Jersey: ABLEX.

Ben-Yishay, Y., & Diller, L. (1983). Cognitive remediation. In M. Rosenthal, E. Griffith, M. Bond, & J. Miller (Eds.), *Rehabilitation of the head injured adult* (pp. 367–391). Philadelphia: F. A. Davis Co.

Bolger, J. P. (1982). Cognitive retraining: A developmental approach. *Clinical Neuropsychology, 4,* 66–70.

Bransford, J. (1979). *Human cognition: Learning, understanding and remembering.* Belmont, CA: Wadsworth.

Bransford, J., Sherwood, R., Vye, N., & Rieser, J. (1986). Teaching thinking and problem solving: Research foundations. *American Psychologist, 41,* 1078–1089.

Brown, A. (1988). Motivation to learn and understand: On taking charge of one's own learning. *Cognition and Instruction, 5*, 311–321.

Brown, A., Bransford, J., Ferrara, R., & Campione, J. (1983). Learning, remembering and understanding. In J. Flavell & E. Markman (Eds.). *Handbook of child psychology* (Vol 3, pp. 77–158). New York: John Wiley & Sons.

Brown, A. L., & Ferrara, R. A. (1985). Diagnosing zones of proximal development. In J. V. Wertsch (Ed.), *Culture, communication, and cognition: Vygotskian perspectives* (pp. 273–304). New York: Cambridge University Press.

Brown, A. L., & French, L. A. (1979). The zone of proximal development: Implications for intelligence testing in the year 2000. *Intelligence, 3*, 253–271.

Brown, A. L., & Kane, M. J. (1988). Preschool children can learn to transfer: Learning to learn and learning from example. *Cognitive Psychology, 20*, 493–523.

Campione, J. C. & Brown, A. L. (1987). Linking dynamic assessment with school achievement. In C. Lidz (Ed.), *Dynamic Assessment* (pp. 83–109). New York: Guilford Press.

Cermak, L. (1984). The episodic-semantic distinction in amnesia. In L. Squire & N. Butters (Eds.), *Neuropsychology of memory* (pp. 55–62). New York: Guilford Press.

Cicerone, K. D. & Tupper, D. E. (1986). Cognitive assessment in the neuropsychological rehabilitation of head injured adults. In B. P. Uzzell & Y. Gross (Eds.), *Clinical neuropsychology of intervention* (pp. 59–83). Boston: Martinus-Nijhoff.

Crossan, C., Barco, P. P., Velozo, C., Bolesta, M. M., Cooper, P. V., Werts, D., & Brobeck, T. C. (1989). Awareness and compensation in postacute head injury rehabilitation. *Journal of Head Trauma Rehabilitation, 4*, 46–54.

Crow, T. J. (1985). The two-syndrome concept: Origins and current status. *Schizophrenia Bulletin, 11*, 475–485.

Davis, E. S., & Radomski, M. V. (1989). Domain-specific training to reinstate habit sequences. *Occupational Therapy Practice, 1*, 79–88.

Embersetson, S. (1987). Toward development of a psychometric approach. In C. S. Lidz (Ed.), *Dynamic assessment* (pp. 141–170). New York: Guilford Press.

Feuerstein, R. (1979). *The dynamic assessment of retarded performers: The learning potential device, theory, instruments and techniques.* Baltimore: Univ Park Press.

Flavell, J. H. (1985). *Cognitive development.* Englewood Cliffs, NJ: Prentice Hall Inc.

Frostig, M., & Horne, D. (1973). *Frostig program for the development of visual perception* (revised edition). Chicago: Follett Publishing Co.

Gange, R. M. (1970). *The conditions of learning* (2nd ed.). New York: Holt, Rinehart, & Winston.

Gange, E. (1985). *The cognitive psychology of school learning*. Boston: Little, Brown.

Gianutsos, R. (1989). Foreword. In M. M. Sohlberg & C. A. Mateer (Eds.), *Introduction to cognitive rehabilitation: Theory and practice* (pp. vii–viii). New York: The Guilford Press.

Giles, G. M. & Wilson, J. C. (1988). The use of behavioral techniques in functional skills training in severe brain injury. *American Journal of Occupational Therapy, 42,* 658–669.

Gick, M. L., & Holyoak, K. J. (1983). Schema induction and analogical transfer. *Cognitive Psychology, 15,* 1–38.

Glisky, E. L., & Schacter, D. L. (1988). Acquisition of domain-specific knowledge in patients with organic memory disorders. *Journal of Learning Disabilities, 21,* 333–339.

Groveman, A. M., Brown, E. W., & Miller, M. H. (1985). Moving toward common ground: Utilizing Feuerstein's model in cognitive rehabilitation. *Cognitive Rehabilitation,* 28–30.

Jensen, M. R., & Feuerstein, R. (1987). The learning potential assessment device: From philosophy to practice. In C. S. Lidz (Ed.), *Dynamic assessment* (pp. 379–402). New York: Guilford Press.

Lidz, C. S. (1987). Cognitive deficiencies revisited. In C. S. Lidz (Ed.), *Dynamic assessment* (pp. 444–478). New York: Guilford Press.

Melamed, L., Rahamani, L., Greenstein, Y., Groswasser, Z., & Najenson, T. (1985). Divided attention in brain-injured patients. *Scandinavian Journal of Rehabilitation Medicine,* (Supplement), *12,* 16–20.

Neisdadt, M. (1990). A critical analysis of occupational therapy approaches for perceptual deficits in adults with brain injury. *American Journal of Occupational Therapy, 44,* 299–304.

Nolen, S. B. (1988). Reasons for studying: Motivational orientations and study strategies, *Cognition and Instruction, 5,* 269–287.

Pedretti, L. W. (1981). *Occupational therapy: Practice skills for physical dysfunction*. St. Louis: C. V. Mosby Co.

Rasch, G. (1960). *Probabilistic models for some intelligence and attainment tests*. Copenhagen: Danish Institute for Educational Research.

Seron, X. & Deloche, G. (1989). Introduction. In X. Seron & G. Deloche (Eds.), *Cognitive approaches in neuropsychological rehabilitation* (pp. 1–15). Hillsdale, NJ: Lawerence Erlbaum Associates.

Sternberg, R. J. (1985). Instrumental and componential approaches to the nature and training of intelligence. In S. F. Chipman, J. W. Segal & R. Glaser (Eds.), *Thinking and learning skills, Vol 2,* (pp. 215–243). Hillsdale, NJ: Lawerence Erlbaum Associates.

Sternberg, R. J. (1986). *Intelligence applied: Understanding and increasing your intellectual skills.* Orlando, FL: Harcourt Brace Jovanovich.

Toglia, J. P. (1989a). Visual perception of objects: An approach to assessment and intervention. *American Journal of Occupational Therapy, 44,* 587–595.

Toglia, J. P. (1989b). Approaches to cognitive assessment of the brain-injured adult: Traditional methods and dynamic investigation. *Occupational Therapy Practice, 1,* 36–57.

Toglia, J. P. (1991). Generalization of treatment: A multicontextual approach to cognitive perceptual impairment in the brain injured adult. *American Journal of Occupational Therapy, 45,* 6, 505–516.

Toglia, J. P. (in press). The contextual memory test manual. New York: New York Hospital—Cornell Medical Center.

Toglia, J. P. & Finkelstein, N. (1991). Test protocol: The dynamic visual processing assessment. New York: New York Hospital—Cornell Medical Center.

Toglia, J. P. & Golisz, K. (1990). *Cognitive rehabilitation: Group games and activities.* Tucson, AZ: Therapy skill builders.

Toglia, J. P. (1990, June). Cognitive rehabilition: Principles and practices. [Supplement manual to workshop conducted at New York Hospital, New York.]

Toglia, J. P. & Fine, S. B. (1990, November). Applying cognitive rehabilitation to mental health: Assessment and treatment strategies for schizophrenia. [Supplement handouts to workshop conducted at New York Hospital—Cornell Medical Center, New York.]

Trexler, L. (1982). Introduction. In L. Trexler (Ed.), *Cognitive rehabilitation conceptualization and intervention* (pp. 3–6). New York: Plenum Press.

Trexler, L. (1987). Neuropsychological rehabilitation in the United States. In M. Meier, A. Benton, & L. Diller (Eds.), *Neuropsychological Rehabilitation,* (pp. 437–460). New York: Guilford Press.

Wilson, B., Cockburn, J., & Baddley, A. (1985). *The Rivermead Behavioral Memory Test.* Reading, England: Thames Valley Test Co.

Vygotsky, L. S. (1978). *Mind in society: The development of higher psychological processes.* Cambridge, MA: Harvard Univ. Press.

6 □□□ □□□ □□□

A Dynamic Approach for Applying Cognitive Modifiability in Occupational Therapy Settings

Naomi Hadas and Noomi Katz

Acknowledgment: We would like to thank Tami Leja, OTR, Shalvata Psychiatric Hospital; Sara Averbuch, M.A., OTR, Loewenstein Rehabilitation Hospital; and Dr. Shlomo Laks Rehabilitation Center Herzelia, for their help and sharing of case examples.

The chapter comprises two main parts. In the first part, the theoretical base, the principles of Feuerstein's dynamic approach for cognitive modifiability in evaluation and treatment of cognitive deficits is presented, including its relationship and relevancy to occupational therapy. In the second part, we describe clinical applications in occupational therapy using instrumental enrichment. The three examples we discuss refer to intervention with brain-injured patients, psychiatric patients, and an adolescent with adaptational difficulties following a physical disability and social deprivation.

Theoretical Base

The dynamic approach for cognitive modifiability, as well as its assessment and treatment was developed by Feuerstein and colleagues between 1950 to 1960 in Israel. Feuerstein's (1979, 1980) work is based on extensive experience with Israeli adolescents who demonstrated mental retardation in intellectual performance due to their diverse cultural origins, disrupted lives, and limited opportunities to learn. His work provided the foundation for a general theory of cognitive competence, coupled with a technology for assessing learning potential (learning potential assessment device, LPAD). Feuerstein's emphasis in this approach is on improving functional deficits in the cognitive process through mediated learning experience (MLE) and instrumental enrichment (IE).

In general the approach is concerned first with the patient's ability to learn and solve problems; second, with examining why this ability fails to develop during early childhood in the absence of environmental enrichment; third, focusing on systematic learning mediated by a caring adult; and fourth, discovering how much later than generally thought possible identified cognitive deficits can be remediated by a formal instructional program.

The method of intervention started in the 1950s with the evaluation and treatment of adolescents suffering from cultural deprivation. Later, it was adapted to populations with learning disabilities or brain injuries, psychiatric patients, and geriatric patients. Recently it was also adapted to normal populations in industrial settings especially in France (Avanjini, 1990).

During the last ten years the approach has been used and adapted by Israeli occupational therapists with various patient populations such as patients with brain injuries, psychiatric patients, and adolescents with behavioral problems.

The Philosophy: Concept of Cognitive Modifiability

Instrumental enrichment represents an active modification approach as opposed to passive acceptance of the performance problems seen in patients with retarded cognition (Feuerstein, 1980). One characteristic of the former approach is the goal of changing the individual by providing him or her with the means to successfully adapt to his or her environment. In contrast, the passive-acceptance approach focuses on changing the environmental conditions to adapt to the low performance level of the mentally retarded individual.

The central issue is of whether the individual is viewed as an open or closed system, since the implications of this view are far ranging. Advocates of the active-modification approach view the individual as an open system that is receptive to change and modification. In this framework, modifiability is considered to be the basic condition of human beings. The individual's manifest level of performance at any given point in his or her development cannot be regarded as fixed or immutable, much less a reliable indication of future performance. This viewpoint has been expressed through the rejection of IQ scores as a reflection of a stable or permanent level of functioning. Instead, and in accordance with the open system approach, intelligence is considered a dynamic self-regulating process that is responsive to external environmental intervention. The view of the human being as an open system is utilized in various occupational therapy theoretical approaches most obvious in the model of human occupation (Kielhofner, 1985).

The assumption that the human organism is open and amenable to change demands a very different method of assessment and evaluation, whose purpose is to evaluate the individual's capacity to learn, and hence, to be modified. The purpose of assessment is to reveal the individual's potential and identify the deficient processes that may be impeding development. Treatment may then be directed at correcting deficiencies, by which the individual will be able to change the course of his or her development.

The aim of the IE program is to modify the individual's cognition by changing his or her internal structures rather than by only changing the environment. To appreciate this process-oriented approach, the therapist should specify the kind of changes the program will aim to produce. The term "cognitive modifiability" was chosen to convey the idea of a process of continuous and self-regulated change set into motion by the program. In the subject with mental retardation, the final process in reversing his or her low manifest level of performance is to cause a diversion from his or her current pattern of development, which requires an active interaction between the individual and the sources of external and internal stimulation. Once activated, the dynamics of modifiability propel the individual along a course of development that could not otherwise be anticipated on the basis of his or her previous performance. Among other factors, cognitive modifiability is a product of highly specific experiences and learning and is a means of adapting to the environment. The survival of any organism depends on its ability to adapt. For the human organism, successful adaptation involves the ability to respond not only to a constant and stable environment but also to situations and circumstances that are constantly changing.

The belief that intervention causes structural change is similar to the sensory integration theory in occupational therapy where changes are assumed to occur within the central nervous system causing adaptive responses to the environment (Ayers, 1979). Toglia (1989, 1991, and in Chapter 4) presents a dynamic approach to cognitive rehabilitation which is based on the same assumptions. In contrast, Allen's (1985) cognitive disability theory is based on the assumption that occupational therapy intervention centers on adapting the task and the environment to the patient's current capabilities. This direction also agrees with current approaches in rehabilitation

(Anthony et al., 1990; Neff, 1985) and may reflect the different target populations of each approach.

The Theory of Mediated Learning Experience

The theory of mediated learning experience (MLE) is the underlying theoretical basis for the concept of cognitive modifiability. The basic assumption in this theory is that the major factor causing cognitive differences among people is the MLE. Deficit or lack of MLE is a stronger explanation than any etiological differences.

Feuerstein conceives the development of cognitive structures in the organism as a product of two interactions between the organism and its environment: direct exposure to sources of stimuli and mediated learning. The first, and the most universal, modality is the organism's direct exposure to all sources of stimulation that it is exposed to from the very earliest stage of development. This exposure changes the organism by affecting its behavioral repertoire and its cognitive orientation. These changes, in turn, affect the organism's interaction with the environment, even when the environment remains constant and stable. Direct exposure to stimuli continues to affect the learning of the organism throughout its life span, to the extent that the stimuli present are varied and novel.

The second modality, which is far less universal and is characteristic of human beings, is mediated learning experience. By MLE we refer to the way in which stimuli emitted by the environment are transformed by a "mediating" agent, a parent, teacher, or therapist. This mediating agent, guided by his or her intentions, culture, and emotional investment, selects and organizes the world of the stimuli for the patient (student, client). The mediator selects stimuli that are most appropriate and then frames, filters, and schedules them. He or she determines when certain stimuli appear or disappear and ignores others. Through this process of mediation, the cognitive structures of the patients are affected. The patient/client acquires behavior patterns and learning sets, which in turn become important ingredients of his or her capacity to become modified through direct exposure to stimuli. Since direct exposure to stimuli over time constitutes the greatest source of the individual's experience, the individual's cognitive development is influenced significantly by whether or not the individual has sets of strategies and repertoire that permit him or her to efficiently use this exposure.

Conceptually the role of the mediator is in some ways similar to the role of the occupational therapist as a facilitator in the original occupational therapy philosophy and habit formation (Meyer, 1922, reprinted 1977; Slagle, 1922), as well as in the model of human occupation (Kielhofner, 1985), and in the sensory integrative approach (Ayers, 1979).

The relationship between MLE and direct exposure to stimuli, the two modalities for the development of cognitive structures, can be set forth as follows: The more often and the earlier an individual is subjected to MLE, the greater his or her capacity will be to efficiently use and be affected by direct exposure to sources of stimuli. On the other hand, less MLE developing individual is offered, both in quantity and quality, the lower his or her capacity will be to be affected and modified by direct exposure to stimuli. Feuerstein and Feuerstein (1991) outline 12 parameters that describe the quality of the MLE. The three main necessary parameters of the MLE are intentionality and reciprocity, transcendence, and mediation of meaning.

Intentionality and Reciprocity: MLE requires a degree of intentionality on the part of the mediator. The voluntary nature of the mediated interaction is evident in certain well-defined instances. The purpose is to increase the intentionality of the recipient and raise his or her awareness of the ways he acts in the same way that the concept metacognition is used by Toglia (in Chapter 4).

Transcendence: An interaction that provides mediated learning must also be directed towards transcending the immediate needs or concerns of the patient by venturing beyond the here and now, in space and time. This approach's premise is that working on transcendence is an integral part of the process of intervention.

Transcendence, in terms of the ability to make generalizations, is done according to MLE during the process of intervention. In contrast, cognitive retraining approaches assume generalization of abilities is a result of the treatment but not essentially a direct part of the process itself (Najenson et al., 1984; Siev et al., 1986).

Mediation of Meaning: In contrast to the first two parameters, mediation of learning deals mainly with the energetic dimensions of the interaction, with why things happen or are done. It raises the individual's awareness and understanding and makes explicit the implicit reasons and motivations for doing things. Mediation of meaning focuses on the interaction of the individual with the environment and aims to increase his or her ability to make choices.

The remaining nine parameters, unlike the first three, are not necessary conditions of MLE, but are considered reinforcing parameters (Feuerstein & Feuerstein, 1991, p. 15). The intentionality of the mediator and the transcendent (generalization) nature of mediated interaction is directed toward building new cognitive structures and broadening the individual's system of needs for functioning.

An individual may lack MLE because of two main reasons: First, the nature of the individual's environment (poverty, cultural deprivation, and disturbed families); second, the individual's condition at a given point in his or her development (learning disabilities, brain injuries, emotional disturbances, and mental retardation). The lack of MLE has the same manifestations regardless of the cause or diagnosis.

The goal of any intervention based on MLE is always to restore a normal pattern of development. The purpose of MLE, as reflected in the instrumental enrichment (IE) program, is never to train the individual merely to master a set of specific skills that will enable him to function only in a limited way. Instead the goal is to change the cognitive structures of the low performer and to transform him into an autonomous, independent thinker capable of initiating and elaborating actions. Thus, the focus is not on a direct functional approach but more similar to a cognitive remediation approach (Neistadt, 1990). Within the intervention process, the therapist works directly on helping the individual mediate structural generalizations.

In short, the goal set for the cognitively low performers according to the theory of MLE is adaptation to a normal environment as opposed to adapting the environment to meet the specific needs of these performers.

The Learning Potential Assessment Device

The dynamic assessment approach was developed to alter the cycle of failure which the low performer experiences in the classical intelligent tests (a static assessment approach). The measurement and remeasurement of an individual's existing capacities should be abandoned in favor of first inducing and then assessing the individual's modified performance within the test situation. By assessing modifiability, we must focus on the cognitive functions found to be directly responsible for the demonstrated deficiencies. We must also continually remember that these deficiencies are experienced by the patient at the input and output phases of the mental act, may be attributable to motivational and/or emotional components, and do not necessarily reflect the individual has a deficient elaborational capacity.

Four major components are changed in the LPAD when it is compared to classic assessment, including (1) The structure of test instruments: Intelligent tests were analyzed for their components and divided into various graded exercises; (2) the test situation and testing procedures: First, the relationship of tester/testee were transformed into teacher/student or therapist/patient (as described in the MLE) and, second, the assessment was not timed, only the length of the whole process was considered; (3) the interpretation of results: the focus is on the change process and the individual's investment in it, and no score is given; and (4) the general orientation of the test is from product to process.

The goals of such a dynamic psychometric evaluation are:

1. to assess an individual's modifiability when he or she is confronted with conditions that aim at producing a change in him or her;
2. to assess the extent of the observed modifiability in terms of the functional levels made accessible to the individual by the process of modification, and the significance of the levels he or she attained in the hierarchy of cognitive operations;
3. to determine how much intervention was necessary to bring about a given amount or type of modification;
4. to determine how much significance the modification achieved in one area can have for other general areas of functioning; and
5. to search for the individual's preferred modalities that represent areas of relative strengths and weaknesses, both in terms of his or her existing inventory of responses and in terms of preferred strategies for achieving the desired modification in the most efficient and economical way.

In using the LPAD, the therapist is not interested in passively collecting data about skills that the patient may or may not possess. Rather he or she assesses general learning modifiability by measuring the individual's capacity to acquire a given principle, learning set, skill, or attitude, depending on the specific task at hand. The extent of modifiability and the amount of treatment investment necessary to bring about the change are assessed respectively by (1) measuring the patient's capacity, first to grasp and then to apply these new skills to a variety of tasks progressively more distant from the one in which the principle was taught; and (2) measuring the amount of explanation and training required in order to produce the desired result. The significance of the attained modification is measured by the patient's developing patterns of behavior that prove his or her efficiency in areas other than those that were actively modified by the training process.

The use of this dynamic approach in assessment assumes that the individual represents an open system that may undergo important modifications through exposure to external and/or internal stimuli (Lidz, 1987). However, the degree of the individual's modifiability through direct exposure to various sources of stimulation is considered to be a function of the quantity and quality of mediated learning experience.

In the context of this theoretical model of cognitive modifiability, intelligence is defined as the capacity of the individual to use previous experience when adapting to new situations. The emphasis is on the use of previously acquired experience. One can measure an individual's modifiability only by using dynamic assessment, which attempts to provide a substitute for the missing experiential background using a concrete and focused intervention, and by providing the patient with the opportunity to demonstrate his or her growing capacities in a progressive way following the focused intervention.

Instrumental Enrichment—An Intervention Program for Cognitive Modifiability

We present instrumental enrichment in this chapter as an intervention strategy for the redevelopment of cognitive structures in the cognitively low performer. It is designed as a direct and focused approach to those processes that, because of their absence, fragility, or inefficiency, are responsible for poor intellectual performance, irrespective of underlying etiology. The IE program consists of more than 500 working pages of paper and pencil exercises, divided into 15 sections (see Table 1). Each part focuses on

Table 1   Instrumental Enrichment Materials

The nonverbal tools
1. Organization of Dots
2. Analytic Perception
3. Illustrations (Cartoons)

Tools requiring limited vocabulary
4. Orientation in Space I
5. Orientation in Space II
6. Orientation in Space III
7. Comparisons
8. Family Relations
9. Numerical Progression
10. Stencil Design

Tools requiring independent reading and comprehension skills
11. Categorization
12. Instructions
13. Temporal Relations
14. Transitive Relations
15. Syllogism

Additional tools
1. Absurdities
2. Analogies
3. Convergent and Divergent Thinking
4. Illusions
5. Language and Symbolic Comparisons
6. Maps
7. Auditory and Haptic Discrimination

a specific cognitive deficiency but can also address the acquisition of many other learning prerequisites. This structured approach assists the therapist (teacher) in his or her choice of the materials to be taught (used) and their sequence of presentation. By knowing the focus of each section, the therapist is able to select and match specific material to the needs and deficits of particular patients/clients. Intervention is either individual or in groups and takes place in approximately 3 to 5 sessions a week (Feuerstein, 1979).

Goals of Instrumental Enrichment

The major goal of IE is to increase the individual's capacity to be modified through direct exposure to those stimuli and experiences that occur throughout life and with formal and informal learning opportunities. In order to attain the major goal of IE during adolescence, the following six subgoals should serve as guidelines for constructing the IE program and its application: (1) Correcting the deficient functions in order to change the structure of the cognitive behavior; (2) Acquire basic concepts, labels, vocabulary, operations, and relationships necessary for IE as represented by the content of the materials, which themselves are purposely content-free; (3) Developing (producing) intrinsic motivation through habit formation (in order to ensure that whatever is taught will become part of an active repertoire, spontaneously used by the individual, one has to ensure that the need for its use will be an intrinsic one rather than a response to an extrinsic system); (4) Producing reflective, insightful processes in the student (patient) as a result of his or her confrontation with both his or her failing and successful behaviors in the IE tasks; (5) Creating task-intrinsic motivation, which has two aspects: the enjoyment of a task for its own sake, and the social implication of succeeding in a task that is difficult even for independent adults; and (6) Providing the cognitively low-performing individual with a self-identity that sees him- or herself as capable of generating information and his or her readiness to function as such, as a result of this self-perception.

Research

Research studies have traditionally centered on children and adolescents with learning disabilities, mental retardation, and cultural/social deprivation. Burden (1987) and Savell et al. (1986) review the research studies conducted about instrumental enrichment effectiveness. The first studies were performed in the 1970s and are reported in Feuerstein (1970). They focus on adolescents who immigrated to Israel from North Africa. The studies attempted to show the effectiveness of the IE program with a pre-post design and a matched control group, which received enrichment in general content areas (the GE group). Their findings showed significant differences in the experimental group over the control group in non-verbal IQ tests. No significant improvement was evidence in self-concept in either of the groups.

However, the original studies were criticized for their methodology and data analysis.

The largest body of data on this topic has been collected in the United States in the late-1970s and covers a few years in five large centers using various populations (Burden, 1987). The findings reinforce the original study's results, showing significant increase of IQ scores (especially on the Raven Matrices) following the IE program. Additional studies with similar methodologies have also shown the same trends in their results.

One longitudinal study was conducted in which 187 subjects of the original group were tested two years later after they entered the Israeli army service. Half of the group was from the IE program and the other half from the GE control group. The results show highly significant differences between the two groups; they display, according to the authors, cumulative gains over time.

In a few additional studies, the effects on noncognitive measures (self-esteem, motivation, locus of control, and the approach to problems) were reported to increase following the IE program (Savell et al., 1986).

Research studies within the adult populations were not conducted until recently. In a few studies, reporting about the effects of IE with college students, results were not significant. According to the authors, this suggests that IE may have more impact during adolescent years, but these results should be verified in additional studies (Savell et al., 1986).

In summary, the theory behind and the practice of the IE program and the LPAD assessment are still under development, and research studies are being conducted in many countries world wide and by different professionals. It has also been recommended for inclusion in the framework of cognitive rehabilitation in the adult brain-injured population (Groverman et al., 1985; Toglia, 1989).

Intervention

In the dynamic approach for cognitive modifiability outlined above, evaluation and treatment are interwoven and are undertaken together during intervention.

Instrumental Enrichment in Occupational Therapy and Target Populations

Instrumental enrichment in Israel has been used with the adult population for the last decade. It is used mainly by occupational therapists who specialize on rehabilitation of adolescent and adult populations with varied dysfunctions (physical, cognitive, emotional, or behavioral). IE is used in conjunction with the evaluation and treatment of daily living skills (ADL), vocational/professional skills, and social skills in occupational therapy, as well as during the process of rehabilitation from the hospital to the community.

The goals of the occupational therapist in this approach are twofold: (a) improvement of underlying structures, and (b) adaptation of the person to his environmental circumstances. Enrichment is used in all three phases of rehabilitation: medical rehabilitation, transitional setting of rehabilitation, and during vocational and social rehabilitation in the community. Regardless of etiology, IE is used with populations who suffer from cognitive, emotional, and/or adaptational dysfunctions. Table 2 presents the goals and methods of treatment in these populations.

The treatment process according to IE to be used in occupational therapy will be demonstrated with three populations: (1) in a brain-injured population suffering from cognitive deficits during medical rehabilitation, (2) in a psychiatric or emotionally disabled population in a transitional rehabilitation setting, and (3) in a population with adaptational difficulties in a community rehabilitation center.

Cognitive Treatment for Brain-Injured Patients Using Instrumental Enrichment in a Medical Rehabilitation Center

The Loewenstein Hospital is a major rehabilitation center in Israel for traumatic head injuries (due to accidents, army service, or various tumors). The average age of the patients is young—about 30 years old. Patients are transferred to the Loewenstein Hospital from acute care hospitals immediately after intensive medical treatment is terminated. Patients arrive to the Loewenstein Hospital at different levels of independence and confu-

Table 2   The Use of Enrichment in Different Populations

Type of Dysfunction	Treatment Goals	Treatment Methods
Cognitive	The improvement of dysfunctional skills: perception, thought, and memory processes	Individual
Emotional	The improvement of personal and interpersonal behavior, and of cognitive flexibility	Group and individual
Adaptational	The improvement of social and cognitive skills; the development of coping mechanisms for adaptation to reality	Mainly individual

sion—from bedridden or sitting in a wheelchair but unable to stand, dress, eat, or wash unassisted, to those seemingly independent, that is, able to get around the hospital and get to treatment sessions on their own.

The treatment of patients at this point revolves around the area of deficit and is adapted to the needs of the injured patient at any given moment (Katz et al., 1990; Najenson et al., 1984). The emphasis here is on treatment not on education; therefore, the use of the enrichment tools is not used exactly as in the IE program. An instrument is not followed through all its exercises. An impaired skill will be exercised with suitable parts (working pages) from different sections. Exercises (not from the enrichment program) at the same level and style may be added. The multitude of materials at graded levels enable systematic and broad treatment of a specific deficit.

Instrumental Enrichment and Spatial Orientation Problems

The treatment relates to four aspects: the individual's physical ability to perform daily living activities, the place (table) where he or she works on the pages of the instrumental enrichment program, the immediate surroundings (hospital, ward), and the nonimmediate surroundings (city, country). The tools of the enrichment program used in treatment, are organized in ascending order of difficulty, as follows:

Orientation in Space I, II, and III: Spatial orientation has three sections that intervene directly in one of the most commonly observed deficiencies of the cognitively disabled performer: his or her limited use of articulated, differential, and representational spatial dimensions.

The first of the three sections deals with spatial orientation relative to one's own body using one's own movements for the frame of reference. The second part adds dimensions of topological space: on, above, below, up, down, and between. The third part deals with an external and stable reference system, the cardinal points of the compass, which is then combined with the first two reference systems. These three parts are directed primarily toward the creation of specific strategies for differentiating the spatial frame of reference from other criteria. They also introduce and demonstrate the relativity of certain systems versus the stability of others.

Organization of Dots: Each of the 26 working pages of organization of dots contains between 14 to 18 exercises. The teacher provides the learner with ample opportunities to engage in various functions, to understand the role they play in the specific exercises, and to become aware of the roles these activities play in their own motor behavior. The motor aspect of the task is to identify and outline, within an amorphous cloud of dots, a series of overlapping geometric figures such as squares, triangles, diamonds, and stars. The molecular components of the task are numerous and reflect a wealth of elements that can directly challenge the difficulties experienced by the cognitively low performer. The exercises therefore are addressed to the correction of a variety of deficient cognitive functions: (1) projection of virtual relationships, (2) conservation of constancy, (3) visual transport, (4) precision and accuracy, (5) summative behavior, (6) planning and restraining impulsivity, (7) discrimination, and (8) segregation of proximate elements.

Analytic Perception: The analytic perception part consists of 38 working pages. In the first units it includes such tasks as subdividing a simple or complex whole into its parts, summing up the number of the components, and finding parts that are identical to the given standard within a complex whole. In order to find a part, the individual must allow sufficient time to completely and accurately perceive the part, transport it visually (or through interiorization) into the field, and engage in a systematic search.

In the exercises of the second unit, the parts of a whole are identified, categorized, and summated. Tasks involve seeking strategies for the recognition, registration, and inclusion of the relevant components into a whole. In the third unit, tasks deal with constructing wholes based on identifiable parts and the closure of figures on a gestalt test by deducing the parts that are missing and identifying them in another setting. The last unit provides subjects with practice in constructing new wholes from the union of some of the parts. Tasks range from pure perceptual exploration to transposition and transformations of the elements.

Instrumental Enrichment in the Development of Thought Processes

The treatment begins with the simple and moves to the more complex: from single to multiple, from individual to the whole community. The IE tools include stimuli in many areas: visual, verbal, and numerical. The IE sections used in the treatment of thought processes from simple to complex are as follows:

Comparisons: Comparisons deal with the development of spontaneous comparative behavior. Comparative behavior is the most elementary building block of relational thinking and, therefore, a primary condition for any cognitive process that will transcend mere recognition and identification.

The comparisons part consists of 22 working pages. The first unit introduces the subject to the concept of commonality and the differences in pictorial and verbal modalities. In the exercises, the subject must compare two items on discrete dimensions, which start with size, form, number, and spatial and temporal concepts and conclude with abstract attributes not immediately perceived (such as function, composition, and power). In the second unit, the subject compares objects to a standard along several dimensions simultaneously. In the exercises of the third unit, the learner is required to establish classes.

Categorization: Categorization is designed to address the lack of, or impairment of, the learner's ability to elaborate on gathered data by using hierarchically higher mental processes for the organization of the data into superordinate categories. Classification is based on successful comparison, differentiation, and discrimination.

The categorization part consists of 31 working pages, divided into units and graded by complexity. The instrument is presented using verbal, pictorial, schematic, and figural modes. It is based on skills and procedures learned in comparisons and leads to the instrumental syllogism section.

Numerical Progressions: The major focus of this part is to train the learner to search for the rules that form the basis of certain experienced events and the relationships that exist between them.

Transitive Relationships: The transitive relations part has 23 working pages. It focuses on drawing inferences of new relationships from those existing between object and/or events, that can be described in terms of "greater than," "equal to," and "less than." In the first five pages of this part, the person is introduced to the concept of ordered sets and the signs used to designate relationships. In the first exercise, he or she is offered strategies for ordering the data and encoding it in such a way as to have the coded information present in the visual field.

Representational Stencil Design: The representational stencil design is an advanced level in the instrumental enrichment program. It capitalizes on functions the subject has acquired in the other parts (e.g., organization of data, analytic perception, comparisons, categorization, spatial orientation, and temporal relationships) and permits their application to situations that require rather complex levels of representational internalized behavior.

The representational stencil design part consists of working pages which require the learner to construct mentally, not through motor manipulation, a design that is identical to that in a colored standard. Colored stencils, of which some are solid and some are cut out, are printed on a poster. The learner recreates mentally the given design by referring to the stencil that must be used, and by specifying the order in which they must be superimposed on each other.

In summary, the adaptation of IE to the treatment of people suffering from head injuries requires that: (1) *the treatment is individualized:* it must be adapted to each person according to his or her specific deficits and conditions; (2) *the treatment focuses on cognitive skill:* using the whole range of materials (Working through all parts of the instrument is not significant; it is more important to use stimuli that are appropriate to the specific deficit); (3) *the treatment is progressive and very slow:* Sometimes it is necessary to add similar exercises to the treatment, even if they are not part of the enrichment program; and (4) *the treatment uses illustration when necessary:* In the spatial orientation working pages, sometimes the therapist must build a three-dimensional model (e.g., with Lego), or cut out a figure of a person from a cartoon and stand it up to provide a concrete illustration. In order to help in the analysis and synthesis exercises, the therapist must cut out the parts and help the patient assemble them again into a design.

Instrumental Enrichment for Psychiatric Patients or Those Who Are Emotionally Disabled

Shalvata Psychiatric Hospital in Israel includes a half-way rehabilitation unit for patient evaluation and preparation for rehabilitation in the community. The patients treated in the unit usually have had a record of psychiatric hospitalization and have usually had diagnoses of various types of schizophrenia. The age range of the population is from 18 to 40 years. The main goal of the unit is to prepare patients for social and vocational rehabilitation in the community. The enrichment program within this unit is done mostly in groups of 4 to 5 patients.

There are three objectives of treatment. The first involves improving the patient's cognitive ability and flexibility in using existing skills; focusing on the process of adaptation to changing situations; and learning of problem-solving techniques, such as decision making, organization, and planning. Second, treatment focuses on improving the patient's social skills and integration into a work group; specifically by moderating impulses, developing the ability to listen as well as to accept orders and criticism; and, finally, to be able to express him- or herself. Third, the treatment tries to raise the patient's awareness of his or her strengths and weaknesses, and to learn how to use his or her assets for adaptation.

To demonstrate a group process, we will describe an example of a group session that centered on awareness to work needs. The working page 9 from the comparison section of the IE program was utilized. [See page example in Figure 6-1.]

Circle the word or words that describe what is common between the sample picture on the left and each of the pictures in the same row.

Sample Picture

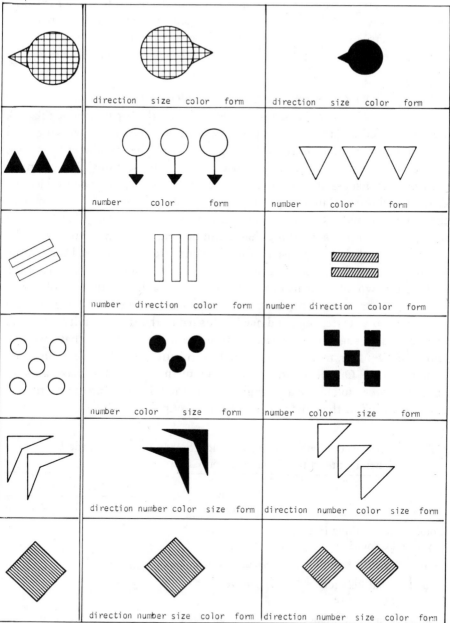

Figure 6-1 Working page 9 from the Comparison section of Feuerstein's Instrumental Enrichment Program.

The purpose of this exercise is to help the patient automatize comparisons, to perceive the basis for classification, and to correct his or her episodic grasp of reality. The patient learns to find similarities and differences between objects, events, and ideas. He or she learns to use concepts and to identify the most essential or characteristic dimensions, while ignoring the irrelevant.

Page 9: Circle the Common Objects

The activity in this group included three parts: First the task was performed as given on the page. Each person received a working page and had to complete it individually. Second, during the session, criteria were pointed out (these have been described in preceding sections). For example, the therapist discussed with the group the concept of objective and subjective criteria, and the explanations/interpretations of these terms by the people in the group was used. *Objective* was defined as (a) "something that I am not involved in," or (b) "something that is not dependent on me." Following the individual work, a group discussion was conducted on the need for criteria when making a choice or a decision. For example, when and why one of the participants would compare two ashtrays on the table according to objective criteria (such as color, shape, size, material, and weight) and by subjective criteria (such as taste, goal, and need). This led to the third activity, in which at the group's suggestion, participants made a list of things that "we can choose in life:" car, mate, house, schools, furniture, where to live, profession, and workplace. Out of the initial list, they further decided to make a list of criteria in order to choose a workplace; they included subjective criteria and compared each of their own criteria to the group's (see Table 3).

Table 3 The Needs that Work Fulfills and Their Importance in the Eyes of Participants in the Rehabilitation Group[a]

Needs	Maslow's Hierarchy	Participants				
		1	2	3	4	5
Comfortable Working Hours; Pay, Good Conditions	Basic Needs	+	0	0	+	−
Tenure, Security, Safety	Security Needs	+	+	+	+	+
Good Personal Relations, Pleasant Atmosphere	Love Needs	+	+	+	+	+
Evaluation and Acceptance	Evaluation Needs	−	0	−	0	+
Interest, Advancement, Development	Self-Actualization Needs	0	0	−	−	+

[a] The first list of needs was compiled by the group participants. The second list is according to Maslow's hierarchy of needs for comparison. The scale as follows: (+) very important; (−) not important; (0) of little importance.

Intervention of this kind, allows the therapists to raise the individual's awareness of himself or herself to his or her needs at any given moment and in comparison to the rest of the group. As Tzuriel (1991) states, the affective motivational factors play an important role in the reciprocal interaction of MLE and cognitive modifiability.

The treatment had two goals: (1) forming an awareness of the practical necessity for activating the cognitive functions treated by this tool; (2) the spontaneous use of cognitive skills for the purpose of adaptation or preparation for the work role.

It is interesting to note, in Table 3, that the needs of belonging, love, and security (second and third in Maslow's Hierarchy of Needs) are the most important needs for all members of the group. Only one participant pointed out the highest need in the hierarchy—self-actualization—as important to him. The causal relationship between needs and cognitive functions was recently stated by Rand (1991). He incorporates the concept of need as one component in an integrative model based on MLE. Need is defined as "an internalized energizing psychological system which is function bound" (p. 80).

Importance of Instrumental Enrichment with the Emotionally Disabled

IE is used in this setting to (1) focus on behavioral elements, both personal and interpersonal; (2) help the individual relate to others (the treatment is done mainly in groups); (3) place emphasis on integration processes, awareness of one's capabilities and their utilization; and (4) to follow the exact order of the IE working pages when appropriate (although pages are often chosen out of order to best suit the needs of the group).

Instrumental Enrichment in a Population with Adaptational Difficulties

The rehabilitation center in Herzeliya is one of the 20 community vocational rehabilitation centers in Israel that serve a heterogeneous population of age, type of injury, and gender. The common denominator for this population is the limitation of employment. The patient's dysfunction can be: cognitive, emotional, physical, developmental/learning, or cultural deprivation, or any combination of the above.

The rehabilitation center has a number of activity centers: diagnosis and reality workshops that aim to develop vocational skills; production workshops on different levels; as well as secretarial, sewing, and cooking workshops. The interdisciplinary team includes social workers, psychologists, counselors, occupational therapists, and placement specialists.

At the center, the two major goals of rehabilitation identified were as: (1) that the client should be able to work in the community either in the open market or in a partially/sheltered or sheltered workshop; and (2) that the client will be able to live independently in the community.

Some of the clients in the workshops also receive a few extra hours of treatment per week based on the enrichment program. They learn basic general educational subjects and, as with everyone else, have sessions with a social worker. The success of enrichment therapy depends on optimal coordination between the various team members.

The goals of enrichment in this framework are as follows: (1) to improve cognitive flexibility and adaptability (this capacity to change will enable the rehabilitation client to adapt to the work reality in his or her community); and (2) to improve and enhance the client's work habits, including his or her ability to follow a time schedule, to produce an end result, to accept orders and criticism, and to work independently.

With these goals in mind, the therapist chooses from the IE working pages the following areas:

Organization of Dots. (This section has already been described.)

Orientation in Space. (This section has already been described.)

Analytic Perception. (This section has already been described.)

Transitive Relations. (This section has already been described.)

Temporal Relations: This section is geared towards retraining the person's perception of time and his or her capacity to register processes and order temporal relationships.

Instructions: Instructions is one of the few sections in the whole program in which verbal factors play an important and central position. Language is emphasized as a system for both encoding and decoding processes on a variety of levels. These range from simple labeling after recognition, to the use of inferred instructions deduced from combining given instructional codes and the presented stimuli. The individual must read and carry out instructions and use the three phases of the mental act in a systematic and orderly way: Input—gathering of the data; elaboration—ordering the object in the required relationship; and output—carrying out the instruction by drawing the required figures.

Syllogism: The mastery of this concept indicates an ability to engage in inductive and deductive reasoning under highly abstract conditions. (Sections such as family relations and cartoons are very rarely used.)

Case Example

One example of treatment involves an adolescent with a mild physical disability since birth and social deprivation which were expressed as adaptational difficulties.

Eli was 15 years old when he started coming to treatment. He was born in Yemen, the third of five children. His father is a plumber, the mother a kindergarten teacher's helper. Eli has had a deformation of his right hand from birth. He is considered the least successful or the "black sheep" of the family. He attended a regular school until the seventh grade and was then referred to neuropsychological and vocational evaluation. His main assessment results indicated that he has psychomotor restlessness (i.e., he uses his right hand only to assist the left; he works quickly but not efficiently; he tires easily; he works impulsively; and he follows only short assignments/tasks). His shape perception is normal, as are his perception of models and memory of simple material. He has more difficulty when planning is required. His thought processes are concrete, yet his logical thought is deficient; he works on a trial-and-error basis and has no self-criticism.

The team's recommendations following evaluation were that Eli should be given simple and short tasks that could be changed easily, and that he should also be provided with cognitive training.

The first phases of rehabilitation included: production workshops, for habit training; a study program in basic education; two-part enrichment which treated Eli's behavior problems (impulsivity, low self-esteem) and his cognitive problems (using strategies, complexity, oral material, attention, and concentration).

At the beginning of the treatment, Eli would hide his right hand and talk very little (and then with a limited vocabulary). His self-expectations were very low—to be a production line worker. While talking, he would not make direct eye contact. His gaze was "scattered," not concentrated, and he looked inefficient.

The second phase of rehabilitation included transferring Eli to the secretarial workshop due both to his request and based on our evaluation that he has the potential to learn. In his studies, he was busy gaining basic knowledge and learning new terms, learning to read and write, and improving his ability to formulate sentences and summarize material.

In the enrichment program with Eli we used working pages from the organization of dots; analytical perception, categorization—knowledge of general terms; instructions—the treatment of impulsivity, concentration, and receiving orders; cartoons—language improvement; and numerical progression. After a year of treatment in the center, at Eli's request he was enrolled into secretarial school. Two years later, Eli is currently working as a teller in a bank. He is independent and does not receive any treatment.

Enrichment is important in a community rehabilitation center because:

(1) the work must be coordinated with the other aspects of treatment the client is receiving; (2) the focus is on adaptation to a general setting, especially to a work environment; (3) the order of the IE sections is not binding: The choice of working pages is done according to the treatment subject; and (4) the treatment is individual: The population in the center is very heterogenic, and sometimes small groups can be formed to emphasize interpersonal relationships and working together.

Summary

Instrumental enrichment is, first and foremost, an approach to understanding the relationships between the individual and other persons, and (only afterwards) is it a treatment method. The enrichment program is special in that it is: *optimistic* (it supports the belief that everyone has the potential to learn and change in every situation, if the right way is found), *holistic* (it considers all aspects of the person: cognitive, emotional, and behavioral), and *flexible* (it can be applied to all ages, to different needs, and various treatment settings). Instrumental enrichment agrees with occupational therapy philosophy and rehabilitation. It relates to the person as a whole despite his or her disabilities, and tries to improve the individual's quality of life and self-esteem.

Implications for Further Development in Occupational Therapy

As mentioned earlier, almost all research has been performed on children and adolescents. Studies on the effectiveness of instrumental enrichment with adult disabled populations should be done. Qualitative methods should be utilized in such studies because they are probably more appropriate for understanding treatment outcomes of this dynamic intervention process. Theoretically, it is important to continue the conceptual work integrating the philosophy and theory of cognitive modifiability and mediated learning experience with occupational therapy principles. Clinically, it is important to analyze tasks and try to combine the IE materials with evaluation and treatment tools and methods utilized in occupational therapy.

References

Allen, K. C. (1985). *Occupational therapy for psychiatric diseases: Measurement and management of cognitive disabilities.* Boston: Little, Brown.

Anthony, W., Cohen, M. & Farber, M. (1990). *Psychiatric rehabilitation.* Boston: Center for Psychiatric Rehabilitation.

Avanjini, G. (1990). *Pedagogies de la mediation.* Autour du P.E.I. programme d'enrichissement instrumental du Professeur Reuven Feuerstein. Lyon, Depot Legal: Chronique Sociale.

Ayers, J. (1979). *Sensory integration and the child.* Los Angeles: Western Psychological Services.

Burden, R. (1987). Feuerstein's Instrumental Enrichment Programme: Important issues in research and evaluation. *European Journal of Psychology of Education, 11,* 1, 3–16.

Feuerstein, R. (1970). A dynamic approach to the causation, prevention, and alleviation for retarded performance. In H. C. Haywood (Ed.), *Sociocultural aspect of mental retardation* (pp. 341–377). New York: Appleton-Century-Crofts.

Feuerstein, R. (in collaboration with Y. Rand & M. B. Hoffman.) (1979). *The dynamic assessment of retarded performers. The learning potential assessment device, theory, instruments, and techniques.* Baltimore: University Park Press.

Feuerstein, R. (in collaboration with Y. Rand, M. B. Hoffman & R. Miller.) (1980). *Instrumental enrichment. An intervention program for cognitive modifiability.* Baltimore: University Park Press.

Feuerstein, R., & Feuerstein, S. (1991). In R. Feuerstein, P. S. Klein, & A. J. Tannenbaum (Eds.), *Mediated learning experience.* London: Freund Publishing House, pp. 3–51.

Groverman, A. M., Brown, E. W., & Miller, M. H. (1985). Moving toward common ground: Utilizing Feuerstein's model in cognitive rehabilitation. *Cognitive Rehabilitation,* May/June, 28–30.

Katz, N., Hefner, D., & Reuben, R. (1990). Measuring clinical change in cognitive rehabilitation of patients with brain damage: Two cases, traumatic brain injury and cerebral vascular accident. *Occupational Therapy in Health Care,* 23–43.

Kielhofner, G. (1985). *A model of human occupation, theory, and application.* Baltimore: Williams & Wilkins.

Lidz, C. S. (1987). *Dynamic assessment. An interactional approach to evaluating learning potential.* New York: The Guilford Press.

Meyer, A. (1922, reprint 1977). The philosophy of occupation therapy. *American Journal of Occupational Therapy, 31* (10), 639–642.

Najenson, T., Rahamani, L., Elazar, B., & Averbuch, S. (1984). An elementary cognitive assessment and treatment of the craniocerebrally injured patient. In B. A. Edelstein & E. T. Couture (Eds.), *Behavioral assessment and rehabilitation of the traumatically brain damaged,* (pp. 313–338). New York: Plenum Press.

Neff, S. W. (1985). *Work and human behavior,* (3rd ed.). New York: Aldme Publishing Company.

Neistadt, M. (1990). A critical analysis of occupational therapy approaches for perceptual deficits in adults with brain injury. *American Journal of Occupational Therapy, 44*, 299–304.

Rand, Y. (1991). Deficient cognitive functions in non-cognitive determinants—An integrating model: Assessment and intervention. In R. Feuerstein, P. S. Klein, & A. J. Tannenbaum (Eds.), *Mediated learning experience*, (pp. 71–93). London: Freund Publishing House.

Savell, J. M., Twohig, P. T., & Rachford, D. L. (1986). Empirical status of Feuerstein's "Instrumental Enrichment" (FIE) technique as a method of teaching thinking skills. *Review of Educational Research, 56* (4), 381–409.

Siev, E., Freishtat, B., & Zoltan, B. (1986). *Perceptual and cognitive dysfunction in the adult stroke patient.* Thorofare, NJ: Slack.

Slagle, E. C. (1922). Training aids for mental patients. *Archives of Occupational Therapy, 1,* 11–17.

Toglia, J. P. (1989). Approaches to cognitive assessment of the brain injured adult: Traditional methods and dynamic investigation. *Occupational Therapy Practice, 1,* 36–57.

Toglia, J. P. (1991). Generalization of treatment: A multicontext approach to cognitive perceptual impairment in adults with brain injury. *American Journal of Occupational Therapy, 45* (6), 505–516.

Tzuriel, D. (1991). Cognitive modifiability, mediated learning experience and affective motivational processes: A transactional approach. In R. Feuerstein, P. S. Klein, & A. J. Tannenbaum (Eds.), *Mediated learning experience*, (pp. 95–120). London: Freund Publishing House.

7

The Process Approach
for Cognitive-
Perceptual and
Postural Control
Dysfunction for Adults
with Brain Injuries

Beatriz Colon Abreu and
Jim Hinojosa

In this chapter, we introduce a process approach for occupational therapy intervention for cognitive-perceptual and postural control dysfunction. The theoretical base for this approach is grounded in information processing theory, learning theories, neuropathology, and the therapeutic use of activities. The theoretical base provides an appropriate foundation for occupational therapy intervention with the adult brain-injured population. We also describe intervention, including screening and evaluation, which emphasizes the use of both qualitative and quantitative strategies. Further, the process approach supports that occupational therapy intervention is unique in its use of activities for the evaluation and treatment of clients with a variety of disabilities. We conclude the chapter with a discussion of the implications for further research and the direction of the development of this approach.

Theoretical Base

The process approach for adults with brain injury is derived from perceptual-cognitive and motor learning theories. In addition, it incorporates the occupational therapist's knowledge and skills of activities to enhance occupational performance. A process approach uses systematic, interactive methods for evaluation and treatment (Abreu, 1990). The approach provides therapists with criteria to use as guidelines for interacting with clients and the use of activity analysis and synthesis. This approach is labeled as a process approach because the therapist needs to continuously adjust the sensitivity of evaluations and interventions to the client's fluctuating abilities (See Figure 1).

Cognitive-Perceptual and Postural Control

Cognition, perception, and motor are typically considered distinct performance components. We discuss each performance component as though it could be isolated from the other, and therefore present them as separate areas of human functioning. In reality, however, they are closely related and may overlap.

Cognition and perception are defined in a variety of ways (Abreu & Toglia, 1987; Bernspang, et al., 1989; Zoltan, Seiv, & Freishtat, 1986). Definitions vary depending upon the clinician's particular theoretical orientation. Clinically, cognition and perception are difficult to differentiate from each other. In reality, it is almost impossible to differentiate between cognitive

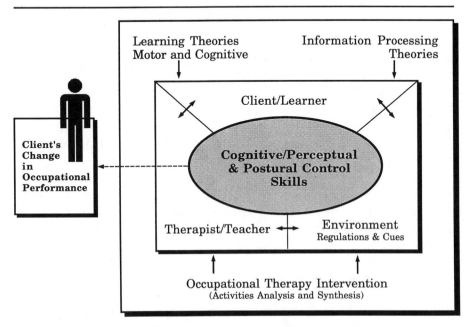

Figure 7-1 A process oriented approach.

and perceptive processing. Both cognition and perception include sensory recognition and interpretation. Further, both are personally subjective processes by which individuals search, acquire, manipulate, and judge sensory information from the environment (Abreu, 1981). Therefore, cognitive-perception has been selected to be used in this chapter to refer to the two processes as one system.

Like every performance component, the motor performance component is divided into numerous minute classifications. Some of these classifications are: reflex integration, coordination, range of motion, strength, and endurance (Mosey, 1981). An alternative functional way of looking at the motor performance component is postural control, which is the ability to perform movement strategies to maintain and regain balance positions. Postural control is defined in this chapter to refer to all the body processes that allow a person to move within the environment.

As previously stated, cognitive-perceptual and postural control are two different systems. However, in this chapter we discuss them as parts of an integrated system, reflecting the importance and influence that each system has on the other. This perspective is based on the assumption that cognitive-perceptual and postural control have common underlying principles and strategies. Both systems underscore the importance of individuals interacting within their environments. In addition, this perspective accepts the assumption that the ability to use language influences the levels of interaction adults have in their environments. Language gives meaning to objects. For example, language allows adults to know what objects are and what objects do (affordances) (Reed, 1988).

In order for the brain to function optimally a harmony must exist between all its cortical and subcortical units (Luria, 1973). This concept highlights the assumptions that the brain works as an integrated whole. Therefore, within the central nervous system each structure affects many other structures. No one section of the central nervous system or its peripheral structures has been identified as exclusively associated with cognition or perception.

Cognitive-perception is primarily a cortical process that allows individuals to acquire and manipulate information. The process requires modulation, classification, organization, and assimilation of information (Abreu, 1985). The focus of our chapter will be on attention, memory, and problem solving. Functionally, cognitive-perception helps individuals adopt cortical and subcortical strategies to maintain or enhance the ability to problem solve and interact with the environment during external and internal distractions (Abreu, 1989).

Under normal conditions, all sensory receptors contribute to movement and posture (Nashner, 1972, 1976). The receptors most associated with postural control are: (a) the ocular receptors, which control the ability to process objects visually; (b) the vestibular receptors, which deal with inertial and spatial qualities in the environment; and (c) the tactile and proprioceptive receptors, which sense the person's supporting surfaces such as the floor or chair seat (Nashner, 1972, 1976). Another important function of these receptors is to help the individual sense the position of his or her joints and how much velocity is needed in his or her movement in order to maintain posture (Schmidt, 1968).

Postural control is primarily a subcortical process that allows an individual to maintain his or her center of mass for righting and/or balancing him- or herself. Functionally, postural control helps an individual to adopt cortical and subcortical strategies to keep his or her center of mass within a stable support base during external or internal disturbances in equilibrium (Abreu, 1989).

The cognitive-perceptual and postural control systems both rely on cortical and subcortical strategies (Abreu, 1990). In return, individuals use these strategies to solve postural control or cognitive-perceptual problems. These problems are solved in an environment that has internally and/or externally generated equilibrium disturbances and disturbances caused by predictable or unpredictable sources. Artificial separation of the cognitive-perceptual system from postural control system does not give credit to the relationship between understanding and action. Both systems share common strategies and principles. Both systems involve the individual interacting with the environment, as a unit, incorporating symbolic language to summon action.

Environment

Environment is the aggregate of relevant characteristics from activities, conditions, circumstances, or objects that surround individuals (Gentile, 1972). Motor theories highlight the impact that environment has on movements and postures (Adams, 1971; 1986; Gentile, 1987; Pew, 1974; Schmidt, 1968; 1975; 1980). The environment plays a role in anticipatory muscle activity, as well as for the timing of the muscular activity (Lee, 1980; 1984; Nashner, 1985). Therefore, the environment has a direct effect on postural control.

An individual's cognitive-perceptual skills enable him or her to understand and apprehend his or her environment. Through cognitive-perception, an individual identifies the critical features of his or her environment that regulate postures. The critical features of the environment are referred to as environmental regulations. An individual who effectively interacts with his or her environment can attend to and adjust to a variety of environmental demands. These demands influence both the postures and movements of individuals. Normally, an individual processes information from his or her environment to move efficiently. He or she processes information from relevant characteristics in the environment and suppresses irrelevant characteristics. The relevant characteristics of the environment are those critical features that have to do with the goal of the movement. In sum, the environment is both influenced by and has an influence on the individual.

Each environment has different processing demands for the cognitive-perceptual and postural control systems. One important facet of an environment is its predictability, which refers to its consistent spatial and temporal characteristics. For example, when sitting at a typewriter, the typewriter does not move and the individual's responses are fixed. An unpredictable environment has characteristics that are variable and changing. For example, when returning a serve while playing tennis, the force and timing of the serve affect the response of the other player. Thus, the unpredictable environment has spatial and temporal characteristics that randomly change.

The environment has a direct impact on the traits of motor behaviors, which are separated into closed and open skills. Closed skills are usually performed in a predictable environment, thus employing feedback which allow for error detection and correction. Predictability of the environment allows individuals to correct motor behaviors based upon direct feedback. Open skills are usually performed in an unpredictable environment, thus typically not providing feedback for error detection and correction. Open skills are characteristic of highly skilled sports in which individuals must have rapid response rates to perform the motor behaviors successfully.

An environment also triggers recognition and recall schemas, which are rules or relationships based on previous experience (Schmidt, 1988). These schemas are part of cognitive-perception and provide individuals with memories of previous experiences in similar environments. They allow individuals to generate movements or postures that would appropriately match the person's environment, tasks, goals, and purposes.

Information Processing

In an attempt to simulate the human nervous system as a machine, engineers developed information-processing theory. Engineers and psychologists, making an analogy between machines (computers) and the way that people think, noted the similarities of computer processing to the thinking process. The information-processing model specifies three stages of sensory processing: (a) detection of the stimulus, (b) discrimination and analysis of the stimulus, and (c) responses based on a hypothesis derived from the relationship between current sensory stimuli and past experiences (Abreu & Toglia, 1987). Note, all this activity occurs in only seconds.

Information-processing theory can be useful for explaining some behaviors typically seen in adults with brain injuries. Information processing considers an individual to be a progammer of information: An individual sequentially processes information in successive stages at various levels within the central nervous system. Each level of processing deals with the same information but in a different way. As information is processed at different transformation levels, new operations are performed on both previous and additional information. Because an individual is the processor of information, the observed performance of the individual is the end result of a sequence of processing stages.

Information-processing theory contains four major assumptions about the processing of information. First, one must attend to the stimulus event in order for it to be registered. Second, registered sensory input is analyzed and the information is interpreted and organized for discrimination. Third, interpreted and organized information is integrated into a repertoire of appropriate responses. Fourth, human responses inherently involve errors. In other words, humans are fallible and therefore no response can be guaranteed to be correct with 100% accuracy. In this manner, information processing highlights important elements for learning.

Information processing identifies the processing stages for cognitive-perceptual functioning. It does not provide insight or explain how the individual evaluates or uses cues from the environment. Therefore, a learning theory is needed to complement the information-processing theory.

Learning

Learning is a change in an individual's capacity to respond to the environment and is associated with practice or experience. Learning theories tend to relate to specific areas of human performance such as cognitive, cognitive social, or motor learning. Within these guidelines, elements of two learning theories will be used as part of the theoretical base: cognitive learning and motor learning.

Motor learning focuses on acquisition of skill movement as a result of practice (Schmidt, 1988). Peculiar to motor learning theories is the belief that motor learning has "a strong ecological emphasis, stressing the notion that our motor system was created through evolution and interactions with the physical characteristics of the environment" (Schmidt, 1988, p. 15). Thus, all motor learning theories recognize the importance of environmental influences on motor acquisition.

Both cognitive and motor-learning theories consider the environment to be an important change agent. Environment is divided into external and internal parts. The internal environment includes the sensation and ideas that generate from one's own inner self. The external environment includes the physical surroundings, consisting of nonregulatory and regulatory aspects. Environmental regulations are the aggregate of relevant characteristics from activities, circumstances, or objects that surround a person (Gentile, 1972). These characteristics regulate the response for an individual task (Lee, 1989). On the other hand, non-regulatory conditions are those characteristics of activities, circumstances, or objects that surround a person but are not critical to regulate the response.

Co-environmental fit refers to the match between an individual and his or her environment. Co-environment has two significant components: congruence and interference. Congruence is the match between an individual's goal and motivation and the environmental regulations. Interference is the degree of variation or difficulty in matching an individual's goals and motivation with environmental regulations. These two concepts help explain the strategies that people use when interacting with their environment. The interplay between congruence and interference determines the degree of difficulty a person will face in performing a task.

Different environments put different demands on individuals. An important environmental variable is the degree of its predictability, including the spatial and temporal features. A predictable environment has critical features that are stationary and temporally fixed, thus allowing for error detection and correction. Thus, it is easier for an individual to deal with predictable environment. Because an unpredictable environment has critical features that are spatially and temporally variable, error detection and correction are more difficult. It may be harder, therefore, for a person to deal with an unpredictable environment because he or she needs to anticipate the response. To function optimally, an individual must be able to respond in both types of environments.

Different environments require different kinds of skills. The skills performed in a predictable environment are closed skills. Closed skills are used when performing tasks in an environment that remains constant, such as when writing, bowling, or washing one's hands. Skills performed in an unpredictable environment are open skills and these are used when individuals cannot effectively plan the response due to the changing nature of the environment. Open skills are characteristic of sports where participants must make on-the-spot decisions (Gentile, 1972; Schmidt, 1975; 1988). Currently, disagreement surrounds what environmental condition is most appropriate for enhancing the acquisition of any type of cognitive-perceptual or motor skill. Some experts advocate the advantages of training in a predictable environment that focus on closed skills (Gentile, 1972; 1987). Other experts propose the use of the unpredictable environment for acquisition of both open skills and closed skills (Schmidt, 1975; 1988). They predict that schema (or rules) are learned more effectively if the experience that leads to their acquisition is variable rather than constant. These experts further propose that an individual learns schemas or rules in practice sequences. These schema or rules are the relationships of previous environmental outcomes what actions were used to produce those outcomes.

Finally, this theoretical discussion focuses on specificity of learning as described by Barnett et al. (1973); Bower, (1981); and Henry, (1968). Each author concludes that optimal learning takes place in an environment that simulates an environment in which the task will be performed. Moreover, the transfer of learning from one task to another is specific: the more similar the environments, the better the transfer of learning. Transfer of learning, therefore, depends on similarities between both task and environment.

Activities

Occupational therapists use a variety of therapeutic activities for assessment and treatment of deficits in cognitive-perceptual and postural control systems (Abreu, 1990; Eggers, 1984; Warren, 1991). Although therapists are using activities to define, describe, and interpret patient disabilities (Allen, 1987), therapists show disagreement on the optimal type of activities and the activities' uses for evaluation and treatment. The primary reason for this controversy is that activities are complex. They are difficult to categorize because of the multiple interrelated elements and multiple dimensions that make up the activities. Furthermore, speed, quantity, time span, sensation, feedback, and activity phase are examples of activity characteristics.

Rehabilitation of adults with brain injuries encompasses the use of therapeutic activities to evaluate and promote function. Activities are often used to address deficits in both cognitive-perceptual and postural control (Abreu, 1985; Ryerson, 1985). Often, therapeutic goals involve activities to relearn cognitive-perceptual or postural control strategies (Abreu, 1990; Eggers, 1984). The use of activities in intervention requires that therapists examine and analyze the activities. First, the therapist engages in activity analysis. During this process the therapist distinguishes the component parts of the activities. Next, the therapist either uses the activities in their current form or synthesizes the activities in a way that is appropriate for evaluation or treatment (Mosey, 1981).

In this chapter, we present guidelines for the use of activities in intervention for adults with brain injuries who experience deficits in cognitive-perception and postural control. Our intervention is guided by the belief that occupational therapy's unique contribution to therapeutic intervention is the skillful, therapeutic use of activities for screening, evaluation, and treatment.

Postulates for Change

This section describes principles used by occupational therapists to manipulate environments to move clients from states of dysfunction to states of function. During this process, function is maintained and interfering behaviors are managed.

Activities, as previously defined, are one important aspect of the environment. Therapists use activities, the client's interactions and responses to activities, and other aspects of the environment to create situations for change. Consistent with information-processing theory, occupational therapists select activities that involve specific processing at particular levels of the central nervous system. If the client attends to the stimulus events of the activities, then registering the stimulus event is feasible. If the client detects the information, then their ability to analyze information for use is feasible. If the client is able to analyze the information, then the client can compare the stimulus events with long-term memories and relate the stimulus to the overall purpose and goal of the activities. All of these postulates are influenced by recognizing the caveat premised in information-processing theory that human performance, by its nature, includes some error.

Being involved in activities (a critical aspect of occupational therapy) intrinsically includes learning, which occurs as clients engage in practice. Through practice or experiences with the activity, the client's capability to respond to or interact with the environment changes. Therapists structure the environment, which includes activities, to facilitate change in the client's repertoire of behaviors. Learning is facilitated when activities are at an appropriate level and challenging to the client. Activities are graded on various continua depending on the client's learning needs. One appropriate continuum, proposed by Fitts (Fitts & Posner, 1967) is a three-phased hierarchical control model for learning. Phase I (cognitive) specifies that a learner's performance is heavily based on cognitive and verbal processes. Phase II (associative) specifies that the learner establishes motor patterns. Finally, phase III (autonomous) specifies that the task becomes automatic.

Target Populations

The process approach for cognitive-perceptual and postural control dysfunction is appropriate for adults with brain injuries and includes individuals with a variety of diagnosis such as head trauma, cerebral vascular accident, and brain tumor.

Adults with brain injuries have a variety of disabilities or impairments secondary to acquired brain damage. Brain damage results in impaired ability to process information from the environment (Luria, 1966, 1973; van Zomeren, Bouwer, & Minderhoud, 1987). Due to the damage to the central nervous system, adults with brain injuries have less available processing capacity than normal, healthy individuals (Diller & Gordon, 1981). This reduced processing capacity impedes their ability to attend to relevant stimuli while simultaneously suppressing irrelevant stimuli from the environment. Unlike normal, healthy individuals who can select what to attend or respond to within a variety of contexts, adults with brain injuries are bound by over- or under-attentiveness and over- or under-responsiveness to environmental stimuli or cues. In addition, adults with brain injuries have fewer effective strategies for problem solving both in cognitive-perceptual and postural control performance areas (Diller & Gordon, 1981; Lee, 1989).

Adults with brain injuries have a variety of deficits depending upon the extent of damage and the locus of the central nervous system lesion. There is no known one-to-one relationship between the locus, the extent, and the functional deficits.

Typically, adults with brain injuries have motor, cognitive-perception, language, and visual deficits. These deficits may come from local or diffuse brain damage. Whether the brain injury is local or diffuse, clients may experience atypical responses to sensory stimuli (Carter, Oliveira, Duponte, & Lynch, 1988), which may result in unusual perceptions and responses to the stimuli. These altered behaviors impair the client's ability to function independently in everyday living (Pelland, 1986). As a group, adults with brain injuries, tend to have difficulty in four major areas: attention, motor performance, sensory reception, speech and language (Abreu, 1981). Regardless of specific deficits, adults with brain injuries tend to have difficulty processing information from their environment.

Adults with brain injuries demonstrate common patterns of motor deficits related to postural control. For example, postural control is related to symmetrical weight bearing and weight shifting (Bobath, 1978; Mizhari et al., 1989). Because brain damage is correlated with the disappearance of symmetrical weight bearing and weight shifting (Bobath, 1978; Mizrahi et brain injuries tend to demonstrate asymmetries in weight bearing and weight shifting. Specifically, they tend to bear weight and shift weight less toward the affected side, which is usually opposite the brain lesion. These asymmetries may also contribute to changes in the client's postural strategies. For example, some clients are unable to perform distal movements that would impair postural control and they develop alternative proximal strategies to maintain posture and balance (Nashner, Shumway-Cook, & Marin, 1983).

Brain damage is associated with impairment of attentional skills, which are necessary for cognitive-perceptual efficiency. The associated impairments include: insufficient alertness, inability to selectively attend to relevant stimulation and filter out irrelevant stimulation, inability to sustain attention over an extended period of time, and inability to shift attention which causes response perseveration (Ben-Yishay, Rattok, & Diller, 1979). Any of these attentional deficits may impair the client's learning or interfere with his or her ability to complete activities of daily living. These attentional deficits may also contribute to a change in the client's cognitive strategies. In addition, some adults with brain injuries visually scan information randomly and appear to use inefficient schemes.

Classification of Specific Impairment

A variety of ways to classify the nature of the specific impairments secondary to brain damage have been proposed. One popular classification system divides the disabilities according to the affected performance components. Psychological, social, motor, cognitive, sensory, and perceptual are examples of classifications. These classifications are considered to be mutually exclusive; therefore, client's dysfunctions are viewed as though they could be divided into separate components. However, in reality, there is considerable overlapping among the components. Additionally, controversy exists regarding what information actually is included in each separate component. To address this issue, occupational therapists have created new components, which involve one or more systems. For example, many therapists use the terms sensory-motor, sensorimotor, perceptual-motor, or psychosocial. To understand the deficits that are secondary to brain injury, therapists need to assume clustering of the components.

The functional approach is an alternative method of classifying the nature of the specific impairments. This approach classifies the client according to deficits within occupational performance areas. Some occupational therapists describe this approach as holistic, because the client is perceived as a whole operative human being. This approach is limited in that it does not recognize that a performance component deficit may possibly be the cause of the client's inability to perform a particular task.

Finally, some occupational therapists feel that one must examine deficits in both the performance components and the occupational performance areas. This approach highlights the assumption that inabilities can be the result of only one or a combination of factors. We chose this approach to use in this chapter. Essentially, the hypothesis states that through the use of activities, occupational therapists can assess both the performance components and the occupational performance areas.

Intervention

Occupational therapists select activities with particular characteristics for both evaluation and intervention. The therapist judges and modifies the characteristics of the activities according to need. Speed, quantity, time span, sensory, feedback, and activity phase are the characteristics that this chapter addresses. Speed is the rate of presentation and performance. Quantity is the number of segments, pieces, items, or steps in the activity. Time span encompasses the duration of presentation and engagement. Sensory refers to the combination of sensory systems that are inherent to the activities or the process? Feedback is more complex because it includes externally generated and self-generated detection and correction. Feedback also includes knowledge of performance and results and is ongoing throughout the cycle of the activities, varying at different stages of the cycle (beginning, middle, or end). Finally, activity phase refers to the cycle that identifies the distinguishing parts of the activities.

Because we view activities as part of the environment, (as discussed earlier), the environment should also be included as an aspect of the activity analysis, during both assessment and intervention. Therefore, occupational therapists should examine the environment for congruencies and potential interferences.

Parallel to our discussion of activity characteristics, the environment has its own equivalent characteristics. The environment may be moving or stationary, and the stability of the environment may determine, to a certain extent, the speed at which activities need to be performed. For example, if the environment is the supporting surface for sitting or standing and it is moving, the processing speed needs to be adjusted. Quantity is the amount of critical stimuli in the environment. Pertaining to sensory, each environment stimulates a different sensory avenue. Feedback subsumes the implicit and explicit environmental rules for actions by affecting expectations for reactions, interactions, or transactions (Cynkin & Robinson, 1990). Finally, environmental conditions may affect the activity cycle.

In the process approach, occupational therapy intervention (including both evaluation and treatment) involves continuous analysis of the client's performance. Occupational therapists use activities as well as standardized assessments to measure changes in a client's functional behavior. During treatment, activities are systematically presented to gradually increase demands on the client's processing. Treatment is conceptualized as a three-phase continuum of detection, discrimination and analysis, and hypothesis generation.

Evaluation Methods

The evaluation assumption for this approach is that traditional naturalistic (qualitative) and experimental (quantitative) methodologies can be used and combined as guidelines for evaluation. When standardized tests and measurements are used, therapists must be sure the attributes of validity and reliability are preserved. The process approach extends the evaluation guidelines beyond the limits of standardized evaluations to allow for the identification of underlying skills through verbal and non-verbal actions and interactions.

Occupational therapy assessment of adults with brain injuries is structured around the use of particular activities and the examination of influential environmental factors. Assessment of function in the cognitive-perceptual and postural control performance components is quantified and judged. Analysis of these results allows the therapist to identify a client's strengths and difficulties. Ultimately, the client's performance directs the therapist's selection of the activities and environments used for treatment. The selection of the specific environments and activities used reflect the therapist's clinical judgments and preferences. Furthermore, the occupational therapist's theoretical orientation and the degree and extent of client's brain injury determine the selection and use of the activities.

Additionally, occupational therapists may employ standardized evaluations, which comprise selected activities from empirical investigations to assess for specific deficits. Systematic investigation is based on the use of a specific set of instructions. The use of these instructions and protocols have been supported by empirical investigations, which have established the reliability, validity, and normative data for each specific instrument. Further, a systematic investigation establishes the populations for which the evaluation is reliable. When determining which normative data is appropriate for use with the client with brain injuries, the therapist must evaluate the sample size and diagnostic categories that were used in the systematic investigation to determine the normative data. Standardized testing is a quantitative aspect of the assessment and only provides some of the information that is needed. It should be noted that whenever standardized tests are administered, standardized procedures should be followed.

Qualitative data is collected during the entire assessment process. This data is collected in two ways. First, the qualitative data is obtained during the client's performance on standardized instruments. The therapist notes observations related to the client's performance. Second, specific qualitative techniques such as interviewing and observation provide qualitative data. Qualitative data analysis requires therapists to use their clinical reasoning skills to formulate a clinical judgment related to the client's performance. This clinical reasoning process involves a series of systematic, analytical steps. It is characterized by reasoning that begins with sorting data into categories, comparing these categories, finding apparent uniformity, and, finally, formulating possible patterns of behaviors. The client's approach to and execution of the tasks are often more relevant than activity completion. The client's approach, execution of the tasks, and appraisal and use of feedback or cues are all critically important.

During both the quantitative and qualitative aspects of the assessment, therapists analyze the environment, the tasks or activities included in the assessment process, and the performance of the client. The interactive, dynamic assessment process outlined earlier reflects the traditional beliefs about assessment that individual differences are as important as standardized norms.

Although the assessment of cognitive-perceptual skills requires a comprehensive battery of tests, two suggested assessment areas have been selected to illustrate this assessment method. Functionally, two important aspects of the cognitive-perceptual performance component are attention and problem-solving skills.

Attention

Attention subsumes the ability to handle increasing amounts of information. Attention dysfunction is characterized by a failure to deal with all the information necessary for optimal task performance.

Attention has four components: (1) insufficient alertness which refers to a lack of readiness of the central nervous system to receive information, or lack of readiness to discharge motor units; (2) impaired selectively, which refers to the inability to choose relevant information and simultaneously suppress irrelevant information, or the inability to selectively use the proper muscular activity and simultaneously inhibit unnecessary muscular activity; (3) poor sustainment, which refers to the inability to maintain focus, concentrate, and persist with an activity or task, or the ability to maintain muscle activity; and (4) inflexibility, which refers to the inability to rapidly shift from one thought or activity movement to another. Characterized by rigidity or perseveration of thought or action (Ben-Tishay, Rattok, & Diller, 1979).

Problem Solving Skills

Both the cognitive-perceptual and postural control involve problem-solving skills. Motor planning aspects of postural control also encompass problem-solving. Problem-solving impairments include: (1) ineffective problem recognition, which refers to the lack of awareness or reflection that an alternative or satisfactory solution is needed; (2) unsatisfactory condition analysis, which refers to the inability to study all the aspects of the problem before attempting a solution; (3) inefficient strategy selection and execution, which refers to the inability to plan and carry out the selected solution; and (4) solution vertification, which refers to the inability to compare the final solution with the original problem.

Evaluating Behaviors and Physical Signs that Indicate Function and Dysfunction

Behaviors and physical signs, if any, that indicate function and dysfunction describe the specific behaviors and/or physical signs that occupational therapists must observe to judge whether the client is functioning closer to function or dysfunction. This is important because dysfunctions are not discrete factors indicating an all-or-none phenomena. The behaviors and physical signs clearly outline the extreme ends of each continuum (see Table 1). These lists of behaviors and physical signs must be used relative to the client's age, socioeconomic status, life style, or other important factors that define function for that particular individual. Therapists use these behaviors to make clinical judgments as to whether a person's behavior is functional or dysfunctional.

It should be noted that specific tests are not recommended in this chapter. The selection of an appropriate assessment is determined by the therapist's clinical judgment, knowledge, and skills in test and measurement. Often, occupational therapists select a nonpsychometric approach and use relevant activities, tasks, and roles to assess a client's cognitive performance. For standardized assessments the readers are encouraged to refer to Mitchel (1985).

When assessing and recording a client's functioning using the process-oriented approach, we recommend scoring performance based on increased accuracy secondary as a result of cuing. This scale is divided into four sections: (1) independence, performs accurately without the needs for cues; (2) limited dependence (50 to 75% accuracy), accuracy depends on cues but cues do not need to be used continuously; (3) modified dependence (25 to 50% accuracy), accuracy depends on continuous cuing; and, (4) dependence (0 to 25% accuracy), accuracy does not increase with cuing.

Reporting the assessment results must include use of clear, concise, and accurate terminology. The therapist's descriptions of impaired performance must contain qualifications that clearly identify the level of function. Inaccurate responses or performances need to be labeled by what influenced the response or performance (e.g., cuing, modification).

Treatment Approach

The process approach as used by occupational therapists is designed to ameliorate or minimize the effects of the dysfunctions. Activities that gradually increase demands on the client's processing are systematically presented. Gradation is from simple to complex, conscious to subconscious, effort to effortless, external to internal control, and internal to external

Table 1 Measures of Function and Dysfunction

Function	Dysfunction	Evaluation Device
Alertness		
Appropriate reaction times, based on the demands of the activity (if fast, respond fast, if slow, respond slow)	Slow or fast delayed reaction time. Difficulty with activities or tests that measure the response in reference to stimuli	Reaction timers, computer software that measures reaction time
Selectively		
Controlled ability to select a stimulus from a noisy (competing) environment	Visually unable to discriminate a figure from a superimposed or embedded background. Difficulty with activities that require visual figure-ground discrimination. Auditorially unable to discriminate a sound from a noisy background. Information may need to be obtained from either an audiologist or speech pathologist. Client is excessively distracted by noises in the environment during conversations. Unable to select the appropriate motor activation to complete a desired action. (Electromyographic study can reveal critical information about the motor unit activation.) When engaged in an activity, a client may delay initiation of a motor response.	Digit span tests and rhythm scales
Sustainment		
Controlled ability to maintain the effort and concentration required for the demands of the task	Unable to maintain long periods of concentration. Cannot complete prolonged visual vigilance tasks. Client has difficulty with activities that require continuous attention for more than 15 minutes.	Vigilance tasks and cancellation tasks

Table 1 Measures of Function and Dysfunction (Continued)

Function	Dysfunction	Evaluation Device
Alertness	Unable to maintain long periods of muscle contraction. Asymmetrical weight bearing and shifting is characteristic of movement. When engaged in activities, the stereotypical motor behaviors of ineffective synergies are exhibited.	
Flexibility Fluently and easily shifts from one thought to another	Difficulty shifting from one thought to another. Poor performance on activities that require changes in formats or sets (shifting from numbers to sets). Perseverates on thoughts or becomes rigid in his/her thinking.	Trail-making tests and Stroop
Fluently and easily shifts from one motor act to another	Difficulty shifting from one motor act to another. Cannot perform reciprocal movements; interactions of body segments producing combined movement of upper and lower extremities. These difficulties are not necessarily due to muscle tone but to motor planning difficulties. During activities the client cannot smoothly move from one posture to another.	
Problem Solving		
Problem recognition Identifies that a problem exists	Unable to identify that there is a problem. Cannot discern the meaning of the instructions when visu-	Activities, role or task that involve the ability to generate solutions for a problem in a variety of categories

183

Table 1   Measures of Function and Dysfunction (Continued)

Function	Dysfunction	Evaluation Device
Problem Solving	ally or auditorially presented with a problem. During an activity, the client does not realize that there is anything astray.	
Condition analysis Discriminates the critical elements needed to solve the problem	Unable to distinguish the critical elements needed to solve a problem. Demonstrates restriction in the number of inputs that he or she can analyze. Does not perceive the whole problem; sees only the parts. Focuses on one feature. Attempts to solve a problem based on overvaluing one salient feature, ignoring other critical features. When engaged in an activity, solely concentrates on one action or one feature of the activity. Focuses on many features that are not critical for the solution of the problem. When engaged in an activity, focuses on irrelevant factors or features and therefore does not select the critical feature on which to focus. Responses are slow and inefficient.	Activities, role or task that involve the ability to generate solutions for a problem in a variety of categories
Strategy selection and execution Smooth, coordinated completion of the task or activity	Impaired or inability to complete the task or the activity.	Activities, role or task that involve the ability to generate solu-

Table 1 Measures of Function and Dysfunction (Continued)

Function	Dysfunction	Evaluation Device
Problem Solving	Selection of ineffective cognitive-perceptual strategies, resulting in solution of the problem with excessive energy and time. No systematic approach to select and execute the solution. Tends to use trial and error and random strategies in an attempt to solve a problem. Selection of ineffective postural control strategies, resulting in motor solution with excessive motor activation or inappropriate motor behaviors. Does not use distal strategies for postural control. May use either excessive or inadequate motor actions to accomplish a task. May over- or undershoot.	tions for a problem in a variety of categories
Solution verification Uses error detection and error correction to improve performance.	Unable to use error detection and error correction to improve performance. Unable to use or has difficulty using feedback to verify knowledge of performance to determine if the problem is being solved satisfactorily. Further, has difficulty using knowledge of results or task completion to determine if the problem was solved satisfactory.	Activities, role or task that involve the ability to generate solutions for a problem in a variety of categories. Solutions are to be checked against the information given to the client

(self) regulation. Drawing from the information-processing concepts in the theoretical base, three phases of treatment can be identified. Phase I (detection) emphasizes the ability of the client to be aware of and detect the stimuli. Phase II (discrimination and analysis) centers on the ability of the client to distinguish, organize, and manipulate sensory information. During phase III (hypothesis generation), the client establishes relationships between the current stimuli and past experiences. These phases do not constitute a fixed hierarchy, as they all occur simultaneously. Therefore, although similar activities may be used during all three phases of intervention, one phase may emphasize one activity more than another.

Phase I: Detection

The activities that are used during phase I—detection—must have instructions that are short and clear to avoid overloading instruction with excessive speech and language. Therapy objectives during this phase are to facilitate the client's awareness and detection of the self-goal and the strategies of the task. Accordingly, important elements of the activities are their salient traits and the regulating factors in the environment. When selecting activities, therapists should determine the appropriateness of the activities relative to the client's status based on recovery level. Cognitive-perceptual and postural control status are also considered with regard to the client's co-environmental fit, that is, the match between the client and the therapeutic environment. It should be noted that the cognitive scale for clients may range from comatose to minimal dysfunction.

Phase II: Discrimination and Analysis

The activities that are used during phase II, discrimination and analysis, must provide feedback to the client. Salient traits of activities and the regulating factors of the environment are now considered relative to the inherent structure of activities. Therapy objectives during this phase are to facilitate the client's consistent discrimination of the self-goal and the strategies of the task in a variety of environments. Accordingly, important elements of the activities (beyond their salient traits and the regulating factors in the environment) are their structure, spatial and temporal demands, and feedback methods. When selecting activities, therapists should determine the activities' appropriateness by matching the client's abilities with the appropriate environment and activities. Therapists need to provide two types of environments. Static environments, which include activities, allow for easier self-detection and correction; they are used to establish basic discrimination and analysis. Dynamic environments, which also include activities, provide less feedback and opportunities for error detection and correction. They are used to promote a more automatic discrimination and analysis response to stimulus events. To be involved in sports, the individual must predict and anticipate the spatial and temporal characteristics of the dynamic environment. Sports and exercises that involve prediction and anticipation are, therefore, highly recommended as therapeutic activities.

Phase III: Hypothesis Generation

The activities that are used during phase III, hypothesis generation, require the client to solve a problem and refine his or her responses. Salient traits of the activities and the regulating factors of the environment, as well as the inherent structure of activities, are considered relative to unique problems and the outcome of the individual's actions. Therapy objectives during this phase are to facilitate the client's cognitive-perceptual introspection skills for categorization, planning, and organization. Accordingly, important elements of the activities are their requirement for organization, abstraction, and memory used to solve a problem. When selecting activities, therapists should determine the appropriateness of the activities by the client's speech and language abilities. Clients are encouraged to communicate (verbally and nonverbally) their strategies to accomplish a task. They are then provided with alternative environments in which to use the same strategies to help them retain the effective strategies.

Phase III, hypothesis generation, is also influenced by cognitive strategies that underlie the client's responses. Cognitive strategies, which can be conscious or subconscious, are organized sets of rules that operate to select and guide the ability to process information (Gagne & Briggs, 1974). Because the strategies that were used prior to the client's brain injury are not readily available, the client's current interactions with the activity and the environment are not always successful. At times, clients may engage in an activity but the engagement does not result in an appropriate adaptive response. Therefore, intervention related to phase III, hypothesis generation, should include strategies that involve conscious awareness of the procedural steps inherent in the activity. Some of these strategies are planning ahead, choosing a starting point, pacing responses, and checking accuracy and quality of the results (Abreu & Toglia, 1987).

Environment

In general, therapists can only design environments or select activities. The client is the one who must interact with the environment for learning to take place (Mosey, 1986). We should note, however, that the therapist is part of the therapeutic environment. As such, the therapist's interactions, including the conscious use of self and the teaching-learning process, are important therapeutic agents.

As occupational therapists intervene with clients, they must be aware that the relationship between activity and environment is not a simple one. The therapist cannot be assured that a specific activity will result in a specific response. Therapists must take the following into account: client expectations or anticipations; habituation to the activity; client's secondary gains for not engaging in the activity or failing; and, other factors related to the client's sociocultural, life style, or personal bias. Further, and most important, therapists need to consider that clients may not want to engage in the activity for personal reasons—just because he or she does not feel like it.

In summary, occupational therapists design therapeutic environments that use activities to match the client's dysfunction in order to promote function. Thus, occupational therapists address the client's disabilities while facilitating the client's strengths. Using a variety of environments and activities, occupational therapists provide clients with experiences they will be able to transfer to the real world when they return.

Case Study

Ms. Rodriguez is a 20-year-old woman who sustained a severe, closed-head injury in a motor vehicle accident 2 years ago. Diagnosis included left skull fracture with right parietal infarct and left vocal cord damage. The last CT scan showed changes in the occipital region bilaterally with slight prominence of left occipital horn of the left lateral ventricle. Cranial nerve lesions sustained at cranial nerve III (oculomotor), VII (facial), IX (glossopharyngeal), and X (vagus). Health professionals documented that Ms. Rodriguez has a variety of visual, motor, voice, and social dysfunctions. Her visual impairments included accommodative insufficiency, nystagmus, gaze paresis, lid retraction, light-near pupillary reflex dissociation (Parinaud's syndrome), and visual acuity impairments (20/200 near vision and 20/70 distant vision). She also had hoarseness due to paralysis of a vocal cord.

Assessment included presentation of specific tasks (computer, activities), an interview, and observations. During the interview, Ms. Rodriguez was alert, oriented in time, person, and place. She initiated conversation, demonstrated turn-taking skills, and responded appropriately to the therapist's face and body language. Although her voice quality was hoarse, she did not have any difficulty communicating her needs. She self-reported in her activity configuration that, on each day, she slept 14 hours, socialized 4 hours, watched television 4 hours, and ate 2 hours.

The therapist observed that she independently completed all basic activities of daily living (feeding, dressing, and personal hygiene). She performed them safely, without modification or assistive devices within a reasonable amount of time. However, she ambulated with only modified independence with a wooden cane, required more than reasonable time to move from one place to another, and was unsafe in unpredictable environments due to postural control impairments. Nonetheless, she could manage her daily static environment. During computer and fine motor activities, the therapist noted that her reaction time was slow; she was unable to maintain concentration for more than 10 minutes; she displayed excessive body and head adjustments during tasks that required close visual attention; she was unable to search and maintain 20 seconds of eye fixation without cues from the therapist; she complained of ocular fatigue and a headache; and she exhibited short-term visual memory impairment as measured by a recall memory task, she could ony recall five out of fourteen items and missed all the background figures. Immediately after the assessment, Ms. Rodriguez was put on an active, home-based treatment program. She received occupational therapy twice a week for 1 hour. Additionally, she received vocational counseling, social services, and physical therapy.

Treatment began with activities that were performed with adapted equipment to increase her awareness and detection to stimuli. The stimuli, auditory and visual feedback, were provided through the use of an adapted seating surface. The adaptation included a light and a buzzer that were triggered whenever she responded off balance and asymmetrical. Activities included computer games, flower arrangements, and a variety of ball games. After 1 month of occupational therapy, she was able to sit on the feedback surface and engage in activities without setting off the alarms.

Since Ms. Rodriguez was verbal and was competent in communication, the occupational therapist was able to use verbal instructions during the second phase of intervention. The training sessions were designed to provide insight about: (1) understanding herself and the problem at hand, (2) understanding the goals of the activities or task, and (3) identification of the strategies to complete the task or activities. Ms. Rodriguez was given activities during treatment sessions without specific instructions. Before she performed the activities, she was asked: "What are the instructions of this activity or task?" "Give me two reasons why you think they are the instructions." and, "What do you need to do to follow the instructions and complete the task?" These questions were designed as a form of reflective mental exercise to assist her in learning how to solve a real or simulated problem and move towards mastery of an activity. After 2 months of variety activities, the occupational therapist determined that treatment should be gradually changed to address phase III, hypothesis generation.

During this phase, Ms. Rodriguez began to take a more active role in the selection of activities. She engaged in increased self-monitoring, resulting in improved error detection and correction. She gradually began to provide alternative solutions to problems or activities presented. The primary role of the occupational therapist during this phase was to reinforce the accuracy of Ms. Rodriguez's perceptions. For example, she determined that she did much better if she performed most activities slowly. Further, she ascertained, with the therapist's assistance, that she needed to focus and concentrate closely to increase her accuracy. After 2 months, she was able to perform at 80% accuracy on the same tasks that were used during the initial assessment.

At the end of 6 months, Ms. Rodriguez was discharged from home-based treatment, but continued outpatient therapy 1 day a week.

Implications for Research Efficacy

Our review of the literature revealed a paucity of research on the use of activity intervention for dysfunction in cognitive-perceptual and postural control in adults with brain injuries. Therapeutic activities tend to be described but not investigated in an empirical manner. However, in one empirical study Abreu (1991), looking at the spatial and temporal characteristics of a reaching activity on postural control after brain injury, determined that healthy and stroke subjects were effected differently, implying that different postural strategies were used by each group. The healthy subjects show strikingly similar patterns of performance across all environmental conditions. On the other hand, the stroke group was not homogeneous. Abreu also proposed that additional studies are needed to examine the impact of environmental regulations on cognitive-perceptual and postural control.

In the future, research studies need to be more concerned with applied research that will focus on determining whether or not the specific treatment was responsible for improved performance. Research designs that are sensitive to individual differences, and that measure change on a repeated basis, may be used to identify clinical change in the client's behavior (e.g., single-subject case study). This may involve developing new and innovative research designs that integrate qualitative and quantitative methods. These new designs must be sensitive to the individual differences characteristic of the brain-injured population. Further, theoretical development by occupational therapists related to the client's occupational performance and change need to be expanded.

The intent of this chapter is to begin to articulate a process approach and to formulate guidelines for using activities with adults with brain injuries. The proposed theoretical base and postulates for change should serve as a beginning point both for intervention and empirical studies.

Summary

This chapter, with its foundation in the use of activities, can enhance the clinical decision-making process of occupational therapists. The information was intended to be clinically useful. Because this is a preliminary set of guidelines, its use may expose some degree of ambiguity. It should be continually revised with new theoretical and clinical information. Additional research should add clarity and information to our knowledge pertaining to occupational therapy's impact on functions for clients with brain injuries. Further, the use of these guidelines may facilitate development of more refined guidelines that will improve and refine our practice.

References

Abreu, A. (1991). An experimental study of the effects of activity predictability on postural control while in a seated position in healthy individuals and in hemiplegic patients after stroke. Unpublished dissertation for Ph.D. New York, NY: New York University.

Abreu, A. (1990). *The quadraphonic approach: Management of cognitive and postural dysfunction.* New York: Therapeutic Service Systems.

Abreu, A. (1989). *Postural control and cognition.* New York State Occupational Therapy Association Workshop Conference, Ronkonkoma, NY.

Abreu, A. (1981). Interdisciplinary approach to the adult visual perceptual function-dysfunction continuum. In B. Abreu (Ed.), *Physical disabilities manual* (pp. 151–182). New York: Raven Press.

Abreu, A. (1985, March). Perceptual-cognitive rehabilitation: An occupational therapy model. *Physical Disabilities Special Interest Newsletter* [AOTA], pp. 1–3.

Abreu, A. & Toglia, J. P. (1987). Cognitive rehabilitation: An occupational therapy model. *American Journal of Occupational Therapy, 41,* 439–448.

Adams, J. A. (1971). A closed-loop theory of motor learning. *Journal of Motor Behavior, 3* (2), 111–150.

Adams, J. A. (1986). Use of the model's knowledge of results to increase the observer's performance. *Journal of Human Movement Studies, 12,* 89–98.

Allen, C. K. (1987). Activity: Occupational therapy's treatment method. 1987 Eleanor Clarke Slagle Lecture. *The American Journal of Occupational Therapy 41*(99), 563–575.

Barnett, M. L., Ross, D., Schmidt, R. A., & Todd, B. (1973). Motor skills learning and the specificity of training principle. *Research Quarterly, 44,* 440–447.

Ben-Yishay, Y., Rattok, J., & Diller, L. (1979). A clinical strategy for the systematic amelioration of attentional disturbances in severe head trauma patients. In Y. Ben-Yishay (Ed.), *Working approached to remediation of cognitive deficits in brain damaged persons* (pp. 1–27). New York: NYU Medical Center, Rehabilitation Monograph No. 60.

Bernspang, B., Viitanen, M., & Eriksson, S. (1989). Impairments of perceptual and motor functions: Their influence on self-care ability 4 to 6 years after a stroke. *The Occupational Therapy Journal of Research, 9,* 27–37.

Bobath, B. (1978). *Adult hemiplegia: Evaluation and treatment.* London: Heinemann Medical Books.

Bower, G. H. (1981). Mood and memory. *American Psychologist, 36,* 129–148.

Carter, Oliveira, Duponte, & Lynch (1988). The relationship of cognitive skills performance to activities of daily living in stroke patients. *American Journal of Occupational Therapy 42,* 449–455.

Cynkin, S., & Robinson, A. M. (1990). *Occupational therapy and activities health: Toward health through activities.* Boston: Little, Brown.

Diller, L., & Gordon, W. A. (1981). Interventions for cognitive deficits in brain damaged adults. *Journal of Consulting and Clinical Psychology, 49*(6), 822–834.

Eggers, O. (1984). *Occupational therapy in the treatment of adult hemiplegia.* London: William Heinemann Medical Books.

Fitts, P. M., & Posner, M. I. (1967). *Human performance.* Belmont CA: Brooks Cole.

Gagne, R. M., & Briggs, L. J. (1974). *Principles of instructional design.* New York: Holt, Rinehart & Winston.

Gentile, A. M. (1972). A working model of skill acquisition with application to teaching. *Quest, XVII,* 3–23.

Gentile, A. M. (1987). Skill acquisition: Action, movement, and neuromotor processes. In J. H. Carr, R. B. Shepherd, J. Gordon, A. M. Gentile, & J. M. Held (Eds.) *Movement science foundations for physical therapy in rehabilitation* (pp. 93–154). Rockville, MD: Aspen Publishers.

Geschwind, N., & Galaburda, A. M. (1984). *Cerebral dominance. The biological foundations.* Cambridge, MA: Harvard University Press.

Gliner, J. A. (1985). Purposeful activity in motor learning theory: An event approach to motor skill acquisition. *American Journal of Occupational Therapy, 39,* 28–34.

Henry, F. M. (1968). Specificity vs. generality in learning motor skill. In R. C. Brown, & G. S. Kenyon (Eds.) *Classical studies on physical activity* (pp. 331–340). Englewood Cliffs, NJ: Prentice-Hall. (Original work published 1958)

Keele, S. W. (1973). *Attention and human performance.* California: Goodyear.

Krefting, L. (1989). Disability ethnography: A methodological approach for occupational therapy. *Canadian Journal of Occupational Therapy, 56*(2), 61–66.

Lee, W. A. (1980). Anticipatory control of postural and task muscles during rapid arm flexion. *Journal of Motor Behavior, 12*(3), 185–196.

Lee, W. A. (1984). Neuromotor synergies as a basis for coordinated intentional action. *Journal of Motor Behavior, 16*(2), 136–170.

Lee, W. A. (1989). A control systems framework for understanding normal and abnormal posture. *American Journal of Occupational Therapy, 43*(5), 291–301.

Llorens, L. A. (1973). Activity analysis for cognitive-perceptual-motor dysfunction. *American Journal of Occupational Therapy, 27*(8), 453–456.

Luria, A. P. (1966). *Higher cortical functions in man.* New York: Basic Books.

Luria, A. P. (1973). *The working brain.* New York: Basic Books.

Magill, R. A., & Hall, K. G. (1990). A review of the contextual interference effect in motor skill acquisition. *Human Movement Science, 9,* 241–289.

Mitchel, J. V. (1985). *The ninth mental measurement yearbook, vols. I and II.* Lincoln: Buros Institute of Mental Measure, University of Nebraska.

Mizhari, J., Solzi, P., Ring, H., & Nisell, R. (1989). Postural stability in stroke patients: Vectoral expression of asymmetry, sway activity and relative sequence of reactive forces. *Medical & Biological Engineering & Computing, 27,* 181–190.

Mosey, A. C. (1981). Occupational therapy: Configurations of a profession. New York: Raven Press.

Nashner, L. M. (1971). A model describing vestibular detection of body sway motion. *Acta Oto-Laryngologica, 72,* 429–436.

Nashner, L. M. (1971). A model describing vestibular detection of body sway motion. *Acta Oto-Laryngologica, 72,* 529–536.

Nashner, L. M. (1972). Vestibular postural control model. *Kybernetic, 10*(2), 106–110.

Nashner, L. M. (1976). Adapting reflexes controlling the human posture. *Experimental Brain Research, 26,* 59–72.

Nashner, L. M. (1985). Strategies for organization of human posture. In M. Igarashi, & F. O. Black (Eds.). *Vestibular and visual control on posture and locomotor equilibrium.* 7th International Symposium of the International Society of Posturography, Houston, Texas (pp. 1–8). Karger Publications.

Nashner, L. M., Shumway-Cook, A., & Marin, O. (1983). Stance posture control in select groups of children with cerebral palsy: Deficits in sensory organization and muscular coordination. *Experimental Brain Research, 49,* 393–409.

Pelland, M. J. (1986). Occupational therapy and stroke rehabilitation. In P. E.

Kaplan & L. J. Cerullo (Eds.), *Stroke Rehabilitation* (pp. 298–320). Boston: Butterworth Publishers.

Pew, R. W. (1974). Levels of analysis in motor control. *Brain Research, 71,* 393–400.

Reed, E. S. (1982). An outline of a theory of action systems. *Journal of Motor Behavior, 14*(2), 98–134.

Reed, E. S. (1988). Applying the theory of action systems to the study of motor skills. In O. G. Meijer, & K. Roth (Eds.). *Complex movement behavior:* The motor-action controversy. North Holland: Elsevier.

Reed, E. S. (1989). Changing theories of postural development. In M. H. Woolacott, & A. Shumway-Cook (Eds.). *Posture and gait across the life span.* (pp. 3–24). Columbia, SC: University of South Carolina.

Ryerson, S. D. (1985). Hemiplegia resulting from vascular insult or disease. In D. A. Umphred (Ed.). *Neurological rehabilitation, vol. 3.* (pp. 475–514). St. Louis, MO: C. V. Mosby.

Schmidt, R. A. (1988). *Motor control and learning a behavioral emphasis.* Champaign, IL: Human Kinetic Publishers.

Schmidt, R. A. (1968). Anticipation and timing in human motor performance. *Psychological Bulletin, 70,* 631–646.

Schmidt, R. A. (1975). A schema theory of discrete motor skills learning. *Psychological Review, 82*(4), 225–260.

Schmidt, R. A. (1980). Past and future issues in motor programming. *Research Quarterly for Exercise and Sport, 51*(1), 122–140.

Schmidt, R. A. (1990). The changing face of motor learning. *Human Movement Science, 9,* 209–220.

Schmidt, R. A., Lange, C., & Young, D. E. (1990). Optimizing summary knowledge of results for skill learning. *Human Movement Science, 9,* 325–348.

van Rossum, J. H. A. (1990). Schmidt's schema theory: The empirical base of the variability of practice hypothesis. *Human Movement Science, 9,* 387–435.

van Zomeren, A. H., Bouwer, W. H., & Minderhoud, J. M. (1987). Acquired brain damage and driving: A review. *Archives of Physical Medicine and Rehabilitation, 68,* 697–705.

Warren, M. (1991). Strategies for sensory and neuromotor remediation. In C. Christiansen, & C. Baum (Eds.). *Occupational therapy overcoming human performance deficit* (pp. 633–664). Thorofare, NJ: Slack Inc.

Zoltan, B., Siev, E., & Freishtat, B. (1986). *Perceptual and cognitive dysfunction in the adult stroke patient* (rev. ed.). Thorofare, NJ: Slack, Inc.

8

□ □ □
□ □ □
□ □ □

A Neurofunctional Approach to Rehabilitation Following Severe Brain Injury

Gordon Muir Giles

In this chapter, I will outline a specialized approach to rehabilitation of patients following severe central nervous system (CNS) trauma. The model was developed for patients with acquired neurological impairments affecting cognitive functioning. It applies to the following diagnostic groups: traumatic brain injury (penetrating/non-penetrating, focal/diffuse), anoxic damage (and other neurochemical imbalances or poisonings causing CNS damage such as carbon monoxide poisoning), infections (e.g., encephalitis, meningitis), some types of vascular events (e.g., aneurysms), brain surgery (e.g., surgery for arteriovenous malformation), and some types of cerebrovascular accidents particularly those with mass effects. We have described this approach as neurofunctional (Giles & Clark-Wilson, 1992). In the World Health Organization (WHO) classification of impairment, disability, and handicap the neurofunctional approach emphasizes the reduction of disability and handicap (WHO, 1980). The neurofunctional approach considers the constraints placed on the patients functioning by the nature of the injury. In addition it considers learning theory in the design and implementation of retraining programs. The focus of the approach is not the retraining of cognitive processes but the retraining of real world skills.

Rationale

Most individuals develop improved function following the acute stage of trauma. The speed of this process in the early stages of recovery demonstrates that a neurophysiological process (or processes) other than learning underlies this recovery. Although the nature of the recovery process is unknown, therapists have attempted to potentiate the process by stimulating the patient. In the early acute period coma stimulation is viewed as an essential component of treatment by many therapists (Giles & Clark-Wilson, 1992). In later stages of acute recovery occupational therapists have attempted to stimulate patients by using tasks of graded difficulty. Hierarchies in various cognitive, behavioral, and physical domains have been constructed and therapist attempt to "move" patients through these (Soderback & Normell, 1986a; 1986b). It has been suggested that the earlier patients can be exposed to this type of acute rehabilitation the greater the recovery (Cope & Hall, 1982). This type of intervention could have an effect both on the speed of improvement and on its overall extent. Alternatively, it could alter the slope of recovery but not the ultimate level of outcome. Of course it could also have neither effect.

Accelerated improvement, whether or not it has durable effects, could result in the patient leaving the hospital earlier and suffering fewer medical and psychological complications. There would, of course, be considerable cost savings. Animal models suggest that there is a considerable effect of early physical intervention. When comparing early and late motor "rehabilitation" in monkeys, delayed intervention resulted in more rapid improvement but the ultimate level of recovery of the early rehabilitation group was never achieved (Black, Markowitz, & Cianci, 1975). There have been no data directly supporting a comparable effect for cognitive functions. Attempts to study the benefits of early intervention with controlled trials on human subjects (Cope & Hall, 1982) have been so complicated by methodological difficulties that results have been uninterpretable (Giles, Fussey, & Burgess, 1988). There are, however, reports of patients removed from nursing homes and admitted to a rehabilitation site whose improvement was so rapid when given appropriate training that it suggests that, at least, some stimulation is necessary to ensure that patients function at the level permitted by their neurological recovery. There is no evidence that one specific form of interaction has a greater effect at this early stage on potentiating recovery more than another.

In the post-acute recovery period therapist have also attempted to directly address the cognitive substrata of perception, attention, memory, judgment and reasoning, and other "skills." The advantage of these basic cognitive interventions, were they to be effective, would be the "trickle down" effect that improvement in basic cognitive skills would have on all aspects of the patient's functioning. So, for example, an improvement in attention would improve the patient's ability to keep track of ongoing events, his or her work performance, etc. The disadvantage of attempting to remediate basic cognitive functioning is that the efficacy of this type of intervention is unproven so that a good deal of the patient's time and effort may be devoted to a pointless task that results in no functional improvement. As an alternative to addressing basic cognitive deficits some therapists have attempted to train brain-injured patients in compensatory approaches to specific deficits (Wilson & Moffat, 1984). Unfortunately patients are often taught techniques without thoroughly considering whether the likely improvment in the patient's quality of life warrants the effort required for them to learn the compensatory strategy. Patients must be able to transfer the compensatory strategy to novel situations encountered in the real world. Brain-injured individuals can often learn strategies but be unable to apply them. The compensatory behaviors that are most successful are those that may be overlearned to the point of automaticity. Compensatory techniques that remain effortful despite overlearning (such as visualization strategies in memory retraining) are usually too demanding to be used outside the training sessions.

As an alternative to the above techniques, specific task approaches train the patient to perform a specific functional behavior. In specific task training the therapist attempts to teach the patient to perform an actual functional task. The intervention may or may not involve task-specific compensatory training. (For example a hemianopic patient who is being taught to cross the street may be trained to overcompensate by turning his or her head to the left[1]). Using the terminology of the WHO (WHO, 1980) what is taught is intended to reduce the patient's disability or handicap. The intervention must address a behavior of clinical importance and to an extent that intervention makes a real difference. In most cases training must be complete enough to be self-sustaining by the time the patient is discharged from the treatment setting.

---

[1] Since there are many activities that involve scanning left to compensate for visual field deficits, it is of course helpful if the patient is taught to do this in as many situations as possible. The neurofunctional approach attempts to restructure the patient's way of approaching the world by training specific routines across many functional settings. We hope that the patient will generalize the skills he or she has learned in functional settings to novel settings (a bottom-up approach).

Theoretical Base

Neurofunctional retraining must consider the learning characteristics of the patient in the design and implementation of programs. Since attention, memory, and problem-solving deficits are central to many of our patients problems these areas must be considered in the development of retraining programs. They are not considered here as areas that will be treated directly but are considered only instrumentally in the design of functional skills programs. I will discuss a theoretical framework for considering these deficits before outlining a system of neurofunctional retraining.

Attention

Automatic and Control Processing

Shiffrin and Schneider (1977) describe attention in terms of attention-dependent controlled processing and attention-independent automatic processing. Controlled processing is capacity limited and is required for new learning to occur. During the learning phase of an activity, the unskilled individual relies heavily on feedback about his or her performance and consciously attends to the activity (controlled processing). This focused attention continues during the practice stage of response acquisition. Once the action is learned, the individual controls his or her performance by a series of "prearranged instruction sequences" which act independently of feedback (automatic processing) and leave the individual free to concentrate on other aspects of the same or different tasks. Automatic processing occurs without conscious control and places only limited demands on the information processing system. Observations of individuals following severe brain injury suggest that activities which were previously automatic are disrupted by brain injury. Levin et al. (1988) administered free recall and frequency of occurrence tasks to patients with severe brain injuries and to a control group. In their first experiment, Levin and associates (1988) found that both free recall (an effortful task) and judgment of relative frequency of occurrence (an automatic task) were impaired in 15 brain-injured patients relative to the control group. In a second experiment, the authors corroborated this finding and showed that frequency estimates were also impaired in a different group of 16 brain-injured patients. Shiffrin and Schneider (1977) have described two types of attentional system break down: divided attentional deficits and focused attentional deficits.

Divided Attentional Deficit

A divided attentional deficit (DAD) (Schneider, Dumais, & Shiffrin, 1984) indicates a failure of the capacity-limited attentional system to accommodate all the information necessary for optimum task performance.

For example, in gait retraining a patient may be able to ambulate with standby assistance, unless a person walks across their visual field or says "Good morning," whereupon they lose their balance. This failure constitutes a divided attentional deficit, because the patient had insufficient attentional capacity to walk and attend to any other information. A study by Stuss et al. (1989) using a complex reaction time task, confirmed the existence of DAD among brain-injured patients. Patients were slow in tasks that require consciously controlled information processing and demonstrated an inability to process multiple pieces of information rapidly. Stuss et al. (1989) found this to be so even in mildly injured patients.

Focused Attentional Deficit

A focused attentional deficit (FAD) typically occurs when an unfamiliar response is required to a stimulus, which already has an over-learned response linked to it (Schneider, Dumais, & Shiffrin, 1984). Continuous attention from the individual may be required to suppress this automatic behavior. Stuss et al. (1989) developed a series of computer tasks designed to assess focused attentional deficits; the central feature of the FAD thus analyzed was the inability to suppress a previously learned complex level of processing when a simpler level of processing was demanded. A complex reaction time computer program task which required multiple discrimination (shape, internal line orientation, color) was followed by a task that appeared outwardly to be the complex task but which actually required a far less complex level of discrimination. Although both patients and controls were informed of the change, the patients were less able than the controls to inhibit the processing of redundant information. The concept of FAD depends to some extent on a Hullian notion of habit strength. For example, when attempting to reach a destination, we may deviate from the correct route to another route of greater familiarity which partially overlaps it. Upon arriving at the familiar (and, in this case, unwanted) destination, we may realize that we reached it on "auto-pilot." Individuals with brain-injury may be extremely inattentive in this sense and have a reduced ability to sustain their attention on new tasks (see, as an example, the discussion of street crossing that follows). Later in this chapter we will suggest that individuals with brain injury are also less likely to spontaneously monitor their behavior on an ongoing basis.

Selectivity

Task performance is influenced by the presence of competing attentional demands (Kewman, Yanus, & Kirsch, 1988). The individual's ability to selectively attend depends on his or her discriminating task-relevant information from competing background stimuli. For example, individuals who have a traumatic brain injury have more difficulty than individuals who are not neurologically impaired in filtering out distracting verbal information from relevant verbal information (Kewman, Yanus, & Kirsch, 1988). Part of their difficulty in maintaining selective attention may be due to their inability to suppress responses to novel or irrelevant stimuli. As a task is practiced, novel and irrelevant stimuli become less distracting as the individual habituates to them (Lorch, Anderson, & Well, 1984). In Solokov's view (1963) habituation occurs because repeated presentation allows the individual to construct a mental representation of the irrelevant stimuli as irrelevant. There is no evidence, however, to suggest that generalization of the habituation process occurs.

Attention and Memory

Long-term memory storage can be conceptualized under the headings procedural and declarative (Tulving, 1983). Declarative memory has its greatest development in humans (Squire, 1986), and information in this store is available to introspection. Declarative memory may be divided into semantic and episodic memory. Episodic memory stores information about temporally dated events and the temporal-spatial relations between these events (Tulving, 1972). It refers to "historical" information specific to the individual. Semantic memory is organized knowledge about the world, which is normally not tied to context (in includes the majority of information learned in institutional education, such as scientific facts and historical dates) (Tulving, 1972). Tulving maintains that the retrieval of information (from the episodic or semantic memory systems) constitutes an episode. One implication of this theory is that the act of remembering is recorded in the episodic memory store thus changing its overall contents. Episodic memory is the type of memory most vulnerable to impairment. Though deficits in acquiring new semantic information probably occur in tandem with episodic memory deficits, semantic memory stores may still be accessed and learning may take place via frequent repetition of to-be-remembered information.

Procedural memory can be thought of as the store of acquired patterns of behavior not necessarily mediated by cognition. Procedural "knowledge" is not available to introspection, information is accessed only through performance. Learning may occur without the subject being aware that learning has taken place. Nissen and Bullemer (1987) examined the attentional requirements of procedural learning to determine whether attention is necessary for procedural learning as it is for introspectively available forms of knowledge acquisition. A computerized serial reaction time task was used. A light appeared at one of four locations. Subjects pressed one key out of a set of four located directly below the position of the light. Learning was evaluated by measuring facilitation of performance on a repeating ten-trial stimulus sequence to which the subjects were naive. In non-neurologically impaired subjects there was considerable improvement in performance when this was the only task, however when given in a dual-task condition (a condition reducing the subjects ability to attend to the task), learning of the sequence (as assessed by verbal report and performance measures) was minimal. Patients with Korsakoff's syndrome were also able to learn the sequence in the single-task condition despite their lack of awareness of the repeating pattern. Nissen and Bullemer (1987) conclude that improved performance in the task, which is dependent on procedural memory, required the subject to attend to it.

There is increasing interest in the role of procedural memory in the acquisition of complex behaviors. Lewicki and co-workers in a series of experiments (Lewicki, Hill, & Bizot, 1988; Lewicki, Czyzewska, & Hoffman, 1987) have examined the ability of individuals to acquire relatively complex procedural knowledge. Their results confirm that nonconsciously acquired knowledge can automatically be utilized to facilitate performance; but, the extreme complexity of the tasks employed in the reports of Lewicki and colleages (1987; 1988) is particularly noteworthy. Although the skill acquisition is likely to be via procedural learning, the tasks were far more complex than those normally thought to be subserved by this memory system.

Problem Solving and Planning

Freedman et al. (1987) examined the ability of patients with closed brain injuries to forward plan, using a relatively simple conditioning paradigm (a shuttlebox-analog avoidance task). When compared to a group of patients after a cerebro-vascular accident, the patients with closed brain injuries demonstrated greater anticipatory behavior deficits. This difference occurred despite the fact that the two groups did not differ on escape behavior, and that the closed brain-injured group had equivalent or better performances in individual tests of the Halstead-Reitan Battery and Wechsler scales. Neither clarifying the instruction, having additional trials, nor enhancing the warning cue appeared to ameliorate the anticipatory behavior deficit. Freedman et al. (1987) suggested that patients with anticipatory behavior deficits would show deficits in situations where current behavior should be regulated on the basis of expected future consequences. Vilkki (1988), using a task similar to the token test but with more ambiguity, found that patients with frontal lobe deficits fail to identify the appropriate categories for sorting. Cicerone, Lazar, and Shapiro (1983) found that subjects with frontal lobe lesions failed to systematically explore a hypothesis (general concept formation) and failed to discard inappropriate hypotheses. They suggested that the deficit may be the result of a disturbance in an attentional control mechanism, which is involved in the ongoing monitoring of feedback from the environment and segregates relevant from irrelevant sources of information. Shallice and Evans (1978) attempted to explicate some of these issues using a novel research protocol. They noticed that many of their patients who had frontal-lobe impairment demonstrated a gross inability to produce adequate cognitive estimates. The authors asked the patients questions that tapped areas of knowledge most people possess but which require material to be accessed and manipulated in novel ways. To answer such questions adequately, the individual must select an appropriate plan for answering the question and mentally check possible answers for error. Examples of the questions included, "On average how many TV programmes are shown on one TV channel between 6:00 p.m. and 11:00 p.m.?" and "What is the length of an average man's spine?" In the latter question, one must compare the spontaneous estimate of an average person's height with the percentage of an individual's height accounted for by his spine. The patients with anterior lesions performed considerably worse than either patients with posterior lesions or normal controls. The authors interpret this finding as a deficit in planning and checking answers against multiple types of data for bizarreness and inconsistency.

Brain-injured individuals may not engage in the internal behaviors necessary for planning and subsequently executing complex dependent sequences of action (Shallice, 1982). In order to carry out complex behaviors that require the initiation of novel behaviors through time, the individual must develop a plan and then initiate a check act/wait cycle (Reason, 1984). Once the plan is developed the individual compares "plan time" with real time in order to determine whether he needs to initiate a plan component or to wait. For example in order to arrive at an appointment 45 minutes across town, a person will intermittently check the time throughout the day so as to leave at an appropriate time. Each time the individual looks at the clock he or she decides if it's time to leave or if he or she should wait. As the time for leaving approaches, he or she will look at the clock with greater frequency and also begin to adjust his or her other activities in order to leave on time. Many of our patients, particularly those with marked frontal lobe impairment appear unable to initiate this type of planning behavior. They cannot develop either action plans or the "drive" required for the check act/ wait cycles. I have found it particularly instructive to observe some severely injured patients doing their laundry. It rapidly became apparent that the severely brain-injured patients were unable to check to see if their laundry was dry. The absence of checking could not be accounted for by memory impairment (the patients, when questioned, were aware that their clothes were in the dryer), nor by lack of knowledge about the laundry procedures involved, nor by lack of motivation. The patients, nonetheless, required an external cue to enable them to initiate the behavior. Many therapists attempt to have the patient practice problem solving and reasoning to overcome these deficits. I believe these types of interventions are misdirected. What the patient cannot do is spontaneously develop and monitor a novel-dependent sequence of actions. Rather than have the patient attempt to improve their responses to novelty, we attempt to have patients overlearn needed behavioral sequences. Some types of novelty can be accommodated by training the patient in the use of a diary or other form of external memory aid (Giles & Shore 1989b; Giles & Clark-Wilson, 1992). The overlearning of frequent checking of the diary must be a component of this retraining.

Intervention

Target Population

Severe brain injury often results in the loss or disruption of patterns of adaptive behavior. Additionally the individual's ability to reacquire adaptive patterns of behavior is impaired. The frequency of disruption of basic self-care skills has been estimated at 5 to 15% (Jennet & Teasdale, 1981; Jacobs, 1988). More complex self-care skills appear to be more commonly disrupted (Jacobs, 1988). The extent and location of brain injury place constraints on human learning but the ability to acquire new behaviors is retained in all but the most profoundly injured.

Assessment

Neurofunctional assessment may make use of a range of evaluation techniques. Methods include observation, questionnaires, checklist and rating scales, and standardized assessment tools. The most important of these methods is observation. Occupational therapists typically assess patients over a wide range of basic areas of functioning that can be divided into sensory, perceptual, motor, cognitive, and affective. A non-exhaustive list of factors to be considered on initial assessment is provided in Table 1. Although observing the patient's performance of functional skills is the central aspect of assessment, a basic skills assessment is necessary because the therapist will need to understand why functional performance breaks down. In addition, certain deficits suggest specific approaches to retraining. For example, if a patient is markedly dyspraxic this will influence how motor retraining is carried out. However, we regard observation of real-life functioning as the primary mode of assessment because there is almost never a one-to-one correspondence between observed cognitive deficits and impaired performance of functional skills. Attempts to produce one-to-one maps are

Table 1   Initial Screening

Sensation	
Vision	Heterotopic ossification
Acuity	Peripheral nerve injuries
Visual fields	Strength
Diplopia	Endurance
Depth perception	Neuromuscular
Color	Ataxia
Hearing	Tremor
Touch	Dyspraxia
Superficial	Spasticity
Deep	Akinesia
Sustained pressure	Bradykinesia
Temperature	Rigidity
Pain	
Proprioception	**Cognitive**
Position sense	Orientation (person, place, and time)
Kinesthetic sense	Attention
	Memory (for current ongoing
Perception	information)
Visual	Planning
Visual neglect	Initiation (level of spontaneously
Visual suppression	occurring behavior)
Form discrimination/constancy	
Visual agnosia	**Affect**
Tactile	Depressed (tearful, psychomotor
Tactile neglect	retardation)
Tactile suppression	Euphoric
Steriognosis	Labile
	Anger/short-temperedness
Motor Skill	Flat or constricted effect
Biomechanical	Insight
Fractures	
Contractures	

in our view misguided (for an alternative view see Arnadottir, 1990). Therapists are often reluctant to observe and are too quick to rescue patients from no or inadequate performance. By ending the observation process too soon, the therapist is prevented from determining whether the patient notices the limitations of his or her performance or if he or she produces any compensatory behaviors (appropriate or inappropriate). The ability to make accurate observations is a skill acquired with training and experience. Most therapists do not emphasize observation, which may be due to lack of appreciation of the importance of establishing a picture of what the client does unconstrained by external cues or demands. Observational techniques can be described as falling under two general categories. The first category is structured observation of specific areas of function: Here the patient is observed (or prompted and observed) in a specific functional skill (the procedures used are described in more detail below). The second category is general observation involving ABC or frequency recordings. This second type of recording is used to develop an overall picture of the patient's behavior and is used specifically to describe and measure inadequate behavioral control or social skills deficits (general baselining techniques are described in more detail in Giles & Clark-Wilson, 1992).

The functional skills assessed by occupational therapists are most often low frequency behaviors. For this reason observation needs to be scheduled. One must remember that this scheduling necessarily affects the patient's behavior. For example, a patient may show adequate performance when prompted to wash and dress but not engage in either behavior spontaneously. Central to the assessment of function is not what the patient can do but what they do normally and habitually. As an example of behavioral observation of an activity let us take street crossing. Initially, the therapist makes a determination of how safe it is to assess this behavior (i.e., a patient who is delusional, aggressive or confused, and given to impulsive behavior might have this aspect of their assessment deferred because of the risk that the patient will evade the therapist and be injured). We typically select a purposive route (e.g., to the coffee shop). The patient is told that the purpose of the trip is to see if they can get to the store safely (and find their way back); thus, they are not specifically cued to safe street-crossing. The therapist then walks with (but a little behind) the patient so as not to give physical cues. The first street to be crossed should be quiet so as to give the therapist an opportunity to estimate performance in a relatively safe environment. The therapist should be ready to stop the patient if he or she is unsafe. If the patient is safe in crossing quiet streets then the therapist may progress with the patient to busier streets, both with and without crossing lights. The therapist should also assess the patient's ability to maintain safety when distracted by conversation. If the patient is initially unsafe (i.e., they do not check for traffic; they inadequately check for traffic; or they check but nonetheless behave inappropriately) the therapist's task is to determine what additional cues are required to elicit safe behavior. For some patients a simple instruction to pay attention to how they cross the street may be adequate. Others may need additional opportunities to practice focusing on safe street-crossing behaviors as outlined by the therapist. Where there is a marked deficit, an identifiable perceptual deficit, or where the individual is unable to respond to general street-crossing stimulation a more structured approach should be considered. The therapist should determine the most appropriate techniques, type of prompts, reinforcers, and frequency of practice. Similarly an appropriate measure of task acquisition should be selected. Progress in assessment is the same for all functional domains from least structured to most structured. Earlier we described factors to be considered in the observational assessment of street crossing. As in other aspects of assessment this should only occur as part of a comprehensive rehabilitation plan.

Neurofunctional assessment determines current level of functioning and assists in the determination of optimal forms of retraining. The neurofunctional assessment is central to the selection of goals and target behaviors required for the rehabilitation team's integrated treatment plan. Neurofunctional assessments should be conducted under conditions as close as possible to those the person will experience following rehabilitation. Neurofunctional assessment, therefore, differs from other types of testing that demand highly standardized conditions. The rigorous control of variables necessary for the pursuit of science is sacrificed in favor of ecological validity. Table 2 is a list of factors to be considered in developing a picture of the individual's behavior in an environmental context. There are many variables that influence performance in real-world situations, for example, the presence of setting events (Giles & Clark-Wilson 1992), cues, or environmental conditions.

Retraining

Having discussed some of the factors which lead to the disruption of functional behaviors, we will now consider how we might retrain a cognitively impaired brain-injured person on a functional task. Let us continue with our concrete example of street crossing and examine how we might train an individual with severe memory impairment to cross the street. During assessment, we determine that the patient has no specific perceptual deficits but that he or she walks across intersections oblivious of the need for checking traffic. Having performed a task analysis, we determine that crossing the street safely consists of stopping at the curbside, looking in both directions, and then walking directly across the street when there are no

Table 2   The Goals of Neurofunctional Assessment[a]

· To identify retained functional skills.
· To identify deficits limiting independent functioning.
· To identify environmental factors that support independent functioning.
· To identify the demands placed on the individual by the environment.
· To identify the strategies used to overcome functional deficits.
· To identify methods that assist the individual relearn functional skills.
· To identify the changes required to enable the individual to function in environmental context.

[a] Reprinted with permission of author and publisher from Giles, G. M., & Clark-Wilson, J. (1992). *Occupational therapy for the brain-injured adult: A neurofunctional approach.* London: Chapman and Hall.

motor vehicles within a certain distance (depending on the patients speed of ambulation and so forth). Having performed the task analysis we can develop a program of verbal prompts, which will elicit from the patient the appropriate behavior and direct the patient's attention to the factors in the task which lead to success or failure. The first time the patient practices street crossing is an "episode." It is processed and the specific to-be-learned activity is associated with the specific street intersection, the passing traffic, and other incidental information. This episode may not be available later for introspection, but a certain priming effect will have occurred. On the second occasion retraining occurs, only certain aspects of the situation will have been held constant, for instance, the specific instructions given. As this street-crossing routine is repeated, always using the same prompts, the street crossing episodes are not retained (or at least are not recallable). The street-crossing memory becomes an abstraction of many specific memory traces, all slightly different, that eventually produces the generalized memory structure of 'crossing streets.' This experience becomes proto-typical and the patient develops a habit of crossing the street in the way which has been practiced. In optimal cases patients no longer choose to cross the street in a certain manner, they just "know" that this is how they cross the street. Initially during treatment there is an attempt to reduce the possibility of failure to a minimum by the cues given (see Warrington & Weiskrantz on cued recall in amnesia 1968; 1974). As performance improves cues may be faded. The task practiced must be ultimately performable given the fixed aspects of the patients deficits (if the therapist attempts to teach behaviors that are beyond the patient's cognitive ability the program will fail).

The functional skills trainer's role is to determine the functional skill to be trained, develop methods which allow the patient to perform the task, with the minimum amount of new learning, and develop a method which directs the patient's attention to the central components of the task.

Programming may be thought to exist on a behavioral—cognitive behavioral continuum. All treatment focuses around modifying the patient's previous responses (Giles & Clark-Wilson, 1988) and replacing them with new and more adaptive ones through practice. More cognitively preserved patients can be assisted to attend to and interrupt inappropriate behaviors and replace them with more adaptive behaviors on their own. What can be taught also depends on the patient's cognitive abilities. Functional skills that require the patient to cope with novelty require a more complex set of cognitive abilities. For example, complete functional use of a diary always involves decisions about what information to write down. Practice in how to make entries and what information to enter reduces the difficulty of these tasks but the patient must, nevertheless, be able to categorize a particular event as one which should be recorded and then initiate the recording.

Training programs that attempt to address a general behavior (such as to reduce a social skills deficit or develop use of a memory book) should include the following three stages. First, training programs should include a cognitive overlearning element, which is an attempt to focus the patient's attention on the behavior or area of skills deficit and to develop a verbal label for the behavior. The therapist discusses the long-term consequences of the behavior or skill deficit with the patient. The therapist emphases its inconvenience and the benefits likely to accrue to the patient from changing it. If the patient has severe deficits this cognitive component may need to be reviewed one or more times per day and may continue throughout and/or beyond the other program elements. Second, training programs should include sessional practice of required behaviors. Here the patient practices the behavior for a short period of time in an environment controlled by the therapist. The patient must be able to produce the behavior with only moderate effort in this controlled environment before progressing to stage three, the 24-hour program approach. In stage three there is an attempt to target each instance of the behavior throughout the day. This type of intervention requires an interdisciplinary team and a high level of staff training. Each time the patient exhibits the target behavior a staff member responds in a predetermined manner usually to have the patient attend to the behavior or categorize it as an instance of the target behavior, suppress it, and replace it with an alternative or incompatible behavior.

In our experience the degree to which a behavior becomes automatic influences its durability. Behaviors that can develop to a high degree of automaticity such as washing and dressing (and which are practiced repeatedly) are extremely robust. Behaviors that must be consciously initiated by the subject (such as using a memory book) require more specific and ongoing environmental support.

Additionally, central to the operation of functional retraining programs is the development of an appropriate rehabilitation culture or holding environment. For a discussion of the development of rehabilitation culture see Giles & Clark-Wilson (1992).

Reinforcement and Skill Building

Reinforcing events increase the likelihood that behaviors that immediately precede them will be repeated. Reinforcers may be primary or secondary. Primary reinforcers are intrinsically desirable (such as social attention, praise, and candy). Secondary reinforcers are points or tokens which may be traded for primary reinforcers. There is some evidence that reinforcement aids learning (Dolan & Norton, 1977; Lashley & Drabman 1974). The reason that reinforcement increases learning is unknown but may be related to the ability of reinforcement to direct attention toward the to-be-learned aspects of the practiced behaviors.

Task Analysis

Task analysis involves a process of dividing tasks into component parts that can be taught as units and chained together into a functional whole. The analysis provides a method of organizing behaviors in order to make them easier to learn. The components of a task analysis may be converted to verbal or visual prompts, and the learner's attention is sequentially directed to each step of the activity. These analyses can be built into subgroups of contiguous core skills and/or identified as functional clusters of behavior. These clusters can be taught as a single instructional step to learners who are more competent. A functional cluster is defined as a sequence of 2 to 4 component contiguous core skills that have a meaningful relationship and constitute an identifiable and potentially teachable segment of a whole task. An example of a core skill might be establishing an appropriate sitting posture. An example of a functional cluster might be all the steps that go into preparing for a wheelchair transfer. When using a task analysis to develop a set of verbal cues, the number of cues depends on the patient's ability. For example, in developing a washing and dressing program some patients require only a few prompts such as "wash your face" to produce complex behavioral chains. Other patients require several prompts, for example, "pick up the wash cloth," "put soap on the wash cloth," "wash your face," and "rinse the wash cloth." O'Reilly and Cuvo (1989) used an interesting variant of this procedure in attempting to train self-treatment of cold symptoms to an anoxic brain-injured adult. They used three levels of cuing: generic prompts (non-specific subject headings), specific prompts (based on a specific step-by-step task analysis), and individualized prompts. Individualized and specific prompt sequences were provided only when the client failed to provide the appropriate behavior to the generic prompt.

When clients can respond to verbal prompts to carry out procedures, we have found it most effective to use a whole task system in which prompts are provided for each step until the task is completed. An exception to this general rule applies to clients who are so slow that attempting to train them in the whole task is too demanding. Where this is the case, specific functional clusters may be selected.

Prompts

Prompts (or cues) are events that facilitate the production of a behavior. A prompt assists an individual to produce the target behavior which may then be reinforced. In many instances prompts are available in the environment but they are no longer sufficient to guide behavior or they have lost their meaning entirely (e.g., arriving at a busy junction no longer cues safe street-crossing routines). The therapist adds additional prompts to those already available in the environment. Therapists can facilitate the learning of skills with a range of differing types of prompts: verbal instructions, written lists, physical touch, or guidance. Once the skill is reliably carried out, the prompt can be faded until performance occurs without the additional aid to initiation.

Shaping

Shaping refers to the reinforcement of closer and closer approximations to the desired behavior. Tasks are graded in difficulty so they are more easily achieved. As competency is demonstrated the task's requirements are increased. For example, one patient I saw would pace the corridors of the treatment facility when not engaged in an activity by staff. The goal of intervention was to have the patient sit with others and engage in appropriate conversation. Initially he was reinforced (with attention and food) if he remained in the unit day room, later he was only reinforced if he was sitting down, and finally only if engaged in appropriate conversation.

Control of a Behavior by Antecedents

For many clinicians, applied behavioral analysis when applied to brain-injured persons has been synonymous with an operant conditioning model. Antecedents may be altered in an attempt to change behavior. This occurs when the environmental conditions are set so that the stimulus events will increase the possibility that the patient will perform the desired behavior. Elsewhere we have reported the use of posters containing specific information in an attempt to "prime" the individual in certain activities (Giles & Clark-Wilson, 1988). The control of specific antecedents may be particularly useful in working with patients with profound memory impairment. Zencius et al. (1989) compared the effect of altering antecedents with the effect of varying consequences in three patients with marked memory disorder following severe brain injury. In the first patient Zencius and co-workers (1989) found that by posting a sign noting break times at the patient's workstation they drastically reduced the number of unauthorized breaks. In another client the most effective way to increase cane usage, a goal of the rehabilitation team, was to provide her with a cane to use during her morning ADLs. This technique was found to be more effective than social praise, a contract for money, or having someone escort her to get the cane when she was found without it. In a third patient the authors found that a map and a written daily schedule were more powerful than a contract for money in increasing therapy attendance. In general, they found altering the antecedents produced behavioral improvement when attempts to alter behavior by changing consequences had proved to be, at best, only marginally successful (for a fuller discussion see Giles & Clark-Wilson, 1992).

Overlearning

Overlearning refers to the practice of a skill well beyond the point where the patient is able to produce the behavior. Overlearning increases the chances that the skill is consolidated—becomes automatic—and reduces the amount of effort required for performance. When a skill becomes automatic, it becomes the easiest behavior to initiate from an array of possible behaviors (i.e., the possibility of an interference error is reduced). The goal of rehabilition can often best be met by having the individual engage in overlearning. For example, a street-crossing program should not be terminated on meeting the functional criteria but on meeting criteria plus a certain number of practice sessions designed to make the behavior automatic. The number of additional sessions required to develop automaticity is unclear. Automaticity is assessed by ongoing monitoring of the patient's behavior in conjunction with distractions.

Fading

Verbal cues may be faded by forming clusters of prompts from the task analysis after the individual has learnt to complete the behavior in response to the original prompts. Another method of fading is to increase the time between completion of the previous behavior and the provision of the subsequent prompt. This delay procedure should only be used, however, when the patient has already developed the skill to the point where they can be 80 to 90% correct. Otherwise he or she is likely to "practice" the propagation of incorrect responses—a situation to be avoided. Questions like "What's next?" or instructions telling the individual to "go ahead" can help the individual initiate the activity and decrease dependence on prompts.

Encore Procedure

When an individual demonstrates an infrequently displayed skill without prompting, he or she can be prompted to produce several more correct responses. For example, CP was learning to attract people's attention appropriately before asking questions or making requests in social skills groups. On any occasion when she responded appropriately by saying the person's name or saying "excuse me" (rather than by screaming or banging objects) and then asking a question, she was given social (and occasionally tangible) reinforcement and was asked to repeat the sequence of behaviors again, whereupon she was reinforced again.

Highlighting

Many individuals after sustaining a brain injury have problems distinguishing the central aspects of a task. Highlighting is a strategy that promotes the discrimination of the crucial elements of an activity by exaggerating the perceptual salience of some stimulus features. Prompts are progressively faded once the patient consistently makes correct discriminations. Highlighting might be achieved by emphasizing phrases, pointing, touching, or by providing specific reinforcement.

More cognitively oriented intervention should not only involve the consideration of the forgoing factors but also should maximize use of the patient's own retained learning ability. The therapist's role becomes to supervise the patient in setting his or her own goals and developing his or her own strategies to perform functional tasks. For example, a patient who has been working on improving his or her community mobility might set himself or herself the task of finding the way to a specific novel location. The patient would then have to develop with the assistance of the therapist, a knowledge of the parameters involved in the task (e.g., available means of transportation, time requirements, cost, route-finding methods, and so forth). Initially, limited time periods should be set aside for individuals to "self-schedule" as they may find the activity stressful, become inactive without continuous support, become sidetracked, or demonstrate behavioral deterioration. As the patient shows increasing competencies, longer periods of time and more complex tasks can be set for the patient. Eventually long periods of the treatment day should be devoted to the patient pursuing his or her own goals while periodically checking in with the therapist who can ensure that he or she remains critically self-aware. The therapist's goal is to set tasks and direct the patient's attention on how his or her current experience can be incorporated into strategies that will improve his or her future functioning. Tasks might include enrolling in evening classes, college programs, or finding social activities. Interactions with individuals after brain injury should be designed to facilitate learning. Two techniques central to this type of intervention are goal statements and debriefing.

Goal Statements

The incorporation of goal statements in each session has a number of advantages in helping brain-injured individuals learn. It may increase participation, help the patient attend to the to-be-learned aspect of his or her activities (this discriminatory aspect may need to be repeated throughout the session), and communicates respect from therapist to patient.

For patients with lack of insight, goal statements orient them to their deficits and provide cues as to how the to-be-undertaken therapeutic activity will help them achieve their own goals. Therapists may wish to present the session as a scientific endeavor, in which either the therapist or the patient is allowed to have incorrect notions but in which an empirical question is examined. With some patients, however, active agreement with the therapeutic intervention is not attainable, and the therapist seeking agreement will only sidetrack the patients and derail the therapeutic endeavor. The therapist is not advised to abandon the goal of developing functional skills by waiting until the patient knows that he or she has deficits. Goal-directing statements (e.g., for 5 minutes at the beginning of each session and interspersed statements throughout) orienting patients to these issues is frequently indicated. For example, saying, "As you know, as a result of your severe brain-injury you have needed some help in washing and dressing yourself. We are working with you every morning so that you can develop a system to be independent. You can now perform all but three of the activities of washing and dressing completely independently."

Debriefing

Regular debriefing about performance (knowledge of results) is indicated in producing positive behavioral change. Telling the patient that he or she has done well is encouraging, but can be nonspecific and damaging if untrue. Feedback about results should be concrete and accurate; written materials that the patient can refer to (such as graphs or logs) should be used whenever possible.

Research Methods and Future Directions

Single case or small group studies have demonstrated the efficacy of functional task training with brain-injured adults in the areas of continence (Cohen, 1986), self-feeding (Hooper-Row, 1988), transfers (Goodman-Smith & Turnball, 1983), personal hygiene (Giles & Clark-Wilson, 1988; Giles & Shore, 1989a), mobility and community skills (Giles & Clark-Wilson, 1992), and social skills (Gajar et al., 1984; Brotherton et al., 1988). Single case and small group designs provide for in depth analysis of the patient's difficulties and allow treatment to be specifically tailored to the patient's needs while maintaining the controls necessary for determining the effects of treatment (Giles, 1989). The background of our own approach as described here is derived from learning theory, neuropsychology, and what can loosely be described as cognitive science. The cognitive component includes models of information processing and includes the newer parallel distributed processing theories now being used to model learning systems (recent ideas that are leading to reevaluations of much of cognitive psychology). Both the theoretical orientation and our treatment methods place our approach on what might be considered the margins of occupational therapy. This is at least partly because much of the inspiration for our work and research has come from outside occupational therapy. It is time that occupational therapists look outside their own discipline for theoretical models that can help provide practical and effective interventions that will help us help our patients.

Occupational therapy must be judged as a technical science on the criterion of whether patients improve function. We must describe the selection of certain types of intervention for certain patients, the effectiveness of the intervention, and treatment effects on overall patient functioning. The detailed and painstaking demonstration of this type of effectiveness is a task that is far from complete.

Conclusion

This chapter has outlined a model for neurofunctional assessment and intervention. The need for the appropriate selection of functional goals has been underlined. We emphasize that the constraints placed on the patient by the brain injury must be considered in the development of retraining programs. We have concentrated on the variables of practice, attention, memory, and the patient's ability to develop action plans. Rather than attempt to address the elusive "underlying cause" of a decrement in functional behavior, we have highlighted the advantages of a more direct approach.

References

Arnadottir, G. (1990). *The brain and behavior: Assessing cortical dysfunction through activities of daily living.* St. Louis, MO: C. V. Mosby.

Bellack, A. S., Hersen, M., & Lamparski, D. (1979). Role-play tests for assessing social skills: Are they valid? Are they useful? *Journal of Consulting and Clinical Psychology, 47,* 335–342.

Black, P., Markowitz, R. S., & Cianci, S. N. (1975). Recovery of motor function after lesions in the motor cortex of monkey. In CIBA Foundation Symposium 34. New Series. *Outcome of severe damage to the central nervous system.* Amsterdam: Elsevier.

Brotherton, F. A., Thomas, L. L., Wisotzek I. E., & Milan M. A. (1988). Social skills training in the rehabilitation of patients with traumatic head injury. *Archives of Physical Medicine and Rehabilitation, 69,* 827–832.

Cicerone, K. D., Lazar, R. M., & Shapiro, W. R. (1983). Effects of frontal lobe lesions on hypothesis sampling during concept formation. *Neuropsychologia, 21,* 513–524.

Cohen, R. E. (1986). Behavioral treatment of incontinence in a profoundly neurologically impaired adult. *Archives of Physical Medicine and Rehabilitation, 67,* 833–834.

Cope, D. N., & Hall, K. (1982). Head injury rehabilitation: Benefits of early intervention. *Archives of Physical Medicine and Rehabilitation, 63,* 433–437.

Dolan, M. P. (1979). The use of contingent reinforcement for improving the personal appearance and hygiene of chronic psychiatric inpatients. *Journal of Clinical Psychology, 35,* 140–144.

Dolan, M. P., & Norton, J. C. (1977). A programmed training technique that uses reinforcement to facilitate acquisition and retention in brain damaged patients. *Journal of Clinical Psychology, 33,* 496–501.

Eames, P., & Wood, R. (1985). Rehabilitation after severe brain injury: a follow-up study of a behaviour modification approach. *Journal of Neurology, Neurosurgery, and Psychiatry, 48,* 613–619.

Freedman, P. E., Bleiberg, J., & Freedland, K. (1987). Anticipatory behaviour deficits in closed head injury. *Journal of Neurology, Neurosurgery, and Psychiatry, 50,* 398–401.

Gajar, A., Schloss, P. J., Schloss, C., & Thompson, C. K. (1984). Effects of feedback and self-monitoring on brain trauma youth's conversational skills. *Journal of Applied Behavior Analysis, 17,* 353–358.

Giles, G. M. (1989). Demonstrating the effectiveness of occupational therapy after severe brain trauma. *American Journal of Occupational Therapy, 43,* 613–615.

Giles, G. M., & Clark-Wilson, J. (1988). The use of behavioral techniques in functional skills training after severe brain injury. *American Journal of Occupational Therapy, 42,* 658–665.

Giles, G. M., & Clark-Wilson, J. (1992). *Occupational therapy for the brain-injured adult: A neurofunctional approach.* London: Chapman and Hall.

Giles, G. M., & Shore, M. (1989a). A rapid method for teaching severely brain-injured adults to wash and dress. *Archives of Physical Medicine and Rehabilitation, 70,* 156–158.

Giles, G. M., & Shore, M. (1989b). The effectiveness of an electronic memory aid for a memory-impaired adult of normal intelligence. *American Journal of Occupational Therapy, 43,* 409–411.

Giles, G. M., Fussey, I., & Burgess, P. (1988). The behavioral treatment of verbal interaction skills following severe head injury: a single case study. *Brain Injury, 2,* 75–81.

Goodman-Smith, A., & Turnbull, J. (1983). A behavioral approach to the rehabilitation of severely brain injured adults: an illustrated case study. *Physiotherapy, 69,* 393–396.

Hooper-Row, J. (1988). Rehabilitation of physical deficits in the post-acute brain-injured: Four case studies. In I. Fussey & G. M. Giles (Eds.). *Rehabilitation of the Severely Brain-Injury Adult: A Practical Approach* (pp. 102–116). London: Croom Helm.

Jacobs, H. E. (1988). The Los Angeles head injury survey: Procedures and initial findings. *Archives of Physical Medicine and Rehabilitation, 69,* 425–431.

Jennett, B., & Teasdale, G. (1981). *Management of head injuries.* Philadelphia: F. A. Davis.

Johnson, D. A., & Newton, A. (1987). Brain injured persons social interaction group: A basis for social adjustment after brain injury. *British Journal of Occupational Therapy, 50,* 11–26.

Kewman, D. G., Seigerman, C., Kinter, H., Chu, S., Henson, D., & Reeder, C. (1985). Simulation training of psychomotor skills: Teaching the brain-injured to drive. *Rehabilitation Psychology, 30,* 11–26.

Kewman, D. G., Yanus, B., & Kirsch, N. (1988). Assessment of distractibility in auditory comprehension after traumatic brain injury. *Brain Injury, 2,* 131–137.

Kreutzer, J. S., Wehman, P., Morton, M. V., & Stonnington, H. H. (1988). Supported employment and compensatory strategies for enhancing vocational outcome following traumatic brain injury. *Brain Injury, 2,* 205–223.

Lashley, B., & Drabman, R. (1974). Facilitation of the acquisition and retention of sight-word vocabulary through token reinforcement. *Journal of Applied Behavioral Analysis, 7,* 307–312.

Levin, H. S., Goldstein, F. C., High, W. M., & Williams, D. (1988). Automatic and effortful processing after severe closed-head injury. *Brain and Cognition, 7,* 283–297.

Lewicki, P., Czyzenska, M., & Hoffman, H. (1987). Unconscious acquisition of complex procedural knowledge. *Journal of Experimental Psychology: Learning, Memory and Cognition, 13,* 523–530.

Lewicki, P., Hill, T., & Bizot, E. (1988). Acquisition of procedural knowledge about a pattern of stimuli that cannot be articulated. *Cognitive Psychology, 20,* 24–37.

Lorch, E. P., Anderson, D. R., & Well, A. D. (1984). Effects of irrelevant information on speeded classification tasks: Interference is reduced by habituation. *Journal of Experimental Psychology: Human Perception and Performance, 10,* 850–864.

Nissen, M. J., & Bullemer, P. (1987). Attentional requirements of learning: Evidence from performance measures. *Cognitive Psychology, 19,* 1–32.

O'Reilly, M. F., & Cuvo, A. J. (1989). Teaching self-treatment of cold symptoms to an anoxic brain-injured adult. *Behavioral Residential Treatment, 4,* 359–375.

Prigatano, G. P., Fordyce, D. J., Zeiner, H. K., Roueche, J. R., Pepping, M., & Wood, B. C. (1984). Neuropsychological rehabilitation after closed-head injury in young adults. *Journal of Neurology, Neurosurgery, and Psychiatry, 47,* 505–513.

Reason, J. (1984). Absent-mindedness and cognitive control. In J. E. Harris, & P. E. Morris (Eds.). *Everyday memory actions and absent-mindedness.* London: Academic Press.

Schneider, W., Dumais, S. T., & Shiffrin, R. M. (1984). Automatic and control processing and attention. In R. Parasuraman, & D. R. Davis (Eds.). *Varieties of attention.* London: Academic Press.

Shallice, T. (1982). Specific impairment of planning. In D. E. Broardbent & L. Weiskrantz (Eds.). *The neuropsychology of cognitive function* (pp. 199–209). London: The Royal Society.

Shallice, T., & Evans, M. E. (1978). The involvement of the frontal lobes in cognitive estimation. *Cortex, 14,* 294–303.

Shaw, L., Brodsky, L., & McMahon, B. T. (1985). Neuropsychiatric intervention in the rehabilitation of head-injured patients. *The Psychiatric Journal of the University of Ottawa, 10,* 237–240.

Shiffrin, R. M., & Schneider, W. (1977). Controlled and automatic information processing: II. Perceptual learning, automatic attending, and a general theory. *Psychological Review, 84,* 127–190.

Soderback, I., & Normell, L. A. (1986a). Intellectual function training in adults with acquired brain damage: An occupational therapy method. *Scandinavian Journal of Rehabilitation Medicine, 18,* 139–146.

Soderback, I., & Normell, L. A. (1986b). Intellectual function training in adults with acquired brain damage: Evaluation. *Scandinavian Journal of Rehabilitation Medicine, 18,* 147–153.

Solokov, E. N. (1963). *Perception and the conditioned reflex.* Oxford: Pergamon Press.

Squire, L. R. (1986). Mechanisms of memory. *Science, 232,* 1612–1619.

Stuss, D. T., Stethem, L. L., Hugenholtz, H., Picton, T., Pivik, J., & Richards, M. T. (1989). Reaction time after head injury: Fatigue, divided attention, and consistency of performance. *Journal of Neurology, Neurosurgery, and Psychiatry, 52,* 742–748.

Tulving, E. (1972). Episodic and semantic memory. In E. Tulving and W. Donaldson (Eds.). *Organization of memory.* New York: Academic Press.

Tulving, E. (1983). *Elements of episodic memory.* Oxford: Clarendon Press.

Vilkki, J. (1988). Problem solving after focal cerebral lesions. *Cortex, 24,* 119–127.

Wilson, B. A., & Moffat, N. (1984). *Clinical management of memory problems.* London: Croom Helm.

World Health Organization. (1980). *International classification of impairment disabilities and handicaps.* Geneva: WHO.

Zencius, A. H., Wesolowski, M. D., Burke, W. H., & McQuade, P. (1989). Antecedent control in the treatment of brain-injured clients. *Brain Injury, 3,* 199–205.

9 ☐☐☐ ☐☐☐ ☐☐☐

Cognitive Rehabilitation: A Retraining Approach for Brain-Injured Adults

Sara Averbuch and Noomi Katz

In this chapter, we describe our ongoing work with patients with traumatic brain injuries at Loewenstein Rehabilitation Hospital. Patients are treated along the whole process spectrum, from the acute phase until they reach a plateau in their progress. Treatment focuses mainly on cognitive training because this area is affected the most by brain damage and has direct implications for function. At the beginning phase of treatment, training is mainly remedial in order to lessen cognitive deficits. In the next phase, our effort is centered on functional treatment and compensations, in order to help the patient adapt to the community with his or her specific deficits.

The chapter includes the theoretical base, the assessment tools, and the cognitive treatment goals and applications we used. We also present a case example and discuss implications for future knowledge development.

Theoretical Base

This chapter's purpose is to describe a cognitive retraining or remediation approach in occupational therapy with brain-injured adults. Our rationale for this approach is based on neuropsychological and cognitive theories (developmental and information processing). Neuropsychology provides the understanding of brain function and the basis and justification for treatment, whereas cognitive theories provide an understanding of the nature of intellectual processes and the developmental sequence. Cognitive theories also influenced the development of the evaluation tools and treatment methods we used. These knowledge bases were then combined with occupational therapy principles of active intervention and philosophical assumptions regarding the quality of life and the importance of independent coping with daily tasks.

Neuropsychological Rationale

The cortex is described as a network of fibers, as "wiring diagrams" (Braitenberg, 1978). Each brain region is involved in various functions and interacts with other regions in completing a specific task. Thus, every normal act is a result of a dynamic balance between all brain structures. According to Luria (1973), "mental functions . . . cannot be localized in narrow zones of the cortex . . . but must be organized in systems of concretely working zones, each of which performs its role in complex functional system" (p. 31). Luria also states that global function is constant, while the relationships among its components are variable and influenced by the specific circumstances under which a function is performed. Thus, the way (or the actions) through which a specific task is performed vary according to circumstances. The system, the "network of fibers," of the higher mental processes in the human cortex constantly change during the child's development and are influenced by his or her environment (learning and training process). The structures of higher mental processes change and with them their relationships to each other, their "intellectual organization" (Vygotsky, 1962). Normal function, therefore, is the result of a dynamic balance between all brain structures.

A brain injury causes a disturbance in the delicate balance between brain structures, which is not only the result of a localized lesion of one of the brain areas. A lesion in each zone or area may lead to disintegration of the entire functional system (Luria, 1973, 1980). In other words, the functional system as a whole can be disturbed by a lesion within a very large number of areas and can be disturbed differently by lesions in different localizations.

Brain damage can also cause symptoms that result from disinhibition of an intact area, not only from the damaged area. Treatment aims, therefore, to regain a balance between the brain structures and to create compensatory strategies for improving function. Because there are several ways to perform cognitive functions, they offer the rationale for training that will create alternative strategies and achieve the reorganization of impaired intellectual abilities.

In summary, "the multiplicity of functions fulfilled by cortical regions, the variety of ways in which complex cognitive functions can be performed, and the different contingencies of learning tasks on an intact brain offer a substrate for the functional reorganization of impaired intellectual abilities" (Rahmani, 1987, p. 5).

The Cognitive Rationale

Cognitive theories study the information processing of the normal intellect. The information an individual has to process comes from three sources: (a) his or her environment, (b) his or her memory, where the information is compared to previous experiences; and (c) the feedback he or she receives after the action (Bourne et al., 1979). Information passes through several stages, during which it is received, registered, and encoded. This processed information is then organized as a schemata. Neisser (1976) defines schema as "that portion of the entire perceptual cycle which is internal to the perceiver, modifiable by experience, and somehow specific to what is being perceived. The schema accepts information as it becomes available at sensory surfaces and is changed by that information; it directs movements and exploratory activities that make more information available by which it is further modified" (p. 54). Schemas enable us to handle large bodies of information by allowing us to compare new stimuli with previous experiences and then modify and change the schema, similar to Piaget's process of assimilation and accommodation (Ginsburg & Opper, 1979).

The normal individual actively seeks and assimilates information in relation to his or her ability to understand and then to remember it. This search is guided by schemata which represent the layout of our memories and knowledge. Perception, thinking, and memory are constantly interacting. Comprehension and memory depend on what and how we perceive. Perception is influenced by our ability to (1) appreciate the relevance of the information, (2) distinguish among hierarchical constellations of attributes characteristic of different information, and (3) distinguish among hierarchical constellations of attributes characteristic of the different information that is perceived. These abilities further rely heavily on previous experiences and accumulated knowledge.

For example, visual identification is strongly affected by the ability to analyze the information according to its hierarchical attributes and previous experiences. Identification is much clearer when we deal with incomplete or partial information, such as in embedded figures. Identification is made by characteristic features, by the prototype of the groups to which the specific item belongs (Rahmani, 1982; 1987). According to Rosch's studies (1975; 1978) the formation and learning of components is based on forming preferential levels of abstraction, selecting prototypes, creating object categories, and determining the degree of category membership. In a similar way, the learning process and memory are strongly affected by the perception process. The various mechanisms of the cognitive functions of perception, thinking operations and memory, provide procedures for cognitive retraining of the impaired intellectual processes in brain-injured patients.

Occupational Therapy for Brain-Injured Patients

Occupational therapists have long treated patients with brain damage caused by traumatic injuries, stroke, and other neurological causes. Recently, however, there has been an increased interest in developing knowledge of the relationships between cognitive deficits and functional performance. In almost all occupational therapy models cognition is considered one of the major performance or competence components that determine occupational performance or human occupation (Allen, 1985; Katz, 1985; Kielhofner, 1985; Mosey, 1986; Pedretti, 1985). Moreover, we believe that cognitive components are the major predictor of rehabilitation outcomes in brain-injured patients; hence, we focus on these assets (Bernspang et al., 1989; Rahmani, 1982).

Various approaches to the treatment of these patients are mentioned in the occupational therapy literature: sensorimotor or neurodevelopmental, transfer of training, behavioral or social, and functional (Giles & Clark-Wilson, 1988; Siev et al., 1986; Zoltan & Ryckman Meeder, 1985). More recently, Toglia (1991) described a multicontext approach. Neistadt (1988; 1990) divided the different approaches of cognitive treatment in occupational therapy into two main categories: (a) the adaptive approach, which emphasizes the functional and practical aspects of everyday activities; and (b) the remedial approach, which emphasizes the training of the cognitive components and their generalization across all activities. The two-phase treatment approach as it is practiced at Loewenstein Rehabilitation Hospital combines these two approaches in the cognitive rehabilitation program, although the retraining phase is central to the process.

Underlying the remedial approach to (or retraining of) cognitive deficits is the assumption that generalization occurs from practice in one modality to other modalities and tasks. The functional approach assumes that brain-injured patients must practice directly every activity they have to perform and that generalization can't be taken for granted. However, using a combination of both during the rehabilitation process seems to be the right approach for adult brain-injured patients. To practice only specific tasks will limit the patient's adaptation; training in tabletop or computer tasks without also practicing real tasks may be inadequate (Abreu & Toglia, 1987; Toglia, 1991).

Furthermore, for occupational therapists the real test of treatment success is performance of purposeful activities in the person's real-world environment. Therefore, even though the main part of treatment in this approach is retraining of cognitive skills, their actual internalization and generalization across tasks has to be tested in real-life situations. Only then is rehabilitation accomplished (Katz, 1988).

Definition of Main Cognitive Concepts

Cognition

"Cognition is the activity of knowing: the acquisition, organization, and use of knowledge" (Neisser, 1978, p. 1). It consists of the intellectual processes that are responsible for function and behavior. Cognition is prerequisite for managing all encounters with the environment. Cognition consists of interrelated processes including the ability to perceive, organize, assimilate, and manipulate information (Abreu and Toglia, 1987). By the same token, cognition (according to Piaget) is equated with intelligent adaptation to the environment. "Cognition is conceived of as a general term that covers attention, perception, thinking operations and memory" (Katz et al., 1989, p. 186).

Perception

Perception is the ability to perceive information and is regarded as the first step and prerequisite to higher function. However, perception relies on the perceiver's experience and previous knowledge. Perception centers on all sensory areas: visual, spatial, auditory, and tactile. In the literature the study of perception focuses largely on visual identification. Visual identification of objects is based on the perceiver's ability to appreciate objects' characteristic features and their relevance (Neisser, 1976).

Thinking Operations

Thinking operations consist of conceptual processes and learning processes and include the ability to categorize, relate information to a hierarchical order, determine the relevance of the information according to a particular situation, sequence information, and solve problems. Problem solving is a behavior directed toward achieving a goal. It involves breaking the goal down into hierarchical tasks that will result in achieving the goal (Rahmani, 1987).

Memory

Memory refers to the capacity for keeping an amount of information in an active state (short-term memory) or the ability to recall or retrieve information from long-term memory. However, information can be used only in an active state and active modes of processing are needed to remember information. Memory is the output of well-processed information from a good thinking process. New material can be learned by visual encoding and/or verbal encoding (Paivio, 1975).

Attention and Concentration

Attention and concentration are the basis of any cognitive performance. Attention is a limited mental resource that can be allocated at the most to a few cognitive processes at a time. Processes that require attention are called controlled processes (Shiffrin & Schneider, 1977). Attention is the ability to focus on specified information at a given time, or to focus on different information at a certain point in time. Concentration is the ability to apply attention over a specific time course (Hoofien, 1987).

Visuomotor Organization

Visuomotor organization is the area that combines perceptual activity with motor response and has a spatial component, including activities such as drawing, copying, building, or assembling. Difficulties in this area are expressed in the performance of ADL tasks and complex activities of any kind (Lezak, 1983).

Intervention

Target Population

The cognitive retraining approach was originally developed for adults with traumatic brain injuries but is now used with almost all neuropsychologically impaired patients. It has also been recently adapted for adolescents with learning problems.

Evaluation

Cognitive rehabilitation theory assumes that most normal adults achieve a basic cognitive task performance. We, therefore, start by assessing the patient's current cognitive task performance. This assessment serves as a baseline for measuring progress, and, together with premorbid information, sensory motor evaluation, and functional status evaluation in daily activities, this assessment forms the basis for treatment planning (Katz, Hefner, & Reuben, 1990). Assessment of cognition includes two batteries, the Lowenstein occupational therapy cognitive assessment (LOTCA) (Itzkovich et al., 1990) and the Rivermead behavioral memory test (RBMT) (Wilson et al., 1985, Hebrew translation Averbuch & Katz.)

Cognitive Assessment Battery

The Loewenstein occupational therapy cognitive assessment (LOTCA) was developed at Loewenstein Rehabilitation Center (LRH) in Israel, to assess basic cognitive abilities of brain-injured patients (Katz et al., 1989; Najenson et al., 1984). Basic cognitive abilities are defined as those "intellectual functions thought to be prerequisite for managing everyday encounters with the environment" (Najenson et al., 1984, p. 315).

The LOTCA battery was derived from clinical experience as well as from Luria's (neuropsychological) and Piaget's (developmental) theories and evaluation procedures (Golden, 1984; Inhelder & Piaget, 1964). The battery provides an initial profile of the cognitive abilities of the brain-injured patient as a starting point for occupational therapy intervention and a screening test for further assessment. It consists of 20 subtests and is divided into four areas: orientation, visual and spatial perception, visuomotor organization, and thinking operations. The battery takes 30- to 45-minutes to administer but can be divided into shorter sessions if necessary. Procedures for evaluating patients with expressive language deficits are included. (See Figure 1 for the LOTCA scoring sheet.)

The battery's measurement properties were established in various ways. Inter-rater reliability coefficients of .82 to .97 for the various subtests were determined, and an alpha coefficient of .85 and above was determined for internal consistency of three areas of perception, visuomotor organization, and thinking operations using two patients groups and a normal control group (Katz et al., 1989). Validity in differentiating between known groups was determined with the Wilcoxon two-sample test which showed that all subtests differentiated at the .0001 level of significance between controls and both the patient groups with traumatic brain injuries and craniovascular accident (TBD and CVA). Initial construct validity was examined using an exploratory factor analysis, which showed a three-factor solution and a total amount of variance explained above 60% (which is substantial) supporting the assumed structure of the LOTCA (Katz et al., 1989). Criterion validity was examined within the CCI group for the visuomotor organization area using the block design sub-test of the WAIS (Wechsler, 1981). A Pearson correlation coefficient of $r = .68$ was found between the score on the block design and the mean score of the visuomotor organization subtests of the

Name: _____S._____

Date: __First x_____Second o__

LOTCA Battery: Scoring sheet
(check the appropriate number)

SUB-TESTS	score low			high		COMMENTS
ORIENTATION						
Time	1	2	3	(X)		
Place	1	2	3	(X)		
PERCEPTION						
Object Identification	1	2	3	(X)		
Shapes Identification	1	2	3	(X)		
Overlapping Figures	1	2	3	(X)		
Object Constancy	1	2	3	(X)		
Spatial Perception	1	2	3	(X)		
Praxis	1	2	3	(X)		
VISUOMOTOR ORGANIZATION						
Copying Geometric Forms	1	2	3	(X)		
Reproduction of a Two-Dimensional Model	1	2	3	(X)		
Pegboard Construction	1	2	3	(X)		
Colored Block Design	1	2	X	(4)		
Plain Block Design	1	2	X	(4)		
Reproduction of a Puzzle	1	X	(3)	4		
Drawing a Clock	1	2	3	(X)		
THINKING OPERATIONS						
Categorization	1	X	(3)	4	5	
ROC Unstructured	X	2	(3)	4	5	
ROC Structured	X	2	(3)	4	5	
Pictorial Sequence A	1	2	X	(4)		
Pictorial Sequence B	1	X	3	(4)		
Geometric Sequence	X	2	3	(4)		
Indicate: Length of time :						
Given in:	⊠ One session			☐ Two or more sessions		

**Based on observation during test performance,
circle the appropriate number:
Attention and Concentration   1   2   3 (4)**

Figure 9-1 The LOTCA scoring sheet.

LOTCA, and a $r = .77$ when time was not measured on the block design. Almost identical results were found for a group of adult inpatients with chronic schizophrenia ($r = .69$ and $r = .78$) (Katz & Hiemann, 1990).

Age-level standards were also determined by testing 240 normal primary school children, with 40 subjects in each age group between 6 and 12 years. Children's performance on the LOTCA was assessed to determine age norms of the various subtests, as well as to verify the hierarchical order in which the various cognitive competencies included in the battery are acquired. Results show a clear developmental sequence in performance along the LOTCA subtests. Performance levels increased steadily with age, while the performance speed of visuomotor tasks decreased concomitant with the increase towards maximal performance (Averbuch & Katz, 1991; Itzkovich et al., 1990). These findings support the battery's assumed hierarchical order and the intended basic level of cognitive abilities measured with the LOTCA. Thus, the measurement properties of the LOTCA were found to be reliable both in agreement between raters and in the internal consistency of its three component areas: perception, visuomotor organization, and thinking operations. The LOTCA was also valid in differentiating between healthy adults and those with brain injuries. This finding, along with the results of a previous study where the performance profile of psychiatric patients was shown to differ from brain-injured patients (Averbuch & Katz, 1988), suggests that the LOTCA can differentiate performance level as well as between patterns of cognitive deficits related to the site of the brain lesions.

On the individual level the LOTCA is used at LRH as a measure of the patient's status over time, that is, as a measure for clinical change. In those cases where deficits were present at initial assessment, the LOTCA is employed as a measure for following up on patients' progress. The assessment should be repeated after an interval of at least 2 months to avoid simple memory carryover. However, learning, as a possible explanation for higher scores, must always be considered because many similar tasks are practiced during treatment. This learning, if generalized, is precisely the purpose of treatment; it should not be regarded as a threat to validity as defined in measurement theory (Katz, Hefner, & Ruben, 1990).

The Rivermead Behavioral Memory Test

Memory deficits are evaluated with the Rivermead behavioral memory test, which is a battery designed by neuropsychologists and occupational therapists at Rivermead Rehabilitation Center in England. The battery was designed to assess memory abilities in everyday tasks: ". . . it is assessing skills necessary for adequate functioning in normal life. . . . can also be used to help therapists identify areas for treatment" (Wilson et al., 1985, p. 4).

The RBMT consists of 11 subtests that assess verbal and visual recognition and recall, learning and recall of instructions, and recall of a spatial root. All subtests use simple and everyday instruments. For example, one of the instructions is to remember to ask when the next appointment is, when the clock rings, or to ask for a personal belonging at the end of the assessment that had been given to the therapist at the beginning of the session.

Treatment

The patient's cognitively impaired functions are one of the most important factors influencing his or her daily living. Therefore, the aims of cognitive retraining are to enlarge and enhance cognitive abilities by providing the tools and reinforcing the patient's ability to cope with everyday tasks of life.

Cognitive Effects of Brain Damage

Brain damage reduces the individual's ability to process the information needed for identification, thinking operations, and remembering and executing everyday tasks. It limits the individual's ability to organize the information required for planning acts. The brain-injured person is limited in the number of items he or she can manipulate simultaneously or sequentially; thus, his or her ability to find various solutions to a given problem is limited. His or her cognitive behavior is concrete and relies strongly on personal experience.

However, brain damage does not affect equally the various cognitive components. The injury always has a predominant effect on one of the cognitive areas. In other words, perception, thinking operations, and memory are not equally impaired. Some sustain more damage, while others, although affected, are less impaired and function better.

Cognitive deficits minimize the brain-injured person's efficiency in every aspect of life: in self-care, social behavior, and in his or her professional life.

Treatment Goals

The general purpose of retraining the perception processes, thinking operations, and memory is to broaden the patient's capacity to handle information and transform it into purposeful activities (Rahmani et al., 1987). Training is expected to lead the patient to a systematic search for information, a process that can be generalized to other tasks.

The therapist's first goal in cognitive treatment is to enhance and strengthen the patient's remaining or less-weakened cognitive abilities. As mentioned earlier, when brain damage is involved not all cognitive functions are equally impaired. By strengthening the intact areas of cognitive ability we create the base for new cognitive strategies.

Creating new alternative strategies is the second goal of treatment. Alternative strategies are different tools, or ways, to receive and accumulate information. The therapist uses alternative strategies to train the patient to systematically perceive information, process it, and act accordingly. The goal is to help the patient acquire the strategy to decide which information is the most relevant to him or her under different circumstances and, accordingly, to be able to solve problems in different ways. Achieving these goals will lead to the creation of new functional patterns, the result of which will be a different behavioral cognitive structure. This will, in turn, improve functional performance.

Treatment Process

The treatment process has two phases. First, the treatment focus is on the cognitive impaired areas. Second, the focus is on adaptation to the environment.

The cognitive treatment is based on the patient's results on the LOTCA and RBMT and his or her premorbid cognitive ability as related by family members in the anamnestic interview.

The training is constructed on different levels in every cognitive area: perception, visuomotor organization, thinking operations, and memory. Each level is characterized by the amount of information present to be processed and its complexity. On each level the patient is trained to develop specific strategies appropriate to the cognitive area and to the particular level. These strategies are the base for the functional scheme, which will help in developing skills to handle more complex tasks and is prerequisite for training at the next more complex level. On each level, once the patient has internalized the given cognitive strategies and can manipulate them on different modalities, he or she will be trained to adjust and adapt them to activities of real life. To clarify, at first the patient will be trained in specific strategies that strengthen his or her intact cognitive skills in order to deal with the impaired cognitive areas. The training will be done in the occupational therapy department with specific tools, similar to those in a laboratory environment. After the strategies are learned and, within the laboratory environment, the patient can use the strategies on different materials, he or she will be instructed and encouraged to transfer them to real-life situations (at first, in the hospital environment in activities of daily living and, later, at home).

The end result of treatment is that the patient integrates the different strategies he or she has learned into schematic patterns and finally into a new functional behavioral system.

For simplicity and clarity, the following description of the treatment process is divided into the different cognitive components. The areas are, of course, interrelated as are the treatment and its effects.

Training of Visual Perception

The first purpose of visual perception training is to reinforce the identification of concrete objects, which is done by showing the patient how to search for information in order to identify objects and to understand the consistent combination of their attributes. The therapist uses different procedures, and they are given here in a hierarchical order, from simple to complex. The complexity depends on the number of stimuli and the clarity of their representation.

First, various concrete, daily objects are presented. At first, they are presented separately and later together. The patient has to search for the relevant attributes that create the object (color, shape, material, etc.) Touch and sound is used as an additional source of information. After the patient has become acquainted with the strategy he is required to use it to identify objects that are grouped together. This task is more complex because parts of the information are hidden.

Second, the patient is trained to identify pictorial and schematic presentations of the objects from step 1. The strategy is broadened by drawing the patient's attention toward the specific features of the objects as they are represented in pictures.

Third, the patient is trained to identify pictures of various degrees of ambiguity. The ambiguity can be either pictures of embedded objects, photos of objects taken from unusual angles, or drawings of objects based on their parts. All these procedures help to develop the patient's ability to identify objects with incomplete information.

Fourth, the patient is taught to discriminate subtle differences between objects. This is done by comparing pictures differing in one or more details, or matching pictures with a large number of variables.

Fifth, finally the patient engages in the most complex task, which is to identify a pictorial situation. This task is not purely visual—it combines more than one cognitive area but can be used for training the specific weak area.

Along each level the patient is trained to use these specific strategies in real life, for example, to identify items according to a list in the supermarket, to find the car in the parking lot, or to identify the needed key.

Training Spatial Perception

The training consist of developing the patient's orientation in the personal space and the extrapersonal space, and in recognizing spatial reversal.

Personal Space. In this task, the procedures used are: identifying body parts and knowing their location; awareness of the body's middle line and its right—left and up—down position. Treatment focuses on helping the patient cross the midline smoothly by using tasks that use these features: for example, all the self-care tasks, such as washing and dressing, etc.

Extrapersonal Space. The treatment purpose here is to identify the position of objects near—far from patients, above—under, and at his or her left—right. The relations between space and person. Training procedures such as arranging the table for dinner, or arranging clothes in the closet are used.

Reversal. In reversal, the purpose is to identify reversed directions in space. First on the trainer's body, while he or she is sitting in front of the patient, and later in the street and finally on the map.

Training of Visuomotor Organization

This area combines the abilities of perception and motor action. Constructional activities, at any level, are the expression of perceptual abilities, praxis abilities, and organization. The patient is trained how to analyze perceptual models, how to plan their reproduction, and finally how to construct them. The main purpose of this strategy is the ability to analyze and synthesize given plans. Various procedures are used in order to train and enhance the constructional strategy.

First the patient must learn how to scan a given model, how to analyze its combination of components. In order to achieve this he or she must copy simple forms or reproduce designs combined of clearly distinct parts. The schema will then be gradually enlarged by more demanding tasks in terms of components. The patient will have to copy complex forms. He or she will be trained to reproduce models that require counting and accurate part or model location, without clear distinction of the compounding parts. Reproducing three-dimensional models, will help the patient as will models in perspective. Finally the patient will have to alter his learned strategy by constructing new strategies according to professional plans.

We should comment that not everyone needs all levels of this activity in their daily life; not all of them will be able to or need to read and reconstruct a plan but almost everyone can learn the simple forms when necessary. What we have described is the extent of our training in occupational therapy. However, when the patient needs these elaborate skills for his or her profession, he or she will be referred on for vocational training.

Training of Thinking Operations

The basis of thinking operations is classification skills and simple logical sequence. In order to develop classification skills, the patient is trained to make the distinction between relevant and irrelevant features of objects. Then he or she must choose the hierarchical order of the relevant features and create simple categories and subcategories, according to the most relevant feature. The features become a criteria for creating a category, and the patient has to be able to shift from one criteria to another. The ability to shift between criteria is the difference between concrete and flexible thinking. These skills in everyday life can be used with activities that require planning and organization, such as shopping, arranging items in drawers or cupboards, and preparing ingredients for cooking, etc.

The logical operations of transitivity and of cause and effect relations are the next step of our training, which is done with different materials and different modalities. Patients will learn to solve logical problems that involve one, two, or more compounding parts; and mathematical problems. Patients will read short stories and answer questions about what they've read, drawing conclusions. Each of these tasks demands systematic strategies of thinking. Sequence is another essential thinking operation. In order to solve a problem, operations have to be done in the right order. This order depends on the patient's ability to sequence. The tasks we use involve arranging pictorial situations and different series of numbers, forms, etc. In order to solve problems, one must have the ability to draw conclusions from one stage to another. One also needs the ability to judge and appreciate the results of his or her solutions. Finally, it is crucial to train these strategies in real problems of everyday life.

Training of Memory

Memory deficits are a major problem for patients with brain injuries. Often they are the only problem the patient notices. Brain-injured patients complain about their lack of memory even when it, objectively, is not their main problem. Memory seems to be the most concrete difficulty; it is easily understood by others and accepted as a very plausible excuse for many other disabilities. However, memory is affected by many cognitive components, and memory problems are the result of other impairments. For example, if patients have difficulties in thinking operations, they will ultimately have memory problems. Information that was not systematically perceived will be stored directly and its retrieval from memory will be incomplete and incoherent. To create functional schemes for learning and remembering, the patient must use other cognitive components, like perception skills, association cues, sequencing and problem-solving strategies. At the same time, the patient will be trained to use adaptive tools, such as note books or tape recorders.

Orientation. The first purpose of training is to help the patient orient him- or her-self to the immediate place and time. The task begins by orienting the patient to the immediate environment of the department and hospital. The therapist administers the training at three parallel channels: first, through conversation the patient is supplied with the accurate information about his or her physical environment and later about his or her time environment. The patient is given the same information in written instructions that are the basis of experiencing everyday tasks. The same bits of information must be given in conversation, writing, and real experience. New information will be added gradually as soon as the patient is able to handle the old information. When training topographic memory of the environment, the therapist instructs the patient to create landmarks of perceptual cues along the way. When training is done in real experiences, the patient has to recite aloud what has been learned by conversation, reading the written instruction, and showing mastery of his or her ability in his or her actions. The training will be enlarged to the outside world and home surroundings, gradually, using the same procedures.

Short-Term Memory. The common expression of short-term memory is when the patient cannot recall an immediate item, usually he or she will be surprised that something has already been presented. To reinforce his or her ability we will use association techniques, the key feature of which is creating familiar associations for the patient. In other words, the point of this procedure is to work intensely on the patient's perceiving and storing processes. These procedures are very useful for recalling names of people, short events, and short bits of information.

Long-Term Memory. Long-term memory loss is seen in the patient's difficulty learning new material from newspapers or professional materials. The major feature of training at this level is content analysis, which consists of dividing the information into concrete meaningful parts, understanding and pointing to the logical sequence of the events, and, thus, creating a framework for arranging and storing information. The frame is the anchor, the landmark of recall. Once the information has been systematically stored it will be much easier to recall if the patient is asked general questions about the learning procedures; for example, What kind of information was it? What was the main topic? What sort of things happened? Was it funny? Was it about people, animals? and so on.

As the patient progresses clinically, the questions become increasingly general, helping the patient to search for the proper information. As mentioned earlier, the patient is trained to use a notebook to register relevant information in it and to use it properly as a reminder while ignoring what is no longer relevant.

Attention

Attention is often presented as a major deficit when discussing cognitive impairment. There are treatment approaches where the main effort is made in developing attention. Attention is a major factor of mental function. However, we regard it as inherent in every cognitive process and assume that by training the patient in specific cognitive processes, his or her attention will be positively affected. Therefore, we don't train attention as an independent entity but use it as part of the different cognitive areas.

Case Study

R.S. is a 44-year-old woman, who is married and has 4 children. She is a family physician. After she suffered headaches for over a year, she found out that she had a meningioma on her left frontal lobe. The meningioma was removed in a bifrontal craniotomy. Two weeks after the operation she was transferred to LRH.

At the first evaluation, R.S. had no motor or sensory deficits, her only deficits were cognitive. The LOTCA assessment showed that her main difficulties lay in thinking operations (see Figure 1 for a profile of the tests). She had major difficulties in choosing the right criteria for categorization. When she chose criteria with the therapist's help, she had fewer problems maintaining them during sorting. Sometimes, during the session she lost the meaning of categorization and worked in an associative way.

In the beginning, R.S.'s appearance was sloppy and neglected. She could wear the same clothes day after day without noticing they were no longer clean. Her behavior was very passive; she showed no affect in her speech and no facial mimics. When describing her situation, she expressed feelings of "not being OK" and feeling helpless.

From the beginning she could work for a long period of time, without losing concentration. She had high motivation and was willing to do anything to progress.

The first goal of therapy was to help her develop basic logical thinking by training her with simple sorting tasks of concrete categories and sequencing. We began by sorting everyday objects by their attributes and learning the meaning of categories. First, we dealt with concrete and everyday categories that differed from one another, for example, clothes and food. We focused on selecting the relevant criteria for sorting and using them in groups of only four or five objects. R.S. learned how to analyze an object, decide what its attributes are and how they relate in hierarchical order, and define what attribute that defines the object is most meaningful, for example, the most meaningful attribute of a pencil is its use for writing. Many concrete objects are defined by their usage. After R.S. was able to sort objects correctly and she had clearly learned how to do it, it was important to train and transfer this ability to activities of daily life. Together with her therapist, she began to organize her schedule for the day. At this point in treatment R.S. became an out-patient and stayed half a day at home. We sorted out the different tasks she has to perform by different criteria, such as when they took place during the day, morning tasks, or activities of personal ADL, and self-care of her children (breakfast, sandwiches for school, etc.), and house-keeping activities. Every group of activities was hierarchically and sequentially arranged and written down. Being at home she had to follow the schedule. She put a great deal of effort into improving her appearance. Once learned, she had no difficulty adapting this skill at home, and her family reported that she constantly improved her home duties.

In further training sessions, we gradually increased her thinking ability to deal with more abstract categories, and began to work on medical study materials. Using the same techniques of searching for the relevant attributes of the object, we began to construct a schema of analyzing a text. The schema consisted of finding the main issues and underlying the important paragraphs; distinguishing between relevant and irrelevant information; writing the characteristics in order of importance to the main issue; and finally drawing conclusions from the given information. At first R.S. had great difficulty locating the important information, she felt that she could not understand the meaning of the sentences. This was quite a shock to her because it was medical material that she had known very well in the past. She needed a great deal of comforting in order to "survive" the nightmare. The training on medical material at this point was at her demand. The turning point occurred when she succeeded in finding the main paragraphs and was able to learn the whole procedure. Manipulating the schema described earlier, she could learn relevant material from her medical books. She responded with joy and fear simultaneously, asking if she would be able one day to return to her practice.

At the same time, she fulfilled all her duties at home as before, except that it took her longer and her performance was less pedantic than before.

At this stage one of the physicians at the hospital volunteered to work with us to assess her real professional abilities. The main problem that occurred was, after hours of training and learning certain material, R.S., was not able to recall it properly. The physician said that "she knows everything but can't use it on her own properly." R.S. said that she felt that she forgot everything. In order to overcome this obstacle, we constructed together an empty chart suitable to her material. It consisted of headlines such as diagnosis, clinical signs, treatment, differential diagnosis, side effects, and so on. We used this method over and over, filling it in with different information according to what she learned. The method helped and she performed significantly better.

R.S. began to help a colleague in his clinic twice a week and worked in the emergency room in the hospital twice a week. In both places she began work under the close supervision of her colleagues. The reports of her performance were positive, she was her own greatest critic. She proved to be a very responsible person. When she felt confident enough, she returned to her work knowing that when she has difficulties she will have to consult another physician colleague.

In summary, a year after the craniotomy she was back home and at work. Her only complaints were of tiredness and of falling asleep early at nights. Her family approved her report adding, however, that she had lost a certain quality of herself. The profile in Figure 1 illustrates her improvement on the LOTCA. The treatment was intensive and progress was achieved in gradual steps with a significant amount of effort and work on the patient's part.

Implications for Further Development

The cognitive approach presented in this chapter centers around the clinical practice. Its development went the route of practice—theory—research and back to practice. Our starting point was the observation of traumatic brain-injured patients' performance whose major dysfunction appeared in the area of cognitive deficits and their effects on function. In spite of the assumption that the retraining approach enlarges the functional schemes and, as such, may be generalized to all functional areas, an adaptive approach should accompany the whole treatment process.

Further knowledge development and clinical applications as well as research studies are needed. We have planned studies to verify the predictive capacity of the evaluation instruments to functional performance in various populations. In addition, the effectiveness of the treatment approach should be investigated in longitudinal studies that are composed of qualitative as well as quantitative methods.

We are currently planning clinical applications that will extend the range of populations treated to patients in prevocational rehabilitation. The purpose is to enlarge the range of vocational possibilities the patient with traumatic brain injuries can acquire, and to adapt the tasks to the patient's abilities. We will analyze prevocational assessment instruments according to the cognitive components in order to ensure each patient the best learning process.

References

Abreu, B. C., & Toglia, J. P. (1987). Cognitive rehabilitation: A model for occupational therapy. *American Journal of Occupational Therapy, 41*(7), 439–453.

Allen, C. K. (1985). *Occupational therapy for psychiatric diseases: Measurement and management of cognitive disabilities.* Boston: Little, Brown.

Averbuch, S., & Katz, N. (1988). Assessment of perceptual cognitive performance: Comparison of psychiatric and brain injured adult patients. *Occupational Therapy in Mental Health, 8*(1), 57–71.

Averbuch, S., & Katz, N. (1991). Age level standards of the Loewenstein occupational therapy cognitive assessment (LOTCA). *The Israel Journal of Occupational Therapy, 1*(1).

Berenspang, B., Viitanen, M., & Eriksson, S. (1989). Impairments of perceptual and motor functions: Their influence on self-care ability 4 to 6 years after a stroke. *Occupational Therapy Journal of Research, 9,* 27–37.

Bourne, L. E., Dominski, R. L., & Loftus, E. F. (1979). *Cognitive processes.* Englewood Cliffs, NJ: Prentice-Hall.

Braitenberg, V. (1978). Cortical architectonic: general and areal. In M. A. Brazier, & H. Petsche (Eds.). *Architectonics of the cerebral cortex.* New York: Raven Press.

Giles, G. M. & Clark-Wilson, J. (1988). The use of behavioral techniques in functional skills training after severe brain injury. *American Journal of Occupational Therapy, 42*(10), 658–665.

Ginsburg, H., & Opper, S. (1979). *Piaget's theory of intellectual development.* Englewood Cliffs, NJ: Prentice-Hall.

Golden, C. J. (1984). Rehabilitation and the Luria-Nebraska neuropsychological battery. In B. A. Edelstein & E. T. Couture (Eds.), *Behavioral assessment and rehabilitation of the traumatically brain-damaged* (pp. 313–338). New York: Plenum Press.

Hoofien, D. (1987). Rehabilitation of attention. In A. Mazzucchi, (Ed.), *Neuropsychological rehabilitation.* Bologna, Italy: Il Mulino.

Inhelder, B., & Piaget, J. (1964). *The early growth of logic in the child.* New York: W.W. Morton.

Itzkovich, M., Elazar, B., Averbuch, S., & Katz, N. (1990). *LOTCA manual.* NJ: Maddak Inc.

Katz, N. (1985). Occupational therapy's domain of concern: reconsidered. *American Journal of Occupational Therapy, 39*(8), 518–524.

Katz, N. (1988). Principles and theoretical approaches in practice. In D. W. Scott, & N. Katz (Eds.), *Occupational therapy in mental health.* London: Taylor & Francis.

Katz, N., Itzkovich, M., Averbuch, S., & Elazar, B. (1989). Loewenstein occupational therapy cognitive assessment (LOTCA), battery for brain-injured patients: Reliability and validity. *American Journal of Occupational Therapy, 43*(3), 184–192.

Katz, N., Hefner, D., & Ruben, R. (1990). Measuring clinical change in cognitive rehabilitation of patients with brain damage: Two cases, traumatic brain injury and cerebral vascular accident. *Occupational Therapy in Health Care, 7*(1), 23–43.

Katz, N., & Heimann, N. (1990). Review of research conducted in Israel on cognitive disability instrumentation. *Occupational Therapy in Mental Health, 10*(4), 1–15.

Kielhofner, G. (1985). *A model of human occupation.* Baltimore: Williams & Wilkins.

Lezak, M. D. (1983). *Neuropsychological assessment.* New York: Oxford University Press.

Luria, A. R. (1973). *The working brain.* England: Penguin Books.

Luria, A. R. (1980). *Higher cortical functions in man.* New York: Basic Books.

Mosey, A. C. (1986). *Psychosocial components of occupational therapy.* New York: Raven.

Najenson, T., Rahmani, L., Elazar, B., & Averbuch, S. (1984). An elementary cognitive assessment and treatment of the craniocerebrally injured patient. In B. A. Edelstein & E. T. Couture (Eds.), *Behavioral assessment and rehabilitation of the traumatically brain damaged* (pp. 313–338). New York: Plenum Press.

Neistadt, M. E. (1988). Occupational therapy for adults with perceptual deficits. *American Journal of Occupational Therapy, 42,* 434–440.

Neistadt, M. E. (1990). A critical analysis of occupational therapy approaches for perceptual deficits in adult with brain injury. *American Journal of Occupational Therapy, 44*(4), 299–304.

Neisser, U. (1976). *Cognition and reality.* New York: W. H. Freeman & Co.

Paivio, A. (1975). Perceptual comparisons through the mind's eye. *Memory and Cognition, 3,* 635–647.

Pedretti, L. W. (1985). *Occupational therapy practice skills for physical dysfunction, 2nd ed.* St. Louis: C. V. Mosby.

Rahmani, L. (1982). The intellectual rehabilitation of brain-damaged patients. *Clinical Neuropsychology, 4*(1), 44–45.

Rahmani, L. (1987). Neuro-cognitive theory and the intellectual rehabilitation of brain damaged patients: an introduction. [Unpublished paper.]

Rahmani, L., Geva, N., Rochberg, J., Trope, I., & Bore, B. (1987). Issues in neurocognitive assessment and treatment. In E. Vakil, D. Hoofien, & Z. Groswasser (Eds.), *Rehabilitation of the brain injured* (pp. 43–60). London: Freund Publishing House.

Rosch, E., & Mervis, C. B. (1975). Family resemblances: Studies in the internal structure of categories. *Cognitive Psychology, 8*, 573–605.

Rosch, E. (1978). Principles of categorization. In E. Rosch & B. Lloyed (Eds.), *Cognition and categorization*. Hillsdale, NJ: Erlbaum.

Shiffrin, R. M., & Schneider, W. (1977). Controlled and automatic human information processing: II. Perceptual learning, automatic attending: A general theory. *Psychological Review, 84*, 127–190.

Siev, E., Freishtat, B., & Zoltan, B. (1986). *Perceptual and cognitive dysfunction in the adult stroke patient*. Thorofare, NJ: Slack.

Toglia, J. P. (1991). Generalization of treatment: A multicontext approach to cognitive perceptual impairment in adults with brain injury. *American Journal of Occupational Therapy, 45*(6), 505–516.

Vygotsky, L. S. (1962). *Thought & language*. Cambridge, MA: MIT Press.

Wechsler, D. (1981). *Wechsler adult intelligence scale*. New York: Psychological Corporation.

Wilson, B., Cockburn, J., & Baddeley, A. (1985). *The Rivermead behavioral memory test manual*. London: Thames Vally.

Zoltan, B. B., & Ryckman Meeder, D. (1985). Head injury in adults. In L. W. Pedretti (Ed.), *Occupational therapy practice skills for physical dysfunction*. St. Louis: C. V. Mosby.

10

Viewing Cognition through the Lens of the Model of Human Occupation

Elizabeth DePoy and Janice Posatery Burke

In this chapter we will introduce the reader to cognitive intervention guided by the model of human occupation (Kielhofner & Burke, 1980). We begin with a brief review of two major conceptualizations of cognition, constructivist and information processing, and then suggest a definition of cognition based on a synthesis of both viewpoints. We then review the model of human occupation, after which we advance an analysis of cognition using the model. The chapter concludes with relevant case studies illustrating the application of the model of human occupation to the treatment of two adults with cognitive dysfunction.

Theoretical Base

Cognition

Many definitions of cognition have appeared in the psychological and rehabilitational literature. Human effort to understand our own brain function has been an enduring theme in our history. Although many definitions of intelligence were posited by theorists prior to the twentieth century, the widespread acceptance of a theory of human cognition did not occur until Piaget (1954) advanced his conception of cognitive growth and development.

Piaget

Jean Piaget, who was trained as a biologist, ultimately turned his attention to exploring the human intellect and learning process (Wolman, 1983). Through observing his own children, he developed a constructivist definition of cognition. In other words, he suggested that cognition is composed of internal structures that organize and provide adaptive mental responses to information. Through these structures and processes individuals can reach equilibrium. Cognition, according to Piaget is therefore defined as a biological process of adaptation through which individuals interact with or "do" in their environment (Piaget, 1954). An enriched environment stimulates the acquisition of higher level thought. However, until an individual is biologically read, he or she does not advance to the next cognitive stage. The work of Piaget focuses on three areas of cognition: structures, processes, and development.

Structural elements. The three basic structures through which individuals produce adaptive responses to intellectual material are schemata, structures, and operations. Schemata are defined as meaningful sensory and motor patterns which can be repeated (Piaget, 1952). Next on the complexity hierarchy are structures, which are composed of schemas. Structures organize intellectual material so that mental activity and doing can be linked together. Operations are the most complex structure through which individuals can mentally represent and manipulate ideas. Through operations, individuals can internalize thought and use symbolism to efficiently organize information.

Processes. Cognitive activity, according to Piaget (1952) occurs through two subprocesses of adaptation: assimilation and accommodation. In assimilation, individuals use their existing cognitive skills to make sense of their environments. In accommodation, the opposite occurs. Individuals must modify existing cognitive structures and processes in order to make sense of input which cannot be understood within existing structures. It is the biological/cognitive process of adaptation, coupled with environmental input that is responsible for cognitive maturation.

Development. Piaget viewed cognitive development as a series of stages that occurred sequentially and hierarchically. Each stage is qualitatively different from the previous stage and cannot be developed until the previous one is mastered. The majority of cognitive development occurs from birth through adolescence. As an individual matures, cognition becomes increasingly interiorized. In adulthood, cognition remains stable and comprises both the appropriate use of cognitive structures and operations from all of the developmental stages.

In the first stage of cognitive development, the sensorimotor stage, Piaget suggests that thinking is equal to sensing and doing. He was one of the first theorists to characterize infant intelligence, which he defined as reflexive. The infant proceeds from a reflexive being to one who is capable of communicating, solving problems, and conceptualizing simple ideas related to what he or she senses and experiences.

In the next stage, the preoperational stage, Piaget suggests that children learn to think symbolically and to communicate with symbols (words). By approximately the age of 7, children enter the concrete operational stage in which they are able to formulate logical thoughts and engage in "thinking in their heads." Thinking and learning become less egocentric and more efficient. In Piaget's most developed cognitive stage, formal operations, individuals are able to reason about ideas, not just about those experiences which have referents in their individual experiences. Thus, thought becomes liberated from concrete experiences and complex abstract reasoning is possible.

Contemporary Constructivism

More recent theorists, such as Flavell (1982), Mossler et al. (1976), and Gelman (1978), have suggested that Piaget underestimated the ability of children to engage in more sophisticated, less egocentric cognition. For example, Gelman (1978) suggests that as children are exposed to diverse opinions, they are better able to understand differences and to demonstrate less egocentricity (within the limitations of the qualitative structures of their cognitive maturation). Studies conducted by Seldak and Kurtz (1981) illustrate simple causal reasoning in 3-year-old children, a notion that Piaget refuted. Most recently, researchers are suggesting that infants as young as 2½ months of age recognize the difference between themselves and the external world and, further, demonstrate object constancy (Raymond, 1991).

On the other end of the age spectrum, Hunter and Sundrel (1989) note qualitative changes in cognition as individuals age. Before the 1970s, the common expectation was that as individuals aged, their cognitive abilities diminished. Theories of cognitive decline were based on measuring intelligence with traditional intelligence scales such as the Weschler Adult Intelligence Scale (Weschler, 1944). Typically, adults would begin to demonstrate a drop in scores in their middle age, with extensive decrease in performance in old age. Labouvie-Vief and Hakim-Larson (1989) challenged the decline model by revealing that as individuals age, their cognition beomes more context dependent. In other words, as opposed to youths, adults organize reasoning and learning within familiar contexts and thus do not perform well when asked to exercise reasoning skills in isolation of meaning. The qualitative changes in midlife and old age were, therefore, described using other investigative means. What emerged was the notion of cognition as a phenomenon that is dynamic and changing in adulthood. As individuals mature, their reasoning not only becomes interiorized but also becomes increasingly embedded in the thinker's experience. The commonsense notion of wisdom seems to be consistent with this view of adult cognition. Intelligence is exercised within a large body of uniquely organized knowledge and experience.

In addition to challenging Piaget's age norms for entering cognitive stages, some theorists have suggested that the formal operational stage is not the highest. Arlin (1977) and Commons et al. (1982), for example, suggest higher stages of reasoning, illustrated by famous thinkers such as Einstein.

Summary of the Constructivist Perspective

The constructivist view of cognition, initiated by Piaget and expanded upon by contemporary theorists defines cognition as mental processes that move sequentially from "doing" to increasingly interior representations and manipulations of human experience and ideas. These processes are adaptive and underlie all human learning, knowledge acquisition, and knowledge organization.

Information Processing Models

With the current popularity of computer intelligence, some theorists have recently posited a view of cognition that differs from that posed by Piaget and other constructivists. Human intellect is viewed as a process of information acquisition, processing, and response. Although there are many different views of cognition representing the information processing perspective, three basic categories of reasoning and learning activity are common to all models: input, storage, and output. As a result of categorizing human cognition into these three areas, the elements of cognition and their relationship to each other has been suggested.

Input. Input may be defined as the acquisition of information. Input is dependent on two basic processes, attention span and organization of information gathering. According to Shaffer (1985), attention span in large part determines the amount of information that can be received and processed at any one time. Thus, a younger individual with a short attention span may illustrate reasoning differently from a more mature individual with a longer attention span. This phenomenon occurs not because of qualitative differences in cognition, as suggested by the constructivists, but as a result of limited and disorganized input and storage (Brown & Deloache, 1981).

However, the ability to attend is not the only factor that determines the nature of input. Systematic and organized information gathering is more efficient than random information acquisition. Once again, the less-mature and less-organized individual is less able to acquire relevant input than the more-organized and logical person.

In summary, input can occur in many different ways. The quality of cognition is dependent on the information that one has available to reason with, rendering input a critical focus for determining cognitive differences in individuals.

Storage. Registration, organization, and memory are the three processes in the category of storage. As information is acquired, stimuli are registered for the next step in processing. Organization of information occurs through the cognitive processes of categorizing and coding information so that it can be stored in the individual's memory banks. Once coded, information can be stored in short-term, or working, memory or relegated to long-term memory. Short-term memory is defined as immediate recall whereas long-term memory is considered to be the permanent collection of information (Shaffer, 1985). Long-term memory is not always accessible, however, and many discussions on enhancing retrieval of long-term information have been advanced in the literature. Within long-term memory, are seated episodic and semantic memory. Episodic memory contains information that is experienced and interpreted idiosyncratically. Semantic memory contains general and abstract knowledge including social norms and language rules.

Output. The output phase of cognition involves the generation of ideas, language, and/or action, with particular attention to problem solving. Output occurs from an active response to a combination of stored and new information which is organized differentially by means of each individual's unique thinking style. Thus, output is dependent on obtaining relevant input and on well-organized and retrievable storage, but the organization of knowledge acquisition and storage contribute to the individuality expressed in human reasoning and learning (Flavell, 1977).

More recently another category of cognition, the construct of metacognition, has emerged (Lezak, 1982). This construct, in large part, is based in the information processing approach to cognition. Metacognition is considered to be an awareness of cognitive style, the host of processes that control whether or not cognition occurs, and the executive functions which guide the initiation and regulation of cognitive activity. In other words, metacognition directs and controls how and when cognition occurs.

In summary, the information processing perspective suggests that cognition is a linear process in which information is input, organized in the human brain, and acted upon in the form of output. The regulatory-awareness function of metacognition oversees the cognitive process. Although differences are recognized among age-related cognitive activity, the notion of stage-specific quality of thinking is not present in the information processing approach. Information processing theorists concern themselves with ways to increase the efficiency of cognitive processes in each phase of thought.

Synthesis of Each Perspective

For our discussion, the definition of cognition will be based on a synthesis of knowledge from the constructivist perspective and the information processing approach. Therefore, cognition is defined as the set of dynamic interactions between human mentation and the environment which give rise to reasoning, learning, knowledge use, knowledge building, and planned engagement with the environment. As one matures, the nature of cognition changes and expands from action to internal representation to contextual knowing. The basic components of cognition are considered to be input, organization and storage, and output.

The Model of Human Occupation

The model of human occupation, developed by Kielhofner and Burke (1980) is a conceptual framework that characterizes the domain and practice of occupational therapy. The model is grounded in Reilly's (1962) tradition of occupational behavior and includes important concepts from the field of neuropsychology, humanism, economics, and the behavioral sciences. The model advances a view of human beings that is anchored on an open systems framework. The individual engages in his or her environment actively through three processes: input, throughput, and output. Input, acquired by person–environment interaction, is derived from environmental feedback. Through-put comprises three subsystems intrinsic to all humans: performance, habituation, and volition. These subsystems are arranged hierarchically with performance being the most basic and volition being the most complex. Performance comprises the basic skills on which human function is anchored. Skill categories included in this subsystem are perceptual motor skill, process skill, and communication-interaction skill. "Perceptual motor skills are the abilities for interpreting sensory information and for manipulating self and objects. . . . Process skills are abilities directed at managing events or processes in the environment, . . . [and] communication-interaction skills are abilities for sharing and receiving information and for coordinating one's behavior with that of others in order to accomplish mutual activities and goals" (p. 33, Kielhofner & Burke, 1985). These skills are organized into roles and routines within the habituation subsystem. The volitional subsystem is defined as the set of energizing and symbolic components which together determine conscious choices for occupational behavior. Within the volitional subsystem are interests, personal causation, and values. The volitional subsystem is, therefore, responsible for the extent to which individuals engage in relevant and meaningful occupational behavior, exert a balance of healthy function, and enact values which control the devotion of time to meaningful occupational function (Kielhofner, 1985).

The three subsystems act together, with the performance subsystem at the forefront, to produce output. Through output, individuals influence their environments and elicit feedback. Thus, individuals are seen as dynamic actors and adaptors to the larger system of their environments. (For a full discussion of the model of human occupation refer to Burke and Kielhofner, 1980; and Kielhofner & Burke, 1985.)

Occupational function, within the model of human occupation, is viewed as a continuum, that moves from achievement to helplessness. The three levels of occupation function include achievement, competence, and exploration. In achievement, individuals demonstrate excellence in their activity, while in competence, individuals exhibit function in concert with usual environmental demands and expectations. Exploration is the level at which individuals learn and develop innovative responses to environmental challenges.

An interruption in occupational function can be presented as inefficacy, incompetence, or helplessness. Inefficacy is a decrease in performance, while incompetence is an inability to enact major life roles. In incompetence, volition and performance are negatively affected as well. The most devastating level of occupation dysfunction, helplessness, refers to an absence or disruption of all life roles with accompanying dysfunction in all subsystems.

Applying the Model of Human Occupation to Cognitive Dysfunction

The model of human occupation, as developed by occupational therapists, has a generalist perspective that can be applied to a wide range of disability groups and dysfunctional behaviors in both children and adults. As it applies directly to cognition, the model has been used to guide intervention with clients with traumatic brain damage, persons with psychiatric disabilities, geriatric persons, and individuals with learning disabilities. The model not only organizes intervention, but also provides a framework that can be used for the full occupational therapy process of assessment, intervention, and evaluation. In this part of the chapter, we will use the model to analyze how occupational function is affected by cognitive disability. A case study will then be presented that illustrates the occupational therapy process of assessment, intervention, and evaluation.

Analysis

The model of human occupation is relevant not only because it provides a framework for understanding the components of cognition, but also because it provides a dynamic systems framework through which we can analyze cognitive process. Essentially, the process of cognition advanced in the earlier definition is consistent with the systems view of human beings posited by the model. Congruent with the information processing nomenclature, cognition (through the model) can be viewed as a feedback loop that includes input, throughput (storage), and output. Further, the trajectory of change, specified in the model as growth and development, guides the occupational therapist to view cognition from a contemporary perspective: as a human capacity that becomes refined and evolves as the individual moves through the life span. Any interruption or disruption in cognition has the capacity to move an individual from occupational function to dysfunction.

Structurally, cognition is seated primarily in the process skill arena of the performance subsystem. According to Kielhofner and Burke (1980), problem solving and planning compose process skill. In other words, within the rubric of the model of human occupation, thinking skills are analogous with process skills. However, both communication-interaction and perceptual-motor skill would also be considered by both the constructivists and the information processing theorists to be part and parcel of cognition.

Looking back at piagetian theory, Piaget and contemporary theorists suggest that cognition cannot be fully interiorized until maturity. Thus, the child and/or the adult exhibiting sensorimotor, preoperational, and concrete operational cognition, problem solves and plans more or less by sensing and doing. The process of organizing information for use in problem solving and planning is seen by both theoretical camps as sensation and perception. In the definition of cognition, advanced by the authors of this chapter, cognition is a systems phenomenon influenced by input and determined by neurological maturation and/or neurological intactness. Thus, the total performance subsystem is involved in cognition. Problem solving and planning are the interior skill processes of cognition, while perceptual–motor and communication–interaction skills make it possible for individuals both to obtain information for processing and to generate output as a result of interior processes. Cognitive skills contained in the performance subsystem include information gathering, memory, reasoning, and communicating and/or "doing" within the environment.

The habitual subsystem provides the context and organization for cognitive skill. Performance skills are organized into functional routines so that thinking is purposeful and pertinent to the life roles in which individuals engage. For example, an adult performing in the self-care role in the morning does not have to call upon his or her high-level process skill to complete the routines necessary to be competent. However, that same individual will need to enact complex problem-solving, planning, and communication-interaction skills in his or her professional role as a occupational therapist. Habituation renders thinking efficient, in that roles and routines define the demand and the domain for the cognitive level and/or processes. Not only does habituation organize the performance components of cognition, but it also provides direction from the cultural layer of the environment regarding the social appropriateness of performance. Thus, in some roles (such as being a learner of a new sport) trial-and-error reasoning is expected, whereas in others (such as being a senior occupational therapy student) trial and error is not desirable or rewarded.

The volition subsystem oversees habituation and performance. Within the model of human occupation, individuals are viewed as self-determining and motivated to engage in purposeful, goal-directed, exploratory, and masterful action within the layers of their environment. Volition is the seat of that motivation, control and regulation. Process skill is the foundation on which habituation and volition are anchored. Conversely, the volition subsystem provides the boundaries, uniqueness, sense of self, and metacognitive abilities that are necessary in order for cognition to be functional, meaningful, and purposeful. What is remembered, processed, and acted upon is guided by the volition subsystem, in the form of interests, sense of self-efficacy (personal causation), and values.

OT Assessment and Intervention

Because cognition is a major determinant of occupational function, it is well within the occupational therapist's professional domain of concern. Occupational therapists have used the model of human occupation to guide all elements of the application of the occupational therapy process to treating adults with cognitive dysfunction (Cubie & Kaplan, 1982). The locus of occupational therapy intervention can be directed to performance, habituation, and/or volition. The ultimate goal of the occupational therapy intervention is to facilitate cognitive competence consistent with cultural, role, and environmental demands so that occupational function can be restored and/or maintained. The following example illustrates assessment and intervention, guided by the model of human occupation, with an individual who demonstrates cognitive impairment as a result of sustaining a closed head injury.

Case Study #1

History. June is a 38-year-old black woman who sustained a mild closed head injury in an automobile accident. Prior to her accident, June lived in an urban house, which she owned. She is the single parent of two teen-aged children. Prior to her accident, June worked in a high level human service position that required a great deal of attention to detail, organization, and planning.

June was referred by her family physician to rehabilitation 2 years post-trauma because, since her accident, she was unable to resume remunerative work. The client had no residual motor deficits, with the exception of mild impairment in fine motor coordination in her left hand.

Assessment. The occupational therapist, working as part of a rehabilitation team, met with the client initially in her home. In a preliminary interview to obtain a sense of the client's goals for herself and her ability to frame future plans, June indicated that she wanted to return to some type of remunerative work but found that she was "scattered and couldn't get it together." A full assessment of the client was planned to ascertain her degree of occupational function in all subsystems. In addition, the environments in which the client functioned were also evaluated. [Note here that even though the client was known to have primarily a cognitive deficit, the model of human occupation expands the assessment and intervention process into other related systems to focus on occupational function, not deficit reduction.]

In the performance subsystem, June's process skill was evaluated by two methods. First, in order to obtain standardized scores of process skills, the team's neuropsychologist conducted a full neuropsychological battery. The neuropsychologist was selected to conduct the standardized evaluation because of her expertise in administering and interpreting standardized assessments of brain function. [The reader should note that the occupational therapist does not necessarily have to perform all assessments to obtain a full picture of the client's occupational function, even though he or she may be capable of doing so. In many cases, other team members will already have information or will possess the expertise sufficient to provide assessment data that most effectively and efficiently meet the team's assessment needs.

The neuropsychological battery included the Wechsler Adult Intelligence Scale (WAIS), the Wechsler Memory Scale, the Mini-Mental Status, the Halstead Reitan Battery and other tests of auditory and visual perception, organization, and executive function. Results revealed that the client became easily frustrated when unable to perform up to her own expectations. June's IQ scores on the WAIS were within normal limits. She demonstrated strengths in auditory understanding, communication skills, and long-term recall. However, her visual spatial skills, short-term recall, and ability to organize complex stimuli from her environment were noted to be deficient. She also had minor difficulties with word retrieval and left-handed motor skills. The clinical patterns exhibited in the neuropsychological examination were consistent with bifrontotemporal brain damage with more dysfunction noted in the right hemisphere.

With the neuropsychological information in hand, the occupational therapist then conducted the second part of the evaluation. She needed to know how these performance deficits affected June's occupational function. In order to ascertain June's level of occupational function, the occupational therapist conducted structured observations in a variety of settings, administered the role checklist (Oakley, 1985), and interviewed the client.

Observations were structured to ascertain the client's occupational function in the home, a simulated work setting, and in a leisure environment. In the home setting, the client was able to care for herself, organize her household, and parent her 16-year-old daughter. She followed a routine schedule of household chores and reportedly rarely deviated from it. However, more extensive observation revealed that the client was unable to follow through with task-oriented activity when unexpected noise (such as her daughter talking on the phone) occurred. After the noise subsided, the client was unable to return to productive activity and retreated to her bedroom for several hours until she reportedly was relaxed enough to resume purposeful activity.

To observe the client in a work environment, a simulated office job was structured at the client's church. The client was able to perform all office skills. However, she once again was unable to follow through with a task if she was distracted by noise in the environment. When distracted, she became angered and, at times, acted socially inappropriately to her coworkers. Her attempts to return to her tasks were thwarted by her inability to remember where she left off.

To test the client in a leisure environment, she was asked to drive to a local shopping mall, as shopping was an activity that she enjoyed, and meet the occupational therapist for lunch. Upon arriving one hour late, the client appeared flustered and stated that she got lost. She indicated that she was unfamiliar with the roads and could not operate her vehicle while looking at new directions. In the mall, the client was unable to navigate the stores since she was unfamiliar with them. Over lunch, the client indicated that the mall was too noisy. She left right after lunch and returned home in a taxicab. Arrangements were made by the client and the occupational therapist to have a relative drive the client's car back to her home.

Over the course of 2 weeks, the client was interviewed extensively to ascertain her history, perceived abilities, interests, desired roles, and perception of her intervention needs. The client indicated a strong desire to work outside of the home, to reduce her current level of frustration, and to engage in a more active social life. She was aware of her memory deficits but did not understand why she became so frustrated.

In summary, in the performance subsystem, the client demonstrated excellent communication-interaction skills, unless frustrated, with the exception of a minor word-finding problem. Process skills were impaired in the areas of short-term memory, visual perception and organization of visual data, auditory recall, and regulatory executive functions. Observation revealed that the client was unable to organize or process input from what she perceived as a chaotic environment.

In the habituation subsystem, the only functional role that the client exhibited was that of homemaker, providing that no interruptions occurred. The role checklist revealed an imbalance of role function. The client saw herself as engaged in self-care and homemaking roles exclusively. This imbalance was not tolerable to the client. While the client was able to develop and follow simple routines, she was unable to adapt the routines to environmental demands. Volitionally, the client articulated interests, but was unable to enact them in the work and social arena due to her cognitive incapacities. Her inability to regulate herself, to demonstrate insight into causes and potential solutions to problems, promoted her sense of perceived incompetence.

In essence, the client was demonstrating occupational dysfunction in all three subsystems in all life roles. The therapist also noted that the client's structural environmental needs were not being met in her home environment, leisure environments, and in potential work environments.

Goals. Intervention goals were developed in four categories: (1) remediating process skill deficits and providing compensatory techniques for those skills that show no change; (2) resuming a balance of meaningful and culturally relevant roles, including worker and player; (3) improving regulatory mechanisms as a means of improving insight and sense of self-control; and (4) modifying the client's environments to promote maximum occupational function.

Intervention. Initially, the occupational therapist worked with the client in her home to reduce the client's anxiety and to work on controlling her distractability. The client was asked to participate in activities which incrementally increased auditory and visual stimulation. For example, in the kitchen, the client began with cooking a simple meal and progressed to organizing and cooking a dinner for four guests. At random times during the day, the occupational therapist would have a colleague call on the telephone in order to test the client's ability to return to a task after being interrupted. If the client became flustered, the occupational therapist would work with the client to establish a routine to move her back into task behavior. All intervention activities that directly treated the client were aimed at improving the client's ability to organize input, to compensate for deficits in memory and perception, and to regulate behavior. Environmental adaptations were also accomplished. In the home, the client and the occupational therapist reorganized the layout so that the client could have a "quiet room." She used this room to reorganize herself and do detailed work, such as writing bills and reading.

In order to help June resume her vocational role, the occupational therapist arranged for June to volunteer at her church. She began working for 4 hours a day, 2 days a week. Initially, the occupational therapist remained with the client in a job coach capacity. As the client was assigned office work, the occupational therapist and the client worked on a compensatory strategy to address the client's memory deficits. The client used a small diary to write each of her responsibilities. She and the occupational therapist would then organize each responsibility into a set of tasks which were to be completed within a set amount of time. After completing a task, the client would check it off in her book and go on to the next. The client ultimately was able to organize her own task analysis and time routine.

Because the actual environment could not be changed to reduce distraction, the occupational therapist introduced an environmental modification for the client that would accomplish the goal: she provided the client with a radio and ear phones. During solitary work, the client was able to filter out unwanted distractions by selecting music that was pleasing and unobtrusive. She also established a regular routine, in which she took frequent work breaks in a quiet area of the church. This time was allotted for regulation and reorganization. As the client became more comfortable with her work, she increased her hours and ultimately took a paid office position in the church.

Similar techniques to those used in the workplace were employed to increase the client's leisure activity. The client joined a health club for the purpose of socialization and exercise. During her exercise, the client wore headphones and did her exercise in a quiet corner of the room. The exercise routine was designed by one of the health club employees so that it could be modified without the intervention of the rehabilitation team.

Summary of Intervention. The assessment revealed that the client was experiencing occupational dysfunction as a result of process skill deficits. While these skills were addressed in treatment, they were not the major focus of intervention. Rather, the aim of intervention was to improve occupational function and a balance of life roles. This overarching goal was done in the context of the client's living and working environments through: (1) the use of activities that called upon improved process skill; (2) the provision and routinization of compensatory techniques for process deficits, and (3) modification of client's living, working, and leisure environments so that the client was able to regulate her own routines and role behaviors within her own living and working arenas.

Case Study #2

[This example demonstrates the application of the model of human occupation to an individual with dementia.]

History. Joe is a 72-year-old white male who was diagnosed with Alzheimer's disease when he was 62. He is now in stage two of the disease, in which he demonstrates poor recognition of family and friends, impaired short-term recall, confusion and disorientation in all three spheres, and agitation in the evening hours. Joe currently lives in a nursing home with a male roommate who has also been diagnosed with dementia. Prior to the onset of dementia, Joe had taken early retirement from a labor position in a paper mill. He has two adult daughters who live in the area and a wife who currently resides alone in the home where Joe and his wife married and raised their daughters. Both daughters are married and work outside of the home. Joe's family is concerned and tried to care for him as long as possible. However, they were unable to adequately care for him in the evening hours. With great hesitance, the family decided to place Joe in the nursing home when he turned 71.

Assessment

The occupational therapist, working as a contracted position in the nursing home, assessed Joe upon his admission to the nursing home 1 year ago. At that time, the Mini-Mental Scale, a modified interest inventory, a picture recognition task of his family and friends, and the KELS were used to formally evaluate Joe. The occupational therapist also interviewed Joe to determine his values and sense of locus of control. Additional evaluation data were obtained from the physical therapist who performed a motor evaluation, the psychologist who performed a full battery of intelligence testing, and the nursing staff who had written daily progress notes on Joe's ADL capacity.

Based on the data the following strengths and deficits were ascertained in occupational functioning: First, in the performance subsystem, Joe showed clear deficits in process skill particularly in the areas of metacognition, short-term recall, judgment, and problem solving. Joe was unaware of the extent of his dementia and often blamed others for playing tricks on him when he misplaced an object or became confused. Strengths were in the areas of communication-interaction; Joe was cooperative and responded to structure, even at nighttime when he became confused and agitated. Motor skills were intact. Second, in habituation, Joe was able to enact self-care and feeding roles with appropriate structure from the nursing home staff. However, he was unable to create a structure of routines for himself and could not function in basic self-care roles without external guidance. He was able to engage in simple work tasks, providing that he was given appropriate structure and the tasks were historically familiar. Joe's major role deficits were in the social arena, because Joe had difficulty remembering his family and friends.

Third, in terms of volition, Joe expressed interest in spectator sports, particularly football and baseball, although he was unable to remember contemporary athletes or teams. Joe was unable to identify any other potent interests. In the initial interview Joe perceived himself as externally controlled due to his placement in the nursing home. He did not articulate any anger or resentment towards his family for placing him there and believed that he would be going home soon. His expectations for returning to his home were unrealistic and confused: he thought that his deceased mother was still alive and would take care of him once he was released from the nursing home.

In summary, upon initial assessment, Joe demonstrated occupational dysfunction in all three subsystems as a result of his dementia. Due to compromised brain function, process skill deficits rendered Joe unable to enact functional roles and routines without extensive external structure. Furthermore, due to the deteriorating nature of Alzheimer's disease, remediation of cognitive activity was not possible. The focus of intervention, relating to a major cognitive deficit, had to be expanded and reconceptualized. [The reader should note that in using the model of human occupation to assess, treat, and evaluate clients may move the focus for intervention away from the presenting problem to another area of occupational function. In this case, the intervention target is the environment, rather than the client's cognition. Thus, the feedback loop and the person-in-environment concept becomes critical in providing meaningful treatment for this client and others with Alzheimer's disease.]

Goals. The following intervention goals were developed to promote occupational function for Joe in all three subsystems:

1. Modify the nursing home environment as a basis to reestablish occupational role function in self-care, social roles, and productivity;

2. Provide compensatory cognitive skills which can be modified as the client's cognitive status changes;

3. Increase client's participation in meaningful structured activity as a basis for promoting occupational competence;

4. Provide simple, structured choices for the client as a basis for promoting a greater sense of internal control.

Intervention. During the year that the occupational therapist worked with Joe, the focus of intervention was in three major areas: environmental modification, providing choices, and providing compensatory skills for memory deficits. To modify the environment, Joe's space was reorganized to include a calendar, a clock, enlarged family pictures with captioned names of relatives, written lists of self-care routines at appropriate locations in Joe's bedroom and bathroom, and a buddy system for navigating the parts of the nursing home outside of Joe's familiar space. The occupational therapist also brought in current baseball cards to cue Joe to the players as he watched baseball on TV. Choices were provided through activity and through food selection. For example, Joe and the occupational therapist worked together on a menu each week that included choices from the basic food groups. In activities such as self-care, Joe would select his clothes from among two outfits that were identified to him. In the area of compensatory skills, the occupational therapist provided Joe with a note pad that contained written instructions for each hour of the day. Joe was also given an alarm watch that contained the day of the week and the date. At hourly intervals, the alarm rang and Joe was cued to look at his notepad. He was able to follow the instructions on the pad. For example, at 11:00 A.M. the note reminded him to meet his buddy in the atrium. His buddy would then accompany him to lunch and guide him to an afternoon activity run by the recreation staff. Using the notepad can be modified to be read to Joe as he becomes unable to read.

In summary, although Joe's occupational dysfunction resulted primarily from a cognitive deficit, the intervention was guided by the model of human occupation and focused on organizing the environment so that Joe could be functional within it. The level of cognitive function was used not as a locus for improvement, but as a guide for the level of activity in which Joe could be expected to engage.

In both cases, the reader can see that although process skill is a major component of occupational function, it was not always the primary focus of intervention. The domain of occupational therapy, defined by the model of human occupation is occupational function. Thus the model provides a foundation for a holistic view of clients in which cognitive deficits are treated within the larger context of environmental layers.

Conclusion

Cognition is an essential component of human occupational function. Using the model of human occupation, assessment and intervention with adults with cognitive dysfunction not only focuses on the cognitive deficits, but also maintains the integrity of the occupational therapy process and focus—that of maximizing occupational function and balancing life roles. Intervention is guided by a human–in–environment perspective which aims not only to "fix the human deficit" but also to enhance the person's fit within the layers of his or her living environment. Using the model, cognitive deficits are approached from a systems perspective in which the effect of the deficit on occupational function as well as an assessment of strengths is ascertained. Intervention can then be directed to remediation, compensation, and integration of occupationally functional roles and routines that fit within the values and interests of the individual being served by the occupational therapist. In providing intervention to adults with cognitive impairments, the occupational therapy process preserves the focus of cognitive and occupational growth and development throughout the lifespan.

References

Arlin, P. K. (1977). Piagetian operations in problem finding. *Developmental Psychology, 13*, 297–298.

Brown, A. L. & DeLoache, J. S. (1978). Skills, plans, and self-regulation. In R. S. Siegler (Ed.), *Children's thinking: What develops?* Hillsdale, NJ: Erlbaum.

Commons, M. L., Richards, F. A., & Kuhn, D. (1982). Systematic and meta-systematic reasoning: A case for levels of reasoning beyond Piaget's stage of formal operations. *Child Development, 53*, 1058–1069.

Cubie, S. H. (1985). Occupational analysis. In G. Kielhofner (Ed.), *A mode of human occupation: theory and application.* Baltimore: Williams & Wilkins.

Cubie, S. H., & Kaplan, K. (1982). A case analysis method for the model of human occupation. *American Journal of Occupational Therapy, 36* (10), 645–652.

Flavell, J. H. (1977). *Cognitive development.* Englewood Cliffs, NJ: Prentice-Hall.

Flavell, J. H. (1982). On cognitive development. *Child Development, 53*, 1–10.

Gelman, R. (1978). Cognitive development. *Annual Review of Psychology, 29*, 297–332.

Hunter, S. & Sundrel, M. (1989). *Midlife myths.* Newbury Park, CA: Sage.

Kielhofner, G. & Burke, J. P. Components and determinants of human occupation. In: Kielhofner, G. (1985). *A model of human occupation: Theory and application.* Baltimore: Williams & Wilkins, pp. 12–36.

Kielhofner, G. & Burke, J. P. (1980). A model of human occupation, part I. Conceptual framework and content. *American Journal of Occupational Therapy, 34,* 572–581.

Labouvie-Vief, G., & Hakim-Larson, J. (1989). Developmental shifts in adult thought. In: Hunter, S., & Sundrel, M. (1989). *Midlife myths.* Newbury Park, CA: Sage.

Lezak, M. (1982). The problem of assessing executive functions. *International Journal of Psychology, 17,* 281–297.

Mossler, D. G., Marvin, R. S., & Greenberg, M. T. (1976). Conceptual perspective taking in 2- to 6-year-old children. *Developmental Psychology, 12,* 85–86.

Piaget, J. (1952). *The origins of intelligence in children.* New York: International University Press.

Piaget, J. (1954). *The construction of reality in the child.* New York: Basic Books.

Raymond, C. (1991). New research challenges the notion of cognitive abilities of infants. *Chronicle of Higher Education, 38*(1).

Reilly, M. (1962). Occupational therapy can be one of the greatest ideas of twentieth-century medicine. *American Journal of Occupational Theory, 16,* 1–9.

Seldak, A. J. & Kurtz, S. T. (1981). A review of children's use of causal inference principles. *Child Development, 52,* 759–784.

Shaffer, D. R. (1985). *Developmental psychology.* Monterey, CA: Brooks-Cole.

Weschler, D. (1944). *The measurement of adult intelligence.* Baltimore: Williams & Wilkins.

Wolman, B. (1983). *The handbook of developmental psychology.* Englewood Cliffs, NJ: Prentice-Hall.

11

Nonverbal Learning Disabilities in the Adult Framed in the Model of Human Occupation

Sharon A. Cermak and Elizabeth Murray

Our focus in this chapter is on identification and remediation of the cognitive-perceptual deficits in the adult with nonverbal learning disabilities. Although most research with the learning disabled has focused on reading and language deficits, in the present chapter we address the cognitive, perceptual, and nonverbal deficits seen in certain subgroups of learning-disabled individuals. These aspects are emphasized because they are the areas most frequently addressed by occupational therapy.

First, we will present information describing learning disabilities in the child and adult. This will be followed by a discussion of nonverbal learning disabilities. Nonverbal learning disabilities will be described in detail so that the therapist can learn to recognize this condition: people with nonverbal learning disabilities often go undiagnosed. An individual may be seen in a mental health setting with a diagnosis of anxiety, depression, or attempted suicide when, in fact, nonverbal learning disabilities may underlie these clinical manifestations (Porter & Rourke, 1985; Rourke, Young, & Leenaars, 1989; Weller & Strawser, 1987). The role of the occupational therapist in the assessment and remediation of the adult with nonverbal learning disabilities will be presented using the model of human occupation as a framework for guiding assessment and treatment. We will also present a case study to illustrate the concepts presented in this chapter.

We assume that the reader is already familiar with the model of human occupation; therefore, we will not describe the model in this chapter (See Kielhofner, 1985, for an indepth description of the model of human occupation). The model of human occupation was chosen because it views the individual in a holistic manner, and the model provides a systematic approach to analysis of the individual's function and dysfunction. Inherent in the model of human occupation is an emphasis on the client's interests, values, and goals. The client's perceptions of his or her needs are central to the formation of therapeutic goals. We feel that an approach that inherently emphasizes empowerment of the adult to act as his or her agent of change is especially critical when working with the higher functioning adult.

Learning Disabilities

Learning Disabilities in Children

The term learning disabilities was initially used to describe children with normal intelligence who had difficulty with academic performance. More recently, learning disabilities have been described by the U.S. Office of Education in the following manner:

> children with specific learning disabilities exhibit a disorder in one or more of the basic psychological processes involved in understanding or using spoken or written language. These may be manifested in disorders of listening, thinking, talking, reading, writing, spelling or arithmetic (Brown & Zinkus, 1979, p. 322).

Although the above is the legal definition of learning disabilities, there have been many different definitions. Three factors have appeared consistently. First is a discrepancy between ability and academic achievement indicated by the student not performing in school as well as would be expected based on his or her given intelligence. A second common factor is the presumption of central nervous system dysfunction. The final factor is an exclusionary factor, which suggests that the learning problems cannot be the result of mental retardation, emotional disturbance, environmental damage, or sensory or motor disability.

Although the most commonly recognized deficits in children are those that pertain to academic success, with attention most often given to the reading and language deficits, there are also nonverbal deficits in abilities such as in spatial perception, the meaning of facial expression, and music and rhythm. In addition to disorders in the perceptual, conceptual, language, or academic areas, individuals with learning disabilities often have associated hyperactivity, attention impairments, and maladaptive behavior.

Learning Disabilities in Adults

In the definition of learning disabilities developed by the National Joint Committee on Learning Disabilities (NJCLD), which is composed of the major professional organizations concerned with the learning disabled, the term learning disabilities no longer refers just to children. Since 1981, the NJCLD has published three major position papers on the impact of learning disabilities on adults and their needs. These statements (NJCLD, 1983; 1985; 1987) addressed the postsecondary educational, vocational, transitional, employment, and psychological/emotional problems of the learning-disabled adult. The Association for Children and Adults with Learning Disabilities (ACLD) emphasized that learning disabilities can affect "self-esteem, education, vocation, socialization, and/or daily living activities throughout life" (ACLD Newsbriefs, 1985). In addition, they differ from the federal definition by including social skills as one of the major areas of difficulty for individuals with learning disabilities. The Vocational Rehabilitation Service also highlighted the need for recognizing the effect of a learning disability on social competence and the need to perform assessments in this area in their revised definition of learning disabilities (Gerber, 1981; Smith, 1988).

Definitions of learning disabilities have also been proposed by the Rehabilitation Services Administration (RSA) for the purpose of including individuals with learning disabilities in vocational rehabilitation programs (Gerber, 1981; Smith, 1988). The guidelines used by RSA state that learning disorders may manifest with deficits in attention, reasoning, memory, communicating, reading, writing, spelling, calculation, coordination, social competence, and emotional maturity. They recognized that these disorders may constitute, in an adult, an employment handicap (Rehabilitation Services Administration, 1990).

Thus, social competence and emotional maturity, two important areas of functioning for employability that may be affected by a learning disability, are now included in the definition as is the recognition that a learning disability may impact on employment. In fact, in a survey a sample of more than 500 adults with learning disabilities reported that their areas of greatest need were improving social relationships and skills, career counseling, and developing self-esteem and confidence (Chesler, 1982).

Incidence of Learning Disabilities

Students diagnosed as learning disabled currently make up the largest percentage of enrollees in special education programs (Adelman & Taylor, 1986). The incidence of children with learning disabilities is estimated from 1 to 30 percent of the school population, depending on the criteria used to determine the disability (Adelman & Taylor, 1986; Lerner, 1976; Brown & Zinkus, 1979); the number of individuals receiving services for learning disabilities has been increasing (Keller & Hallahan, 1987).

The incidence of learning disabilities in the adult population is not known. Learning disabilities is a fairly newly recognized condition, and there have been few long-term longitudinal studies. Nevertheless, research with adolescents and adults with learning disabilities has now indicated that, for the most part, children do not outgrow learning disabilities (Cannon & Compton, 1980; Cruickshank et al., 1980; Kenny & Burka, 1980) and these problems tend to persist (NJCLD, 1983; 1985; 1987; Polloway, Smith, & Patton, 1984; Smith, 1988; Spreen, 1988). In recent years there has been a significant increase in the number of adults referred for evaluation and re-mediation of learning disabilities (Vogel, 1989).

Life Span Learning Disabilities

The definition of learning disabilities proposed by the ACLD states that *throughout life* the condition can affect self-esteem, education, vocation, socialization, and/or daily living activities (ACLD, 1982; NJCLD, 1985; 1987). Increased awareness of the continuing needs of adults with learning disabilities has led to the revised definitions of learning disabilities, the increase of support services in postsecondary setting, and the accessibility of vocational rehabilitation services. However, the manifestations of a learn-ing disability may change over the years (Rourke, 1988a). A student diagnosed as having a deficit in word recognition skills in the second grade may be diagnosed as having a reading comprehension problem in the seventh grade. A student described as hyperactive in second grade may be described as socially maladjusted as an adolescent. Rarely is a learning disability mani-fested only during adolescence or adulthood. Although the actual diagnosis may not be made until adolescence or adulthood, there is usually a history of academic and/or social problems. One must recognize, however, that the task demands and settings of the adult with learning disabilities are no longer school-based. Adults with learning disabilities tend to be viewed within the context of the occupational (e.g., social and vocational) behaviors of non-learning disabled adults (Polloway, Smith, & Patton, 1984).

Subtypes

Historically, learning disability was viewed as a unitary phe-nomenon, implying that there was one best approach to remediation. How-ever, as early as the 1960s, Johnson and Myklebust were arguing for the presence of subtypes of learning disabilities (Johnson & Myklebust, 1967). We now recognize that persons with learning disabilities form a heterogeneous group, and since the 1970s research in learning disabilities has been attempting to describe subtypes of disabilities.

Studies of subtyping have varied in both the measures that they use to assess dysfunction and the subtypes that have been found. Two commonly used measures are the Wechsler Intelligence Scale for Children-Revised (WISC-R) (Wechsler, 1974) or the adult version of this test, the Wechsler Adult Intelligence Scale-Revised (WAIS-R) (Wechsler, 1981). These tests provide both a verbal score, based on tests that require verbal abilities, and a performance score, which is derived from visual-perceptual and visual-motor tests. Many persons with learning disabilities demonstrate a difference between their verbal and performance scores. Hypothetically, a verbal score significantly lower than a performance score indicates a learning disability that is primarily language-based, while a performance score significantly lower than a verbal score suggests poor nonverbal skills (Strang & Rourke, 1985; Thompson, 1985). Subtyping research has used both the WISC-R and the WAIS, as well as other measures of language abilities and visual-perceptual and visual-motor tests, in order to describe the strengths and weaknesses in subtypes of learning disabilities.

Most of the subtype studies have suggested implications for differential intervention, based on the patterns of strengths and weaknesses noted (Bergman, 1987; Rourke, 1985; Weller & Strawser, 1987). However, the effectiveness of these differential approaches to remediation has not been documented to date (Forness, 1988; Kavale & Forness, 1987). Also, although an individual may be considered to manifest a certain sybtype of learning disability, not everyone with that subtype would have identical problems: individual characteristics and environmental factors could be expected to have a significant effect on the function of each individual (Fisk & Rourke, 1983).

Nonverbal Learning Disabilities

Nonverbal learning disabilities are a form of developmental learning disabilities that have been described as "the reverse of dyslexia" (Badian, 1986). Verbal skills are generally intact, and, in fact, persons with nonverbal learning disabilities tend to be talkative and to rely on auditory and verbal skills for learning. However, children and adults with nonverbal learning disabilities demonstrate deficits in visual-spatial abilities and organizational skills. Their learning is compromised by difficulties with nonverbal problem solving, concept formation, and cause-and-effect relationships. Although problems with self-esteem are frequently found in persons with learning disbilities, deficits in social interaction and in perception of social situations are particularly associated with individuals who have nonverbal learning disabilities. Because they have relatively strong verbal skills, children with nonverbal learning disabilities may not be identified until the elementary grades. The problems these children have, however, affect their ability to learn and engage in social interaction throughout the school years, and these effects persist into adulthood.

Spreen and Haaf (1986) followed subgroups of children with learning disabilities into adulthood and found that, although those subjects who had primarily linguistic impairments as children did not show these same impairments as adults, those who had visual-perceptual deficits continued to manifest these perceptual problems when they were adults. Snow and his associates (Snow, Koller, & Roberts, 1987) also noted a subgroup of learning-disabled adolescents and adults who demonstrated poor perceptual organization, as indicated by low scores on several performance subtests of the WAIS.

Areas of Deficit

The individual with nonverbal learning disabilities has been noted to have deficits in several areas. These will be described in the following sections.

Cognitive Style

Individuals with nonverbal learning disabilities have problems in organizational skills and in simultaneous thinking, or the ability to consider several aspects of a problem at once (Brumback & Staton, 1982; Rourke, 1989). They prefer a sequential, step-by-step approach to learning and may become overwhelmed if given too much information at once because they frequently find it hard to organize and synthesize material (Davidson, 1983; Rourke, 1988b; 1989). Often persons with nonverbal learning disabilities are good at learning and remembering specific details, but they have trouble developing overall concepts or making inferences from information (Rourke, 1982; Strang & Rourke, 1985). Additionally, some researchers have suggested that deficits in attention are associated with nonverbal learning disabilities (Rourke & Fisk, 1988; Voeller, 1986).

Problem Solving

Rourke and his associates have highlighted nonverbal problem solving as a major deficit in persons with nonverbal learning disabilities (Rourke et al., 1989). Because they have a strong preference for a sequential, step-by-step approach to tasks and the difficulty with simultaneous thinking, persons with nonverbal learning disabilities often are unable to generate alternative solutions to a problem and may find it difficult to modify their strategy when an approach is not effective. Even when a strategy has proven effective in one situation, they may have difficulty generalizing this strategy to other appropriate situations or in "deselecting," or not using a strategy when it is ineffective or inappropriate for a given situation. Frequently these subjects are described as rigid and overly dependent on rules and regulations (Semrud-Clikeman & Hynd, 1990). Problems in understanding cause-and-effect relationships make it difficult for them to generate hypotheses about possible outcomes, thus further limiting their problem-solving abilities and their ability to anticipate and understand the consequences of their behavior.

Visual Perception

A major aspect of nonverbal learning disabilities is a deficit in visual perception, particularly in visual-spatial skills. People with these disabilities have problems putting parts of an object together and visualizing what objects would look like in different orientations (Tranel, Hall, Olson, & Tranel, 1987). As mentioned earlier, they frequently have a Performance IQ that is significantly lower than their Verbal IQ (Abramson & Katz, 1989; Rourke, 1982). Additionally, persons with nonverbal learning disabilities have been found to have problems making judgments about the space surrounding them when they are moving or when an object is moving toward them. They may have a particularly poor sense of direction (Rourke et al., 1989; Tranel et al., 1987).

Many visual-spatial tasks are performed most efficiently when one can mentally try out several solutions at once and anticipate the end product. Thus, the cognitive style of the person with a nonverbal learning disability can also affect his or her ability to perform visual-spatial tasks.

Language and Communication Skills

Verbal skills are generally considered an area of strength in individuals with nonverbal learning disabilities. These persons are generally quite talkative and often have a good vocabulary (Rourke, 1988b). They also usually have strong rote memory for verbal information (Rourke, 1989; Rourke et al., 1989). However, in this population, more subtle language problems have been noted. They have weaknesses in pragmatic skills, such as the ability to maintain a conversation and convey information in a concise and organized manner (Rourke, 1989). Their speech may be tangential, and they may have a tendency to overuse jargon. They are frequently described as overly verbal (Semrud-Clikeman & Hynd, 1990). Prosody, or the rhythm and "melody" of speech is another area of deficit commonly identified in this population (Brumback & Staton, 1982; Tranel et al., 1987). They may also have problems in paralinguistic skills, or the nonverbal aspects of communication, including decreased eye contact and lack of gestures while speaking (Tranel et al., 1987).

In addition to problems with expressive language, persons with nonverbal learning disabilities have been noted to demonstrate deficits in the comprehension of complex or abstract language. They may have difficulty making inferences out of what is said to them and, thus, often miss the point the speaker is trying to make (Thompson, 1985). Further, just as they may be poor in using nonverbal cues to communicate, they also frequently do not "read" others' nonverbal cues (Murray, 1991; Strang & Rourke, 1985).

Neuromotor and Motor

Individuals with nonverbal learning disabilities have been reported to be awkward or clumsy as children, and adults have described themselves as "clumsy" and "nonathletic" (Tranel et al., 1987). Motor impersistence, or difficulty in sustaining a motor activity, has been reported (Voeller & Heilman, 1988). Problems with spatial awareness also affect the ability to move the body efficiently through space. Additionally, a few studies have indicated the occasional presence of left-sided signs in this population, such as arm or hand posturing when under stress, or especially poor fine motor coordination with the left hand (Abramson & Katz, 1989; Rourke, 1988b).

Academic Skills

Persons with nonverbal learning disabilities often have a history of academic problems. The outstanding academic difficulty associated with nonverbal learning disabilities is a deficit in arithmetic. Problems are noted in the ability to understand mathematical concepts and to apply these concepts in skills such as measurement, telling time, and the use of money (Abramson & Katz, 1989; Badian, 1986; Davidson, 1983). Deficits also are reported in arithmetic computation and particularly with written calculations (Rourke, 1982).

Reading skills are generally higher than arithmetic skills. Word recognition may be strong and, at first, the problems in children with nonverbal learning disabilities are often missed in the early grades because reading skills are age appropriate. However, as the demands of reading comprehension increase, their problems often become more evident (Rourke, 1988b; Thompson, 1985). Although they may be able to retrieve factual information from their reading, children with nonverbal learning disabilities have trouble synthesizing information and making inferences from what they have read (Rourke, 1982). Questions such as, "What is the main idea?" and "What do you think will happen next?" tend to be particularly hard for them to answer.

Social-Emotional

Persons with nonverbal learning disabilities have been reported to have a variety of social and emotional problems, ranging from shyness and introversion (Tranel et al., 1987; Weintraub & Mesulam, 1983) to chronic anxiety and depression (Bergman, 1987; Brumback, 1988; Rourke et al., 1989; Tranel et al., 1987). In fact, the emotional problems are what usually bring the adult with nonverbal learning disabilities into treatment. Several authors have suggested an increased incidence of suicide in this population (Bigler, 1989; Fletcher, 1989; Rourke et al., 1989).

The cognitive style of persons with nonverbal learning disabilities may affect their social and emotional skills. Because they tend to attend to details rather than the overall picture, they frequently overreact to specific situations or problems and have trouble placing these situations in perspective. Problems with understanding cause-and-effect relationships may result in a difficulty in recognizing the consequences of their own actions (Rourke et al., 1989). Thus they may have a tendency to blame others for their own problems and lack insight into their own behavior. They may have a strong perference for familiar, routine social situations, and have difficulty in thinking of alternative strategies or solutions to problems, which may result in a tendency to be rigid and inflexible. Often they dislike and avoid any new social situation.

Language and communication deficits also affect social skills. Persons with nonverbal learning disabilities are often unaware of the rules of conversation. Their contributions to a conversation may be tangential, and they may leave out information needed to follow their train of thought, unaware that the listener is lost. Problems with summarizing and synthesizing lead to a conversation full of details but one that often does not "get to the point." Additionally, they may have trouble understanding ideas expressed by others, particularly when this requires drawing conclusions or making inferences. Subtle humor, for example, may be lost on them. Problems with the nonverbal aspects of communication further affect social interaction. As mentioned earlier, persons with nonverbal learning disabilities tend to have poor eye contact (Weintraub & Mesulam, 1983; Tranel et al., 1987), poor prosody or intonation in speech, and limited use of gesture for communication (Rourke, 1989). Additionally, they may misinterpret body language and intonation in the speech of others and, thus, have difficulty reading others' emotions and knowing how to react to them (Brumback & Staton, 1982; Rourke et al., 1989). Because of their poor conversational and interpersonal skills persons with nonverbal learning disabilities may end up isolated, as others avoid spending time with them.

Effects on Occupation

Post-Secondary Education

Persons with nonverbal learning disabilities generally have a history of academic problems that begin in the elementary grades. As adults their problems can continue to interfere with academic learning, both in college and in vocational or technical programs. Difficulty in understanding mathematical concepts and poor visual-spatial abilities can affect more technically related subjects such as carpentry and mechanics, as well as higher level mathematics and science courses.

Study skills may generally be poor. The type of reading assigned in many courses requires an ability to synthesize and summarize information, determining the main concepts that are presented. These skills also are needed in order to take adquate notes in class. Often the student with a nonverbal learning disability is unable to determine the main ideas presented in a lecture and instead attempts to write down everything that is said. Their written assignments may resemble a long string of detailed information with no obvious point to be made or conclusion to be reached.

Adults with nonverbal learning disabilities would be expected to need more time than the typical student to study and to complete assignments. However, planning and budgeting time tends to be one of their areas of weakness. Persons with nonverbal learning disabilities frequently have trouble anticipating how long it will take to complete a task or assignment. While this problem interferes with studying to some degree at any age, it can be a particular problem in higher education, when there is much more flexibility in the scheduling of classes and often more options for free time.

Vocation

Because of deficits in problem-solving, persons with nonverbal learning disabilities may find it hard to assess their vocational skills adequately and may end up in jobs for which they are not well-suited. While they may be able to handle fairly structured, routine jobs, professions that require workers to provide their own organization and structure would be hard, and they would have difficulty dealing with unexpected situations or problems that arise (Rourke et al., 1989). If they fail at a job they may blame others for their failure and, consequently, not learn from their mistakes. This, combined with limitations in the ability to plan long-term career goals, could lead to a series of job failures.

Merely obtaining a job for these individuals can be difficult. Poor communication skills would hamper most job interviews, and problems synthesizing information may make it hard to emphasize the important qualities a person brings to the job. Communication problems can also interfere with relations with colleagues on the job.

Rourke and his associates (Rourke et al., 1989) suggest that persons with nonverbal learning disabilities may end up taking less-demanding jobs than those for which they were trained. However, as they point out, these jobs often require a high level of visual-spatial or visual-motor coordination, something that these individuals often lack.

Self-Maintenance Skills

Self-maintenance skills include the ability to maintain a home and to manage finances. Self-maintenance is an area that can be problematic for the adult with a nonverbal learning disability. Merely keeping track of the many tasks that need to be done (such as cleaning, laundry, and planning and preparing meals) requires organizational skills that they may lack. They may tend to focus on the many details required in each task and thus feel overwhelmed. Deficits in mathematics may affect their ability to develop a budget. Additionally, as planning for the future may be problematic, persons with nonverbal learning disabilities may have trouble staying within their budget and saving for unexpected events.

In order to prepare a meal one must plan ahead, so that all the dishes being served are ready at the same time. This type of planning and organization may prove difficult. Skills that require measurement, such as sewing, home repair, and basic carpentry, may also be limited. These skills require a sense of how parts fit together in order to visualize how the completed project will appear. Additionally, fine motor incoordination may interfere with many of these tasks.

Recreation and Leisure

As their communication and other social skills may be poor, persons with nonverbal learning disabilities are often described as being socially isolated. Consequently, their choices in recreational and leisure activities would tend toward those that can be done individually, rather than group activities. Motor clumsiness, as well as poor group interaction skills, would most likely prevent participation in group sports, such as baseball or soccer. Sports such as running and swimming, which can be performed individually and require less precise coordination and planning, may be more popular choices for those who wish to engage in more physical activity. Unfortunately, as Rourke et al. (1989) have suggested, the activity level in the adult with nonverbal learning disabilities may be decreased. Shyness and possible depression may make these adults avoid social contact. Leisure time may be spent in more passive solitary activities, such as watching television or reading. Although they may enjoy hobbies such as gardening or collecting coins, they may avoid sharing these interests with others through either informal or organized groups.

Hypothesized Etiology

Nonverbal learning disabilities are commonly thought to reflect a developmental deficit of the right hemisphere. The right hemisphere has been described as superior to the left in *holistic* (gestalt) thinking, or thinking in terms of complex wholes, rather than parts (Kumar, 1973). The right hemisphere is also thought to more easily process information simultaneously than the left hemisphere, and it may use a more intuitive approach to problem solving, considering several alternatives at one time. The right hemisphere also has been shown to be superior with tasks that require spatial perception and constructional abilities (Lezak, 1983; Luria, 1980). Thus, the deficits in spatial perception and cognitive style seen in children and adults with nonverbal learning disabilities appear to reflect deficits in right hemisphere function.

The language problems associated with nonverbal learning disabilities may also reflect right hemisphere dysfunction. Many patients with lesions of the right hemisphere lack intonation and rhythm when speaking. Further, they frequently have little depth or organization to the content of their speech, although they may be quite talkative (Lezak, 1983). Difficulty in drawing inferences and understanding complex stories or humorous material have also been reported in patients with right hemisphere lesions (Rivers & Love, 1980; Wapner, Hamby, & Gardner, 1981).

In addition to demonstrating a style that reflects possible right hemisphere dysfunction, some studies have documented the presence of motor asymmetries, with posturing on the left side during stress in individuals with nonverbal learning disabilities (Brumback, 1988). These asymmetries are also suggestive of dysfunction in the right hemisphere.

Semmes (1968) has hypothesized that differences in the neural organization of the two hemispheres may parallel functional differences. Based on research with brain-injured patients she concluded that the right hemisphere is more diffusely organized than the left and, thus, has an advantage in synthesizing unlike inputs. She has proposed that this organization may give the right hemisphere an advantage in synthesizing inputs from a variety of sources.

In a similar vein, Goldberg and Costa (1981) have hypothesized that the right hemisphere has more association areas than the left, thus allowing it to specialize in synthesizing and integrating information from various sources. They suggested that the greater proportion of white matter found in the right hemisphere also indicates that there may be a larger amount of interregional integration in the right hemisphere than in the left.

Rourke (1988b) also viewed the right hemisphere as more intermodal and integrating than the left. Observing that the skills the right hemisphere is specialized for generally demand complex inputs from several sources, Rourke has hypothesized that the right hemisphere is dependent on the connecting white fibers of the brain for both learning and maintaining skills. According to Rourke, although the left hemisphere also is dependent on these connecting fibers for learning new skills, once learned, these skills become less dependent on multiple inputs.

Assessment and Remediation of Nonverbal Learning Disabilities

In this chapter, we will utilize the model of human occupation as a guide for describing assessment and treatment planning of the adult with nonverbal learning disabilities. The model of human occupation is being presented because it addresses all the areas of concern in the adult with nonverbal learning disabilities. Its framework serves as a guideline for the therapeutic course of action. For details on application of the model of human occupation, the reader is referred to Cubie and Kaplan (1982), Duncombe and others (1988), Kaplan (1984), and Kielhofner (1985).

Components of Assessment and Remediation

Assessment and remediation is a problem-solving process in which the therapist selects relevant information about the client and integrates it with a theory of the individual's unique occupational function and dysfunction. Rogers and Kielhofner (1985) identified five steps in the treatment planning process: (1) identifying clinical questions; (2) collecting data, (3) creating an explanation of the occupational function or dysfunction, (4) identifying and selecting from among treatment options, and (5) evaluating outcomes and adjusting therapy. Areas 1 through 3 form the basis for the assessment phase, and areas 4 and 5 form the basis for the treatment phase.

Identifying Questions for Clinical Assessment

From the model of human occupation, five major areas guide the process of collecting information on the client's strengths and weaknesses. These include an examination of the client's volitional status, habituation status, performance status, performance history, and environmental supports or constraints. Each will be discussed with a review of the particular problems expected in the adult with nonverbal learning disabilities.

Performance

Performance evaluation includes assessment of the individual's skills and underlying components of these skills. Table 1 provides questions that guide an assessment in this area. Performance deficits typically may occur in several areas, although the severity and extent of the problems vary from one individual to another.

Table 1 Performance Questions for Assessment

Skills

Does the person demonstrate the ability to communicate and interact effectively with others in self-care, work, and play activities?

Does the person have the ability to problem solve, plan, and organize personal behavior and the immediate environment in order to accomplish self-care, work, and play tasks?

Does the person have the ability to receive and interpret sensory data and organize motor activity in order to accomplish self-care, work, and play tasks?

Skill constituents

Are the person's symbolic processes intact? Does he or she have a cognitive limitation? Does the person show evidence of a poor internalization of rules to guide behavior?

Does the person have an intact nervous system? Is there evidence of damage to, or developmental delay in, the nervous system? Are there problems of sensory processing and integration?

Does the person have an intact musculoskeletal system? Does the person have functional strength and range of motion? Is there any disturbance of muscular, skeleal, or joint integrity?

From: Rogers, J., & Kielhofner, G. (1985). Treatment planning. In G. Kielhofner (Ed.), *A model of human occupation. Theory and application* (pp. 136–146). Baltimore: Williams & Wilkins. (With permission of the author and publisher.)

Perceptual-Motor Skills. Adults with nonverbal learning disabilities generally demonstrate deficits in visual-spatial abilities. In the school years, they commonly have academic deficits in arithmetic and in understanding mathematical concepts, which are associated with deficits in visual-spatial perception. They experience difficulty later in the use of money (including budgeting and banking), in skills such as measurement, and in other activities that involve numbers and spatial concepts. Additionally, adults with nonverbal learning disabilities frequently have been described as clumsy and nonathletic.

Process Skills. Learning in the adult with nonverbal learning disabilities is compromised by difficulties with nonverbal problem solving, concept formation, and cause-and-effect relationships. Individuals with nonverbal learning disabilities have difficulty considering several aspects of a problem at once and may become overwhelmed if given too much information at once. Although they often are good at remembering specific details, they have more difficulty developing overall concepts and drawing inferences.

Communication/Interaction. Although their verbal skills have generally been considered an area of relative strength, individuals with nonverbal learning disabilities have deficits in communication skills. These

Table 2   Habituation Questions for Assessment

Roles

What roles has the person filled (or will fill) in the past, present, and future?

What are the person's expectations of himself or herself for each current or anticipated role? Are they reasonable and commensurate with what others expect or
would be likely to expect?

Does the person experience an overload or conflict of roles, or does he or she have
too few roles to organize their use of time?

Habits

How organized is this individual's use of time? What is the nature of a typical day?

Does this person exhibit habits (e.g., promptness and attentiveness) necessary for
role performance?

How flexible is this person? Can he or she adapt easily to changing circumstances?

From: Rogers, J., & Kielhofner, G. (1985). Treatment planning. In G. Kielhofner (Ed.), *A
model of human occupation. Theory and application* (pp. 136–146). Baltimore: Williams
& Wilkins. (With permission of the author and publisher.)

individuals often have difficulty communicating in a concise and organized
manner. They have problems with the nonverbal aspects of communication,
including eye contact, appropriate distancing, and use of gesture. Just as
individuals with nonverbal learning disabilities may function poorly when
using nonverbal cues to communicate, they also have difficulty interpreting
the nonverbal cues given by others. Relationships with others have consistently been described as poor for this group of individuals.

Habituation

The therapist should examine habituation to show possible
sources of organization and disorganization of routine behavior. The questions indicated in Table 2 can guide assessment of habituation. Individuals
with nonverbal learning disabilities typically have difficulty meeting expectations of others in terms of their role as student, worker, and family member.
Typically, individuals with nonverbal learning disabilities have difficulty
with organization, which contributes to their inability to enact roles. Habits
of time use are a major problem, for these persons are unable to prioritize
and organize their activities efficiently. Individuals with nonverbal learning
disabilities are frequently described as rigid and overly dependent on rules
and regulations. They often have difficulty generalizing strategies from one
situation to another, demonstrating rigid or poorly adaptable habits.

Volition

Examination of the client's volitional status provides information about the individual's motives for occcupation. The therapist must
determine how "values, interests and personal causation influence [the in-

Table 3 Volitional Questions for Assessment

Personal causation

Does the person feel in control or does he or she feel controlled by external forces?

Can this person identify personal skills and liabilities?

Does this person feel his or her skills are relevant to his or her life situation and/or identify areas of needed skill development?

Does the person expect success or failure in various aspects of his or her life?

Are these views of personal causation realistic, given the person's actual abilities, environment, prognosis, and other assets and liabilities?

Values

What occupations, if any, have meaning for the person and why does he or she find them meaningful?

What standards of performance has this person internalized and how do they guide his or her action?

What is this person's relative orientation to past, present, and future and what beliefs does he or she hold about how time should be used? Are they realistic and reflective of the culture at large and/or the person's subculture?

What goals does this person have?

Is the person's value system appropriate for his or her developmental level?

Interests

Can this person identify degrees of liking or disliking for various occupations?

What is the pattern of occupations this person enjoys? Is it reflective of a balanced life-style?

Is this person's report of interest based on experience with the occupations and does his or her interest lead to participation in the activities?

From: Rogers, J., & Kielhofner, G. (1985). Treatment planning. In G. Kielhofner (Ed.), *A model of human occupation. Theory and application* (pp. 136–146). Baltimore: Williams & Wilkins. (With permission of the author and publisher.)

dividual's] choices of action, inaction, or overaction" (Rogers & Kielhofner, 1985, p. 137). Guiding questions are presented in Table 3. Because individuals with nonverbal learning disabilities have experienced failure in peer relationships so often, their belief in self-competence for handling problems is often diminished. They often expect failure and have such a diminished belief in their personal effectiveness that these individuals may feel they have little control over what happens to them (decreased personal causation). [See Schunk, 1989, for a fuller understanding of the importance of how one's personal beliefs about one's capabilities to organize and implement actions influence the ability to attain designed levels of performance.] Because individuals with nonverbal learning disabilities have difficulty in understanding cause-and-effect relationships, they have difficulty generating hypotheses about possible outcomes. This limits their ability to anticipate and understand the consequences of their behavior. In addition, they typically set unrealistic goals and find no meaning or interest in leisure and work. Indi-

Table 4   Environmental Questions for Assessment

What is the physical and social press for performance in this person's environment? That is, what performance demands are made by objects, tasks, and other persons in the environment? Do these provide an appropriate level of challenge for the person? Are these demands relevant to the person's needs and goals?

What values will be used as standards to judge the person's competence?

What supports exist or may be needed in the environment to maintain this person's competence in spite of limitations?

Does the environment foster or deprive the person of a sense of internal control?

Does the person have opportunities to practice new roles and habits in a variety of contexts?

From: Rogers, J., & Kielhofner, G. (1985). Treatment planning. In G. Kielhofner (Ed.), *A model of human occupation. Theory and application* (pp. 136–146). Baltimore: Williams & Wilkins. (With permission of the author and publisher.)

viduals with nonverbal learning disabilities frequently have been described as anxious or depressed, and some have suggested that they are at greater risk for depression and suicide.

Environmental Constraints and Supports

In order to evaluate the individual's ability to function, the therapist must know the context in which the individual is expected to perform. Environmental questions for assessment are presented in Table 4. Due to difficulty with problem-solving and the tendency to be rigid and overdependent on rules, the client often performs better when the environment is structured and consistent.

Performance History

How the client has performed his or her various roles in the past can provide the therapist with useful information about what factors may promote or constrain successful performance. The occupational history gives an indication of the roles performed, length of time at each, and the degree of success and satisfaction. Information regarding leisure is valuable for understanding the impact of nonverbal learning disabilities on social life and recreation. Because occupational therapists are concerned with understanding the total quality of life, they are interested not only in the client's school and work but also with his or her peer relationships, interpersonal relationships, and the degree of satisfaction the adult experiences with his or her life. Several developmental, educational, and occupational history forms are available to serve as guidelines for assessment in this area (e.g., see Kielhofner, 1985).

Methods of Collecting Data

Evaluation will be most effective if it can be designed to answer a series of questions. The therapist must prioritize the areas for evaluation based on the client's interests, values, roles, and on the goals he or she has established with the client. A critical aspect of assessment is the selection of appropriate evaluation methods and tools. Assessment should not be limited to academic areas exclusively nor to the formal, standardized measures available. The adults themselves can provide valuable information during interviews or from questionnaires, rating scales, and checklists. Other sources of information are formal testing and observational data. Research on nonverbal learning disabilities suggests that stragegies of reasoning, planning abilities, and problem attack should be assessed. However, there are few, if any, standardized tests that can measure such components of cognitive performance effectively. Observing individuals while they perform tasks and through interviews can provide insight into their problem-solving abilities. An evaluation can be strengthened by comparing performance on tasks with varying degrees of structure, as learning problems may be less evident on highly structured tasks. These individuals may also be more successful in naturalistic settings rather than a testing situation because of redundant cues in the environment (Johnson & Blalock, 1987).

Information is often available in other professionals' reports and can be used by the therapist. If the client has had a neuropsychological evaluation, much of the information on the client's performance abilities may be provided in that assessment.

Constructing an Explanation of Occupational Function and Dysfunction

We use the information from our assessment to describe how clients do or do not function effectively in their daily occupations. Clients with nonverbal learning disabilities may be affected in a variety of ways. They may demonstrate limited ability to manage their roles as student, worker, and family member. Their skill repertoires may be limited. Their limited social interactional skills, work habits, and organization may interfere with their occupational performance. Poor problem solving may interfere with the ability to set and achieve realistic goals. Additionally, when things go wrong they may have a tendency to blame others for their lack of success. Table 5 summarizes the characteristics frequently identified in the adult with nonverbal learning disabilities.

Table 5   Occupational Status for the Adult with Nonverbal Learning
Disabilities

Performance
Deficits in visual-spatial abilities
Verbal expression generally good, often masking deficient problem-solving skills and
    making client appear more functional than he or she actually is
Nonverbal aspects of communication problematic
Interpersonal skills are deficient

Habituation
Difficulty meeting role expectations of others
Difficulty with organization
Problems with time use
Rigid and overdependent on rules and regulations
Study and work habits poor

Volition
Expect failure
Lack belief in personal effectiveness
Limited ability to anticipate and understand consequences of their behavior
Set unrealistic goals
Diminished ability to find meaning or interest in leisure or work
Narrow range of interests

Environment
Performance better when the environment is structured and consistent
Incongruence between social demands of the environment and skills of the individ-
    ual

Identifying and Selecting from among Treatment Options

The critical focus of intervention should be on strategies for coping with various daily demands that may create difficulties for the adult with learning disabilities. We must examine how the adult adapts and deals with specific life tasks and challenges, and we must identify what factors facilitate success or lead to failure (Polloway, Smith, & Patton, 1984). The ultimate goal of the intervention program is to enable clients "to engage in a balanced routine of work, play and daily living tasks appropriate for their environments, their disabilities and their developmental levels" (Cubie, Kaplan, & Kielhofner, 1985, p. 157).

Assessment of the client's performance and habituation subsystems generally provides evidence of problems that can be addressed. For example, the therapist may discover that the patient has poor visual-motor integration, poor visual-spatial abilities, poor problem-solving abilities, and poor use of time. By identifying these problems, the therapist could begin to initiate the following kinds of treatment: activities to improve visual-motor integration, cognitive-retraining procedures, and planning for time use. Although each of these modalities potentially is appropriate for the corresponding problem, the therapist must decide if and how each should be implemented. The therapist must couple information on the client's performance and habituation subsystems with information on both the client's volition and the social and task environments in order to make decisions regarding treatment. The therapist must know what is personally meaningful to and socially valued by the client and must utilize the patient's own concerns and values as a guiding principle in the clinical decision-making process. To empower the learning disabled adult to act as his or her change agent, "the therapist provides the [individual] with the knowledge needed to participate effectively in decision making. The therapist presents the possible options for treatment, projects the outcomes of each option, explains how the outcomes are achieved, and outlines a time sequence for goal attainment" (Rogers & Kielhofner, 1985, p. 145). However, individuals with nonverbal learning disabilities may not see themselves as successful and as having an effect on their environment. They need successful experiences to begin to believe in their own causality (Duncombe, personal communication, May 10, 1991).

Evaluating Outcomes and Adjusting Therapy

Once a therapeutic course of action is chosen its effectiveness must be assessed, in order to examine whether the outcomes of treatment are those desired by the client and therapist. Ongoing assessment is critical to evaluate therapeutic efficacy. If the desired goals or outcomes are not obtained, the therapist should determine whether the original objectives need to be modified or revised, or whether the therapeutic means were not optimal for attaining the goals. New goals and/or new procedures may then be chosen. When the desired outcomes are obtained, the therapist and client together may set new goals or may agree that the client's occupational status has reached the desired functional level.

Case Study: Mark

Mark is a 28-year-old man who was referred to the Dunhofner Mental Health Center due to depression secondary to being placed on probation at his current job working on an assembly line at a candy factory. His employer indicated that Mark is often late for work. He interrupts his co-workers during critical aspects of their work by talking about topics not related to the job (such as the movie he saw on television the previous night). Due to his tardiness and his constant attempts at socialization, he has been consistently below his quota on the assembly line.

Mark currently lives at home with his parents, who are concerned that he does not appear to have the skills needed to live independently.

The Assessment Process

As a part of the initial intake process, Mark, his parents, and his employer were interviewed for information on his past history and current status. The clinical questions in Tables 1 through 4 served to guide this process.

HISTORY

OCCUPATIONAL. Mark completed high school but dropped out of college after his first year. He had trouble organizing his time and found his required science courses to be particularly difficult. Mark has had previous clerical jobs but has not worked at any one job for more than a year. His previous supervisors reported that he could handle routine work in a satisfactory manner, but he had difficulty with making decisions and handling problems that arose on the job. For example, when he worked as a receptionist, he became extremely stressed when he did not know the answers to questions. Additionally they noted that he had trouble getting along with his co-workers. He often was observed arguing with them, and he was the target of many of their practical jokes.

DEVELOPMENTAL AND ACADEMIC. Mark's parents did not have any major concerns about him as a young boy. They did note that he had more trouble learning to dress himself than his older brother did and that he always seemed to be disheveled. However, he learned to talk at an early age, and many of their friends commented on how verbal he was.

Mark had no difficulty with reading in the primary grades. Problems arose later, however, when he needed to summarize or synthesize what he read. Although he was good at remembering details, he was poor at making inferences or answering "why" questions. Math was always particularly difficult for Mark. Although he was able to memorize his number facts he had trouble applying these to everyday situations, such as learning to tell time and managing money. Mark's teachers noted that his handwriting was messy. He had problems organizing his work and was usually late handing in his assignments.

VOLITION AND HABITUATION

Mark is a very verbal young man who is depressed about his difficulty keeping a job. In order to assess volition and habituation he was given an Interest Checklist, Role Checklist, Time-Use Inventory, Vocational Preference Assessment, and Leisure Interest Survey (see Kielhofner, 1985, for a description of these tools).

VOLITION. Mark values having a job and is proud of his present position. He does not understand why he was placed on probation, as he feels that he is doing a good job and trying very hard. He also does not understand why he has had so much difficulty keeping a job in the past.

Mark is involved in few activities outside of work. He usually watches television in his free time. Occasionally he goes to the movies or a ball game with his parents or brother. He follows baseball closely and knows a great deal about the teams and players. Mark states that he enjoys cooking. His mother, however, is reluctant to allow him to cook, as he makes a mess of the kitchen and does not clean up adequately. Mark also reports that he had enjoyed bowling when he was in high school and often was the high scorer on his team. He presently does not engage in this activity because he has "no friends to bowl with." During the interview Mark was asked about goals for the future. Mark's main goal for himself is to keep his job. He also hopes that by the time he reaches 30 he will have his own apartment. He expressed his frustration that he was unable to make and keep friends and stated that one goal would be "to have friends to do things with."

HABITUATION. Mark's primary roles are those of son and worker. Although he is 28 years old, his parents still take a major role in structuring his life and in meeting his needs (e.g., food, housing). His mother prepares most of his meals and does his laundry. When Mark began working he tried to manage his own finances. However, he frequently spent more money than he had, buying items on credit and ordering from catalogs. His parents have had to cover his debts several times. Finally his mother took over his finances. She now gives him a daily allowance, and he requests money to pay for any major expenses.

Mark likes external structure in his life. He does better when rules are clear-cut and do not change. Interviews with his parents and employer indicated that Mark needed a great deal of structure in order to maintain a schedule. He did not seem to comprehend how long tasks would take to complete. For example, he might begin preparing for a 6 o'clock meal at 5 minutes to 6.

PERFORMANCE

NEUROPSYCHOLOGICAL ASSESSMENT. The tests we administered as part of the neuropsychological evaluation are described in Appendix B. Results of the neuropsychological evaluation indicated a marked discrepancy between the verbal and visuospatial domains in many areas of cognitive functions. On the WAIS-R, Mark's Verbal IQ was 105, which was 21 points higher than his Performance IQ of 84. His verbal learning and memory were in the average range, but his visual memory was severely impaired. His speech and language skills were in the average range, although melodic contour was somewhat reduced. Mark's performance on tests of visuocon- struction were moderately to severely impaired. Performance on the Rey Osterrieth Complex Figure indicated a piecemeal approach to drawing with a focus on detail. Twenty-minute delayed recall further supported this anal- ysis. Mark's eye contact and gestural communication were poor. We noted that Mark could correctly interpret the emotional content of simple static facial expression made by the examiner, but when the examiner made mul- tiple facial expressions in rapid sequence (more similar to the natural context in which facial expressions occur), Mark was not able to interpret the emo- tional content. Academic difficulty on the Woodcock-Johnson was seen in arithmetic but not in reading or spelling. In addition, arithmetic was the lowest subtest score on the Verbal Scale of the WAIS-R.

OCCUPATIONAL THERAPY EVALUATION. In addition to obtaining information on habituation, volition, and environment which was obtained primarily through checklists and interviews, the occupational therapist was concerned with certain aspects of Mark's performance, particularly his fine motor and perceptual abilities. Several standardized tests were administered (see Appendix A for a description of these tests).

On the Developmental Test of Visual Motor Integration, Mark success- fully completed 17 of the shapes resulting in a score in the lowest 5%. In the more complex designs, he did not articulate shapes that were joined but rather drew them as two separate shapes. Mark was not able to successfully achieve interlocking of forms. As also noted by the neuropsychologist on the Rey-Osterrieth Complex Figure, Mark's approach to copying shapes was very piecemeal.

On the Hooper Visual Organization Test, Mark scored in the mildly deficient range. Mark's scores on the Purdue Pegboard test were in the low average range with his right hand (standard score = -0.8) and in the deficient range with his left hand (standard score = -1.6), and with both hands together (-1.5). Mark's performance on the assembly task was also poor (-1.2).

Mark completed the Grooved Pegboard test in 106 seconds with his right preferred hand and 140 seconds with his left nonpreferred hand. Although the time for each hand was in the low average range, the "between hand" discrepancy was greater than is expected. The average between hand discrep- ancy in a normative sample is 7 seconds, whereas Mark's difference was 34 seconds.

The MacQuarrie Test for Mechanical Abilities consists of 7 subtests which include eye-hand coordination, speed of finger movements, and the ability to visualize space. Mark's overall score placed him at the 11th percentile, with subtest scores ranging from the 1st to the 60th percentile (6 of the 7 subtests were below the 25th percentile).

In summary, Mark clearly showed difficulty in fine motor performance with his left hand being somewhat less coordinated than his right hand. Consistent with the findings of the neuropsychology assessment, difficulties were also noted with perceptual and perceptual motor performance.

ENVIRONMENT

Mark lives with his parents. His father is an accountant, and his mother works part-time at an employment agency. His older brother lives nearby, and occasionally he and Mark attend sporting events together.

Mark does little to help around the house. As mentioned earlier, his mother prepares his meals and launders his clothes, and his parents manage his finances.

Mark's parents would like to move into a smaller apartment. However, they cannot do this while Mark is living with them. They would like to help him become more independent so that he could live on his own, but so far they have not facilitated independence. His mother is a very organized and orderly woman and has trouble with Mark's disorganized approach to tasks. For example, although he enjoys cooking he is allowed to prepare meals only occasionally, as the meals are always late and, "he doesn't clean up the kitchen the way he should."

As he does not drive a car, Mark's opportunities to participate in social activities and his choice of employment are limited. When Mark was 16 years old his father did attempt to teach him to drive, but both Mark and his father were overwhelmed by the task and gave up. Mark has not explored learning to drive since then.

OCCUPATIONAL FUNCTION AND DYSFUNCTION

Due to inadequate social skills Mark does not have friends and feels isolated and alone. Mark's daily routine at home does not provide him with opportunities to develop competence; as a result, he has feelings of inadequacy and lack of control. Although he has the goal of living independently, Mark does not have the skills to do so, nor can he articulate a plan to acquire these skills. He had a lack of insight into his problems at work and does not understand how his behavior contributes to his current situation. He is, however, highly motivated to keep his present job.

TREATMENT PLAN

The evaluation team met with Mark to discuss his evaluation results and plan a course of action. The following goals were set with Mark: (1) improve relationships with peers; (2) increase independent functioning in budgeting, self-care activities, and household maintenance tasks; and (3) develop performance abilities needed to keep a job. To enact these goals four approaches were undertaken. First, Mark was referred to the local Association for Children and Adults with Learning Disabilities (ACLD) so that he could meet and socialize with other adults with learning disabilities. Second, Mark was referred to a program provided by Vocational Rehabilitation Services (VRS) that worked with both employers and employees. Third, Mark participated in an evening cooking group run by the occupational therapists at the Mental Health Center, whose goals included improvement of socialization skills and development of organizational and planning skills. Finally the staff at the Mental Health Center worked with Mark and his family to set up a schedule to promote increasing responsibility and independent function at home.

Although the assessment revealed moderate to severe problems in spatial skills and mild problems in fine motor coordination, these deficits were not interfering with Mark's present job or his current life tasks. Thus no remediation was initiated at this time. However, one of Mark's long-term goals is to be able to drive, and some research has indicated a relationship between spatial skills and driving ability (Sivak et al., 1984; Sivak et al., 1981). Therefore, the potential impact of his spatial deficit on his driving ability will be more fully investigated before Mark begins planning for this goal.

Outcome

After a period of 4 months the evaluation team met with Mark to evaluate his progress and make any adjustments in his program. Mark had begun to assume increased responsibilities at home. He was doing his own laundry and had full responsibility for the planning and preparing of dinner for his family every Wednesday night. His mother initially had been frustrated because Mark left the kitchen a mess. The occupational therapist met with Mark and his mother, and together they made a list of the essential steps in cleaning up the kitchen. Mark used this list to check himself when he had finished. Although the kitchen was not as neat as his mother would have liked, she agreed that it was acceptable and the meals were improving. Additionally, Mark began making his own lunches to take to work each day. Mark reported that when he initially started making his lunch he frequently "ran out of time" in the morning and went without lunch. However, since the occupational therapist suggested that he prepare his lunch the night before, he "has not missed a single meal."

Mark was very excited about the friends he was making through the ACLD. He reported that he had joined their bowling group and was "bowler of the week" last month.

Although his production at work is still somewhat slow it has improved. He has become more aware that his talking interrupts his co-workers and is making an effort to refrain from conversation while he is on the production line. Mark was taught to covertly ask himself "does this relate to my performing my job or my co-workers performing their jobs?" prior to engaging in interaction while working on the assembly line. [For further information on applying cognitive strategies see Simmonds, Luchow, Kaminsky, & Cottone, 1989.] Mark and his supervisor have met several times with personnel from VRS, and Mark now views his supervisor as an ally and supporter. He feels more comfortable in asking for assistance when problems arise on the job.

In general, Mark reports feeling more competent in his abilities and feels he has begun to make friends and establish goals for the future. He has set as a goal that, over the next 6 months, he will take over managing his finances and learn to drive.

Implications for Future Work in Nonverbal Learning Disabilities and Occupational Therapy

Typically, learning disabilities have been associated primarily with academic learning and the school-aged child. Only recently have clinicians recognized that learning disabilities are a lifelong condition, with varying needs at different ages/stages. Occupational therapy, with its emphasis on the individual's work, play/leisure, and daily living skills can make a unique contribution to improving the functional performance of the adult with learning disabilities. As the unique needs of the adult with learning disabilities become known, the role of occupational therapy will become more clearly defined. Occupational therapists need to be involved in delineating the needs of the adult with learning disabilities. Occupational therapists working with individuals with nonverbal learning disabilities should document, by case studies, their assessment and treatment approaches.

The utility of different occupational therapy treatment approaches with persons with nonverbal learning disabilities needs to be examined. For example, visual-spatial deficits are a primary characteristic of the adult with nonverbal learning disabilities. Occupational therapists need to examine and document whether or not the visual-spatial deficits are related to deficits in activities of daily living, work, and play/leisure. In addition to examining more routine tasks, such as dressing skills, therapists should examine complex activities of daily living (such as the management of one's finances). Therapists need to examine whether the focus of intervention should be remediation of the underlying spatial deficits, improving specific functional skills, teaching cognitive strategies, modifying task demands, or a combination of these. [For a more complete discussion of analysis of occupational therapy approaches for perceptual deficits, see Abreu & Toglia, (1987); Neistadt (1988, 1990), and Toglia (1991).]

Summary and Conclusions

Nonverbal learning disabilities are a pervasive disorder manifested throughout the life span. Although the manifestations are often subtle, they may, nevertheless, interfere with almost all aspects of occupation. Until recently, this disorder has been little recognized and the symptoms have often been viewed as reflecting psychiatric disorders. Occupational therapists must recognize that some patients presenting with depression or suicidal tendencies may have underlying nonverbal learning disabilities and their histories should be examined carefully.

There is little written in the occupational therapy literature about evaluation and treatment of the adult with nonverbal learning disabilities. In fact, only within the last twenty years has the need for continued services for the learning disabled adult been recognized. Occupational therapy has much to offer the adult with nonverbal learning disabilities. Our focus on self-care, work, and play/leisure addresses the multiple needs of these individuals.

Acknowledgments

Our appreciation is extended to Linda Duncombe, M.S., OTR, and Gary Kielhofner, D.Ph., OTR, for their critical reviews of this manuscript. This chapter was prepared under the auspices of the Neurobehavioral Rehabilitation Research Center, a center for scholarship and research in occupational therapy at Boston University funded by the American Occupational Therapy Association and the American Occupational Therapy Foundation.

References

Abramson, R., & Katz, D. (1989). A case of developmental right-hemisphere dysfunction: Implications for psychiatric diagnosis and management. *Journal of Clinical Psychiatry, 50(2)*, 70–71.

Abreu, B. C., & Toglia, J. P. (1987). Cognitive rehabilitation: A model for occupational therapy. *American Journal of Occupational Therapy, 41*, 439–448.

Adelman, H. S., & Taylor, L. (1986). *An introduction to learning disabilities.* Glenview, IL: Scott Foresman & Co.

Association for Children and Adults with Learning Disabilities. (1982, September/October). ACLD Vocational Committee survey of learning disabled adults: Preliminary report. *ACLD Newsbriefs*, 10–13.

Badian, N. (1986). Nonverbal disorders of learning: The reverse of dyslexia? *Annals of Dyslexia, 36*, 253–269.

Bergman, M. (1987). Social grace or disgrace: Adolescent social skills and learning disability subtypes. *Journal of Reading, Writing and Learning Disabilities International, 3*, 161–166.

Bigler, E. (1989). On the neuropsychology of suicide. *Journal of Learning Disabilities, 22(3)*, 180–185.

Brown, J. S., & Zinkus, P. W. (1979). Screening techniques for early intervention. In M. I. Gottlieb, P. W. Zinkus, & L. J. Bradford (Eds.), *Current issues in developmental pediatrics: The learning-disabled child* (pp. 315–342). New York, NY: Grune & Stratton Inc.

Brumback, R. A. (1988). Childhood depression and medically treatable learning disability. In D. L. Molfese & S. J. Segalowitz (Eds.), *Brain lateralization in children: Developmental implications* (pp. 463–506). New York: Guilford.

Brumback, R. A., & Staton, R. D. (1982). An hypothesis regarding the commonality of right hemisphere involvement in learning disability, attentional disorder, and childhood major depressive disorder. *Perceptual and Motor Skills, 55*, 1091–1097.

Cannon, I. P., & Compton, C. L. (1980). School dysfunction in the adolescent. *Pediatric Clinics of North America, 27*, 79–96.

Chesler, B. (1982). ACLD vocational committee completes survey on LD adult. *ACLD Newsbriefs, 146(5)*, 20–23.

Cruickshank, W. M., Morse, W. C., & Johns, J. S. (1980). *Learning disabilities: The struggle from adolescence toward adulthood.* New York: Syracuse University Press.

Cubie, S. H., & Kaplan, K. (1982). A case analysis method for the model of human occupation. *American Journal of Occupational Therapy, 36*, 645–656.

Cubie, S. H., Kaplan, K. L., & Kielhofner, G. (1985). Program development. In G. Kielhofner (Ed.), *A model of human occupation: Theory and application* (pp. 156–167). Baltimore: Williams & Wilkins.

Davidson, P. (1983). *Mathematics learning viewed from a neurobiological model for intellectual functioning. Final report. Vol. 1.* Washington, DC: National Institute of Education (DHEW).

Duncombe, L., Howe, M., & Schwartzberg, S. (1988). *Case simulations in psychosocial occupational therapy, 2nd ed.* Philadelphia: F. A. Davis.

Fisk, J. L., & Rourke, B. P. (1983). Neuropsychological subtyping of learning-disabled children: History, methods, implications. *Journal of Learning Disabilities, 16,* 529–531.

Fletcher, J. M. (1989). Nonverbal learning disabilities and suicide: Classification leads to prevention. *Journal of Learning Disabilities, 22*(3), 176–179.

Forness, S. R. (1988). Reductionism, paradigm shifts, and learning disabilities. *Journal of Learning Disabilities, 21,* 421–424.

Gerber, P. J. (1981). Learning disabilities and eligibility for vocational rehabilitation services: A chronology of events. *Learning Disability Quarterly, 4,* 422–425.

Goldberg, E., & Costa, L. (1981). Hemisphere differences in the acquisition and use of descriptive systems. *Brain and Language, 14,* 144–173.

Johnson, D. J., & Blalock, J. W. (1987). *Adults with learning disabilities: Clinical studies.* Orlando, FL: Grune & Stratton.

Johnson, D., & Myklebust, H. R. (1967). *Learning disabilities.* New York: Grune and Stratton.

Kaplan, K. (1984). Short-term assessment: The need and a response. *Occupational Therapy in Mental Health, 4,* 29–43.

Kavale, K., & Forness, S. (1987). The far side of heterogeneity: A critical analysis of empirical subtyping research in learning disabilities. *Journal of Learning Disabilities, 20,* 374–382.

Keller, C., & Hallahan, D. (1987). *Learning disabilities: Issues and instructional interventions.* Washington: National Education Association.

Kenny, T. J., & Burka, A. (1980). Coordinating multiple interventions. In H. E. Rie & E. D. Rie (Eds.), *Handbook of minimal brain dysfunctions: A critical view* (pp. 645–665). New York: John Wiley & Sons.

Kielhofner, G. (1985). *A model of human occupation: Theory and application.* Baltimore: Williams & Wilkins.

Kumar, S. (1973). The right and left of being internally different. *Impact of Science on Society, 23,* 53–64.

Lerner, J. (1976). *Children with learning disorders.* Boston: Houghton Mifflin Co.

Lezak, M. D. (1983). *Neurological assessment.* New York: Oxford University Press.

Luria, A. R. (1980). *Higher cortical functions in man, 2nd ed.* New York: Basic Books.

Murray, E. A. (1991). Hemispheric specialization. In A. G. Fisher, E. A. Murray, & A. C. Bundy (Eds.), *Sensory integration: Theory and practice* (pp. 171–200). Philadelphia: F. A. Davis.

National Joint Committee on Learning Disabilities. (1983). Learning disabilities: The needs of adults with learning disabilities. A position paper of the National Joint Committee on Learning Disabilities. Baltimore, MD: NJCLD, The Orton Dyslexia Society.

National Joint Committee on Learning Disabilities. (1985). Adults with learning disabilities: A call to action. A position paper of the National Joint Committee on Learning Disabilities. Baltimore, MD: The Orton Dyslexia Society.

National Joint Commission on Learning Disabilities. (1987). Adults with learning disabilities: A call to action. *Journal of Learning Disabilities, 20,* 172–175.

Neistadt, M. E. (1988). Occupational therapy for adults with perceptual deficits. *American Journal of Occupational Therapy, 42*(7), 434–440.

Neistadt, M. E. (1990). A critical analysis of occupational therapy approaches for perceptual deficits in adults with brain injury. *American Journal of Occupational Therapy, 44*(4), 299–304.

Polloway, E., Smith, J., & Patton, J. (1984). Learning disabilities: An adult developmental perspective. *Learning Disability Quarterly, 7,* 179–187.

Porter, J. F., & Rourke, B. P. (1985). Socio-emotional functioning of learning disabled children. A subtypal analysis of personality patterns. In B. P. Rourke (Ed.), *Neuropsychology of learning disabilities: Essentials of subtype analysis* (pp. 281–301). New York: Guilford Press.

Rehabilitation Services Administration (1990 September 28). Program assistance circular RSA-PAC-90-7 (Available from U.S. Department of Education, Office of Special Education and Rehabilitation Services, Washington, DC 20202).

Rivers, D. L., & Love, R. J. (1980). Language performance on visual processing tasks in right hemisphere lesions cases. *Brain and Language, 10,* 348–366.

Rogers, J. C., & Kielhofner, G. (1985). Treatment. In G. Kielhofner (Ed.), *A model of human occupation: Theory and application* (pp. 136–146). Baltimore: Williams & Wilkins.

Rourke, B. P. (1982). Central processing deficiencies in children: Toward a developmental neuropsychological model. *Journal of Clinical Neuropsychology, 4,* 1–18.

Rourke, B. P. (1985). *Neuropsychology of learning disabilities: Essentials of subtype analysis.* New York: Guilford.

Rourke, B. P. (1988a). Socio-emotional disturbances of learning-disabled children. *Journal of Consulting and Clinical Psychology, 56,* 801–810.

Rourke, B. P. (1988b). The syndrome of nonverbal learning disabilities: Developmental manifestations in neurological disease, disorder, and dysfunction. *The Clinical Neuropsychologist, 2,* 293–330.

Rourke, B. P. (1989). *Nonverbal learning disabilities: The syndrome and the model.* New York: Guilford Publications.

Rourke, B. P., & Fisk, J. L. (1988). Subtypes of learning-disabled children: Implications for a neurodevelopmental model of differential hemispheric processing. In D. L. Molfeses, & S. J. Segalowitz (Eds.), *Brain lateraliza-*

    tion in children: Developmental implications (pp. 547–566). New York: Guilford.

Rourke, B. P., Young, G. C., & Leenaars, A. A. (1989). A childhood learning disability that predisposes those afflicted to adolescent and adult depression and suicide risk. *Journal of Learning Disabilities, 22,* 169–175.

Schunk, D. H. (1989). Self-efficacy and cognitive achievement: Implications for students with learning problems. *Journal of Learning Disabilities, 22,* 14–22.

Semmes, J. (1968). Hemispheric specialization: A possible clue to mechanism. *Neuropsychologia, 6,* 11–26.

Semrud-Clikeman, M., & Hynd, G. W. (1990). Right hemispheric dysfunction in nonverbal learning disabilities: Social, academic and adaptive functioning in adults and children. *Psychological Bulletin, 107*(2), 196–209.

Simmonds, E., Luchow, J. Kaminsky, S., & Cottone, V. (1989). Applying cognitive learning strategies in the classroom: A collaborative training institute. *Learning Disabilities Focus, 4,* 96–105.

Sivak, M., Hill, S. S., Henson, M. A., Butler, B. P., & Silber, S. M. (1984). Improved driving performance following perceptual training in persons with brain damage. *Archives of Physical Medicine and Rehabilitation, 65,* 163–167.

Sivak, M., Olson, P. L., Kewman, D. G., Won, H., & Henson, D. L. (1981). Driving and perceptual/cognitive skills: Behavioral consquences of brain damage. *Archives of Physical Medicine and Rehabilitation, 62,* 476–483.

Smith, J. O. (1988). Social and vocational problems of adults with learning disabilities: A review of the literature. *Learning Disabilities Focus, 4,* 46–58.

Snow, J. H., Koller, J. R., & Roberts, C. D. (1987). Adolescent and adult learning disability subgroups based on WAIS-R performance. *Journal of Psychoeducational Assessment, 5,* 7–14.

Spreen, O. (1988). Prognosis of learning disability. *Journal of Consulting and Clinical Psychology, 56,* 836–842.

Spreen, O., & Haaf, R. (1986). Emprically derived learning disability subtypes: A replication attempt and longitudinal patterns over 15 years. *Journal of Learning Disabilities, 19,* 170–180.

Strang, J. D., & Rourke, B. P. (1985). Adaptive behavior of children who exhibit specific arithmetic disabilities and associated neuropsychological abilities and deficits. In B. P. Rourke (Ed.), *Neuropsychology of learning disabilities: Essentials of subtype analysis* (pp. 167–183). New York: Guilford.

Thompson, O. M. (1985). The nonverbal dilemma. *Journal of Learning Disabilities, 18,* 400–402.

Toglia, J. (1991). Generalization of treatment: A multicontext approach to cognitive perceptual impairment in adults with brain injury. *American Journal of Occupational Therapy, 45,* 505–516.

Tranel, D., Hall, L., Olson S., & Tranel, N. (1987). Evidence for a right-hemisphere developmental learning disability. *Developmental Neuropsychology, 3*(2), 113–127.

Voeller, K. K. S. (1986). Right-hemisphere deficit syndrome in children. *American Journal of Psychiatry, 143,* 1004–1009.

Voeller, K. K. S., & Heilman, K. M. (1988, September). Motor impersistence in children with attention deficit-hyperactivity disorder: Evidence for right-hemisphere dysfunction. [Paper presented at the 17th annual meeting of the Child Neurological Society, Halifax, Nova Scotia, Canada.]

Wapner, W., Hamby, S., & Gardner, H. (1981). The role of the right hemisphere in the apprehension of complex linguistic materials. *Brain and Language, 41,* 15–33.

Wechsler, D. I. (1974). *Examiner's manual: Wechsler Intelligence Scale for Children—Revised.* New York: Psychological Corp.

Wechsler, D. I. (1981). *Examiner's manual: Wechsler Adult Intelligence Scale—Revised.* New York: Psychological Corp.

Weintraub, S., & Mesulam, M. M. (1983). Developmental learning disabilities of the right hemisphere: Emotional, interpersonal, and cognitive components. *Archives of Neurology, 40,* 463–468.

Weller, C., & Strawser, S. (1987). Adaptive behavior of subtypes of learning disabled individuals. *Journal of Special Education, 21*(1), 101–115.

Appendix A   Tools to Assess Performance in the Cognitive, Visual-Perceptual, and Visual-Motor Domains

Title	Content	References/source
Purdue Pegboard Test (standardized test)	This test of motor dexterity involves placing pegs in a board with the right hand, the left hand, both hands simultaneously, and then both hands in an assembly task. The score is the number of pegs inserted in a specified time.	Purdue Research Foundation (1948). *Examiners manual for the Purdue Pegboard.* Chicago: Science Research Associates. Lafayett Instruments (1968). Lafayette, IN.
Grooved Pegboard (standardized test)	This manipulative dexterity test requires more complex visual-motor coordination than most pegboards. The test consists of a	Klove, H. (1963). Clinical neuropsychology. In F. M. Forster (Ed.), *The medical clinics of North America.* New York: Saunders.

Appendix A   Tools to Assess Performance in the Cognitive, Visual-Perceptual, and
Visual-Motor Domains (Continued)

Title	Content	References/source
	small board with a set of slotted holes angled in different directions into which grooved pegs must be fitted.	Matthews, C. G., & Klove, H. (1964). *Instruction manual for the Adult Neuropsychology Test Battery*. Madison, WI: University of Wisconsin Medical School.
MacQuarrie Test for Mechanical Abilities (standardized test)	This paper and pencil test consists of 7 subtests that measure manual speed and fine motor control (3 subtests), visuospatial function (3 subtests), and speed and accuracy of visual tracking (1 subtest).	MacQuarrie, T. W. (1953). *MacQuarrie Test for Mechanical Abilities*. Monterey, CA: CTB/McGraw Hill.
Developmental Test of Visual Motor Integration Third Revision (standardized test)	This paper and pencil test involves copying 24 geometric shapes (Norms through age 19)	Beery, K. (1989). *The VMI: Developmental Test of Visual-Motor Integration*. Cleveland: Modern Curriculum Press.
Rey Osterrieth Complex Figure Test	The subject is required to copy a complex figure and later to reproduce that figure from memory. The subject's approach to the task (organization) is analyzed.	Lezak, M. (1983). *Neuropsychological assessment, 2nd ed.* (pp. 395–402). New York: Oxford University Press.
The Hooper Visual Organization Test (standardized test)	The test consists of 30 pictures of cut-up objects. The objects are shown one at a time and the subject must name each object.	Hooper, H. E. (1958). *The Hooper Visual Organization Test*. Los Angeles: Western Psychological Services.
Wechsler Adult Intelligence Scale-Revised (standardized test)	This test includes 11 subtests that provide a full scale score, a verbal scale score, and a performance score. The verbal scale is pri-	Wechsler, D. (1981). *WAIS-R Manual*. New York: Psychological Corporation.

Appendix A   Tools to Assess Performance in the Cognitive, Visual-Perceptual, and
Visual-Motor Domains (Continued)

Title	*Content*	*References/source*
	marily based on language tasks, whereas the performance scale is primarily based on visual-perceptual and visuo-motor tasks.	
Woodcock-Johnson Test of Achievement (standardized test)	This test consists of a standard battery, containing 9 tests, and two supplemental batteries, each containing 9 achievement measures. The test provides in-depth analysis of reading, mathematics, written language, and knowledge.	Woodcock, R. W., & Mather, N. (1989). *Woodcock-Johnson Tests of Achievement.* Allen, TX: DLM Teaching Resources.

Index

References followed by a t or f represent tables or figures, respectively.

Ability
  crystallized, 55
  fluid, 55
Academic skills, of adults with nonverbal learning disabilities, 265
Accommodation, definition of, 79
Achievement, definition of, 246
ACL. See Allen Cognitive Level test
ACLD. See Association for Children and Adults with Learning Disabilities
Activities. See also Process approach
  concept of, 60
    use of, 62–63
  levels of, 60–61
  therapeutic, for brain-injured adults, 174
Activities of daily living (ADL) assessment process, 68–75
  case example of, 71–74
  case review in, 69–70
  family or caregiver interview in, 70
  future development of, 74–75
Activity analysis
  based on information processing, 60–63
  with ceramic bowls, 92–94
  of cognitively disabled older adults, 27–29
  hierarchy for, 60
  of mental patient, 92–97
    case example, 94–97, 95t, 96f
  of physically disabled, 32
Adaptation, cognitive, 79
Adaptational difficulties/dysfunction, instrumental enrichment (IE) for, 161–163
  case example, 162–163
  goals of, 154t, 161–162
  methods for, 154t
Adaptive approach, to occupational therapy for brain-injured, 222
ADL. See Activities of daily living assessment process
Adults. See also Brain-injured adults; Older adults

learning disabilities in, 260
  incidence of, 261
nonverbal learning disabilities in, human occupation model of, 258–289
Alertness, measures of, 182t–183t
Allen, C.
  cognitive disability frame of reference
    in gerontological rehabilitation, 22–50
    in psychiatry, target population for, 63
    in short-stay private psychiatric hospital, 51–76
  cognitive disability theory, 17, 35–36, 146
  definition of disability, 53
Allen Cognitive Level (ACL) test, 10, 36–37, 55
Allen Cognitive Level (ACL) test-Problem Solving, 10, 64
Arithmetic skills, of adults with nonverbal learning disabilities, 265
Arthritis, limitations imposed by, 30
Assimilation, definition of, 79
Association for Children and Adults with Learning Disabilities, definition of learning disabilities, 260–261
Attention
  assessment of, 180
  automatic and controlled processing in, 198
  after brain injury, 198–201
  at cognitive level 1, 38, 57
  at cognitive level 2, 38, 57
  at cognitive level 3, 40, 57–58
  at cognitive level 4, 42, 58
  at cognitive level 5, 43, 59
  at cognitive level 6, 44, 59
  components of, 180
  definition of, 224
  depression and, 56–57
  foundations of, 59
  and memory, 200–201

processes that require, 224
process of, 55–59
selective, 56
    active, 56
    feature–integration theory of, 57
    passive, 56
selectivity of, 199–200
strategies and behaviors of, 114t
training of, 234
Attention deficit/dysfunction
in brain-injured adults, 176–177
characteristics of, 180
divided, 198–199
focused, 198–199
in schizophrenia, 60
Attention getting, 56
Automatic actions, description of, 4t
Awareness, types of, 129
Awareness training techniques, 126
use of, 129–130

Behavior(s)
control of, by antecedents, 210–211
development of, training program for, 208
functional, environmental docility hypothesis of, 26
shaping of, 210
that indicate cognitive function and dysfunction, evaluation of, 181
Behavioral problems, occupational therapy for, dynamic approach to, 145
Bottom-up approach, for rehabilitation after severe brain injury, 197
Brain
normal function of, 220
right hemisphere of, functions of, 268–269
Brain damage/injury
effects of, 220, 228
severe
    attention after, 198–201
    neurofunctional assessment of, 203–206
    problem solving and planning after, 201–203
Brain-injured adults. *See also* Cognitive disability
areas of difficulty for, 176
attention deficits in, 176–177
cognitive rehabilitation for
    neurofunctional approach to, 206–213
    retraining approach to, 219–239
deficits in, 176
instrumental enrichment (IE) for, 154–158
motor deficits in, 176
occupational therapy for, 174, 177–178, 222–223
    adaptive approach to, 222

approaches to, 222
bottom-up approach to, 197
characteristics of, 177–178
dynamic approach to, 145
neurofunctional approach to, 195–218
process approach to, 167–194
remedial approach to, 222
secondary disabilities or impairments in, 175–176
classification of, 177
therapeutic activities for, 174
Brain tumor
intervention for patient with, process approach to, 175
problem solving and planning with, 201–202

Caregiver interview, in activities of daily living (ADL) assessment process, 70
Categorization, in development of thought, 156–157
Central nervous system trauma. *See* Brain-injured adults
Centrism, definition of, 81
Ceramic bowls, activity analysis with, 92–94
Cerebrovascular accident
intervention for, process approach to, 175
problem solving and planning after, 201
Chain of actions level(s), 61
Chance, conception of, test of, 88
categories of response, 90t
Children, learning disabilities in, 259
incidence of, 260–261
Co-environment, components of, 173
Co-environmental fit, 173
Cognition. *See also* Information processing
assessment of, tools for, 289t–291t
constructivist view of, 243
contemporary, 242243
decline in, theories of, 242–243
definition of, 107, 168–169, 223, 240–243, 245
development of, 81, 147, 241–242
    concrete operational stage of, 242
    formal operational stage of, 242
    preoperational stage of, 242
    sensorimotor stage of, 242
dynamic model of, 108f
    multicontext treatment approach based on, 126–137, 127f
    summary of, 113
    theoretical foundations for, 107–113
human occupation model of, 240–257
information processing models of, 243–245

input phase of, 243–244
interior skills of, 247
output phase of, 244–245
processes of, 241
scope of, 105
storage phase of, 244
structural elements of, 241
structure of, 79
style of, in adults with nonverbal learning disabilities, 263
Cognitive, definition of, 8
Cognitive adaptation, definition of, 79
Cognitive assessment battery, 85–89
according to conceptual domain and developmental stage, 86t
categories of response, 90t
example results, 95t
for retraining approach, 225–227
Cognitive deficit. *See* Cognitive disability
Cognitive disability, 121
categorization of, 116–118
compensatory strategies for, 125–126,
197
definition of, 8, 53
effects of, 79, 228
on occupational function, 246–247
evaluation of, methods for, 10–11
implications of, 17–19
intervention for, 10–17
approach to, 11–17
goals of, 13
legal definition of, 7
long-term care for, 15–17
effects of, 19
goals of, 18
indications for, 17
patients who require, 16
in older adults, rehabilitation of, 22–50
literature review, 23–27
post-acute care for, 11–12
terminology for, 12
rehabilitation for. *See* Cognitive rehabilitation
in short-stay psychiatric hospital, intervention for, 63–75
stabilization process, 14–15
target population, 910
temporary, 8
Cognitive disability frame of reference
in gerontological rehabilitation, 22–50
in psychiatry, target population for, 63
in short-stay private psychiatric hospital, 51–76
Cognitive disability theory, 17, 35–36
assumption of, 146
clinical application of, 3637
goal of, 12
Cognitive dysfunction
behaviors and physical signs that indicate, evaluation of, 181
classification of, 109

definition of, 113–118, 117t
instrumental enrichment (IE) for, 153
methods and goals, 154t
measures of, 182t–185t
model of, 110f
physical signs that indicate, evaluation
of, 181
postulates for change, 175
Cognitive function, 79
behaviors and physical signs that indicate, evaluation of, 181
classification of, 109
definition of, 113–118
evaluation of, by process approach, scale
for, 181
measures of, 182t–185t
model of, 110f
physical signs that indicate, evaluation
of, 181
underlying elements, 114t–115t
Cognitive learning, theory of, 172–173
Cognitive level(s), 2
attention according to, 38, 40, 42–44,
57–60
descriptive model of, 2, 3t
functional activities associated with, 89
goal-direction actions according to, 38,
40, 42–44
information processing according to,
57–60
measuring changes in, 64–68
sample questions and rationale for,
65t
sample script for, 66t
motor actions according to, 38, 40, 42–
44
rehabilitation according to, 37–44
sensorimotor model of, 3t
Cognitive modifiability
concept of, 145–147
theoretical basis for, 147–149
dynamic approach for
intervention with, 153–163
in occupational therapy, 144–166
target population, 145
theoretical base for, 144–153
intervention program for, 151–153
Cognitive organization
definition of, 79
Piagetian framework, 77–103
Cognitive-perceptual control, 168–170
in brain-injured adults, 176
environmental regulations, 170–171
motor performance component of, 169
process of, 169
Cognitive-perceptual dysfunction
detection of, by process approach, 186
discrimination and analysis of, by process approach, 186–187
intervention for, process approach for,
167–194

case study, 188–190
environment for, 187–188
evaluation methods of, 178–181
hypothesis generation in, 187
implications for research efficacy, 190
intervention with, 177–178
target populations, 175–177
treatment approach for, 181–190
Cognitive-perceptual skills, assessment of, 180
Cognitive Performance Test (CPT), 37, 45
Cognitive rehabilitation, 1315. *See also* Occupational therapy
according to cognitive level, 37–44
deficit specific approach to, 105–107
discharge criteria for, 15
domain-specific, 124–125
dynamic approach to, 104–143, 146
effectiveness criteria for, 45
functional approach to, 124–126, 222
gerontological, 22–50
literature review, 2327
multicontext approach to, 126–137, 127f
neurofunctional approach to, 195–218
for patients with poor learning potential, 124–126
for patients with potential for learning, 126–137
potential for, dynamic assessment of, 112
reductionist approach to, 105–107
retraining approach to, 219–239
successful, requirements for, 45
terminology for, 13–15
timing of, effects of, 196
traditional approach to, 105–107
Cognitive retraining approach. *See* Retraining approach
Cognitive therapy
for depression, 84
goals of, 228–229
for post-acute patient
advantages of, 196–197
disadvantages of, 197
for schizophrenia, 84
Coma, description of, 4t
Communicationinteraction skills, 247
of adults with nonverbal learning disabilities, 264–265, 271–272
definition of, 245
Comparisons, use of, in development of thought, 156–157
Competence, definition of, 246
Concentration, definition of, 224
Conceptual domains, 80
definition of, 80
Constructivism, 243
contemporary, 242–243
definition of, 81–82
Controlled process, definition of, 224

Coordination limitations, compensatory strategies for, 33–34
CPT. *See* Cognitive Performance Test
Custodial care program, 16
participation in, methods for, 16–17

DAD. *See* Attention deficit/dysfunction, divided
Data analysis, qualitative, 179
Debriefing, use of, 213
Decentrism, definition of, 81
Deductive reasoning tests, 123–124
Deficit specific approach, to cognitive rehabilitation, 105–107
limitations of, 106–107
Dementia. *See also* Senile dementia
definition of, 23
Dementia patient
application of human occupation model to, 253–255
cognitive level of, 63
community care for, 25
home care for, 25
institutionalization of, reasons for, 25
intervention for, issues in, 24–26
Depression
and attention, 56–57
cognitive level of, 63
cognitive therapy for, 84
Developmental stages, definition of, 80
Developmental Test of Visual Motor Integration, third revision, 290t
Discharge criteria
for post-acute patient, 12
for rehabilitation patient, 15
Discharge recommendations, for post-acute patient, 12
Documentation. *See also* Recordkeeping
for post-acute patient, 12
Domain-specific training, 124–125
Dynamic interactional approach
for cognitive modifiability
intervention with, 153–163
in occupational therapy, 144–166
for cognitive rehabilitation, 104–143, 146
implications for future research, 137–139
theoretical base for, 144–153
for therapy for behavioral problems, 145
for therapy for brain-injured, 145
Dynamic interactional assessment, 67, 118–139, 180
in activities of daily living (ADL) assessment process, 71
examples of, 120–124
limitation of, 120
of potential for rehabilitation, 112
treatment with, 124–137
Dynamic model, of cognition, multicon-

text treatment approach based on, 126–137, 127f
Dynamic visual processing assessment, 120–122
sample cues used in, 121t

Education, post-secondary, effects of nonverbal learning disabilities on, 266–267
Emotional deficits, in adults with nonverbal learning disabilities, 265–266
Emotionally disabled, instrumental enrichment (IE) for, 158–161
goals of, 154t, 161
methods for, 154t
Encore procedure, 211–212
Environment
of adults with nonverbal learning disabilities, 274
and cognitive-perceptual and postural control, 170–171
cultural, definition of, 112
holding, development of, 208
interaction with, 173–174
physical, definition of, 112
therapeutic, 187–188
Environmental constraints and supports, assessment of, 274
questions for, 274t
Environmental docility hypothesis, of functional behavior, 26
Equilibration, definition of, 80
Error evaluation, use of, 126
Exploration, definition of, 246
Exploratory actions, description of, 6t–7t
Extrapersonal space, perception of, training of, 231

FAD. See Attention deficit/dysfunction, focused
Fading, of cues, methods of, 211
Family interview, in activities of daily living (ADL) assessment process, 70
Featureintegration theory, of selective attention, 57
Feuerstein, R., dynamic approach for cognitive modifiability, 144–166
theoretical base for, 144–153
Fluid horizontality conservation test, 87
categories of response, 90t
Fried, Yehuda, *Intellectual Regression in the Schizophrenic with Paranoia*, 101–103
Frontal lobe lesions, problem solving and planning with, 201–202
Functional approach, to cognitive rehabilitation, 124–126, 222
Functional capability, assessment of, 32
Functional capacity, evaluation of, 32
Functional retraining programs, for cognitively impaired brain-injured, 206–213
Functional skills
assessment of, 205–206
retraining of, 207
Functional skills trainer, role of, 207

Genetic epistemology, definition of, 78
Geometric figures classification test, 88
categories of response, 90t
Gestalt thinking, 268–269
Goal-directed actions
at cognitive level 1, 38
at cognitive level 2, 38
at cognitive level 3, 40
at cognitive level 4, 42
at cognitive level 5, 43
at cognitive level 6, 44
description of, 5t–6t
Goal statements, 212–213
Grooved Pegboard test, 289t–290t

Habituation, 246–248
of adults with nonverbal learning disabilities, 272
assessment of, 272
questions for, 272
Hallucinations, reasons for, 102
Head injury/trauma. *See also* Brain-injured adults
intervention for
instrumental enrichment (IE) for, 157–158
process approach to, 175
Hearing impairment/loss, limitations imposed by, 30
Heart conditions, limitations imposed by, 30–31
Helplessness, definition of, 246
Hemiplegia, compensatory strategies for, 32–33
Highlighting strategy, 212
Holding environment, development of, 208
Holistic (gestalt) thinking, 268–269
The Hooper Visual Organization Test, 290t
Human occupation
input process, 245
output process, 245–246
through-put process, 245–246
Human occupation model, 240–257
analysis with, 247–248
application of
to cognitive dysfunction, 246–247
to dementia, case study, 253–255
assessment with
components of, 270
environmental questions for, 274t
habituation questions for, 272t
identifying questions for, 270–274

methods of collecting data for, 275
  performance questions for, 271t
  volitional questions for, 273t
case studies, 249–255
of nonverbal learning disabilities in
  adults, 258–289
occupational therapy assessment and
  intervention with, 248
remediation/treatment with, 270
  adjustment of, 277
  case study, 277–283
  components of, 270
  evaluating outcomes of, 277
  identifying and selecting options for,
    276–277
  theoretical base for, 240–245
  use of, 256
Hypertensive disease, limitations imposed
  by, 30

IE. *See* Instrumental enrichment
Impairments
  definition of, 14
  examples of, 9
Impossible, understanding of, 81
Individual
  functional capacity and capability of, 32
  as open or closed system, 145–146
  structural capacity of, 108–109
Information gathering, 247
Information processing
  activity and task analysis based on, 60–
    63
  at cognitive level 1, 57
  at cognitive level 2, 57
  at cognitive level 3, 57–58
  at cognitive level 4, 58
  at cognitive level 5, 59
  at cognitive level 6, 59
  concepts of, 53–55
  crystallized and fluid abilities for, 55
  definition of, 53
  environmental characteristics of, 111–
    112
  individual characteristics of, 108–111
  model of, 109–111, 110f
  schema of, 221
  stages of, deficient processing strategies
    and behaviors according to, 117t
  strategies of, 109
  task characteristics, 112–113
Information processing deficits, in schizophrenia, 59–60
Information processing models
  of cognition, 243–245
  of sensory processing, 171
Information processing theory, 54, 171–
  172
  assumptions of, 172
Instructions, reading and carrying out, for
  development of thought, 162

Instrumental enrichment (IE)
  for adaptational difficulties/dysfunc-
    tion, 161–163
    case example, 162–163
    goals of, 154t, 161–162
    methods for, 154t
  for brain-injured, 154–158
  for cognitive dysfunction, 153
    methods and goals, 154t
  for development of thought processes,
    156–158
  for emotionally disabled, 158–161
    goals of, 154t, 161
    methods for, 154t
  goals of, 152
  for head-injured, 157–158
  materials for, 151t
  in occupational therapy
    goals of, 154
    implications for further use, 164
    target populations, 153–154
  for psychiatric patients, 158–161
    goals of, 161
  research studies, 152–153
  spatial orientation problems, 155–156
Instrumental enrichment (IE) program,
  145146, 151153
  aim of, 146
  special features of, 164
Intelligence, development of, 102
Intelligence quotient (IQ) scores, interpretation of, 146
Interaction skills. *See* Communication-interaction skills
International Classification of Diseases
  (9th Revision, 1980), 1
*International Classification of Impair-
  ments, Disabilities, and Handicaps* (1980), 1
IQ scores. *See* Intelligence quotient scores

Knowledge
  declarative, 109–110
  procedural, 109, 200
Korsakoff's syndrome, memory in, 201

Language skills. *See also* Communication-
  interaction skills
  of adults with nonverbal learning dis-
    abilities, 264–265
LAPD. *See* Learning potential assessment
  device
Learning
  specificity of, 174
  theories of, 172–174
Learning ability
  assessment of, 8
  evaluation of, 9–10
Learning difficulties, classification of, 9
Learning disabilities
  in adults, 260

in children, 259
definition of, 260–261
incidence of, 260–261 legal definition of, 259
life span, 261
nonverbal, 262–269
   in adults, human occupation model of, 258–289
subtypes of, 261–262
Learning potential assessment device (LAPD), 145, 149–151
Leisure, effects of nonverbal learning disabilities on, 268
Loewenstein Hospital, cognitive treatment for brain-injured patients with instrumental enrichment (IE) in, 154–158
Loewenstein occupational therapy cognitive assessment (LOTCA) battery, 225–227
   scoring sheet, 226f
LOTCA. *See* Loewenstein occupational therapy cognitive assessment battery
Lower Cognitive Levels (LCL) test, 37

MacQuarrie Test for Mechanical Abilities, 290t
Mania, acute, cognitive level with, 63
Manual actions, description of, 5t
Maslow's Hierarchy of Needs, 160t, 161
Mediated learning experience (MLE), 145
   intentionality and reciprocity in, 148
   intervention based on, goal of, 149
   lack of, 149
   mediation of meaning in, 148
   theory of, 147–149
   transcendence in, 148
Mediator, role of, 147–148
Medical rehabilitation center, cognitive treatment for brain-injured patients with instrumental enrichment (IE) in, 154–158
Memory, 247
   attention and, 200–201
   declarative, 200
   definition of, 224
   long-term, 200
      training of, 233–234
   procedural, 200–201
   short-term, training of, 233
   strategies and behaviors of, 114t–115t
   topographic, training of, 233
   training of, 232–234
Memory book, use of, training program for, 208
Mental health
   cognitive therapy in, 82–84
   occupational therapy in
      intervention with, 85–89

with piagetian framework, 77–103
   development of, 84–85
   implications for further development of, 97–98
   theoretical base for, 78
principles of, 91–97
research for, 89–91
Metacognition, 109, 244
aspects of, 129
skills of, 109, 129
MLE. *See* Mediated learning experience
Modes of performance
description of, 4t–7t
ordinal scale of, 3
Motor actions, 36
   at cognitive level 1, 38
   at cognitive level 2, 38
   at cognitive level 3, 40
   at cognitive level 4, 42
   at cognitive level 5, 43
   at cognitive level 6, 44
   imitated, 36
   spontaneous (self-initiated), 36
Motor deficits
   in adults with nonverbal learning disabilities, 265
   in brain-injured adults, 176
Motor learning, theory of, 172–173
Motor skills. *See* Perceptualmotor skills
Multicontext approach, to cognitive rehabilitation, 126–137, 127f
   case examples, 131137
   components of, 127
   levels of transfer distance in, 128t

National Joint Committee on Learning Disabilities (NJCLD), definition of learning disabilities, 260
Necessary, understanding of, 81
Need(s)
   definition of, 161
   Maslow's hierarchy of, 160t, 161
Negligence, definition of, 7
Neurofunctional approach
   rationale for, 196–197
   to rehabilitation after severe brain injury, 195–218
      intervention with, 203213
      research methods and future directions, 213–214
      retraining in, 206–213
      target population, 203
      theoretical base for, 198–203
Neurofunctional assessment
   goals of, 206t
   initial screening for, 204t
   observational techniques for, 204–205
   of severely brain-injured, 203–206
Neuromotor deficits, in adults with nonverbal learning disabilities, 265
Neuropsychology, focus of, 52–53

Nonverbal learning disabilities, 262–269
adults with
  areas of deficit in, 263–266
  assessment of, 270
    components of, 270
    environmental questions for, 274t
    habituation questions for, 272t
    identifying questions for, 270–274
    methods of collecting data for, 275
    performance questions for, 271t
    volitional questions for, 273t
  environment for, 274
  human occupation model of, 258–289
  occupational function and dysfunction of, constructing explanation of, 275
  occupational status of, 276t
  occupational therapy for, 284
    implications for future work in, 283–284
  remediation/treatment of, 270
    adjustment of, 277
    case study, 277–283
    components of, 270
    evaluating outcomes of, 277
    identifying and selecting options for, 276–277
  effects of
    on occupation, 266–268
    on post-secondary education, 266–267
    on recreation and leisure, 268
    on self-maintenance skills, 268
    on vocation, 267
  etiology of, hypothesized, 268–269
Numerical progressions, in development of thought, 156–157

Observational techniques, for neurofunctional assessment, 204–205
Occupation. *See also* Human occupation
  effects of nonverbal learning disabilities on, 266–268
Occupational function
  effect of cognitive disability on, 246–247
  interruption in, 246
  levels of, 246
Occupational status, of adults with nonverbal learning disabilities, 276t
Occupational therapist, as facilitator, 147–148
Occupational therapy
  for adults with nonverbal learning disabilities, 284
    implications for future work in, 283–284
  assessment and intervention with, human occupation model for, 248
  for behavioral problems, dynamic approach for, 145
  for brain-injured, 174, 177–178, 222–223

adaptive approach to, 222
approaches to, 222
bottom-up approach to, 197
characteristics of, 177–178
dynamic approach to, 145
neurofunctional approach to, 195–218
process approach to, 167–194
remedial approach to, 222 for cognitively disabled, 15–16. *See also* Cognitive rehabilitation; Cognitive therapy
cognitive modifiability in, dynamic approach for, 144–166
  target population, 145
instrumental enrichment (IE) in, 153–154, 164
for long-term care, 15–16
  primary outcomes, 16
in mental health, 85–89
piagetian framework for, 77–103
principles of, 91–97
research, 89–91
for post-acute patient, primary outcomes, 11–12
principles of, 175
in psychiatry, theoretical base for, 51–53
for rehabilitation, 13
  primary outcomes, 13
test of treatment success in, 223
Occupation dysfunction
human occupation model of, 246–247
levels of, 246
Older adults
cognitive capacities and limitations in, assessment of, tools for, 36–37
cognitively disabled
  activity analysis of, 27–29
  activity of, meaning of, 28–29
  compensatory strategies for, 27–28
  functional assessment of, 27
    special aspects of, 29–31
  operations of, 27–28
    results of, 28
  rehabilitation for, 22–50
    literature review, 23–27
limitations of
  chronic conditions that cause, 30
  functional, 30–31
  interventions for, 30–31
physically disabled
  compensatory strategies for, 32–34
  rehabilitation for, 31–34
Operations
  definition of, 62, 79
  levels of, 62
Organic brain syndrome, cognitive level in, 63
Organization, cognitive, 77–103
Orientation, training of, 233

Orienting reflex, 56
Overlearning, 211

Paranoid schizophrenic, intellectual regression in, 101–103
Perception. *See also* Cognitive-perceptual control
definition of, 168–169, 223
Perception process, 221–222 retraining of. *See* Retraining approach
Perceptual-motor skills, 247
of adults with nonverbal learning disabilities, 271
definition of, 245
Performance
of adults with nonverbal learning disabilities, 270
evaluation of, 270–272
questions for, 271t
Performance history, assessment of, 274
Performance skills, 247
categories of, 245
Personality disorders, cognitive level with, 63
Personal space, perception of, training of, 231
Physical disability
activity analysis of, 32
compensatory strategies for, 32
changing method of performance, 34
changing position of individual, 32–33
changing property of materials and tools, 33–34
changing resistance, 33
in older adults, rehabilitation for, 31–34
Piaget, Jean, definition of cognition, 241–242
Piagetian framework
defining concepts of, 79–82
occupational therapy in mental health with, 77–103
development of, 84–85
evaluation process, 85
further development of, implications for, 97–98
principles of, 91–97
research, 89–91
target population, 85
theoretical base for, 78
Planned actions, description of, 7t
Planning, after brain injury, 201–203
Positioning. *See also* Postural control
dysfunctional, compensatory strategies for, 32–33
Possible, understanding of, 81
Postural actions, description of, 4t
Postural control, 168–170
in brain-injured adults, 176

definition of, 169
environmental regulations of, 170–171
process of, 170
receptors associated with, 169–170
Postural control dysfunction
detection of, by process approach, 186
discrimination and analysis of, by process approach, 186–187
intervention for, process approach for, 167–194
case study, 188–190
environment for, 187–188
evaluation methods of, 178–181
hypothesis generation in, 187
implications for research efficacy, 190
intervention with, 177–178 target populations, 175–177
treatment approach for, 181–190
Postural limitations, compensatory strategies for, 32–33
Posture, poor, etiology of, 32
Probability, quantification of, test of, 89
categories of response, 90t
Problem solving
in adults with nonverbal learning disabilities, 263–264
after brain injury, 201–203
concepts of, 54
definition of, 223
measures of, 183t–185t
strategies and behaviors of, 115t
Problem-solving behavior, description of, 54–55
Problem-solving impairments, 180
Problem-solving skills, 180
assessment of, 180
Process approach
evaluation with
methods for, 178–181
scale for, 178–181
implications for research efficacy, 190
to intervention for cognitive-perceptual and postural control dysfunction, 167–194
intervention with, 177–178
target populations for, 175–177
theoretical base for, 167–175, 168f
treatment with, 181–190
case study, 188–190
phase I, 186
phase II, 186–187
phase III, 187
Process skills
of adults with nonverbal learning disabilities, 271
definition of, 245
Prompts, use of, 209–210
Psychiatric hospital. *See* Short-stay private psychiatric hospital
Psychiatry

instrumental enrichment (IE) in, 158–161
  goals of, 161
occupational therapy in, dynamic approach for, 145
remedicalizaiton of, 51–52
use of cognitive disability frame of reference in
  clinical applications of, target population for, 63
  at short-stay private hospital, 51–76
Psychotic disorders, cognitive level with, 63
Purdue Pegboard Test, 289t

Quality of life, definition of, 45

RBMT. *See* Rivermead Behavioral Memory Test
Reach limitations, compensatory strategies for, 34
Reading skills, of adults with nonverbal learning disabilities, 265
Reality, definition of, 81
Reasoning, 247
Recordkeeping. *See also* Documentation
  for rehabilitation patient, 15
Recreation and leisure, effects of nonverbal learning disabilities on, 268
Reductionist approach, to cognitive rehabilitation, 105–107
Referral criteria
  for post-acute patient, 12
  for rehabilitation patient, 13–14
Rehabilitation. *See also* Cognitive rehabilitation
  gerontological, for physical disabilities, 31–34
Rehabilitation culture, development of, 208
Rehabilitation Services Administration (RHA), definition of learning disabilities in, 260
Reinforcement, for skill building, 208–209
Remedial approach, to occupational therapy for brain-injured, 222
Remediation approach. *See* Retraining approach
Retraining approach
  cognitive assessment battery for, 225–227
  cognitive rationale for, 221–222
  to cognitive rehabilitation for brain-injured adults, 219–239
  concepts of, definition of, 223–224
  evaluation with, 224–228
  implications for further development, 236–237
  intervention with, 224–228

neuropsychological rationale for, 220–221
  target population for, 224
  theoretical base of, 219–224
  treatment with, 228–236
    case study, 234–236
    goals of, 228–229
    process of, 229–236
Rey Osterrieth Complex Figure Test, 290t
RHA. *See* Rehabilitation Services Administration
Rivermead Behavioral Memory Test (RBMT), 227–228
Role reversal, use of, 126
Routine Task Inventory, 10
Routine Task Inventory (RTI), 37
RTI. *See* Routine Task Inventory

Safety hazards, 14
Schema, definition of, 79
Schizophrenia
  attention deficits with, 60
  cognitive impairment with, 83–84
  cognitive level with, 63
  cognitive therapy for, 84
  information processing deficits with, 59–60
  with paranoia, intellectual regression in, 101–103
Scratch pad assembly task, 10–11
SCS. *See* Survey of Cognitive Skills Self-estimation, 129
  use of, 126
Self-maintenance skills, effects of nonverbal learning disabilities on, 268
Self-questioning, use of, 126
Self-regulation, definition of, 80
Senile dementia, 23–24. *See also* Dementia
  incidence of, 24
  limitations imposed by, 30
Senile dementia patient, intervention for, issues in, 24–26
Sensorimotor associations, 35–36
Sensorimotor model, of cognitive levels, 3t
Sensory cues, 35
Sensory integration theory, 146
Sensory processing
  information processing model of, 171
  stages of, 171
Shalvata Psychiatric Hospital, 158
Short-stay private psychiatric hospital
  cognitive disability in patients at, intervention for, 63–75
  use of cognitive disability frame of reference in, 51–76
Size comparisons test, 87–88
  categories of response, 90t
Skill building, reinforcement for, 208–209

Skills
  academic, of adults with nonverbal
    learning disabilities, 265
  of cognition, interior, 247
  cognitive-perceptual, assessment of, 180
  of communication, of adults with non-
    verbal learning disabilities, 264–
    265
  communicationinteraction, 247
    of adults with nonverbal learning dis-
      abilities, 271–272
    definition of, 245
  functional
    assessment of, 205–206
    retraining of, 207
    trainer of, role for, 207
  of language, of adults with nonverbal
    learning disabilities, 264–265
  metacognitive, 109, 129
  perceptualmotor, 247
    of adults with nonverbal learning dis-
      abilities, 271
    definition of, 245
  of performance, 247
    categories of, 245
  problem-solving, 180
    assessment of, 180
  process
    of adults with nonverbal learning dis-
      abilities, 271
    definition of, 245
  self-maintenance, effects of nonverbal
    learning disabilities on, 268
  social, deficit of, training program for
    reduction of, 208
Social-emotional deficits, in adults with
  nonverbal learning disabilities,
  265–266
Social skills deficit, reduction of, training
  program for, 208
Spatial orientation problems, for brain-injured adults, 155–156
Spatial perception, training of, 231
Specific task training, 197
Stencil designs, for development of
  thought processes, 156–157
Subject's weight conservation test, 86
  categories of response, 90t
Substance abuse, cognitive level with, 63
Survey of Cognitive Skills (SCS), 6768
Sustained actions, description of, 5t
Syllogism, mastery of, for development of
  thought, 162

Tactile limitations, compensatory strategies for, 33
Task analysis
  based on information processing, 60–63
  use of, 209

Thinking, holistic (gestalt), 268–269
Thinking operations
  basis of, 232
  definition of, 223
  training of, 232
Thought. See also Thinking
  development of, instrumental enrich-
    ment (IE) for, 156–158
  dimensions of, 35
Toglia category assessment, 122–123
Transitive relationships, in development
  of thought, 156–157

Validity
  factual, 80
  logical, 80
Visual identification, process of, 221–222
Visual limitations, compensatory strategies for, 33
Visual perception
  of adults with nonverbal learning dis-
    abilities, 264
  assessment of, tools for, 289t–291t
  training of, 230
Visual processing, strategies and behaviors
  of, 114t
Visuomotor organization
  assessment of, tools for, 289t–291t
  definition of, 224
  training of, 231–232
Vocation, effects of nonverbal learning disabilities on, 267
Volition, 248
  of adults with nonverbal learning dis-
    abilities, 273–274
  assessment of, 272–274
    questions for, 273f
  definition of, 246
Volume conservation, example activity of,
  92
Volume conservation test, 87
  categories of response, 90t

WAIS-R. See Wechsler Adult Intelligence
  Scale-Revised
Wechsler Adult Intelligence Scale-Revised
  (WAIS-R), 262, 290t–291t
Wechsler Intelligence Scale for Children-
  Revised (WISC-R), 262
Weight conservation test, 86
  categories of response, 90t
Wilcoxon two-sample test, 225
WISC-R. See Wechsler Intelligence Scale
  for Children-Revised
Woodcock-Johnson Test of Achievement,
  291t

Zone of proximal development, definition
  of, 111–112